Children's Writer®
Guide to 2002

Editor: Susan M. Tierney

Contributing writers:
Joan Broerman
Marnie Brooks
Toni Buzzeo
Barbara Cole
Jan Fields
Sandy Fox
Donna Freedman
Maureen Garry
Vicki Hambleton
Mark Haverstock
Jackie Horsfall
Veda Boyd Jones
Marni McNiff
Josephine "Joi" Nobisso
Mary C. Northrup
Darcy Pattison
Patricia Curtis Pfitsch
Ruth Sachs
Sandy Stiefer
Susan M. Tierney
Carolyn P. Yoder

Copy editor: Cheryl de la Guéronnière

Editorial and research assistants:
Barbara Cole
Maureen Garry
Joanna Horvath

Publisher: Prescott V. Kelly

1-800-443-6078. www.writersbookstore.com
e-mail: services@writersbookstore.com

Printed and bound in Canada.

Table of Contents

Publishing
2002

Book Publishing

The Year Nonfiction & Young Adult Turned Golden

By Toni Buzzeo

Some are born in the year of the dragon, some in the year of the ox or the rat. Children's publishing is having a rebirth with the year of nonfiction, marked by the launch of the Robert F. Sibert Award and the publication of a host of extraordinary nonfiction titles for children. Children's nonfiction is clearly in ascendancy.

Not to be entirely eclipsed, however, is young adult fiction. So recently catapulted into the limelight by the launch of the Printz Award, YA now holds its own share of attention in the children's publishing field and its own share of the market. New formats and styles continue to emerge as established authors and newcomers find a growing audience among teens and adult readers of YA literature. Meanwhile, the traditional workhorses of children's publishing, middle-grade and picture book fiction, have changed in response to market demands, striving to keep pace with tastes and trends and with an increasingly culturally diverse American population.

While we don't yet know the long-term effects of the terrorist attacks of September 11 and the aftermath on children's publishing, we do know from publishers and booksellers alike that many parents and children have turned to books to help them confront the events and their feelings. Booksellers and librarians rushed to put together a collection of books that would answer informational needs and offer comfort. Some speculate that we will see more room for the *quiet* book again in children's publishing in the years to come, but it is certainly too soon yet to tell.

Despite recent events, however, and no matter the genre, children's publishing continues to be strong. While industry projections have shown a slowed growth rate in publishing overall, the news is better in the juvenile segment, with a strong projected growth in children's paperback sales and modest growth in trade hardcover. Kids books continue to demand attention in the marketplace.

True Books: Nonfiction Comes into Its Own

On a balmy Washington, D.C., morning months before September 11, the first Sibert Award was announced to a

Nonfiction's New Honor

The Association for Library Service to Children, a division of the American Library Association, established the ALSC/Robert F. Sibert Informational Book Award to honor the author of the most distinguished informational book published during the preceding year. Marc Aronson won the first Sibert for his acclaimed portrait of an ambitious hero, *Sir Walter Ralegh and the Quest for El Dorado* (Clarion Books). The award "has given me a kind of authority and stamp of approval, a certain standing, a sense of arrival. . . . It's given me courage and a big canvas," says Aronson, who now has solid plans for a trilogy about colonial America; the first book in the trilogy will be about Sir Walter Ralegh. "It also opens doors to new books. People will now be more interested in what I do."

In addition to *Sir Walter Ralegh,* the Sibert committee also named four honor books: *The Longitude Prize,* by Joan Dash, illustrated by Dusan Petricic, (Frances Foster Books), which also won the *Boston Globe-Horn Book* Award for nonfiction; *Blizzard! The Storm That Changed America,* by Jim Murphy, (Scholastic Press); *My Season with Penguins: An Antarctic Journal,* by Sophie Webb (Houghton Mifflin); and *Pedro and Me: Friendship, Loss, and What I Learned,* by Judd Winick (Henry Holt). It is interesting to note that Aronson edited Winick's graphic-book memoir of Pedro Zamora while still working at Henry Holt.

Nina Lindsay, 2002 Sibert Award Committee Chair, feels hopeful about the power of the Sibert to continue to transform children's nonfiction. "The criteria for the Sibert award," she says, "call attention to strengths of nonfiction that other award criteria, such as the Newbery, do not. For instance, organization, ancillary matter, the perception of author authority, all become very important. I think that the Sibert will get librarians and other critics thinking and talking more about these aspects of nonfiction. We've been coached in how to evaluate stories—plot, characterization, etc.—much more, and when we put that eye to nonfiction, we don't always find its best or worst aspects." Lindsay points out that nonfiction fans are far fewer than fiction fans in the general population, a fact echoed among the population of the nations' librarians. Yet, she notes, "as we become more practiced in appreciating nonfiction as the Sibert gains steam, we'll be able to highlight it more in our collections, and recommend it to our readers."

hushed crowd at the American Library Association (ALA) Midwinter Conference—right along with the Caldecott (awarded to another nonfiction book), the Newbery, and the Coretta Scott King Award. It was the dawning of a new day for *true* books, as the kids call them.

Marc Aronson, Vice President and Publisher of Cricket Books and Open Court Books at Carus Publishing, and coincidentally the winner of the Sibert Award for *Sir Walter Ralegh and the Quest for El Dorado,* says, "People tend to view nonfiction as dusty and sleepy. But I think it's about getting kids to think and putting them in touch with thinking. It needs to have a freshness of vision." This was the year children's publishing seemed to rededicate itself to that freshness of vision in nonfiction.

What, then, did the year's tragic events and the Sibert mean for children's and YA nonfiction? The events of September 11 have clearly highlighted the need for quality nonfiction for children. Parents and children are hungry for ways to deal with the reality of horrific events.

Emma Dryden, Vice President and Editorial Director of Margaret K. McElderry Books, for instance, cites a marked sales increase for *Firefighters A to Z,* by Chris Demarest (McElderry). "The fact that the author/artist is himself a volunteer firefighter gives great credence to *Firefighters A to Z,*" Dryden says. "The book has proven to be a safe way to introduce children to what firefighters actually do, while not scaring them with unnecessary images of innocent people or animals

Jennifer Owings Dewey

Antarctic Journal

Four Months at the Bottom of the World

in distress or mortal danger."

The face and uses of nonfiction have changed in any case, says Judy O'Malley, Editor of Cricket Books. "Nonfiction is no longer concerned with *just the facts.* The best of this genre sees all parts of human history, past and current, as shaped story, meticulously documented with notes and sources, so that these books model critical thinking, careful research, and good writing."

Nina Lindsay, 2002 Sibert Award Committee Chair, agrees. She points to the increasing number of books about scientists in the field as good examples, including Jennifer Owings Dewey's *Antarctic Journal: Four Months at the Bottom of the World* (HarperCollins) and new titles in Houghton Mifflin's Scientists in the Field series, such as *Swimming With Hammerhead Sharks,* by Kenneth Mallory. Such books, Lindsay says, "illuminate the

Teen Reading Habits

A recent National Education Association (NEA) survey found that kids 12 to 18 *are* reading. Overall, 41 percent in the survey of 509 young people read more than 15 books a year and 56 percent read more than 10 books. Between middle-schoolers and high-schoolers, the younger kids do better: 70 percent of middle-schoolers and 49 percent of high-schoolers read more than 10 books a year.

Adolescents are reading in about the same amounts for education and entertainment, according to the NEA survey: 46 percent said most reading was for school, but 42 percent read for pleasure. 87 percent characterized reading as "relaxing"; 85 percent as "rewarding and satisfying"; and 79 percent as "stimulating or interesting."

Parental support of reading varies culturally, at least in the kids' eyes. 52 percent of African-American teens in the survey said their parents encourage their reading; 47 percent of Hispanic teens said the same; and 43 percent of white respondents.

(Source: National Education Site: www.nea.org/nr/nr010302. html. The poll was performed by Peter D. Hart Research Associates.)

practical side of the scientific process for young people." They are also well-written and teach kids how to think while also telling a story.

O'Malley sees differences in teen nonfiction. "One welcome change we're seeing more in nonfiction is a tone of respect for young readers' need and desire to know about the world. This is apparent in books that deal honestly with tough subjects from violence to racial strife." Books such as *Things I Have to Tell You*, edited by Betsy Franco (Candlewick), give teens their voices in the publishing marketplace as well.

O'Malley continues: "Some of the most intriguing of these books include those that broadcast the authentic voices of teens who have strong views about social issues that confront them daily, be they immigrant teens, biracial teens, gay and lesbian teens, or just kids trying to figure out the world around them."

Aronson agrees. "Teenagers are immensely interested in the world. Teachers and booksellers think that busy teens with heavy course loads only read fiction; however, if publishers do nonfiction that plays to the intellectual interests of teens, it will be read. They are interested in themselves and look for books that capture something in their lives. The opportunity exists to give them a look at something fresh in the world—to see themselves in a new way."

A champion of quality YA fiction and nonfiction, Aronson plans to capture that opportunity. He is launching a sub-imprint of Cricket Books called Marcato (a musical term meaning *with*

Nonfiction Publishers:
Middle-Grade & Young Adult

Company	Description	* Annual submissions	* Titles last year
ABDO Publishing	Middle-grade. Biographies, leisure, nature, science, reference, social studies.	300 queries	170
Atheneum Books	Nonfiction for all ages. Biographies, nature, science, history, multicultural, sports.	20,000 queries	80
ATL Press	YA. Astronomy, biochemistry, biotechnology, computers, earth science, food, medicine, polymers.	100-150 queries	12
Avisson Press	Publishes YA nonfiction only. Biography series, history, multicultural and ethnic.	500 queries	7
Avon Books	Middle-grade and YA. Social issues, computers, history, sports, education, popular culture.	1,500 queries	300
Bantam Double-day Dell	A large house with many divisions. The only nonfiction Bantam publishes is YA.	2,000 queries	300
Barron's Educational Series	Nonfiction for all ages. Currently seeking YA nonfiction. Nature, science, animals, social issues, travel, art.	1,700 submissions	90
Behrman House	Nonfiction for middle-grade and YA, of Jewish interest.	700+ submissions	9
Bethany House	Evangelical Christian publisher for all ages and categories. Looking for nonfiction for YA girls.	250 queries	61
Boyds Mills Press	Up to middle-grade nonfiction.	9,700 submissions	50
Candlewick Press	Nonfiction for all ages.	14,000 submissions	180
Carolrhoda Books	Published 70 middle-grade nonfiction books last year on science, geography, history, social issues, sports.	3,050 submissions	106
Centering Corporation	Middle-grade and YA titles on coping with grief, divorce, infertility, adoption, special needs parenting.	120 queries	12
Chelsea House	Specializes in middle-grade and YA nonfiction. History, the classics, African-American studies, parenting, culture, more.	350 submissions	369
Chicago Review Press	Middle-grade and YA. Activity books and general nonfiction.	1540 submissions	32

Number of submissions and titles for all ages and categories published, not limited to nonfiction.

Nonfiction Publishers:
Middle-Grade & Young Adult

Company	Description	Annual submissions	Titles last year
Children's Press	Middle-grade. Biographies, science, geography, social studies, sports, career. Hi/lo books.	2,000 queries	400
Chronicle Books	Middle-grade. History, social issues, nature, science.	22,500 submissions	45
Clarion Books	Nonfiction to middle-grade. Nature, ecology, history, holidays, multicultural.	1,100 submissions	60
Clear Light	Middle-grade and YA biographies, nature, history, religion, on Southwest and Native American cultures.	250 queries	25
Contemporary Drama Service	YA books on theater, speech.	1,600 queries	60
Creative Editions	YA. Nature, environment, animals, sports, biographies.	40 submissions	5
Cricket Books	Middle-grade and YA. History, biography, math, science, social issues, sports.	1,500 submissions	12
Crossquarter Publishing	YA. Biography, how-to, health, fitness, metaphysics, environment, cross-cultural understanding.	180 queries	7
Crown Books	Nonfiction for all ages. Social issues, history, sports, science, nature.	1,500 submissions	25
Dawn Publications	Middle-grade and YA titles on nature.	2,800 submissions	8
Dial Books	Nonfiction for all ages on all subjects.	1,000 queries	35
Dorling Kindersley	Nonfiction for all ages. Wants queries for middle-grade nonfiction and biographies.	2,000 submissions	150
Dutton Books	Nonfiction for all ages. History, nature, biography.	2,500 queries	101
Eakin Press	Nonfiction for all ages on Texas and the Southwest.	1,200 queries	70
Enslow Publishers	Specializes in middle-grade and YA nonfiction. Social issues, health, history, science, multicultural.	1,000 queries	200

Nonfiction Publishers:
Middle-Grade & Young Adult

Company	Description	Annual submissions	Titles last year
Falcon Publishing	Nonfiction for ages 5 to 18. Nature, animals, environment, the outdoors, history, Western Americana.	100 queries	150
Farrar, Straus & Giroux	Middle-grade and YA. Science, nature, social issues.	7,000 submissions	80
Frederick Fell	YA self-help and how-to's.	4,000 queries	35
Feminist Press	Middle-grade. Multicultural, biographies.	800 queries	15
Free Spirit	Middle-grade and YA on family, social issues, stress management, self-awareness.	4,000 queries	20
Front Street Books	YA. History, family, social issues.	2,000 submissions	16
Girl Press	Middle-grade and YA. Popular culture, entertainment, social issues, business, travel, humor.	100 queries	11
Graphic Arts Center	Nonfiction for all ages on people and wildlife of Alaska, the Northwest, Canada.	350 submissions	23
Greenhaven Press	YA anthologies on literature, history, culture, teen issues, current issues. By assignment only.	25	120
HarperCollins	Nonfiction for all ages. Entertainment, science, history, geography, humor.	15,000 submissions	500
Hazelden Foundation	Middle-grade and YA. Self-help. Alcohol and substance abuse, health, social issues.	250 submissions	15
Hendrick-Long Publishing	Nonfiction for all ages on Texas and the Southwest.	500 queries	8
Holiday House	Nonfiction for ages 4-18. History, social issues, science, biographies.	8,000 queries	60
Henry Holt and Company	Nonfiction for all ages. History, math, nature, science, technology, multicultural.	7,600 submissions	63
Houghton Mifflin	Middle-grade and YA nonfiction. Current events, history, multicultural.	13,000+ submissions	90

Nonfiction Publishers: Middle-Grade & Young Adult

Company	Description	Annual submissions	Titles last year
Impact Publishers	Specializes in middle-grade and YA nonfiction. Self-help, social issues, self-esteem, relationships, multicultural.	400 queries	11
Just Us Books	Middle-grade. Biographies. Black history, culture, and experiences.	not available	4
Lark Books	Middle-grade. Crafts and activities: knitting, crocheting, sewing, mosaics, weaving, paper, nature crafts.	100 queries	55
Lerner Books	Nonfiction for ages 7-18. Social issues, history, science, geography, environment, sports, arts, entertainment, biographies.	400 submissions	200
Arthur A. Levine Books	Nonfiction for early readers to YA. History, nature, environment, multicultural.	120 queries	45
Little, Brown and Company	Nonfiction for all ages. History, nature, crafts, environment, social and family issues.	2,000 submissions	94
Lucent Books	Specializes in middle-grade nonfiction. Politics, culture, society, science, history, current issues, biographies.	250 queries	170
Magination Press	Middle-grade and YA. Grief, divorce, learning disabilities, family issues.	400 submissions	10
Mayhaven Publishing	Nonfiction for all ages. Travel, nature, cooking, history, the West.	1,000+ queries	10
Margaret K. McElderry Books	Nonfiction for all ages, on all subjects, for 2004-2005 publication.	4,000 queries	26
Meadowbrook Press	Nonfiction to the middle-grades. Family activities, crafts, cooking, humor, parties.	700 queries	15
Milkweed Editions	For ages 8 to 13 only. Explores ethical, cultural, aesthetic issues.	5,000 submissions	15
The Millbrook Press	Primarily nonfiction; middle-grades the core audience. Science, history, environment, arts, sports, crafts, biographies.	not available	125
Mitchell Lane Publishers	Authorized biographies of well-known figures for readers 5 to 18. On assignment.	80 submissions	25
Morgan Reynolds	Specializes in middle-grade and YA nonfiction. Music, science, history, sports, biographies.	700 submissions	24

Nonfiction Publishers:
Middle-Grade & Young Adult

Company	Description	Annual submissions	Titles last year
National Geographic Society	Nonfiction for all ages. History, biographies, reference, science, technology, animals, geography, nature.	350+ submissions	40
Naturegraph Publishers	Middle-grade and YA. Paperbacks on natural history.	400 queries	3
The New England Press	Middle-grade history and regional subjects.	500 queries	5
NorthWord Press	Middle-grade. Natural history, animals, nature, environment.	20 queries	20
The Oliver Press	Specializes in middle-grade and YA nonfiction, especially biography series.	60 queries	8
Parachute Press	Ages 5-18. Humor, science. A packager.	440 submissions	100
Peachtree Publishers	All ages. Southern regional publisher. Nature, history.	9,000 queries	20
Perigee Books	Imprint specializing in middle-grade and YA nonfiction.	450 submissions	75
Philomel Books	YA nonfiction. Biographies, first-person essays.	1,500 queries	25
Piñata Books	YA nonfiction on Hispanic history, Hispanic women's literature, sociology, anthropology, literary criticism.	3,900 submissions	30
Pineapple Press	Florida regional publisher. Middle-grade nonfiction. History, sports, or travel relating to Florida.	1,440 queries	24
The Place in the Woods	Middle-grade multicultural nonfiction. Biographies, special education, history.	1,300 submissions	4
Pleasant Company	Middle-grade. Animals, crafts, hobbies, games, health, family, advice, sports.	not available	60
Prima Publishing	How-to and self-help for all ages. Also: Biographies, natural health, computers, cooking, sports, entertainment, more.	1,200 queries	200+
Publish America	YA. Current events, entertainment, health, history, multicultural, religion, social concerns, special education, self-help.	8,600 submissions	300

Nonfiction Publishers:
Middle-Grade & Young Adult

Company	Description	Annual submissions	Titles last year
Rosen Publishing	Middle-grade and YA nonfiction only. History, science, health, arts, sports, more.	350+ submissions	500+
SeaStar Books	Middle-grade. Animals, nature, environment, history, religion, social issues.	1,200 submissions	21
Simon & Schuster	Ages 4-12. Math, science, nature, history, social issues, biographies.	2,500 queries	75
Small Horizons	Self-help for all ages. True-life heroes, family, multicultural.	100 queries	2
Sports Publishing	Middle-grade. Sports, athletes.	350 queries	80
Sterling Publishing	All ages. Reference, how-to, nature, sports, science, crafts.	500 queries	200
Third World Press	All ages. Ethnic and multicultural.	600 submissions	12
Megan Tingley Books	All ages. Self-help, hobbies, crafts, multicultural.	600+ queries	23
J.N. Townsend Publishing	To age 14. Books about living with animals.	60 submissions	9
Tricycle Press	Birth to age 12. Real life issues, cooking, gardening.	15,000 submissions	21
Twenty-first Century Books	Specializes in YA nonfiction. Health, medicine, science, technology, history, politics, government, sports, studying.	100 queries	50
UXL	Specializes in middle-grade references. History, current events, multicultural, health, science, careers.	not available	20
VGM Books	YA career books.	200 queries	40
Viking Children's Books	Nonfiction for all ages. Biographies, science, nature, history.	3,000 submissions	75
Walker and Company	Nonfiction to the middle-grades. Social issues, history, biographies.	2,400 submissions	29

Nonfiction Publishers:
Middle-Grade & Young Adult

Company	Description	Annual submissions	Titles last year
Wayne State University Press	Middle-grade nonfiction on regional Midwestern history, African-American life, American Jewish civilization, film, TV, more.	280 submissions	50
White Mane Publishing	YA. History, Civil War.	360 queries	14
Albert Whitman & Company	Nonfiction to the middle-grades. Family life, social issues, multicultural, biographies.	4,800 submissions	30
Wiley Children's Books	Middle-grade and YA nonfiction. Arts and crafts, sports, multicultural, history, math, science, nature.	300 queries	20
Windward Publishing	Paperbacks for all ages on nature, animals, natural history, agriculture, horticulture, recreation, science, sports.	60 submissions	10
Winslow Press	Nonfiction for all ages.	1,300 submissions	21
Woodbine House	For disabled or special needs children from 4-18.	2,000 submissions	8
Workman Publishing	Nonfiction for all ages. Nature, environment, science, sports, cooking, games.	3,000 submissions	40

Publishing by the the Numbers

Publishing industry figures for sales over the past year and projections for the coming year are always slow to generate, and sometimes difficult to pin down. This year's numbers are perhaps even less "stable," given the state of the economy and the world. Nonetheless, children's books continue to lead in strength in publishing, with projections of growth—though smaller than in the past few years. Below are the numbers provided by three firms that compose industry reports, Veronis Suhler, PricewaterhouseCoopers, and Ipsos-NPD.

■ **Veronis Suhler**
- Growth projection of sales of juvenile books for the year ahead:
    Spending on trade books to increase 1.9%, to $18.1 billion
    On children's paperbacks: 8.1%
    On children's hardcovers: 1.9%

- Growth projection over five-year period, spending on consumer books:
    2.4%, to $20 billion.

In the preceding three years, the increases had been dramatic, with children's book sales increasing more than any other publishing segment, culminating in a 14.5% increase.

■ **PricewaterhouseCoopers**
- Growth projection of sales of juvenile books for the year ahead:
    Spending on trade books to increase 5.1%, to $18 million

- Growth projection over five-year period, spending on consumer books:
    Compound annual growth of 4.5%, to $21.4 billion.

■ **Ipsos-NPD**
- In a survey of 12,000 households, the source of book purchases for children under 14 shifted slightly:
Book purchases from "special markets," such as book clubs, book fairs, and direct mail, increased 2 percent to 36 percent of dollars spent. Bookstore purchases decreased 2 percent, to 25 percent.
Educational and nonfiction titles both increased in dollars spent. Fiction, activity books, and reference books decreased.

Source: Based on reports in *Publishers Weekly,* the *Veronis Suhler Communications Industry Forecast,* and *Subtext.*

a distinct accent). Asked about Marcato's publishing program, Aronson reports, "I won't shy away from more experimental books. Judd Winick, author of *Pedro and Me: Friendship, Loss, and What I Learned* (Henry Holt), a Printz Honor book, will publish a new book in the line. I'll also publish issue books and definitely sports—but the inner experience of sports. I'm also very interested in the arts." Aronson adds, "I tend not to want to do books anyone else can do. I want the books to reflect how I see the world."

For many years, nonfiction was synonymous with the publishing lines of the *institutional* houses, the companies that sold to schools and libraries. But, as Aronson points out, in the past, nonfiction was defined by curriculum content areas, and publishers published a book on every curriculum subject. When a nonfiction author proposed a book to a trade publisher, and was asked what was available in the market, there was always something already in print on the subject. Now, with greater attention to newer nonfiction styles in the *trade* houses, "there can be more of a focus on *how* it's written," says Aronson.

Content is no longer all. Style optimizes content. As Lindsay notes, "The best teaching books are the ones in which the author is obviously enthused about his or her subject, as is evidenced in all the Sibert winners."

Meanwhile, the practical objectives of educators—standardized testing—are fueling a call for nonfiction. "Testing requires analysis of expository writing," says Aronson. "Kids need to practice that skill." They can't practice it on fiction, and so, the need for nonfiction is only likely to increase. Middle-grade and picture book nonfiction continue to be strong categories, but in books with fresh style—and publishing style also influences the outcome of nonfiction.

Lindsay says, "Historical books seem to be taking two very different directions. There are still more and more picture-book-style biographies, usually with fictionalized dialogue and drama, that really do make history fun for a young audience, but don't give much insight into the process of history and historical research. At the same time, more authors of longer historical books are including author's notes, annotated source notes, etc." She adds, "I've had a couple of interesting conversations with nonfiction authors on this subject, indicating that the decision about the level of notation often resides with the editor or publisher, not the author, and that an author might turn out two very different looking historical treatments from two different publishers."

Also on the increase is more heavily illustrated nonfiction and beautiful bookmaking. Two notable examples are *Shipwrecked! The True Adventures of a Japanese Boy,* by Rhoda Blumberg (HarperCollins), and *The Lamp, The Ice and the Boat Called Fish: Based on a True Story,* by Jacqueline Briggs Martin, illustrated by Beth Krommes (Houghton Mifflin). Both titles were under consideration by the ALA's Association for Library Services to Children (ALSC), specifically by its Children's Notables Committee, and received strong reviews.

Illustrated picture book biographies continued strong, particularly in sports. *Hank Aaron: Brave In Every Way*, by Peter Golenbock and illustrated by Paul Lee (Gulliver Books), was a beautiful example. "Biography is another area of nonfiction in which I think we've seen some fascinating breakthroughs in books that look honestly at lives of people who have made a difference," says O'Malley. "No longer idealizing or reverential, biographies for readers of all ages now take frank looks at men and women in the context of the times, places, and situations that shaped them."

Finally, of course, was the refreshing fact that a nonfiction book won the Caldecott medal, a rarity. *So You Want to Be President?* (Philomel), illustrated by David Small in a mix of watercolor, ink, and pastel chalk, was written by Judith St. George. Many nonfiction enthusiasts, like Lindsay, were delighted by this turn of events.

"I think it's fantastic that this year's Caldecott was nonfiction. Of course, it's in picture book format and the illustrations are of equal importance with the text in terms of conveying the information with a certain mood. Illustrations can be vital in an informational book."

Lindsay goes on to speculate about the future, a future that appears to shine brightly for nonfiction. "I hope we see soon a Sibert medal and a Caldecott or Newbery medal on the same book. I think we will. Librarians always talk about medal contenders towards the end of the year, and the people serving on those committees listen. As more and more people start talking about the Sibert, and as former Sibert committee members start serving on the Newbery or Caldecott, I think we'll see nonfiction take a stronger place in these prestigious awards. Now that the American Library Association is publicly recognizing excellence in informational books for children, I think it can only do good for the market." In fact, it already has.

YA Fiction's Second Golden Age
Like nonfiction, young adult literature has benefited by the creation of its own award, the Printz. Since the first Printz award was given to Walter Dean Myers's *Monster* (HarperCollins) last year, the profile of YA has been high.

Lauri Hornik, Editorial Director at Dial Books, agrees. "In general, YA publishing is quite strong now, and certainly much higher profile than it was even five years ago. People grumble about recent articles (in the *New York Times* and *Washington Post*) that have

A YA Trend Is Born?

Identifying the start of a trend is sometimes a most difficult proposition. The concurrence of two or more books of a similar format, theme, or type may be mere coincidence—or, as it may seem, the beginning of a trend. Such is the case with the second-person voice in young adult literature.

Alix Reid, Editorial Director at HarperCollins, says, "I think that thanks to *Bright Lights, Big City,* writers and publishers were scared off from the second-person singular for many years. But recently, several extremely talented writers have been exploring this voice in YA fiction, as a way of capturing the alienation that teenagers feel—from their parents, from their peers, and even from themselves."

You Don't Know Me, by David Klass (Farrar, Straus & Giroux); *Freewill,* by Chris Lynch (HarperCollins); and *Damage,* by A.M. Jenkins (HarperCollins) all use the second person. While *You Don't Know Me* employs this voice only sporadically to address various characters directly, both *Freewill* and *Damage* are written fully in second-person singular, creating a subtle detachment from the main character that serves the theme in both novels.

In commenting on the effectiveness of the narrative style in *Damage,* Reid says, "A.M. Jenkins's use of the second-person voice brilliantly conveys her protagonist's overwhelming depression. Austin Reid, high school football star, has everything going for him, but he can't seem to get out of bed in the morning. He feels guilty for not feeling happy, but he just can't feel happy; his emotions are so overwhelming that he almost feels numb. Amanda's use of the second person immediately tells the reader that there is something *wrong* with Austin—that the way he views the world and himself is not as a complete person, but as a splintered entity. It's hard to imagine how else the book could have been written!"

made a big deal about the gritty or racy subject matter in current YA fiction. But I see these articles as a sign that there's new interest in the genre from folks outside of the children's book world. Bookstores are beginning to move their YA selections out of the children's book corners and they're even expanding these sections. The ALA has finally created an award specifically for YA writing. Publishers are getting jazzier—much more inventive—with their cover and marketing approaches. And these things are paying off: Laurie Halse Anderson's *Speak* (Farrar, Straus & Giroux) was on the *New York Times* best-seller list, for example."

That's good news for the writers and editors of YA fiction, once a much harder sell but now everyone's darling. This, despite the untimely demise of the Teen People Book Club after only a year. Hornik says, "It's an exhilarating time for me, an editor who has always focused much of my attention on YA publishing. When I moved from Bantam Doubleday Dell to Dial,

the author I was most strongly encouraged to bring with me was Nancy Werlin. What a satisfying thing that is—to have your YA authors wooed by your new company and to be fully supported in your desire to grow your imprint's YA list! Dial was publishing only the very occasional YA title before I got here; now after less than two years, 10 to 15 percent of our list is YA and I don't see any reason to stop there. Two of the fall Dial titles that got the most hurrahs from booksellers are YAs: Richard Peck's *Fair Weather* and Nancy Werlin's *Black Mirror*."

What are the trends, then, in this hot genre? As the two new titles that Hornik points to above prove, both historical and mysteries/thrillers continue to occupy a strong spot. The Edgar Award for the Best Young Adult Mystery went to *Counterfeit Son,* by Elaine Marie Alphin (Harcourt), a riveting blend of the thriller with the realistic/edgy YA genre that has held strong for several years.

Realistic YA surfaced again, splendidly, in this year's Coretta Scott King Award winner, *Miracle's Boys,* by Jacqueline Woodson (Putnam). The long awaited arrival of Chris Crutcher's newest novel, *Whale Talk* (Greenwillow), satisfied those who like their YA fiction gritty and true.

Fantasy continues to play strong across the age categories. The second annual Printz Award went to *Kit's Wilderness,* by David Almond (Delacorte), whose first book, *Skellig* (Delacorte), splashed him on the American YA literary scene by winning a Printz Honor. All eyes are now on his new release, *Heaven Eyes* (Delacorte), written for a slightly younger audience. Garth Nix's *Lirael: Daughter of the Clayr* (HarperCollins), the anticipated sequel to the popular *Sabriel* (HarperCollins), was met with tremendous enthusiasm by the teens at the Best Books for Young Adults Teen Session at last year's Midwinter ALA conference. Finally, Hyperion's *Artemis Fowl*, by Eoin Colfer, has taken fantasy in a new direction, combining traditional fairy legend with the high-tech crime world for a raucous ride.

Verse Forms

Unconventional formats, characters, or subjects like those often found in fantasy, are an easy sell to teens, who are always looking for something new and fresh. While the contemporary novel in verse is certainly not a new concept in YA literature, having a history at least back to Virginia Euwer Wolff's 1993 novel *Make Lemonade* (Scholastic) and gaining a solid footing with Karen Hesse's Newbery Medal-winning *Out of the Dust* (Scholastic), they have now burst onto the scene in significant enough numbers to be called a trend.

Seven years later, Wolff has published the sequel to *Make Lemonade,* entitled *True Believer* (Atheneum), and promises a third for a trilogy. Sonya Sones, whose novel in verse *Stop Pretending: What Happened When My Big Sister Went Crazy* (HarperCollins) was an ALA Best Book for Young Adults and a Top Ten Quick Pick, published *What My Mother Doesn't Know* (Simon & Schuster), the delightful, sassy story in verse of a girl's romantic and sexual awakening.

David Gale, Editorial Director of Simon & Schuster Books for Young Readers and Sones's editor, comments on the surge in novels in verse, calling them a natural outgrowth of novels that are in essence collections of short stories that work together, such as a title of a few years ago, *Doing Time: Notes from the Undergrad,* by Rob Thomas (Simon & Schuster). "There is also more acceptance of poetry among teens, and most novels in verse have an emotional intensity that poetry allows," Gale says. Ron Koertge's *The Brimstone Journals* (Candlewick) takes an even more unconventional approach, telling in verse the story of 15 high school students in modern America from 15 discrete viewpoints.

Another trend in YA format is the explosion of fiction written as diaries or journals. Dryden, at Margaret K. McElderry Books, says, "I am intrigued by and enthusiastic about YA novels written in a journal format. On the one hand, the journal format offers the author many opportunities for delving deeply into the voice and mind of a character; on the other hand, the format can limit the author by preventing any in-depth exploration of feelings and moods of characters other than the journal writer."

The imposed limitation in point of view often makes for a stronger connection between reader and main character. In Kelly Easton's *Life History of a Star* (McElderry), says Dryden, "Kristen's moods and interpretations of things and people around her are critical to the arc of the story; we get to know those moods and interpretations intimately and immediately by virtue of the story being told in the journal format. The journal format gives Kristen's story an intensity that it otherwise might not have if the story were written in the third person, from the perspective of an outside narrator. The journal format allows us to hear a voice and know a person without anyone else's tone, mood, or opinion getting in the way."

But it is also a limitation that a skilled writer will work around. As Dryden points out, "Easton cleverly overcomes any limitations the journal entry format may cause by calling upon her own playwriting background to include dialogue in Kristen's journal entries. This dialogue is set up in a play format, with the speaker's name and a colon in front of their speech. So even though we cannot know what characters other than Kristen are feeling or experiencing, Easton does let us hear

the real voices and real words of other characters and we come to know them a bit better that way."

Light and breezy novels in diary format have been notably strong, from Louise Rennison's *On the Bright Side, I'm Now the Girlfriend of a Sex God*, a sequel to the Printz Honor Book *Angus, Thongs, and Full-Frontal Snogging* (both from HarperCollins) to *Princess in the Spotlight,* by Meg Cabot (HarperCollins), a sequel to *Princess Diaries* (HarperCollins), made more popular by the Disney movie release.

The diary format is used to strong effect in books with a bit more emotional weight as well. Cynthia Leitich Smith uses journal entries as part, but not the whole, of her first novel, *Rain Is Not My Indian Name* (HarperCollins). HarperCollins Executive Editor Rosemary Brosnan finds that the entries add a rich dimension to the novel. "I think the journal entries are intriguing: They jump back and forth in time, they touch on matters that are truly important to Rain, and they give readers a window into her soul. The journal entries let the reader see into Rain's past, into events that happened before the book opens. Sometimes it's easier for Rain to write in her journal about things that are important to her—about special times with her mother, for instance—than for her to talk about these things during the course of the book."

The journal is an essential device of *Breathing Underwater*, by Alex Flinn (HarperCollins). In this first novel told from the violent protagonist's point of view, Nick abuses his girlfriend until her parents have a restraining order

Middle-Grade Fiction Publishers

Following each of the publishers is the number of children's books, including middle-grade fiction, published on last year's list.

■ **Alef Design Group:** Jewish religious fiction. 1 title.

■ **All About Kids:** To age 10. Story picture books in many genres. 9 titles.

■ **Atheneum Books for Young Readers:** Many genres, including adventure, fantasy and science fiction, historical, mystery. 80 titles.

■ **Augsburg Books:** Evangelical Christian, religious & inspirational fiction. 22 titles.

■ **Avon Books:** HarperCollins. Adventure, historical fiction, mysteries, family & social fiction. 300 titles, many licensed or reprints.

■ **Barron's Educational Series:** Sells to the school & library market. 60 titles.

■ **Bethany House:** Evangelical Christian; series fiction. 57 titles.

■ **Blue Sky Press:** Scholastic Inc. Adventure, folklore, historical, humor, multicultural, and more. 17 titles.

■ **Boyds Mills Press:** Genres include adventure, ethnic, multicultural. 50 titles.

■ **The Brookfield Reader:** Historical fiction, adventure, folklore, suspense, sports, and other genres. 2 titles.

■ **Candlewick Press:** Most genres, including adventure, fantasy, folktales, nature. 180 titles.

■ **Carolrhoda Books:** Contemporary, historical, mystery, multicultural, and more. 106 titles.

■ **Clarion Books:** Houghton Mifflin. Many genres, including adventure, folk and fairy tales, science fiction. 60 titles.

■ **Coteau Books:** Canadian authors only; any genre except horror. 10 titles.

■ **Cricket Books:** Currently reviewing middle-grade fiction; genres include contemporary, fantasy, historical, multicultural. 12 titles.

■ **Crossway Books:** Evangelical Christian. 20 titles.

■ **Dial Books for Young Readers:** Literary fiction wanted. 35 titles.

■ **DiskUs Publishing:** Online publisher. 15 titles.

■ **Dorling Kindersley:** All genres. 150 titles.

■ **Down East:** New England regional publisher now expanding into other regions. 9 titles.

■ **Dutton Children's Books:** Penguin Putnam. All genres. 101 titles.

■ **Eakin Press:** Regional publisher; fiction on Texas and the Southwest. 30 titles.

■ **Ebooksonthe.net:** Online publisher for all ages, all genres.

■ **Educators Publishing Service:** Ethnic, multicultural, other genres. 30 titles.

■ **Eerdmans Books for Young Readers:** Christian; inspirational and religious fiction, retellings of classic tales. 12 titles.

Middle-Grade Fiction Publishers

■ **E.M. Press:** Regional titles for Maryland, Virginia, Washington, DC area; many genres, including animal and holiday stories. 2 titles.

■ **Farrar, Straus & Giroux:** Contemporary, fantasy, humor, mystery, other genres. 80 titles.

■ **The Feminist Press:** Ethnic, multicultural fiction with strong female characters. 4 titles.

■ **Fondo de Cultura Economica USA:** Spanish language titles for the American market; many genres. 40 titles.

■ **Formac Publishing:** Canadian; most genres, including sports. 20 titles.

■ **Forward Movement:** Episcopalian; contemporary fiction with Christian themes. 16 titles.

■ **Frances Foster Books:** Farrar, Straus & Giroux. Selective, literary list. 16 titles.

■ **Front Street Books:** Highest quality; looks for new authors. 16 titles.

■ **Laura Geringer Books:** HarperCollins. Variety of genres, including stories about nature, fantasy, historical. 14 titles.

■ **Greenwillow Books:** HarperCollins. Animal stories, contemporary, other genres. 49 titles.

■ **Guardian Press:** Online subsidy publisher of many genres. 26 titles.

■ **Gulliver Books:** Harcourt Brace. Contemporary adventure and light fantasy wanted. 30 titles.

■ **Hampton Roads:** Inspirational, metaphysical, visionary fiction. 5 titles.

■ **Harcourt Children's Books:** All genres. 165 titles.

■ **HarperCollins:** All genres. 500 titles.

■ **Hendrick-Long Publishing:** Fiction on Texas and the Southwest. 8 titles.

■ **Holiday House:** Wants literary novels. 60 titles.

■ **Henry Holt and Co.:** All genres. 63 titles.

■ **Houghton Mifflin:** Welcomes new writers, but a competitive market; all genres. 90 titles.

■ **Imperial International:** Educational, including hi/lo. 15 titles.

■ **Just Us Books:** Black history and culture. 4 titles.

■ **Key Porter Books:** Canadian; animals, nature, environment. 11 titles.

■ **Alfred A. Knopf Books for Young Readers:** Contemporary, historical, multicultural, and other genres; high-quality. 60 titles.

■ **Kudlicka Publishing:** Online publisher. 20 titles.

■ **Lerner Publications:** Specializes in nonfiction, but does some fiction. 200 titles.

■ **Arthur A. Levine Books:** Scholastic. Currently wants genre-oriented middle-grade fiction. 45 titles.

■ **Little, Brown and Co.:** All genres, high-quality. 94 titles.

■ **MapleInk Publishing:** Online publisher. 25 titles.

Middle-Grade Fiction Publishers

■ **Margaret K. McElderry Books:** Simon & Schuster. Looking for middle-grade fiction for 2004-2005 list. 26 titles.

■ **Meadowbrook Press:** Many genres; specializes in anthologies. 4 titles.

■ **Moody Press:** Christian; Westerns, Bible stories, fantasy, historical, mystery. 80 titles.

■ **National Geographic Society:** Some fiction, including a middle-grade mystery series; nature, the environment. 40 titles.

■ **Naturegraph Publishers:** Native American lore, folktales, myths. 3 titles.

■ **New Leaf Press:** Christian; religious themes. 10 titles.

■ **Orchard Books:** Scholastic. All genres. 30 titles.

■ **The Overmountain Press:** Appalachian folklore, regional fiction. 5 titles.

■ **Owl Books:** Canadian authors. 10 titles.

■ **Pacific Press Publishing:** Seventh-day Adventist; Biblical ideas must be conveyed. 30 titles.

■ **Parachute Press:** Packager; concentrates on horror titles. 100 titles.

■ **Paulist Press:** Catholic; chapter books for middle-graders with Catholic themes. 12 titles.

■ **Peachtree Publishers:** Atlanta company; regional, multicultural. 20 titles.

■ **Pelican Publishing:** Louisiana company; holiday, fantasy, folklore, historical, regional. 99 titles.

■ **Perfection Learning:** Hi/lo in many genres, including sports. 100+ titles.

■ **Philomel Books:** Penguin Putnam. Any genre, but must be very fresh and new. 25 titles.

■ **Piñata Books:** Hispanic people and culture. 10 titles.

■ **Pitspopany Press:** Jewish; religious, ethnic, multicultural, adventure, science fiction, other genres. 7 titles.

■ **The Place in the Woods:** Multicultural. 4 titles.

■ **Pleasant Company Publications:** Books for girls; animals, contemporary, historical. 60 titles.

■ **G.P. Putnam's Sons:** Penguin Putnam. Contemporary, multicultural, and other fiction. 36 titles.

■ **Saint Mary's Press:** Catholic; religious, contemporary, fantasy, historical. 4 titles.

■ **Scholastic Book Group:** All genres; high standards. 500 titles.

■ **SeaStar Books:** Many genres, especially contemporary and historical. 21 titles.

■ **Silver Moon Press:** Looking for titles on American history, especially colonial times, and very suspenseful mysteries. 6 titles.

■ **Silver Whistle:** Harcourt, Inc. Folktales, inspirational, adventure, contemporary. 14 titles.

Middle-Grade Fiction Publishers

■ **Simon & Schuster Books for Young Readers:** High-quality, all genres. 75 titles.

■ **Sports Publishing:** Fiction about sports and athletes. 80 titles.

■ **Starlight Writer Publications:** Online publisher. Time travel, romance, humor, other genres. 12 titles.

■ **Third World Press:** African, African-American, and Caribbean life. 12 titles.

■ **Megan Tingley Books:** Little, Brown. Particularly looking for strong female characters. 22 titles.

■ **Torah Aura Productions:** Jewish themes. 18 titles.

■ **Tor Books:** Fantasy and science fiction. 25 titles.

■ **Tricycle Press:** Particularly looking for middle-grade fiction. 21 titles.

■ **Viking Children's Books:** Penguin Putnam. High-quality, all genres. 75 titles.

■ **Walker and Co.:** Contemporary, historical, other genres. 24 titles.

■ **White Mane Publishing:** Specializes in historical fiction, almost all about the Civil War. 14 titles.

■ **Albert Whitman & Co.:** Humor, historical fiction, mystery, other genres. 30 titles.

■ **Winslow Press:** Looking actively for middle-grade fiction in many genres, including regional, fantasy. 21 titles.

■ **Wright Group:** McGraw-Hill. Classroom use, many genres. 225 titles.

■ **Zonderkidz:** Christian; inspirational fiction, romance, humor, mystery. 60 titles.

issued against him. The journal is an effective stylistic tool, a court-ordered device that allows Nick to reveal the backstory of his stormy relationship with Caitlin while the narrative line moves forward in the present, after the restraining order is issued. Like Easton and Smith, Flinn uses the journal format to enhance revelation of character in a manner that more firmly connects the reader to the protagonist.

Finally, short story anthologies have burgeoned in the YA publishing market. Hornik, who acquired one of those popular anthologies, *On the Fringe*, edited by Don Gallo, agrees. "Yes, the short-story anthology is definitely a genre that has exploded in the last few years. Editors find the projects attractive because they allow us to publish acclaimed authors who would otherwise be out of reach. The focus on one particular theme makes for easy marketing, often especially to schools—though I'm not sure that anthologies are finding their way into as many classrooms as we'd like. When I acquired *On the Fringe*, it was with the strong hope that the book would be useful to high school teachers who wanted a way to discuss more easily the issue of ostracism and its repercussions. So far it's selling nicely, and I like to think that a large portion of the buyers are teachers."

Other notable recent YA anthologies include *The Color of Absence, 12 Stories about Loss and Hope,* edited by James Howe (Atheneum), and *Love and Sex, 10 Stories of Truth,* edited by Michael Cart (Simon & Schuster). Gale, also editor of *Love and Sex,* comments, "Many kids like themed short story collections devoted to an interesting topic with a variety of views." As an editor, he shares Hornik's appreciation for the opportunity to publish authors not regularly on his list.

Middle-Grade Fiction Continues Strong and in Demand

Middle-grade fiction has long been a strong segment of children's publishing, and while middle-grade didn't dazzle as YA did in the past year, it has continued with a hardy showing and is attracting new interest. Four trends are apparent in middle-grade fiction, though none entirely new: the continued popularity of historical fiction, ongoing popularity of Southern regional voices, a rise in humor with substance, and a predictable continuation of interest in fantasy.

Historical fiction got a boost when the Newbery Medal was awarded to *A Year Down Yonder,* by Richard Peck (Dial), the Depression-era sequel to Peck's *A Long Way from Chicago,* which won a Newbery Honor. In demand for this age, too, has been fiction about World War II. Avi's *Don't You Know There's a War on?* (HarperCollins) focuses on life on the home front during World War II, while Harry Mazer's *A Boy at War: A Novel of Pearl Harbor* (Simon & Schuster) personalizes the infamous bombing by focusing on a 15-year-old boy who witnessed the attack, knowing his father was on the *U.S.S. Arizona* at the time.

But historical fiction for middle-graders also went beyond the most commonly popular eras in American history. Of particular note were Linda Sue Park's *A Single Shard* (Clarion),

Other Industry Trends

Not surprisingly, in this era of television and media-driven culture, media tie-ins in children's books continue. Television tie-ins such as the Kipper (Simon & Schuster) and Arthur (Little, Brown) lines continued to grow, as did the number of books by celebrity authors. Last year saw the publication of *Just the Two of Us,* by actor and musician Will Smith, illustrated by Kadir Nelson (Scholastic); *Marsupial Sue,* by John Lithgow, illustrated by Jack E. Davis (Simon & Schuster); and *Growing Up Is Hard,* by radio and television analyst Laura Schlessinger, illustrated by Daniel McFeeley (HarperCollins).

Movie tie-ins proved equally strong. Random House released 17 children's books in several formats from flip book to storybook based on Disney's summer movie *Atlantis: The Lost Empire,* and Tim Burton's remake of *Planet of the Apes* engendered titles from comic books to adult and juvenile novelizations of the movie, as well as a reissue of the original book by Pierre Boulle.

which is set in twelfth-century Korea, and *Storm Warriors*, by Elisa Carbone (Knopf), a novel about the U.S. Lifesaving Service in 1895 on Pea Island off the North Carolina coast. Both titles were strongly reviewed and under consideration by the ALSC's Children's Notables Committee.

Southern regional fiction continued to hold sway in the middle-grade market as well. Caitlyn Dlouhy, Senior Editor at Atheneum Books, values the use of the Southern voice in children's fiction. "If done extremely well," she says, "it can be so warm and honest (yet full of subtlety) that it is easy for the reader to empathize with, if not flat out fall in love with, the characters. A strong Southern voice contains a flavor that is just so pure and true. It isn't influenced by what's hip or what's trendy or what's on MTV. It can create the same kind of effect on readers, as though they've been eating several meals of gooey, decadent desserts, and now all they yearn for is a cool,

crisp apple, or a ripe peach. And oftentimes, the issues within these types of novels are of a less frivolous nature, because the characters have a more timeless quality to them. I think that's why *Dovey Coe* has been so warmly received—the author created a character whose voice is as true as she is to herself, and readers respond to that."

The riveting first-person voices of Dovey in the Edgar Award-winning, *Dovey Coe,* by Frances O'Roark Dowell (Atheneum), and of India Opal Buloni in the Newbery Honor book *Because of Winn-Dixie,* by Kate DeCamillo (Candlewick), are strong evidence of a solid trend. The same might be said for the Southern voice in such new titles as *Love, Ruby Lavender,* by Deborah Wiles (Harcourt), with its feisty Ruby and her wise old grandmother, Miss Eula. It's no wonder then that Southern fiction for children continues to gather a following.

Humor, of course, is a perennial of

children's novels. One need only think of Winnie the Pooh and Ramona for proof. But humor in middle-grade fiction now often has an added punch—humor with substance, if you will. Kathy Dawson, Executive Editor of G. P. Putnam's Sons, reflects on her own childhood experiences with humor in fiction: "I had almost no sense of humor as a child. I was very serious, so I didn't look for any humor in books then. But I did read emotionally true, poignant books that were peripherally, now that I think of it, very funny. *Harriet the Spy*, by Louise Fitzhugh, Constance Greene's *A Girl Called Al*, and the rest, even some of Judy Blume's books, had humor. I didn't actually pick up on the humor in those books as a kid, but when I go back and read them now, it's so clearly there."

That trend toward serious topics laced with humor has escalated, most notably in Jack Gantos's award-winning Joey Pigza books, published by Farrar, Straus & Giroux, including *Joey Pigza Swallows the Key* and the Newbery Honor winner *Joey Pigza Loses Control*, a book more poignant and less raucously humorous than the first.

As Dawson expresses it, "In some ways, I guess I feel that is the role of humor in the middle-grade fiction I love: dessert, but not the main course. The books I love aren't *funny*. They are much more than that, and yet there's humor too. I would say what I look for is *smart humor*: humor that tells a deeper truth as it makes you laugh, humor that emerges from painful situations. Paula Danziger talks a lot about that connection between pain

and humor. I think the best humor comes from truth or pain, which are sometimes one and the same. I see humor in middle-grade fiction playing the same role as it does in life. Humor draws us in, humor makes us feel closer to other people, or characters, humor makes us remember we're only human."

Dawson cites a middle-grade title she edited that exemplifies her points about humor, including the fact that humor is largely about timing, beats, and also underscores the increase in substantive humorous fiction. Dawson says, "In *Notes From a Liar and Her Dog* (Putnam), Gennifer Choldenko did not set out to write a funny book, and she's surprised when people tell her it's funny. In fact, half the people who read the book cry and half laugh. I think it depends on whether or not the reader has sisters, and where they fall in the line up: oldest, middle, or youngest. But that just goes to show

how subjective humor really is. Gennifer was able to get close to difficult sister issues without getting heavy or depressing, and I think that's often the role of humor—it can make serious issues more digestible."

Finally, fantasy continued the trend in middle-grade fiction begun with Harry Potter. While we recover from the first movie and await the fifth installment in the Harry Potter books, readers are still gleefully gobbling up fantasy and publishers are still cheerfully publishing it. Eva Ibbotson's books have taken center stage in the middle-grade fantasy world with the release of *An Eva Ibbotson Collection: Which Witch?, The Secret of Platform 13, Island of the Aunts,* three titles in a single volume (Dutton), as well as her *Dial a Ghost* (Dutton).

Stephanie Owens Lurie, President and Publisher, Dutton's Children's Books, muses, "Eva is now a *Publishers Weekly* and *New York Times* bestselling author, thanks in large part to the fact that booksellers are recommending her books as post-Harry Potter reading. Of course, she was around long before Ms. Rowling!"

Other authors and publishers have benefited from the Harry-wake as well. SeaStar launched a new series with Robin Jarvis's *The Dark Portal: Book One of the Deptford Mice Trilogy* and followed up with the sequel, *The Crystal Prison.* Additionally, Nancy Springer published a female protagonist fantasy entitled *Rowan Hood: Outlaw Girl of Sherwood Forest* (Philomel). As with YA, the market for middle-grade fantasy shows no signs of diminishing.

Picture Book Market Tightens

The children's book market has grown tighter in one of its most conspicuous and enduring categories, however: picture books. Lurie comments, "We have heard that the market for hardcover picture books is getting more and more difficult. The preschool area in particular is suffering; the demographic isn't there right now." The baby boom echo is now reverberating through those middle grades and young adults; the numbers of very young children in the U.S. has declined for the time being.

The market in picture books is therefore seeking out the one-of-a-kind work that will capture hearts young and old. Editors are on a search for such titles as the Caldecott Honors *Olivia,* written and illustrated by Ian Falconer (Atheneum), and *Click, Clack Moo, Cows that Type,* illustrated by Betsy Lewin and written by Doreen Cronin (Simon & Schuster). *Short* and *fun* are the traits picture book editors are repeating most. "People are choosing entertainment over edification in trade picture books these days," opines Lurie. "Many don't have time to study and puzzle out a subtle or complicated book when they are in the bookstore. Books have to be *loud* to compete with television, the Internet, video games, and movies."

Certainly, many books considered by the ALA award committees bear out that truth. *Car Wash,* by Sandra and Susan Steen, illustrated by G. Brian Karas (Putnam); *Five Creatures* by Emily Jenkins and illustrated by Tomek Bogacki (Farrar, Straus & Giroux), which was the *Boston Globe-Horn Book* Honor Book in the picture book category; and *The Great Gracie Chase: Stop that Dog!* by Cynthia Rylant, illustrated by Mark Teague (Blue Sky Press), all fit the short and fun description. No ponderous texts there. No heavy requirement of the reader. Just a romp, whether through a car wash, a family's character traits, or the entire town.

"Bookstore visits have shown me that humor is popular at the moment," says Lurie. "For older picture book readers and middle-graders, the humor is often edgy and off-the-wall, as in the shows they are watching on the Cartoon Network. Many preschool books, even concept books, are light and funny too. We've had success with a picture book called *Dog's Colorful Day: A Messy Story About Colors* and *Counting,* by Emma Dodd (Dutton), in which readers can identify the colors that land on a *blobby* white dog that gets increasingly messy as the day goes on. Picture books with a gimmick that adults and children can appreciate together, such as *If You Take a Mouse to the Movies,* by Laura Numeroff, illustrated by Felicia Bond (HarperCollins), or *What Dads Can't Do,* by Douglas Wood and illustrated by Doug Cushman (Simon & Schuster), are selling well."

Humor is likely to continue strong as families seek to escape the horrors of the terrorist attacks and all that followed. Dryden notes that families are seeking *bibliotherapy,* as sales for one McElderry title, written by Robie H. Harris and illustrated by Jan Ormerod, have proven. "Since September 11, 2001, interest in and sales of *Goodbye Mousie* have increased," Dryden notes.

"As a fictional picture book about a child who loses his beloved mouse, a story like *Goodbye Mousie* makes talking about death and the perfectly normal stages anyone goes through when someone they love has died a bit easier for adults as well as for children."

Fractured nursery rhymes and fairy tales are in publishing vogue now, too. *Beware of the Storybook Wolves,* by Lauren Child (Arthur A. Levine), and *The Three Pigs,* by David Wiesner (Clarion), both capitalize on the threads of familiar fairy tales and on visual jokes for their humor, to create successful—and sophisticated—books that appeal to adult readers as well as child listeners.

The Stevens sisters' romp through nursery rhymes, *And the Dish Ran Away with the Spoon,* by Janet Stevens and Susan Crummel Stevens (Harcourt), exhibits just the sort of intellectual *gimmick* that Lurie cites as a

E-Publishing Begins to Make Inroads

"Our goal is to become the Amazon of children's e-books. Our goal is that if someone is looking for an e-book, they'll come to us," says Harold Underdown, Vice President, Editorial, of ipicturebooks.com, the Time Warner Trade Publishing affiliate launched last year and dedicated to providing high-quality e-books. Authors and illustrators should not feel left behind if they are not yet involved in e-publishing, Underdown says. "It's very early in the game and no one knows where it will go." While the e-book announcement-of-the-day frenzy has passed, there are no standardized e-book formats. Underdown hopes that e-publishing will settle into two: one for illustrated books and one for text only.

Right now, there are three levels of endeavor in the e-book market, Underdown says—by large houses, individuals, and new ventures. Big publishers, such as Random House, are simply experimenting, using e-books as a form of marketing, and coordinated by the marketing departments. In November, Random House launched Random View Books, calling it the company's "first e-book publishing program." The line so far consists of e-book versions of successful middle-grade and young adult titles by authors such as Christopher Paul Curtis, Patricia Reilly Giff, Gary Paulsen, and Philip Pullman at a price of $3.99.

Underdown says big houses might also give away as many as 20,000 copies of a complete .pdf version of one of the new books in a series they are launching. The big houses are also archiving electronic copies of books they acquire, but as for moving wholeheartedly into electronic markets, Underdown says, "Fairly limited things are going on."

Beyond the big houses, many individuals with just a little money are buying sites, setting up shop online, and calling themselves e-book publishers. "Writers need to tread warily," Underdown warns. It requires very little money and absolutely no experience to call oneself an e-book publisher.

feature adults appreciate in the picture books they share with kids.

Diverse Books, Diverse Kids

After the boom in multicultural publishing of the early to mid-1990s, anyone looking at children's publishing must pause to wonder about the state of multiculturalism in the current market. According to some, what was certainly once a trend is now just daily business. "I think multiculturalism is now just part of publishing rather than a trend," says Brosnan. "We know there is a need for multicultural books and that all children should be able to see themselves represented in books. I think the big push of the early nineties has calmed down, but we are still publishing great multicultural books. I made a commitment long ago to publishing new voices, writers of

E-Publishing Begins to Make Inroads

Many of these publishers are doing very little, if anything, to protect books from being copied. They are posting them in non-secure formats and trusting people to be honest in downloading, employing an acknowledged honor system. "Be nervous," Underdown cautions writers and illustrators. Similarly, he warns authors and illustrators to be wary of e-book publishers who charge the cost of conversion for out-of-print books. That, he says, is another brand of vanity press. "Steer clear of these companies," he advises.

In between the large publishers and the mom-and-pop enterprises, may lie a middle ground; Underdown speculates that ipicturebooks.com might be the only company occupying that ground at the moment. Their twofold aim is to license books from publishers (allowing publishers to experiment in the e-books market with a solid structure in place), and to purchase and launch original projects.

Underdown, author of the popular Purple Crayon website (www.under-down.org) for children's authors and illustrators, plans to create an E-books Primer at his site, telling readers what electronic publishing is, explaining the different formats, and keeping them abreast of what's happening in e-publishing.

Authors may want to pay some attention to the Rosetta Books case, however. In a ruling handed down last year, Judge Sidney Stein of the U.S. District Court for the Southern District of New York found that Random House backlist contracts for eight titles to which they hold print rights do not include e-book rights. Rosetta Books, he ruled, may continue to sell e-book editions of those titles. Contracts on these books, of course, were written long before anyone envisioned electronic books. Therein lies the problem. For those signing contracts in this century, it is wise to always pay close attention to the electronic rights section and negotiate.

color, and writers from other countries, and I try to honor that commitment. It's one of the most important things I do in my career."

Andrea Davis Pinkney, Editorial Director of Hyperion Books for Children agrees. She speaks of a long tradition of books related to multicultural topics in the history of children's publishing. Hyperion's multicultural imprint Jump at the Sun has "a targeted phi-losophy, focus, and sales and marketing strategy." She sees the benefits of a distinct line devoted to multicultural publishing as twofold: It helps Hyperion attract some of the most notable authors and illustrators in the field, such as Bell Hooks and Toni Morrison, and it gives readers a clear place to find some of the best African-American titles published.

HarperCollins, Brosnan reports,

"launched a Hispanic list in fall 2001, and I am coordinating that for the children's division. The new imprint is called Rayo, and it features books in Spanish, bilingual books, books in English by Hispanic writers—anything we think will be of interest to the Hispanic market. It's very exciting!"

Philip Lee, Publisher of Lee & Low Books, takes a slightly different view: "The multicultural publishing boom has cooled. The number of multicultural children's books published has actually declined for three straight years, according to the Cooperative Children's Book Center at the University of Wisconsin, Madison, which tracks data on multicultural children's books." The last data available shows that "there were 147 books by or about African-Americans, 54 Asian-American, 42 Latino, and 39 American Indian. That is just 288 books out of more than 5,000 published."

But Lee's company, a children's publisher entirely dedicated to the publication of multicultural books, is growing. "At Lee & Low, we've expanded our publishing program. We now publish about 14 books a year compared to 5 books a year when we launched our first list in 1993, including board books, as well as reissues of out-of-print, award-winning picture books and young adult titles."

Among recent highlights are a poetry collection, *Love to Mama: A Tribute to Mothers,* edited by Pat Mora, which celebrates Latino mothers and grandmothers, and *Rent Party Jazz,* by William Miller, illustrated by Charlotte Wiley-Webb, a story set in the 1930s about an African-American family raising money to pay rent.

Lee points out that there is good reason for his publishing house to take a single focus. "It is important to recognize the growing need for multicultural books. It is not a fad. The census data tells us that the U.S. is getting more diverse and publishers, large or small, need to provide more materials that reflect this diversity. We have to start with publishing good books, but we also have to do a better job reaching the readers. Good multicultural books, while they may be about a particular culture, should be able to cross cultural boundaries and inform and entertain readers of all backgrounds."

Pinkney says, "Our program continues to grow. I don't know that it should be called a trend, though. We meet a need that is twofold. We offer the world books that hold up a mirror for children of color to view their own experience and we offer a window through which the general public can look at a culture other than their own."

Whether responding to the demographics of the population, the tastes of consumers, or the quest for excellence on the part of librarians and educators, children's publishing continues in its strong commitment to support what is new and fresh. We continue to see many of the most talented authors and illustrators of our time sharing their talents on the pages of children's books with a passionate commitment to intellectual inquiry, to story, and to fun. Kids are the beneficiaries—and so then are we all.

Passing the Torch: From McElderry to Dryden, from Hirschman to Duncan

By Toni Buzzeo

At the turn of the twentieth century, women were nearly invisible in publishing while men thoroughly dominated the industry. Yet within two decades, the first juvenile trade department was established at Macmillan in 1918 and women took the helm. These women, strong and independent leaders, were visionaries who nurtured the development of children's literature. As the twentieth century drew toward its close, many women continued to captain the ship. Two of them, Margaret K. McElderry and Susan Hirschman, had long been among the most revered children's editors.

In so many ways, McElderry and Hirschman changed the face of children's books. Throughout illustrious careers, each edited some of the finest children's books. Between them, their imprints, Margaret K. McElderry Books and Greenwillow Books, have garnered 3 Newbery Medals, 7 Newbery Honors, and 11 Caldecott Honors.

Each of these women has hand-picked her successor, recently passing the torch to another, younger protégé of note, a woman dedicated to carrying on the dream. Emma Dryden now serves as Vice President and Editorial Director of Margaret K. McElderry Books. Virginia Duncan followed Susan Hirschman as Vice President and Publisher of Greenwillow Books.

Friendship, Above All Else

The seamless passing of the torch at each imprint has been made possible by the collaboration of the extraordinary women involved and their shared vision. Yet, when asked what they've most enjoyed about their collaboration over the years, it is friendship they all cite first.

"What I've enjoyed most," says Hirschman, "is knowing Virginia. When we first met, I knew we could work together and that I would admire her as a colleague. But I didn't know that I would love her as a friend. That has been the best." In turn, Duncan treasures her friendship with Hirschman. "I have enjoyed working with Susan and, as she likes to say, hearing about how things were done before I was born and while I was growing up. Working together has mostly been just plain fun."

Dryden couldn't agree more. "I have enjoyed growing as an editor and publisher under Margaret's guidance, advice, and leadership, but I have particularly enjoyed the friendship that has developed between us. We have a friendship that is both professional and personal—and it is that relationship that I cherish above all else." McElderry boils the satisfaction down to that one gift. "The real friendship with Emma Dryden that developed and which I treasure is what I've enjoyed most about working together."

Not only are McElderry and Dryden friends, but they share similar tastes in children's books, which has helped to ensure a smooth transition. "Basically," says McElderry, "our tastes are much alike, both in judging texts and pictures." Dryden agrees. "Margaret's and my taste do tend to be quite alike. We both have a good sense of humor and we tend to particularly like deeply felt characters and a vivid sense of time and place in any story we read." They also share a vision.

Margaret McElderry: The Vision Realized

"My vision was, always has been, and still is to publish the best I can find—both in texts and pictures," says McElderry, former Vice President and Publisher, now Editor-at-Large, of Margaret K. McElderry Books. In her long and esteemed career, that vision helped to shape the field of children's literature as she worked with such greats as Eloise Jarvis McGraw, Margot Benary-Isbert, Antonio Frasconi, Helen Oxenbury, and Susan Cooper.

It also led her to more than a half-century of involvement in work with children's literature in translation. Early in her career, she published German and Japanese postwar novels for children and introduced Americans to writers from England, Australia, and South Africa. In fact, McElderry was one of the first children's book editors to make scouting trips to European publishers, writers, and artists. Happily, Dryden shares McElderry's vision. "I hope to continue to publish books of the highest possible quality in text, artwork, design, and production. I also hope to maintain relationships with foreign publishers, to import picture books and novels from abroad in order to keep the list well-balanced between domestic and foreign projects."

Margaret McElderry was born and grew up in Pittsburgh, Pennsylvania. She attended college at Mount Holyoke, graduating in 1933 with a major in English Literature. Yet it was her second Bachelor of Arts degree, in library science from Carnegie Library School, that set her on a path in children's books. Starting as a children's librarian at the New York Public Library in 1934, McElderry served with legendary Anne Carroll Moore for nearly nine years before she left to join the Office of War Information Overseas Branch in London during World War II. In 1945, she was transferred to Brussels with the United States Information Service as Chief of Special Projects.

It wasn't until November 1945, on returning to New York City, that McElderry began her career in children's publishing. She became Editor of Children's Books at Harcourt, Brace and Company and was one of a legendary generation of women editors in the post-World War II boom years. It didn't take long for McElderry to make her mark. In 1952, she was the first editor to have two books win the Newbery (*Ginger Pye,* by Eleanor Estes) and Caldecott (*Finders Keepers*, illustrated by Nicolas Mordvinoff with text by William Lipkind) in the same year.

Despite 26 successful years as Editor of Children's Books, shepherding other Newbery and Caldecott Medal and Honor winners to publication, in 1971 William Jovanovich asked McElderry to take an early retirement. Fortunately, for the children's book world, she instead accepted an offer to join Atheneum Books as Consulting Editor and Director of Margaret K. McElderry Books, the first children's book imprint to bear an editor's name. In 1984, when Atheneum became part of Macmillan, McElderry became Vice President and Publisher of Margaret K. McElderry Books until her retirement in 1998.

What made McElderry such an extraordinary force in children's books for so many years? Looking back on McElderry's long career, Dryden reflects, "Margaret brings a sense of history to the job, which translates itself into a clear respect for the work she does, a clear respect for the authors with whom she works, and a clear sense of commitment to and pride in her work and the people with whom she works. Margaret also brings herself to the job—her political beliefs and her sense of humor, for example—which makes for an honest and open working environment."

Emma D. Dryden, Assuming the Torch

For her part, Emma Dryden says she has enjoyed growing as an editor and publisher under McElderry's guidance, advice, and leadership. "As an editor," Dryden says, "I've learned an enormous number of things from Margaret, such as the importance of respecting and valuing the author/ editor relationship; how to trust and follow my instincts; and how to write rejection letters that result in receiving "thank you" notes in return. But probably the most valuable thing I've learned from Margaret is the importance of taking extra time to make the author or artist happy."

That belief has come into play as Dryden has worked with such esteemed authors and illustrators as Richard Scarry, Robie H. Harris, Jan Ormerod, David Catrow, Demi, Louise Borden, Chris Demarest, and S.D. Schindler. In her commitment to continue to find and nurture new talent, Dryden has acquired first projects from Kelly Easton, Joan Hiatt Harlow, Kate Hovey, Dianne Ochiltree, Lea Wait, and Karma Wilson. McElderry praises Dryden for her instincts about people: "Her evaluation of people and of their creative possibilities is a great strength."

Dryden, who was born and raised in New York City, started college at Vassar, studying poetry there with Nancy Willard. Before graduating from Smith College with a Bachelor of Arts in English language and literature, she spent the summer working as an intern at Viking Children's Books. She spent her first four years after Smith working at Random House Children's Books before she began to edit with McElderry in 1990. In 1998, Dryden assumed leadership of Margaret K. McElderry Books, becoming Senior Editor and Director.

Looking back over her years working with McElderry, Dryden says, "As a publisher, the most valuable thing I've learned from Margaret is to expect the marketplace to fluctuate and not to panic, but to ride consistently through the up times and the down times, for one necessarily follows the other over and over again. As the director of an imprint bearing Margaret McElderry's name, another valuable lesson I've learned from Margaret is to be proud enough of the imprint and of myself, to care about every single aspect of the book-making process. As a manager of a department, I've learned from Margaret how important it is for those of us who work together in the imprint to feel comfortable and close to one another, as though a family."

McElderry echoes her protégé. She says that working with Dryden has confirmed something she always knew: that those working together every day in children's publishing can be as close as a happy family.

Susan Hirschman, A Legendary Career

Virginia Duncan, whom Susan Hirschman, retired founder and Publisher of Greenwillow Books (an imprint of HarperCollins), chose to succeed her, has incredible respect for her predecessor. "Susan brings an energy, passion, and humor to her work and to the office that is almost indescribable. Working with Susan—and traveling with her to the ALA and IRA conventions, sales conferences, and the Bologna Book Fair—has been a remarkable experience. She is open to the world, to people, and to every manuscript that comes through our door. Her standards are also very high. I was terrified on my first day at Greenwillow, but by the second I felt as though I had been here for years and years. Susan does that. She makes you feel at home."

Susan Hirschman was born in New York City and grew up there. She attended Wellesley College, graduating in 1953, certain she wanted to be a children's book editor. Toward that end, she accepted her first job at Alfred A. Knopf in 1954, serving as a secretary for one year. She spent her mornings working for a children's book editor and afternoons working for the library promotion director.

After this brief internship, she left for Harper and Brothers (later Harper & Row) children's book department, where her real career began. She began as a reader of unsolicited manuscripts, looking for even a single good sentence. For 10 years, she worked there under Ursula Nordstrom before becoming Editor in Chief of the children's book department at Macmillan in 1964. A decade later, in 1974, when all Macmillan department heads were told to cut their lists in half and fire 50 percent of their staffs, Hirschman left in protest and launched her Greenwillow imprint (named after Elizabeth Coatsworth's book *Under the Greenwillow Tree*) at William Morrow and Company.

Hirschman is known for her strong belief in cultivating authors, not books, and sees the strength of any list in its creators. Among Hirschman's authors at Greenwillow were some of the biggest names in the business. She was responsible for launching the careers of Kevin Henkes, Arnold and Anita Lobel, Ann Jonas, Chris Crutcher, Diana Wynne Jones, Tana Hoban, and Jack Prelutsky. Over the years, she has also worked with Aliki, Donald Crews, Sid Fleischman, Pat Hutchins, Ezra Jack Keats, Robin McKinley, Peggy Parish, James Stevenson, Nancy Tafuri, Vera B. Williams, and Charlotte Zolotow.

When asked about her vision for Greenwillow, Hirschman says, "When Greenwillow was founded in 1974, I wanted to be a publisher of the highest quality books for children of every age. I wanted people to forget we were new, and to see us as a traditional publisher. That didn't really take very long. What I wanted was to publish books for kids, not for their parents or any other adults. That's what we've tried to do over the years, whether picture books or young adult novels. We've tried to keep readers in mind." That Greenwillow, an imprint known for its child-friendly books, has accomplished.

Virginia Duncan, Sustaining the Vision

As her retirement approached, Hirschman hired Virginia Duncan, in 1997, as Executive Editor at Greenwillow. When asked what special sensibilities Duncan brought to the job, Hirschman says, "Virginia is smart as a whip. And patient and calm and kind. She knows her own mind, and yet is open to the opinion of others and listens fairly and well. She is an extremely talented line editor, but can also see the whole and relinquish control when necessary. Perhaps most important, she is wonderful to work with, and her colleagues all over the house as well as all our authors and artists know and appreciate this immense gift."

Born and raised outside of Boston, Massachusetts, Duncan attended college at the University of Virginia, earning a Bachelor of Arts degree in English. She began her publishing career in 1985 at Macmillan as an assistant in the subsidiary rights department. She moved on to positions as Editorial Assistant, Associate Editor, and then Editor at Bradbury Press. Finally, she was named Editor in Chief of Four Winds Press in 1991. When Simon & Schuster purchased Macmillan, Duncan was named Executive Editor at Simon & Schuster Books for Young Readers, where she remained until coming to Greenwillow. When Hirschman retired on August 1, 2001,

Duncan was named Vice President and Publisher of Greenwillow Books. Hirschman feels comfortable having left her imprint in Duncan's care. "I admire her totally as a publisher, and I think her editorial vision is superb," she says. "It makes me enormously happy to leave Greenwillow in her hands."

For her part, Duncan says that she learned much from Hirschman during their years of collaboration that she will carry forward into her tenure. "I have learned to trust my instincts, for big things and little things. I also have learned to worry less and act faster. Susan has taught me that if you do things right away, they get done and if you think about them too much, they often don't. She has shown me the importance of allowing our authors to have a family feeling about Greenwillow and the house in general. I always believed in this—but never knew it. Now I do, and I see what it means."

Those authors and illustrators who have a family feeling about Greenwillow and their editor, Duncan, include all of the Greenwillow regulars plus those newer to the list, including Sandra Belton, Brian Karas, Jane Kurtz, Lynne Rae Perkins, Lisa Westburg Peters, Lynn Reiser, Peter Sis, Karen Romano Young, and Amy Bronwen Zemser. Thinking about her authors and illustrators, Duncan says, "When Susan was here, my favorite thing to do at work was sit in her office and listen to publishing stories. My second favorite thing to do was look at a picture book dummy with Susan. One of the most interesting things to me is realizing that so much of what I believe in, and the reason I came into the field in the first place, has not changed." Duncan's belief in the creators of children's books and their vision shines brightly at Greenwillow, just as Hirschman hoped it would.

The Future: The Flame Burns Brightly

The future of both Margaret K. McElderry Books and Greenwillow appears bright. While Hirschman is taking advantage of full retirement at 70, making good on the travel plans she long anticipated, McElderry defines retirement as four days a week in the office, arriving later and leaving earlier than her colleagues.

For their part, Dryden and Duncan haven't missed a beat. They continue to publish wonderful children's books, carrying on the lessons learned from the *grandes dames*, while keeping both eyes on the future.

When asked about plans for the future of her imprint, Duncan says, "I hope to maintain the Greenwillow goal of publishing the very best books possible. I want those books to be for children—really for children—as they always have been. I have adored meeting and getting to know so many of the Greenwillow regulars over the past four years, and I look forward to continuing to publish them, as well as those authors and artists who are newer to the list, and those we haven't met yet."

Dryden echoes Duncan's goal of publishing wonderful books and making room for new talent. "I hope to continue to publish the books I love, whether that means having a best-seller or taking a financial risk now and again. I hope to continue to find new voices and new visions for the imprint, to offer first-time authors and artists a chance. I hope to keep the imprint a solid and viable business within the larger business of which it is part." And, she adds from the heart, "I hope to make Margaret McElderry proud."

Editor David Gale: A Novel Passion

By Toni Buzzeo

When people in the children's writing community are asked to name the top young adult book editors in the business today, David Gale's name makes the list every time, frequently in the top slot. Gale's name is synonymous with honest, risk-taking YA books. As Editorial Director of Simon & Schuster Books for Young Readers, he acquires and edits hardcover trade books, from picture books through novels, but YA novels are his passion. Editing novels is what he loves.

Gale has dedicated the bulk of his career to children's publishing. He holds masters' degrees in the teaching of reading and in children's literature and was previously employed as Executive Editor at HarperCollins Children's Books, Senior Editor at Bantam Doubleday Dell Books for Young Readers, and Associate Book Review Editor of *School Library Journal*. Prior to that, he worked in textbook publishing, on elementary school reading programs. At Simon & Schuster, however, he feels he's found a home. "Simon & Schuster is the perfect place to be. Editorial, design, marketing, publicity, sales, and subsidiary rights are all in place and functioning smoothly," he says. "In other places, at any given time, at least one of these departments can be somewhat problematic."

What Gale most loves about his job, besides the books themselves, is discovering new authors. "I discovered Rob Thomas, Chris Lynch, Lori Aurelia Williams, and now Rachel Cohn," he says, referring to his latest discovery, the author of the new first-person YA novel *Gingerbread* and two more to come. He also "rediscovered" Ellen Wittlinger. Wittlinger, author of two previous YA novels, won the 1999 Lambda Literary Award and a 2000 Michael L. Printz Honor for her novel *Hard Love*, which Gale edited.

Voices and Viewpoints

It's *voice* Gale first looks for in a novel. Listen to the opening of *Gingerbread*, for instance, to hear what drew him in:

> My so-called parents hate my boyfriend, Shrimp. I'm not sure they even believe he is my boyfriend. They take one look at his five-foot-five, surfer-shirt-wearin', baggy-jeans-slouchin', *Pop Tart*-eatin,' spiked-hair-head self and you can just see confusion firebombs exploding in their heads, like they are thinking, Oh no, Cyd Charisse, that young man is not your homes.
>
> Dig this: He is.

Voice: fresh, distinctive, and above all else, authentic, that's what Gale looks for. He has an ear for an authentic voice that will resonate with teens. "I don't have a preference for first-person over third-person point of view," he says, "but the voice must be the distinctive voice of a memorable character. What I like about Rachel Cohn is that her writing is like that of Francesca Lia Block, but much more grounded. And I love the main character in *Gingerbread*."

In addition to voice, Gale looks for an unusual premise. "I want a situation that demands much from the character." He points to *Takeoffs and Landings,* by Margaret Peterson Haddix. In this deeply psychological novel, told in alternating viewpoint chapters, the two oldest children of a motivational speaker hate each other. When they accompany their mother on a two-week cross-country trip, they must confront each other and the truth about their father's death eight years before. It's a challenging situation, one that draws the reader in.

Another unusual, intriguing situation underlies Wittlinger's *The Long Night of Leo and Bree*. On the anniversary of the murder of Leo's sister, his mother shows him photographs of her body, taken by the murderer. When Leo flees the house, he sees a girl on the street and wonders why she couldn't have been the murder victim instead. In a desperate move to untangle his feelings, Leo grabs Bree and holds her hostage through one long night.

A Guy Thing

In addition to YA novels, Gale also enjoys editing middle-grade novels, looking, once again, for the distinctive voice and intriguing situation. He points in particular to *The Beloved Dearly,* by Doug Cooney. Gale originally encountered the story as a play Cooney had written for youth theater, and that was later produced by the Lincoln Center Institute, with music by Elizabeth Swados. Gale saw the potential in this comedy about 12-year-old Ernie's pet-funeral business and his hireling, Swimming Pool, the official "crier." He asked Cooney if he'd be interested in trying it as a novel. The results, Gale says, are better than he could even have hoped, funny and emotionally resonant.

Gale makes a significant contribution to children's novel editing, in part, because of his gender, he believes: "With so many female editors, librarians, and teachers—and moms who buy books—it's important for someone to recognize boys' requirements in books. To hold a boy's interest, a book has to have action. And the voice must be authentic to a guy!"

Despite his love of novels, Gale also does edit picture books. "Picture books are fun," he says. "They're just not my love. They require a whole other set of editing skills, different from novel editing. For instance, I can tell an author what the writing needs, but I don't have the vocabulary to tell an illustrator what the art needs. I work closely with the art director, who is able to understand what I think is needed and communicate that to the illustrator." He manages quite well, editing a variety of picture books. This variety is reflected in recent and forthcoming titles he's edited. *Tub-Boo-Boo*, by Margie Palatini and illustrated by newcomer Glin Dibley, is the farcical story of a boy and his family who get stuck in a bathtub faucet. *The Master Swordsman & The Magic Doorway: Two Legends from Ancient China*, retold and illustrated by the incomparable Alice Provensen, brings two stories of artistry to life. *Shoeless Joe and Black Betsy*, by new author Phil Bildner and illustrated by C. F. Payne, is the story of the early days of baseball great Shoeless Joe Jackson and his relationship with his special baseball bat.

Gale doesn't anticipate ever doing anything else besides children's book editing. "What else," he asks with a quizzical look, "would I do?" The children's literature community answers hopefully, "Nothing!"

Wendy Lamb: Promoting Authors' Visions

By Toni Buzzeo

Wendy Lamb shone with her characteristic warmth and enthusiasm at the Random House Children's Books launch party for her new imprint, Wendy Lamb Books, hosted at the annual American Library Association conference in San Francisco. Formerly Executive Editor of Delacorte Press Books for Young Readers, Lamb is now Vice President and Publishing Director of her eponymous imprint. During the 2002 launch year, she is publishing 12 titles, with plans to publish between 10 and 15 books annually thereafter, generally 12 books in three seasons. They will be primarily middle-grade and young adult novels, with some sophisticated nonfiction, such as young adult biography, and occasional picture books.

"It was flukiness that led me here," Lamb reports. "I've followed an unconventional career path." After majoring in creative writing at Brown University, she worked at Harper Junior Books and Viking Children's Books. She left publishing to attend the Writer's Workshop at the University of Iowa, and later pursued her interest in writing musical theater. She supported her writing by working as a freelance editor for many years. In 1996, she finally settled into full-time editing at Delacorte Press.

Editorial Achievements

Lamb is recognized as one of the finest children's book editors in the business. She was recipient of the 1999 *Literary Marketplace* Award for Editorial Achievement in Children's Publishing and has edited numerous prize-winning novels. They include *Bud, Not Buddy,* by Christopher Paul Curtis, winner of the 2000 Newbery Medal and Coretta Scott King Award; *The Watsons Go to Birmingham—1963,* also by Curtis, winner of a Newbery Honor and Coretta Scott King Honor; *145th Street: Short Stories,* by Walter Dean Myers, winner of a *Boston Globe-Horn Book* Fiction Honor; and *Under the Blood-Red Sun,* by Graham Salisbury, which was awarded the Scott O'Dell Award for Historical Fiction.

Other celebrated authors Lamb has worked with are Gary Paulsen, Peter Dickinson, and Patricia Reilly Giff. Paulsen's newest title, *Caught by the Sea*, is a riveting nonfiction read. Paulsen recalls his personal history as a sailor, in a book that is impossible to set down once begun. "This is vintage Gary Paulsen," says Lamb, "funny, hair-raising, entertaining, and packed with information." Lamb has a brand-new title with another of her male authors, Graham Salisbury. *Lord of the Deep* is a powerful coming-of-age novel set in the waters off the Hawaiian islands. Lamb loves this book "because it's such a rare combination of real action writing and a powerful emotional story, and because it's beautifully written."

Add to these titles Dickinson's *The Ropemaker*, which Lamb calls "a complex, challenging fantasy from a brilliant writer, one of the best in England," and *All the Way Home,* by Giff, a heartwarming middle-grade novel about the friendship between 11-year-old Brick and Mariel, in Brooklyn and upstate New York in 1941."This is such a satisfying story," Lamb says, "told from two points of view. Pat has a way of bringing us back into the past without ever going into the zone of nostalgia, because her kids are so real, and we see life truly through their eyes."

Nurturing the New
"At my imprint, I will continue to publish many of these writers while also nurturing new talent," Lamb says. In fact, above all else, she has come to be known for her willingness to undertake that nurturing. For years she ran the Delacorte Press Contest for a First Young Adult Novel, begun by George Nicholson in 1983. Among the 12 books to be published in the first year of Wendy Lamb Books, 4 are first novels. "My job is to find new people and bring them along as well as tending my current authors."

Jaira Placide, an Assistant Editor at Morrow Junior Books, is one of those new writers. Her *Fresh Girl* has a wonderfully believable and singular voice. Placide creates a fictional Haitian family whose words and lives sing with uniqueness. The novel, says Lamb, is "very ambitious, subtle, brave, full of warm and vivid characters. The girl's secret is that she was raped by soldiers during a coup. This is dealt with in an extraordinary scene—honest, but not graphic." Lamb adds, "I can't wait to see what Jaira does next."

Of Lamb's first year's 12 titles, 8 are YA, including *Island Boyz,* by Graham Salisbury, a new collection of short stories by the author of *Blue Skin of the Sea* (Delacorte). "There is a terrific range here," Lamb says. "Sandy is such a natural at short stories." Also on the list are *Dr. Franklin's Island,* by Ann Halam (May 2002). Lamb acquired this intense novel for ages 14 and up from the U.K. "It's a doozy!" Lamb promises. "Three British teenagers survive a plane crash only to fall into the hands of Dr. Franklin and his experiments in genetic engineering—combining humans and animals. Some of this is startling and disturbing yet it also conveys the joy of being a fish, or a bird. But overall it's a story of friendship, about what binds humans to each other." Lamb hopes that it's timely as well, in the light of the stem-cell research controversy.

Finally, well-loved author Donna Jo Napoli contributes a book to the launch year with *Daughter of Venice.* "It was a treat to explore Venice through the eyes of a noble girl from 1592 Venice," says Lamb, "and I really grew to love Donata. I was in Venice in April and went to all the places mentioned in the book, and to the museum of the city, the Museo de

Correr. The more I learned about life at that time the more remote it seemed, and I was amazed by Napoli's achievement in creating this real girl who truly connects to readers today."

Promote Progress

As exemplified by *Daughter of Venice*, and as is true for so many editors, Lamb is drawn in by voice. "I want authority in the storytelling voice," she says. She wants kids who sound like kids, whose voices give life to books. Beyond that, Lamb says, "I want books that are fun and books I can learn from. I also like stories where a child has some power." She cites Curtis's *Bud, Not Buddy* as a good example of a kid with power to change the course of his own life, as is Giff's *All the Way Home*. "I publish a lot of male authors," she says, "and I have a personal interest in black history in America," both exemplified by Lamb's work with Christopher Paul Curtis and Walter Dean Myers. Finally, she says, "I would like to find books that address the meaning of faith in kids' lives today." There are too few written, she thinks.

Lamb is very clear about her role as an editor. "It is definitely my job to promote progress in a writer. I am trying to publish books that will interest readers long after we're gone," she says. "To do that, I need to help an author deepen a book so that it will last." In that effort, she looks for ambition in an author, an ambition deep enough to drive him or her to revise. For her part, she tries to assist authors in finding the deep emotional source for the story to keep them going. Always, she lives by this rule: "The author is the star, not the editor."

When Lamb first approaches a manuscript, she tries to grasp the author's vision, to understand the story the author hopes to create. "I try to understand the book he or she is trying to write," she says, "not my own vision of the book." She does that by clarifying and strengthening plot, language, characterization, and voice. Then, she says, "I read from the point of view of the intended reader. I ask myself when I am bored, confused, or distracted. We have to make sure the reader never has an opportunity *not* to turn the page!" If the author is treated as a star, still, "The most important person in the process is not the author, editor, or agent, but the reader."

Lamb muses, "Each writer demands a different role from the editor. The editor is there to keep the spine or shape of the book clear. She must always give her author the belief that he or she *can* write the best book. Fifteen different editors would produce 15 different books!" Thankfully, for those of us in the children's writing community, Wendy Lamb continues to be one of those editors producing memorable books.

The Paperback Writer

By Vicki Hambleton

"Dear Sir or Madam will you read my book,/ It took me years to write will you take a look,/ And I need a job,/ So I want to be a paperback writer, paperback writer./ I can make it longer if you like the style, I can change it round,/ If you really like it you can have the rights,/ It could make a million for you overnight,/ If you must return it you can send it here,/ But I need a break,/ And I want to be a paperback writer,/ Paperback writer."

"Paperback Writer,"
John Lennon and Paul McCartney

My childhood bookshelf held the family hand-me-downs: *Winnie-the-Pooh, Mary Poppins, Now We Are Six, Treasure Island,* and all of Louisa May Alcott's titles. As I grew older, I added the Nancy Drew books, hardcovers with no book jackets, and wonderfully painted covers. Paperbacks never graced those shelves until I was in high school. Now 30 years later, on my daughter's bookshelves are the hand-me-downs, along with some cherished hardcover picture books. But all the rest are paperbacks, even her collection of Nancy Drew. Walk into any children's section of any bookstore today to be overwhelmed by the sheer number of books—most of them paperbacks.

The journey to those paperback shelves takes one of several routes: as *series books* originating with paper covers, sometimes for the trade market, but usually mass-market; *reprints* of hardcovers; *trade standalone* (non-series) titles; and *mass-market standalone* titles.

Children's paperbacks as a business advanced by leaps and bounds on the first of these routes with the unprecedented success of such series as R.L Stine's Goosebumps, Sweet Valley High, the Baby-Sitter's Club, and others. Even today, several years after Goosebumps and other series hit their peaks, it's not unusual for one of those series titles to end up on the best-seller list with numbers like 180,000 sold.

Those series changed choices for children's publishers. Now the market is changing again. "In some ways, the series business is segmenting," explains Craig Walker, Vice President and Editor-in-Chief of Scholastic Paperbacks. "Instead of there being a megaseries that everybody has to read, there is a tendency for kids to narrow down their interests. We are finding that a number of series will do well, but none to the extent that they did in the past."

Fiction continues to have the strongest paperback presence, but nonfiction is making a bigger name for itself. Nonfiction standalones are gaining in strength. Standalone children's fiction often gets a strong second wind when re-issued in paperback with new marketing thrusts. On *Publishers Weekly (PW)* best-seller's list as *Children's Writer Guide* went to press, 8 out of the top 10 fiction titles were paperbacks. That's distinct from *PW*'s list of the top 10 series and tie-ins. Publishers are also turning to teens to sell more paperbacks, especially in nonfiction. Several companies are entering into joint ventures in this expanding market.

While book publishing growth has slowed in the past year, children's books, and especially paperbacks, remain the strongest market segments. The last annual statistics available showed juvenile paperback sales up about 20 percent over the preceding year. Over the course of the last months, the year-to-date sales numbers varied for juvenile paperbacks, sometimes up as much as 13 percent, sometimes dipping. Given the economic and world events of late last year, the final figures are difficult to predict. But the paperback revolution continues to unfold.

Cost & Availability

The paperback revolution in publishing really began in the mid-twentieth century, escalated quickly in the 1960s when more titles at cheaper prices proliferated, and hit the children's market head on with the explosion of series in the 1990s. Companies such as Scholastic—with its book clubs and book fairs selling titles consisting overwhelmingly of paperbacks—took full advantage.

Walker cites the paperback price point as a factor, and a big one. Publishers take advantage of the lower cost of paperbacks in a variety of ways. Scholastic re-releases hardcover books in paperback in time for summer reading programs. The lower price of mass-market books, versus trade paperbacks, has meant increased sales over the last years at outlets such as discount stores, toy chains, price club outlets, book clubs, even supermarkets. "Big chain stores like Walmart are strictly looking for value, and you would be hard put to try to sell a single title trade paper to them," says Walker.

Mass-market books have in the past seemed to appeal more to younger readers, or the adults who buy for them, than trade books because of cost.

Now that is sounding echoes among teen consumers. Mass-market paperbacks may sell well to young adults not just because of cheaper prices, but because they are available in more places teens go: the supermarket, Kmart, chain drug stores, and the like, rather than the traditional bookstore.

All About Series

Without doubt, the paperback market has proved to be very successful for dozens and dozens of fiction series for children of all ages, from beginning readers to teens. But the phenomenon of series that stretch to hundreds of titles is disappearing, and being replaced by what editors refer to as *trios* and *quartets*. Readers' tastes have changed and the generally slowing economic times are making children's book publishers re-position.

Ellen Krieger, Vice President and Associate Publisher of Paperback Books for Simon & Schuster, says companies are responding to a softer market. "That is the reason we are seeing so many trios and quartets. But also, I think the series market has gotten very crowded. It became hard to launch a new series. As a publisher you also have to be willing to commit to a certain number of titles; you have to put serious marketing dollars behind it; and let's face it, it's hard to find shelf space for a series that may run to zillions of titles. That being said, of course we are all still looking for the next series that will really take off. Series titles can still do well if they are the right fit. For example, our Fearless series by Francine Pascal is doing very well."

Simon & Schuster also publishes a number of media-tie-in series. Books based on the television programs *Buffy the Vampire Slayer, Sabrina, Charmed,* and *Angel* are all ongoing series with traditional bimonthly release schedules.

Series tied to television or films continue to hold a special place in the paperback market—so much so that Walker notes, "We fashion a lot of our series introductions very closely after media-like presentations. For example, our new series, T*Witches, which came out this year, is doing very well. Many people comment that the books remind them of a TV show."

Fiction series often offer the best opportunities for new writers to get a foot in the door to a major publishing house. Most series that extend to a number of titles have more than one author and many are done by new writers. Some series are ghostwritten by authors, new and experienced. Be realistic, however, about proposing new paperback series. "Series have to have a really great idea to make it when they are by a first-time author," says HarperCollins Senior Editor Abigail McAden.

Fiction on Its Own

It remains true that few publishers go straight to paperback with individual titles. "We do few single title original paperbacks, and only then if they are by a name author. I don't think we'd be doing a new author any favors by originating his or her book as a paperback," says McAden.

Stephen Fraser, Editorial Director of Trophy and Tempest Paperbacks, HarperCollins Children's Books, agrees.

"We will almost never publish a single title in paperback, and almost never by a first-time author. For one thing, it is too hard to place a one-off title in stores. And, it wouldn't be fair to the new author either. If I buy a first novel I feel in all fairness to the author, it should be a hardcover first. You want the book to be reviewed, and you want to help the author build a name in the marketplace."

If most fiction single titles begin as hardcover books, how do publishers decide which books go to paper? There is no one answer. At Scholastic, all hardcover fiction books go to paper. "We always think a fiction piece will have two lives," Walker says. "Even if a book doesn't sell well as a hardcover, we'll put it in paper."

At HarperCollins, criteria are different. "In recent years," says Fraser, "we have become particularly stringent about what makes a book ideal for paperback. It must have strong sales, good reviews, and it is often a book by an author we are trying to build."

Sometimes the decision to take a novel to paper is determined more specifically by the market. Walker says, "This summer we re-released some novels in paper that we just felt needed an extra boost and that were good for summer reading tables. Several of our titles that were so-so performers did very well because of this promotion."

A series of novels by the author Maud Hart Lovelace originally published in the 1940s was re-issued in paper by HarperCollins. "When Bette Midler mentioned on a television program how much she loved reading the Betsy Tacy books when she was young, we decided to repackage all of them immediately," says Fraser.

Another benefit of paperbacks for publishers is a chance to redesign covers, to make them catchier and fresher. "We are so graphically sophisticated, especially kids," says Walker. "Even a mid-90s title: Forget about putting it out there with the same cover. Kids won't even begin to buy it." It's not unusual to see a paperback appear with a number of different covers, to fit almost every taste or color preference.

The Other Side: Nonfiction Paperbacks

If fiction paperback publishing still leans towards series, or trios and quartets, nonfiction goes the other way, with many single titles going straight to paper, often by previously unknown authors. It's no secret that the phenomenal success of the *Chicken Soup for the Teenage Soul* books from Health Communications had children's publishers sitting up and taking notice. Since the first title was released in 1997, the books have sold more than 10 million copies. "Every acquisition meeting I go to, someone says, we need to do a Chicken Soup series!" says Fraser.

"Self-help books have been so popular in the adult market," says Walker, "that it is no surprise that these types of books are now making it down to the teen and middle-grade level." Teen buying power is no secret. It plays a big part in publishers' renewed interest in the teen market. Publishers are responding to the hunger on the part of teens to discover who they are and how they fit in, especially in light of life post-September 11. Almost every major house that publishes teen titles has begun to market nonfiction titles that deal with the real world.

Scholastic joined forces with *Teen* magazine to publish a paperback series entitled Real Teens about the real life adventures of a group of high school kids. HarperCollins launched a line of fiction and nonfiction in conjunction with *Seventeen* magazine. Penguin Putnam Books for Young Readers partnered with Alloy Online, a popular teen website, to create Alloy Books.

With six books now in print, Real Teens is written in a diary format by a group of eight high school students. The books' appeal is that they feature "real teens, real issues, real life." Each cover features an artistic black-and-white photo of teens. Scholastic advertises them on its website with the lure: "The diaries you are about to read are real. Names, places, and other details have been changed to protect the teens involved. But what they have to say all really happened."

Alloy Books, described as "surprisingly in-your-face nonfiction, innovative fiction, and cutting-edge design," run the gamut from the predictable nonfiction topics of beauty, love, and entertainment, to such current *in* subjects as dreams, spirituality, astrology, and numerology. On the fiction side, a book heavily advertised on the Alloy website is *The Sisterhood of the Traveling Pants,* by Ann Brashares. The story follows the lives of four best friends who share a pair of magic jeans for the summer. The jeans, found in a thrift shop, come to represent the girls' sisterhood, a developmentally and culturally hot topic for teen girls. Another book selling well is *SLAM*, a collection of poetry by young women.

For Judy Galbraith, President and Publisher of Free Spirit Publishing, a small house with about 18 to 20 titles a year, the interest in nonfiction topics by young readers is nothing new. She has been publishing nonfiction for teens and middle-graders since starting her company in 1983. "When I started, I had virtually no competition in this area and I kept thinking, 'why haven't the big guys been doing this?' You could go to any bookstore in America and there would be hundreds and hundreds of self-help titles for adults on how to live better lives—everything from career and hobbies to fitness to mental health, to relationships. It seemed to make sense that teens would want to read the same kinds of books."

Stick Up for Yourself is a Free Spirit self-help paperback for middle-grade kids that deals with the topics of self-esteem and assertiveness. *Fighting Invisible Tigers* is a teen title on stress. "We have even been asked for self-help books for preschool and elementary children," says Galbraith. Asked if it is good or bad for her company that big houses like HarperCollins and Scholastic are jumping deep into the nonfiction market, she responds, "I think this is an area that has room to grow, and where Free Spirit will always be a leader."

The Next Challenge

As paperback markets become even more popular, particularly as a way to reach teen readers, the challenge all publishers face is getting books in places where readers will find them and buy them. Central to that is a problem that has plagued bookstores for years—namely the placement of young adult books. "Everyone knows that a teen wouldn't be caught dead looking for a book in the kiddie section," says Simon & Schuster's Krieger, "but in most stores, teen books are either in or right next to the children's department."

Publishers agree that with more titles coming out in categories like nonfiction that are hot with teens, the problem will probably be taken more seriously. Teen books may soon be found next to the magazines, or adult paperbacks, or by the chain bookstore's coffee shop. There is even talk of books being sold in Gap stores.

Fraser concedes, "We are all trying to sell books to the same audience. We are always trying to better the competition." In the next year it may be trios and quartets, and self-help. After that, who knows? But while publishers are repositioning and deciding what to publish in paperback, the paperback writer will have a job.

Magazine Publishing

Time to Clean House

By Vicki Hambleton

News headlines tell one story of magazine publishing: Advertising numbers dropping, titles consolidating or folding, false starts. Through it all, however, Nina Link, Chief Executive Officer of Magazine Publishers of America (MPA), remains confident of an upturn, despite negative numbers.

After nearly five years of almost unchecked growth, the children's magazine market has begun to clean house. The titles that remain will do so because they stand out and improve.

With an economic downturn no one can deny—after the many recent years of upturns in juvenile magazine and book publishing—and the almost unforeseeable consequences on all businesses in the extended aftermath of the September 11 tragedies, no one is making predictions without qualifiers. But the changing perspective that had begun even before that date has everyone in the magazine business thinking about how to build a better product. While adult magazines depend largely on advertising revenues, children's publications know

that success, business and literary, is measured by different standards. The *products*, from teen fashion titles to classroom magazines to high-end specialized publications for kids, are in a period of redefinition.

At a conference of the MPA held in New York after the terrorist attacks, Link told magazine executives, "Magazines have always been there—a part of that American spirit . . . fostering the exchange of ideas, shaping opinion, providing historical perspective, moving people to act. Ever since Benjamin Franklin and Andrew Bradford published the first American magazines three days apart in 1741, magazines have educated, inspired, and entertained."

A New Face

Some of the biggest news from the most established magazines is hard not to see in the light of recent world events. Still, economic trends were undoubtedly a preceding, primary cause for the marketplace changes.

Mademoiselle closed after 67 years. The title for older teens and early twenties had undergone a makeover two years ago under a new editor. It had been rechristened "the magazine for the *me* years." Given world news and the economic climate, the *me* generation is now openly facing larger concerns than fashion and lifestyle. It's also worth noting that *Glamour*, Condé Nast's biggest success story for a comparable audience, announced less than a month after the September 11 events that it would refocus its content on health and financial issues, rather than fashion, beauty—glamour—beginning the next month.

Even before September, competition had toughened among magazines and publishers. Editors were forced to recognize the limits on the number of publications that could target a single audience. Nowhere was this more evident than among teen titles. For the past several years, the number of new magazines designed for adolescents (girls primarily, but not exclusively) increased almost exponentially. When it seemed no new teen magazine could find room in the market, at least two appeared. Now even the most established teen titles are taking good, hard looks at themselves and devising ways to stand out from the pack, to remake themselves.

Parenting titles have been among the strongest markets in the history of publishing. Like teen magazines, another always seems to be launching. Unlike teen magazines, the parenting market generally has been stable. Some newer, smaller publications clearly target under-served readerships, such as parents with special needs kids. Others approach the audience from a different angle, like *Scientific American Explorations*. Regional parenting publications usually service their well-defined markets well enough to live long and happy lives. But some new parenting publications with readerships only superficially defined did fail, despite the backing of major players in the industry.

The school and library market has also had a big name come into more active play—the National Geographic Society. The last major company to challenge the dominance of Scholastic and Weekly Reader was Time, Inc., with *Time For Kids*. Given Time's success, the new *National Geographic for Kids*, and to a lesser degree other publications, may well find a place in the lucrative school market.

In the consumer children's market, a strong company is becoming even more robust. Now more than a year old, the Carus Publishing/Cobblestone Publishing combination is also strengthening with steps toward the educational arena.

New for School

The splashy news about Time challenging Scholastic and Weekly Reader dates to the early 1990s. Today, *Time For Kids* is well entrenched in the classroom. It and the Scholastic magazines showed muscle with their coverage of the September 11 attacks and their aftermath. (See "Reporting Tragedy to Children," page 59.)

Another giant on the horizon eyed the lucrative classroom sale and made its move. In this market, clout and money clearly talk, and National Geographic has both. In a year that marked the twenty-fifth anniversary of *World*,

Reporting Tragedy to Children

Rebecca Bondor is the Editorial Director of Classroom Magazines for Scholastic, a company practically synonymous with kids, education, and current events. She talks about how the publisher decided to handle coverage of the terrorist attacks on America:

"Clearly this is an ongoing story, one we will deal with in the months ahead as we did with our initial coverage. First, we made sure that the way we approach the news is age-appropriate. What we have in our third-grade magazine is different from what we feature in the sixth-grade magazine, which differs from material in *New York Times Upfront*. This extends to text and photographs. We would never scare or alarm children at any age. Part of our role in covering this story is to be as compassionate, thoughtful, and careful as we can.

"In the issue of *Scholastic News* immediately after the attack on the World Trade Center, we featured a photo of a little girl on her father's shoulders, holding a small American flag with the caption 'United We Stand.' Inside we used a question-and-answer format; we thought it would give kids a clear, immediate understanding of what happened. We pulled in our teacher advisors, asked them the kind of questions they were getting in the classroom, and tried to answer those questions. We consulted with Dr. Bruce Perry, an expert on children and violence, and he appeared in a section featuring tips for kids on how to deal with their feelings: Talk to their friends, don't watch the events on television over and over again, and try not to direct anger at the wrong people. In that way, we touched on the bias that could potentially result from the event.

"In subsequent issues, we discussed how America responded to the attacks. We explained the approaches our government is using to respond. We talked about the bombing, but also our humanitarian efforts: We had pictures of American soldiers and of Afghan refugees. In our additional coverage is an article on Islam. Charts and graphs show how Islam is the second-fastest growing religion in the world. Things like that deepen their understanding and give the kids a really big picture of the situation.

"These kids have never lived through a war, so we need to provide some context for them, in particular in *Scholastic Jr.* and *Scholastic News*. We did an article on the bombing of Pearl Harbor to give them some historical perspective. For older kids, ones reading *Upfront*, there were questions about the draft. They are applying for college and they are wondering how the conflict might affect travel, how it might affect enlisting in the army if they want to, questions like that. We are doing our best job to give information that is both informative and responsible."

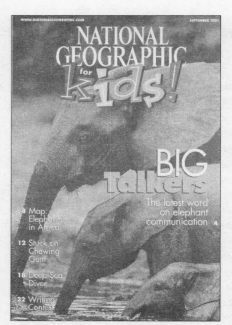

its subscription-based publication for ages 8 to 14, the company announced a new 24-page classroom magazine, *National Geographic for Kids,* to appear six times a school year and target grades three through six. Editor Mary Dalheim says the magazine will "offer science and social studies content along with reading and writing units."

National Geographic has enjoyed success with *World,* which targets homes and characterizes its articles as "entertainment-based." *National Geographic* magazine itself has been the source of thousands of school projects over many years, so the move into the school market seems a natural. Each 24-page issue of *National Geographic for Kids* includes three nonfiction articles on science and social studies topics related to the curriculum, such as living in space, seen through the eyes of a space station commander;

the history of chocolate; the many faces of masks and their uses; pandas; cliff dwellers of Mesa Verde; genetically altered food; the winter Olympics; women athletes; penguins; dinosaur discoveries; Mars; sneakers. Regular departments include Geo News, Think Science!, Online Adventure, History Highlights, Writing Workshop, and Photo Finish.

Accompanying teachers' guides provide more information on the topics, and also identify skills and curriculum areas related to each part of the magazine. The *National Geographic for Kids* website offers games and activities that extend the print magazine coverage.

Dalheim says that the magazine received considerable notice in schools across the country from the beginning. "We have a special subscription offer where if a school orders at least 200 subscriptions, the cost per student will only be $1 per child. We're excited because that makes the publication accessible to children in almost every school."

Digging & Asking

While competition with the giants is never easy, the school market continues to be top on the list for Cobblestone Publishing, which last year became part of the Carus Publishing family, home to such magazines as *Cricket* and *Muse.* According to Managing Editor Lou Waryncia, numbers continue to look good for all the company's magazines, and two new titles are joining the family.

Launched by the Archaeological Institute of America (AIA) three years

Science & Social Studies Magazines at a Glance

Science Publications

■ **ChemMatters:** Ages 14-18. Published by the American Chemical Society. Makes chemistry exciting by connecting concepts to daily life. Of particular interest: Inorganic chemistry, and topics related to winter. www.acs.org

■ **Current Science:** Ages 10-14. Weekly Reader classroom magazine on the earth, physical, and life sciences, and technology. Shows science as real life; stimulates readers to think, ask questions, experiment. Website for all Weekly Reader publications on this page: www.weeklyreader.com

■ **Dolphin Log:** Ages 7-13. Focuses on ecology, marine biology, natural history, and the environment. The Cousteau Society. www.dolphinlog.org

■ **Odyssey:** Ages 10-16. Covers science and math, particularly astronomy and space. Articles are informational, but also cover people, and the magazine includes experiments and projects. Website for all the Cobblestone magazines on this page: www.cobblestonepub.com

■ **Science Weekly:** Ages 5-13. Educational newsletter in seven editions for grades K-8. Articles and activities cover space, weather, biology, oceans, photography, physical science, and more. www.scienceweekly.com

■ **Science World:** Juniors and seniors. Scholastic classroom magazine on science, technology, health, medicine, the environment. www.scholastic.com

■ **SuperScience:** Ages 6-14. Theme-based Scholastic classroom magazine on scientific topics from telescopes to global warning to genes to virtual reality. Website for all Scholastic publications: www.scholastic.com

History/Social Studies Publications

■ **American Girl:** Ages 8-12. A general interest publication with a strong tie to history, and contemporary topics for girls. www.americangirl.com

■ **AppleSeeds:** Ages 7-9. Cobblestone, theme-based magazine tied to the social studies curriculum but covering a variety of subjects.

■ **Calliope:** Ages 8-14. Cobblestone themed magazine on world history.

■ **Cobblestone:** Ages 8-14. Covers American history in themed issues.

■ **Crinkles:** Ages 8-14. Educational, theme-based magazine on history, culture, and also science and other topics. www.crinkles.com

■ **Faces:** Ages 8-14. Cobblestone magazine on people and their cultures: religion, customs, political systems, geography, architecture, and more.

■ **Footsteps:** Ages 8-14. Cobblestone magazine on African-American history.

■ **New York Times Upfront:** Ages 14-18. Current events publication that is a collaboration between Scholastic and the *New York Times*. Politics, government, technology, the arts and sciences are also covered. www.nytimes.com/upfront

■ **Read:** Ages 11-15. Weekly Reader publication that covers a wide range of current topics and history, with an emphasis on classroom discussion.

■ **Scholastic News:** Grades 1-3 and 4-6. Weekly classroom publication in two editions on current events, as well as history, science, and other topics.

ago, *Dig* magazine was purchased by Cobblestone. "AIA decided that they were no longer in a position to publish the magazine and wanted to find a good home for it," explains Waryncia. "They asked us if we were interested, and we said *yes*." Plans for changes at the subscription-based magazine lean heavily toward the educational market. "Currently, most of the subscribers are consumers," Waryncia says, but "we want to start making *Dig* very viable for the school market as well."

The new *Dig* is being edited by Rosalie Baker, who already edits the highly successful *Calliope*. Baker says the early issues of *Dig* will closely follow the direction of the original publication. Changes in approach and content will not appear for a year or more, although they are being developed.

Also in the works at the Cobblestone/Carus family is *Ask* magazine, edited by Carus's Alice Letvin. *Ask* (*Arts and Sciences for Kids*) targets children in grades two to four and is theme-based. The magazine will cover a wide range of topics in all the major subject areas, including the arts, natural history, history, and science. Letvin is posting a theme list on the magazine's website (www.cobblestonepub.com).

"The biggest challenge for me," says Letvin, "has been to define the middle magazine between *Click* and *Muse*. *Muse* and *Click* are such distinctive magazines, with their emphasis on inquiry and learning about the world in a way that is really engaging. My job has been to develop as distinctive a magazine for kids between 7 and 10. *Click* looks at how the world works, while I think *Muse* focuses on controversy, true cutting-edge science. But with *Ask,* what we are beginning to see emerge is a magazine that will focus on questions that a child or investigator in the field would be curious about; then, the articles will model how a scientist would investigate that question. *Ask* will be a broad-based cultural magazine, but with an emphasis on science and discovery." (For more information on Carus Publishing, see the sidebar, "Carus, Cricket, Cobblestone: A Growing Empire," page 73.)

A New Model in the Family

Just as in book publishing, the question of the purchaser—the adult, whether parent, grandparent, teacher, or other—of a children's title always plays a part in titles for younger readers. As magazines for kids look for ways to appeal to parents, one idea that has gained strength is the publication that is purposely geared toward both parents and kids.

An early model, and enormous success, is *FamilyFun*. Now a decade old, the magazine is devoted to activities that families can do together. *Family Life,* published by the Parenting Group of Time, Inc., was a similar example until AOL Time Warner announced its closing in the final weeks of last year. *FamilyFun* aims primarily at parents with children 5 to 12. *Nick Jr.* came along for parents with younger children. It has enjoyed tremendous success and in turn has served as a model for newer magazines that look at parenting fun time, less than at the problem-solving or disciplinary sides.

Nick Jr.'s tag line is "a place where kids play to learn and parents learn to play." The description might also serve to describe what is fast becoming a whole new category of parent publications. "We see this is a whole new category of magazines for parents," says Christine Arrington, Publishing Director of the new *Scientific American Explorations.* "This new breed of parenting magazine incorporates information for parents and kids and brings them together in activities and adventures." Other magazines in this newly refined category are *Martha Stewart Kids* and Scholastic's *Parent & Child,* a publishing venture with Binney & Smith, manufacturers of Crayola crayons and one of the original partners of *Crayola Kids.*

Nick Jr. initially launched in part to fill the gap left behind in the marketplace when Meredith Publishing closed the doors on *Crayola Kids.* Material for parents and for parents and kids together is listed in *Nick Jr.* with symbols designating which skills the activity helps build: social, cognitive, problem-solving, physical, and creative. One issue, for example, featured a survey of

parents of two-to-five-year-olds on how they play with their kids; the regular feature Five Things to Do With . . . offered simple crafts for seashells; a parents' article examined the latest philosophies on preschools; and the kids get their own magazine in a magazine, *Noodle,* with games, stories, and puzzles.

"I think we all are trying to remind parents how much fun it is to play and discover new things together," says *Explorations'* Arrington. A recent article in the *New York Times* noted that many elementary schools are cancelling class field trips in response to the situation in the world and this could likely be a boon to magazines filled with ideas for having fun closer to home.

Explorations describes itself as a "valuable tool for parents and grandparents" that wants to instill a love of science and technology in children. The fall issue featured a lead article on why America is failing its children when it comes to science.

Steady as She Goes

The dawn of the new millennium has turned into broad daylight, revealing some sights that publishing eyes would prefer invisible: possible increased postal rates, a struggling economy, national tragedy. In light of uncertain times, what better place to turn for consolation than the tried-and-true? Here is a roundup of what editors at some well-established children's magazines had to say.

Children's Better Health Institute, Editor Daniel Lee: "I'd say we are operating on a very new status quo for us. I'd almost call it *lifeboat* status. We are doing some serious belt-tightening at our magazines. We are only using stories and activities that tie very closely to our message, namely health and fitness. In the past, we have been able to stray a bit from that for a really good story, but no longer. We are doing much more of our editorial in-house and making use of our inventory to a greater degree. At least the lifeboat is not sinking! No magazines are in danger of folding any time soon."

Guideposts for Teens, **Editor Betsy Kohn:** "This has been a good year for us. We have done well in direct mail tests and the magazine is having a trial run on newsstands in select WalMarts. The test runs for another six months. *Guideposts* survives tough times well, or certainly has in the past, because everyone is looking for inspiration.

"What we need most now are action-adventure stories. We are particularly interested in stories told from the point of view of a minority or Jewish teen. I never see enough light stories and humor—for example, stories about the major events in teens' lives, like prom night or cheerleading, homecoming, moving to a new school, getting a job, or getting a driver's license. We are overstocked with stories about illnesses and accidents. The stories, whether light or serious, need to have the same elements: The narrator faces a conflict and at the outcome that person is changed in some positive way by an action he or she has taken.

"We continue to look for material for the *Guideposts for Kids* website. But I caution writers that the pay scale is somewhat less since, for the Web, we only buy electronic rights. I am always looking for Q & As with celebrities. We just had Sammy Sosa for example, and with the Olympics coming up, interviews with these athletes are high on my wish list."

Hopscotch, Boys' Quest, Fun for Kidz, **Editorial Assistant Diane Winebar:** "This has been a good year for us and our biggest news really is the launch of our third magazine: *Fun for Kidz.* The first test issue has gone out and the premier issue appears in January. We really consider it a companion piece to our two existing magazines, *Hopscotch* and *Boys' Quest,* and it will appear in the months that the other two do not. *Fun for Kidz* is all about activities. They really drive the magazine. For example, we have an issue about the great outdoors, and one of the stories is about an uncle who takes his nephew for a walk in the woods. They find all sorts of animal tracks, so one activity for this issue is on how to make animal tracks using plaster of paris. Like our other publications, this one is built around themes. A theme list will be on our website, www.funforkidz.com. Other than that, things are pretty much status quo here. We always enjoy humor and never get enough of it. And while we work from themes, it is not unheard of for us to create a theme because we receive an incredible story."

Pockets, **Editorial Assistant Patty McIntyre:** "We'd like to see more of the stories we run for our younger readers, those between the ages of five and seven. These are no more than 600 words and we do have trouble getting enough quality stories for this feature. We also have a new feature called God in My Life, which is actually written by children but could certainly be helped along by an adult. These are stories that are about how children are aware of God in their lives, how He has been helpful to them in some important way."

Ranger Rick, **Editor Gerald Bishop:** "In terms of our needs, we continue to work almost exclusively with the freelancers we have been using for quite some time. Our magazine is so visually driven that we don't really have a need for manuscripts anymore. It's more a question of writing to explain the pictures."

While articles and departments are aimed at the older generations, the magazine also has a Family Time section full of activities for everyone.

In a representative issue, the Why and How section took a look at the cookie cutter shark, with a game about how science discovered the mystery of this creature. How It Works looked at vacuums, and Cheap Science Thrills offered ideas for making your own blimp. Just for Kids section offers puzzles, a mystery story, neat science facts, and games. Spotlight showcases a particular museum, such as the Montreal Science Museum. Part of *Explorations*'s goal is to help parents get over the typical American science phobia, and see that science is found in everyday life experiences and events.

For the kids alone, *Fun for Kidz* is a new magazine from the publishers of *Hopscotch* and *Boys' Quest*. It is an activity-based magazine that is appearing in the "off" months the other two bimonthlies do not run. All three are theme-based.

Any mention of crafts and home life means that the queen of home style can't be far behind. Yes, Martha Stewart now publishes not one, but two magazines aimed at parents: *Martha Stewart Baby* and *Martha Stewart Kids*. Stewart's new magazines are less about parenting and more about style, and given her track record, parents can be expected to line up to learn about how to make homemade gifts and homemade baby food.

Next Chapters in Parenting

Publications with circulations topping the one million mark, like *Parents, Parenting, Baby Talk,* and *Child,* continue to dominate in a country where approximately 4 million babies are born each year. But regionally, more than 150 publications target parents and maintain a strong, stable presence.

While many regionals started out as venues for local advertisers more than serious journalistic ventures, over the years that has changed. *Chicago Parent,* one of the nation's oldest regionals, is an example. "Over the six years that I have been editor here," explains Sharon Bloyd-Peshkin, "I have watched regional parenting publications become much more sophisticated. They really have grown into serious magazines and the people editing them have developed some serious sophistication as journalists."

Recent years have seen an increase in the number of publications that target parents with special needs children. They run the gamut from magazines for alternative families to publications for parents of ADHD children, to families who homeschool. While none of these publications will ever compete with a *Parents* or *Child,* they have no aspirations to do so. Like the regionals, they are instead focused on doing what they do best: targeting a very specific audience.

One special interest area that seems sure to continue its growth—and need for materials both in print and online—is families who homeschool. A recent article in *Time* estimated that in 1999 (the most recent year for which figures are available), 850,000 students were learning at home, compared to an estimated 345,000 five years earlier. Magazines founded in the early 1990s, like *Homeschooling Today*, will have to make room for a growing crop of competitors. Yahoo lists no fewer than nine magazines on homeschooling, including a newsletter specifically targeting Jewish homeschoolers. Online zines include *Eclectic Homeschool Online* and *Homeschooling Fun*.

The other edge of the sword, however, is that magazines that refine their aims too narrowly and yet try to compete in a large marketplace do not fare well.

One title that started off with a bang was *Offspring*, from the publishers of *Smart Money*. Within weeks of the magazine hitting newsstands, editors of *Offspring* were appearing on national morning programs like *Today*, touting their expertise. But even the limelight wasn't enough to convince readers to buy. After costing Hearst Magazines and Dow Jones a reported $5 million, the title shut down after only three issues. *Offspring* never managed to define what it would bring parents that they did not already have; from the start, its editorial mission remained unclear. In the premiere issue, Managing Editor Steven Schwartz described the magazine as "an attempt to bring together a community of action-oriented parents of all-aged children looking for the information they need to make a difference." Presumably no one quite figured out who those parents were.

Like *Offspring*, the new magazine *dads* launched with a guaranteed circulation of 200,000, and plans were for the title to appear six times a year.

"Our magazine is called *dads*, and our mission is to help fathers be better dads," stated Editor and managing partner Eric Garland as the magazine launched. "Our target audience are professional men who have reached a certain level in their professional careers, and want to have the same kind of success at home with their families. Today's dad is not the same as the father of say 20 years ago." The publication premiered with none other than baseball superstar Cal Ripkin on the cover. But celebrity covers couldn't save *dads*; it too folded after three issues. Dads may not be the same as they were 20 years ago, but they still aren't running to the newsstand to buy magazines.

Working mothers began to look for a new place to hang their hats as *Working Mother* and its sister publication *Working Woman* were put up for sale. *Working Woman*, after 25 years in

Special Interest Magazines

These special interest magazines aim at particular audiences, whether they are association members, professionals, parents of children with special needs, or others. More general interest religious, regional, educational, and parenting publications are not included. The numbers following each listing are the publications' circulations.

- **ADDitude:** For parents of children with attention deficit disorder. www.attitudemag.com. Circulation not available.
- **Adoptive Families:** For those who have adopted and plan to adopt. www.adoptivefamilies.com. 25,000.
- **AIM:** A literary magazine that aims to eliminate racism. www.aimmagazine.org. 7,000.
- **Alateen Talk:** For children whose lives are touched by alcohol abuse. www.a-anon.alateen.org. 4,000.
- **Catholic Forester:** Lifestyle magazine for members of a fraternal insurance society. www.catholicforester.com. 100,000.
- **Challenge:** For teachers and parents of gifted children. 14,500.
- **Child Care Information Exchange:** For child-care professionals. www.ccie.com. 26,000.
- **Children's Advocate NewsMagazine:** On children's issues in California. www.4children.org. 15,000.
- **Children's Voice:** For readers interested in child welfare issues. www.cwla.org. 20,000.
- **Circle K:** Magazine of a service organization that stresses leadership and community. www.circlek.org. 15,000.
- **Dimensions of Early Childhood:** Refereed journal for childhood professionals. www.southernearlychildhood.org. 19,000.
- **Dovetail:** A newsletter for interfaith Jewish and Catholic families. www.dovetailpublishing.com. 1,200.
- **educational Horizons:** Official publication of Pi Lambda Theta, on social, educational, and cultural issues. www.pilambda.org. 13,000.
- **Gifted Education Press Quarterly:** For all concerned with educating gifted children. www.giftededpress.com. 1,500.
- **Green Teacher:** Helps educators and parents teach children about the environment and global issues. www.greenteacher.com. 6,000.
- **Home Education Magazine:** Educational information for home schoolers. www.home-edmagazine.com. 60,000.
- **Homeschooling Today:** Practical information for home schoolers. www.homeschooltoday.com. 25,000.
- **Joey:** Lifestyle e-zine for gay teens. www.joeymagazine.com.

Special Interest Magazines

■ **Juco Review:** Association publication for members of the National Junior College Athletic Association. www.njcaa.org. 2,700.

■ **Keynoter:** Publication of the Key Club International, the world's largest high school service group. www.keyclub.org. 200,000.

■ **Kids Courier:** A children's newspaper from the National Children's Literacy Project to encourage reading and writing. www.kidscourier.com. 525,000.

■ **Leadership for Student Activities:** For student leaders and their advisors. www.nassp.org. 51,000.

■ **Multicultural Review:** Journal on diversity for educators and librarians. www.mcreview.com. 5,000.

■ **Reunions:** A magazine targeted to anyone organizing reunions of any kind. www.reunionsmag.com. 12,000.

■ **SAA Families:** The publication of the Stepfamily Association of America. www.saafamilies.org. 1,000.

■ **Small Farmer's Journal:** Quarterly for farm families. www.smallfarmers journal.com. 20,000.

■ **Student Assistance Journal:** A narrowly targeted educational publication on successful assistance programs for children at risk. Suite F, 1270 Rankin Drive, Troy, MI 48083. 10,000.

■ **Teaching Exceptional Children:** From the Council for Exceptional Children, for professionals who work with children with all kinds of special needs. www.cec.sped.org. 55,000.

■ **Today's Father:** With all the publications directed at mothers, and parents in general, few target fathers as this quarterly does. www.fathers.com. 35,000.

■ **Transitions Abroad:** Helps young adults and adults find opportunities to study and work abroad. www.transitionsabroad.com. 20,000.

■ **Twins:** For parents of multiples. www.twinsmagazine.com. 56,000.

■ **U Magazine:** Quarterly of the United States Automobile Association, on how parents can teach children about money and being good consumers. www.usaa.com. 360,000.

business, ceased publication. There is talk of bringing it back after a hiatus, but most insiders think it is unlikely. *Working Mother* fared better, and with the exception of the editor, staff remained intact. Carol Evans, the original publisher of *Working Mother*, joined forces with MCG Capital to oversee a restructuring. "I'm proud to be the first woman owner of these magazines," says Evans. It continued its publishing schedule, but whether *Working Mother* survives or is sold depends on the refocus going on everywhere.

Teen Fatigue?

Launch fatigue was everywhere, including among markets for teens, still among the largest growing population categories in the U.S. While teen publications still sell to advertisers, the economic downturn had ripple effects felt even in the foundations of the teen market—*Teen, Seventeen*, and *YM*. Lynn Lehmkuhl, President of *Teen*, admits that all the fashion teen books were "experiencing the hit of saturation."

YM faced the challenge by introducing a redesign under new Editor Annemarie Iverson. As a result, *YM* is one of the few titles to show a sizeable jump in ad pages last year. The magazine is published by Gruner + Jahr, who bought out the publication *Jump*. Published by Weider Publications, *Jump* premiered five years ago and tried to position itself as a magazine designed to appeal to "independent thinkers." It never found its stride.

The *YM* success is largely credited to Iverson, who then moved on to *Seventeen*. The added list of *Jump*'s subscribers helped, but more important to *YM*'s success was the clear focus the magazine developed thanks to Iverson. The magazine targets the younger teen and depends heavily on a strong shot of celebrity stories—Britney Spears on the cover, *NSync on a movie set, Sarah Michelle Gellar on her high school horrors. Issues devote four of six coverlines to celebrity stories. The other topics featured on the cover? No surprise—boys and makeup. An indication of the average reader's age is clearly given in one regular column, Grade the Boys: Gross or Good. The younger teen market continues to be loyal to its magazines, while older teens stray to adult titles for the fashion-savvy, like *Vogue*.

Another category leader, *Teen* struggled to regain its footing after advertising pages fell 7.1 percent and newsstand sales dropped off more than 22 percent, according to figures from the Audit Bureau of Circulations (ABC). Late last year, readers of the popular magazine saw a whole new look, inside and out. *Teen* has given up most of the traditional teen girl trappings: Gone are the articles about eating disorders and acne, teen love and celebrity worship. Instead, *Teen* is determined to devote itself to *shopping*. All the content, according to Editor in Chief Tommi Lewis Tilden will be "style-based." Every article in a layout will feature an 800-number or a web address to support the shopping.

The challenge for *Teen* will be to find a place of its own, now that it and its rival *Seventeen* are published by the same company, Primedia. *Seventeen* raided *YM* to hire away Iverson. She is Editor in Chief and Editorial Director of Primedia's Teen Magazine Publishing Unit, which also includes *Tiger Beat, Teen Beat,* and *16 Magazine.* Tommi Lewis Tilden, Editor in Chief of *Teen* and Editorial Director of *Teen Prom* and special issues, clarifies changes: *Teen Beat* and *Tiger Beat* are changing to a quarterly frequency, but the content remains the same. *Bop* and *All About You* both suspended publication.

According to John Loughlin, CEO of Primedia Consumer Media and Magazine Group, "Primedia is focused on extending its leadership in the teen market and further building our teen magazine brands through integration and the development of new and innovative editorial content."

Some analysts foresee more teen magazines folding. Martin Walker, an industry consultant and head of Walker Communications, expects other spin-offs from adult fashion magazines to be among the first to fall, preceded only by magazines covering the travel industry. *Mode,* a women's fashion magazine whose teen spin-off, *Girl,* moved from print to the Web to survive, is one that has now disappeared.

CosmoGirl! has continued to find success after its first year, with ad pages up 7.8 percent, but *Teen Vogue,* introduced at about the same time has not fared so well. It is still appearing on newsstands, but only twice a year for the moment. Despite the dangerous waters, Hachette Filipacchi is jumping into the teen pool with four issues a year of *ElleGirl* planned. Editor Brandon Holley says *ElleGirl* will go after the older teen market, especially girls who love to shop. Nearly two-thirds of the content will be devoted to style and fashion.

As new titles come and go, *Teen People* continues to live up to its reputation as one of the most successful launches ever. The celebrity publication lost Christina Ferrari, the original editor of *Teen People* and credited with much of the title's success, who resigned to live in Europe. Barbara O'Dair, formerly with *Harper's Bazaar* was tapped to succeed Ferrari and has no intentions of making any immediate changes at *Teen People.* O'Dair makes the point that *Teen People* is very different editorially from other teen titles; nevertheless it will still compete for the same readers and advertisers.

Other teen magazines that did not make it to the new year include *Entertainmenteen* and *hot!* Still holding its own is *TeenStyle,* but at a steep step down from the major titles in its category. Last year the teen magazine for boys, *MH-18,* launched as a bimonthly but it dropped back to four issues a year. Editor Jeff Csatari described the decision as "prudent, considering the downturn in advertising," but he hoped to see the magazine back to six issues a year by the end of the year. Instead, a short time later, *MH-18* closed.

The publishers of *Girls' Life,* for ages 10 to 14, announced plans last year to launch a title for teen boys. The decision was later made to target an older audience instead. Editor Miguel Vilier says *Adam* will appeal to college-age men, and men starting careers. "And our goal is to be a more intellectual title than the ones that currently target our audience," says Vilier.

An unfinished story at *Children's Writer Guide*'s press time is typical of the times: The Illinois-based H & S Media new teen title was selling like hotcakes when it hit the market last year. Like a junior *O (*Oprah Winfrey's magazine), the teen celebrity twins' *Mary-Kate and Ashley* was apparently on its way to success, until the recent news that H & S Media is reportedly $1 million in debt and looking for a buyer for its magazines.

How different from the stalwarts— the *Highlights for Children, Boys' Life, Spider*, and Children's Better Health Institute magazines. These don't sell advertising, don't change their formulas dramatically, but they all meet with continued, if more measured success than flashy new titles. Good magazines are really about good ideas, whatever the size of the publication, from the 3-million circulation *Highlights* to the 15,000-strong *Hopscotch*. In changing times, these models of clean, timeless publishing are welcome in our homes. They are also welcoming of writers.

Profile of a Growing Empire:
Carus, Cricket, Cobblestone

By Vicki Hambleton

A call to the New Hampshire offices of Cobblestone Publishing is answered by a new recording: "Thank you for calling Carus Publishing, home of Cobblestone Publishing, Cricket Books, and Open Court." A little more than a year ago, Carus Publishing bought Cobblestone and its family of magazines. The transition has embraced new ideas, new faces, and new publications. The union has made Carus one of the largest publishers of children's educational magazines, with a total of 16 magazines: *AppleSeeds, Ask, Babybug, Calliope, Cicada, Click, Cobblestone, Cricket, Dig, Faces, Footsteps, JAM, Ladybug, Muse, Odyssey,* and *Spider.*

Cricket Books continues to prosper and under the direction of its Vice President and Publisher, Marc Aronson, will begin to publish more nonfiction for middle-grade and young adult readers. Aronson has also launched his own Cricket Books imprint, Marcato.

Marianne Carus, founder of the growing empire, says, "I would like to retire someday, but I don't think that's likely any time soon. As if we don't have enough going on, we are looking forward in 2003 to the thirtieth anniversary of *Cricket* magazine!"

New Magazines, New Directions

Carus's merger with Cobblestone and its hiring of new staff in the Carus, Illinois, offices have meant the company has been able to expand into a range of new directions, with three new magazines debuting last year alone.

Alice Letvin is the Editorial Director in charge of the nonfiction magazines *Click* and *Muse,* but she also works closely with Marianne Carus on the fiction magazines. Her previous experience was with the Great Books Foundation. "Great Books Foundation is a national organization," Letvin explains, "and its primary focus is on junior grade books. It puts excellent literature in the hands of children. I was involved in making selections for the program and in making children familiar with literature at a young age." As well as her experience dovetails with the fiction published by Carus, Letvin has spent much of her first year at the company working on two nonfiction launches, *Ask* and *JAM.*

"These new magazines have been my biggest challenges," Letvin explains, "but they have been a wonderful experience and we are very proud of what we have accomplished." *Ask* stands for Arts and Sciences for Kids, and will cover a wide range of topics under a variety of disciplines, including history, science, the arts, and culture. "Working on *Ask* has been really wonderful," says Letvin. "*Muse* and *Click* are such distinctive magazines, with their emphasis on inquiry and learning about the world. *Ask* is written for kids between the ages of 7 and 10 and it will have its own unique approach."

A visit to www.cobblestonepub.com reveals some detail on the niche *Ask* intends to fill. "Our brand-new magazine is full of everything: history, natural history, science, the arts, and surprises . . . kids will explore the world with inventors, artists, thinkers, and scientists of the past and present. They'll discover how the ideas that shape our lives were formed." Sample themes include: what is art?; sports: ancient, modern, and future; from squire to knight: training in the Middle Ages; and marking the year end: from ancient ritual to *The Nutcracker.*"

"What we found when we began, in terms of definition," says Letvin, "was a magazine that focuses on questions that a child or an investigator in the field would be curious about. The articles will then model how a scientist would investigate that question."

Kids' Business

Letvin has also been hard at work with the Junior Achievement organization, creating a new magazine for ages 9 to 13, *JAM* (for *Junior Achievement Magazine*). This is not the first time Carus Publishing has partnered with another organization to produce a magazine. *Muse* is produced jointly by the Smithsonian and the Cricket Magazine Group.

Marianne Carus is very excited about the new partnership and thinks it will be an important link for future directions the company may wish to pursue. "*JAM* is going to be very interesting for us," she explains. "It covers some important ideas. It's about kids and business and the kinds of business they are interested in. These days, economics is a very important area for kids to study. They need to have at least a basic knowledge of economics to succeed today."

JAM does not appear on the Carus website, but the magazine for kids 9 to 13 can be found on the Junior Achievement website, www.ja.org. The goal of *JAM* is to help kids "be inspired to set their sights high by reading about entrepreneurs of all ages; get the inside scoop on business and careers; explore everything from the economics of baseball to marketing dinosaurs; and to have fun with comic strips, puzzles, interviews, and activities." *JAM* appears six times a year during the school year and is distributed through Junior Achievement's chapters.

"Economics and business perhaps aren't the most natural things for kids to think about," says Letvin, "so the challenge is to pick topics that will spur their curiosity and at the same time afford us a chance to teach them something about economics."

Another new magazine for Carus Publishing is *Dig*. "I have always loved *Dig*," says Carus enthusiastically, "and I am so excited that it has come to us." *Dig* was purchased last year from the Archaeological Institute of America and is under the guiding hands of Cobblestone Publishing Managing Editor Lou Waryncia. "We are very excited about the magazine," he says, "and feel we are in a position to make it a wonderful magazine. Rosalie Baker will be the magazine's editor and I think she is perfect for the job." Carus agrees: "Rosalie Baker is doing a wonderful job, and I know archaeology is one of her passions." Baker also edits *Calliope* and *Footsteps*.

Excellence and passion could be the bywords of the entire company, and no one who works there hesitates to say so. "We know what high quality is," says Jack Olbrych, Publisher of the Cricket Magazine Group. "We create material that is stimulating and challenging, we do not talk down to children, and we do not rely on market surveys to tell us what kids like. We will lead the rest of the industry to higher standards of excellence."

On the Book Front

Five years ago, Carus Publishing began to move into book publishing and that expansion has continued. The move was a natural one, given the company's close relationship with so many well-known children's authors, thanks to *Cricket* magazine. At the time, Carus had said: "Our book venture will be a new challenge and opportunity for our many loyal Cricket Magazine Group authors who would love to get into book publishing. Some think it's crazy to start a children's book line in today's publishing environment, but they said the same thing about launching a children's magazine 25 years ago."

Originally, Carus partnered with Stephen Roxburgh, President and Publisher of Front Street Books, in the venture. Although Roxburgh will continue to act as a consultant, the overall book group is now headed up by publisher and author Aronson. Aronson won the first American Library Association Robert F. Sibert Award, given to the year's most distinguished informational children's book, for his *Sir Walter Ralegh and the Quest for El Dorado*. "Marc Aronson is just so passionate about books," says Carus.

At least two of Cricket's books are already receiving notable attention. *Seek* is by Paul Fleischman, who won the Newbery award for *Joyful Noises*. The story of a high school student named Rob who is assigned to write his autobiography, *Seek* mixes pieces of that life story with voices Rob has heard over the years—that of his mother, grandparents, teachers, and his father, a radio disc jockey Rob never met. The book is unique in that it can be read as a novel or performed as a play. Also receiving rave reviews is *Jon Riley's Daughter*, by Kezi Matthews, which is the first-person story of a troubled girl coming to terms with her life, attitudes, and options.

Aronson is clearly devoted to expanding Cricket Books and taking it in new directions in terms of fictional forms, as exemplified in the Fleischman novel, and with more nonfiction titles, Aronson's personal passion. In a speech to the Association of Children's Librarians, Aronson outlined his description of history and the important role it plays today. The entire speech is available at www.bayviews.org.

> "What is knowledge? It is human beings trying to make sense of what goes on around us. Nonfiction is the record of that effort. . . . It is the play of mind, and there is nothing potentially more interesting. . . . The real challenge of history today is to create a kind of mobile, a structure in which all of the parts matter, all of the stories count, all of the voices are heard. . . . It sounds like those multi-voiced novels that have become so popular in recent years in the hands of Walter Dean Myers, and Paul Fleischman . . . and others. . . . And that is just about right. History should be of its time. It should be fresh and lively. It should be open to new ways of seeing the past and telling the story. It should, in other words, be quite as challenging, engaging, and inspiring as fiction."

Strength of Minds
Carus describes the strength of her company as a meeting of many minds. "We all of us have so many different interests and experience with different subject matter, that we can play off each other and get each other's advice on our projects." She points out some of the newer members of her editorial staff who are strong members of a team that already includes such well-known names in children's magazines as Editors Deborah Vetter, Paula Morrow, and Art Director Ron McCutchan. "Heather Delabre has worked for two years now as the Assistant Editor of *Spider*," says Carus. "We have Tracy Schoenle working with Debbie Vetter on *Cicada* and *Cricket*. Meggy Hamil is sort of our girl Friday and she helps all of us out and has started editing on her own as well. She is just out of college, so she tells us what teens would like. She is still close enough in age to know!"

Carus is beginning to plan events for *Cricket*'s thirtieth anniversary, and two new anthologies of material from the magazine, one on dragons due out this year and another of Middle Eastern stories. Her mission is much the same as it has always been: to find the best writers and bring their work to children of all ages.

Mary Dalheim: New *Kid* on the Block

By Vicki Hambleton

National Geographic Kids, the newest magazine from the National Geographic Society, is the company's first venture into the world of classroom magazines. Heading up the new magazine as Editor is Mary Dalheim, who describes her position as "the perfect job for me."

Dalheim's whole life has prepared her for just such a place. Ask her where she grew up and she laughs and says, "Nowhere and everywhere. My dad worked for an oil company, and so we moved every two-and-a-half years." The world around her was something Dalheim never took for granted; along the way she developed a passion for teaching and writing. "I was always a camp counselor in the summers," she recalls, "and so it seemed natural to major in education at college." College was Notre Dame, where she earned her bachelor's degree in elementary education, and minored in English and science.

After graduating, Dalheim taught middle school—every subject. "I taught in grades five through seven, and really loved what I was doing, but at the same time, I felt that I had talents that I wasn't using." So Dalheim gave up her teaching and earned an M.A. in journalism at the University of Missouri, which gave her the skills she needed to pursue her love of writing, and gave her an edge in education. "I would strongly recommend to anyone starting out as a writer to consider a degree in journalism," she says, "but I think you also need to develop skills in another area you can use in your journalism career," as Dalheim did in education. "My career definitely accelerated because of my master's in journalism. It helped me move more quickly in my career, compared to others I knew who started at the bottom and worked their way up the ranks at various publishers."

Basic Training

Dalheim next went to work at *Highlights for Children* as an Assistant Editor. Her job entailed planning the editorial for third-grade readers and she continued to work with kids in schools. "After I stopped teaching full-time, I knew I wanted to stay in contact with kids and keep my education skills fresh. While I was working in publishing, I kept going back to this one school in Pennsylvania where I worked a few days every year teaching second grade."

After getting her "basic training" at *Highlights,* Dalheim worked for a number of years for Holt, Rinehart, and Winston, where she was one of the editors responsible for the revision of the Holt Basic Reading Series. From there she moved to Scholastic, beginning as Senior Editor of *Instructor;* she went on to become Executive Editor. Dalheim and the *Instructor* staff were awarded EdPress's prestigious Golden Lamp award for outstanding adult education magazine of the year. Dalheim continued her career at Scholastic, first at *Teachers and Computers*, and then as Editorial Director of professional materials for Scholastic.

It was during her time at Scholastic that Dalheim first heard hints of National Geographic's interest in creating a magazine for classroom use. From that time forward, Dalheim followed the progress of the idea, even when it was shelved. "As far back as the '70s, National Geographic was thinking about the classroom. They always thought they should be in schools, but the education market is a tough place to make money. At one point, they even came to Scholastic about whether to pursue the idea of a classroom publication."

In the 1990s, Dalheim's career took her to Washington, D.C., where she worked as Editor in Chief of *Careers* magazine, followed by a stint as Manager of the Publications Department and Editor of the American Society for Engineering Education's *Prism* magazine. Dalheim won her second Golden Lamp Award at *Prism*.

On Its Way
While her career continued to flourish, Dalheim never forgot about National Geographic's ideas for a classroom magazine. "The editors at the Society got to know me very well," she says. "When I moved to Washington, I went knocking on their door and actually ended up working on a number of prototypes for what has become *National Geographic Kids*."

Finally, National Geographic decided the time was right to move forward. "They took a good, hard look at their readership, and realized that the core group was aging and that the time might be right to develop a product for young children that would help nurture a new audience." When the decision to move ahead was made, Dalheim was ready and waiting. She was hired as editor for the new publication.

"It has been a wonderful experience since the start," she explains, "in part because I was able to have an entire year to test and develop our editorial, and that is such a rare and wonderful opportunity." The magazine targets students in grades three through six, but the core audience is grades four and five. Part of Dalheim's job in the planning year was to review curriculum standards for these grades around the country. "We found that there were quite a number of places where the curriculums met and overlapped in the different grades," she explains.

The first feedback Dalheim and her staff received from teachers about the magazine was rewarding: "We are pretty on target with our age and interest level." Dalheim has most of the first year's editorial planned but is waiting for additional feedback to plan further. "For one thing, I think we will devote more editorial to the study of world culture in the coming year," she says. "Given current events, I think a publication like ours is perhaps more important than ever."

Dalheim distinguishes between *National Geographic Kids* and the Society's other kids' magazine, *World,* by explaining that while both are designed to inform and entertain, "*World* describes its content as "edutainment," but *Kids* is more closely tied to the curriculum and written with teaching and teachers in mind. (Each magazine comes with a teacher's guide.) Dalheim thinks that *Kids* not only fills an important niche, but that it is unique. "I don't think we really have any competition," she explains. "*Time For Kids*, Scholastic's publications, and those of Weekly Reader are mainly current events magazines. We are more tied to the curriculum, but we also take an interdisciplinary approach, covering science, geography, culture, just like the adult *National Geographic*." The November/December issue of *National Geographic Kids* featured an article on pandas, another on genetically altered food, and another on the cliff dwellers of the Mesa Verde. The magazine website offers additional editorial, and links to other resources.

Kids Teach Back

Dalheim laughingly describes a *typical* day at *National Geographic Kids*: "*Typical* means we all do a little bit of everything. We have a very small staff so we juggle several issues at the same time. Today, for example, I am planning our April/May issue, editing March, and writing captions for January/February and looking at layouts at the same time. This afternoon, we have kids coming into the office to give us feedback. I even do what I call *bus stop surveys*—I show kids at a school bus stop the covers. Usually I give them three choices and ask them which they like best. We are learning things we never expected to from the kids. We recently showed some readers Olympics covers. One was of a really fast skier and you could see the speed in the way the photo was taken. We thought kids would love that one, but it was not the favorite. They seem to go for clearer pictures, and here we thought we were giving them a cutting-edge photo!"

Dalheim says her classroom and education experience are invaluable to her work at *National Geographic Kids*. She uses them every day. "I write a lot of the magazine, particularly some of the columns, and every time I work on an article, I think about the classroom and how I would teach the subject and use the magazine to help me. I have teachers who work as writers for me, as well as people who are just fabulous writers, but I think they are missing a piece by not having a little bit of both experiences."

Mary Dalheim

"Really, *National Geographic Kids* is the perfect job for me, and I feel very fortunate. I get to use all my skills on a regular basis, and it is so rewarding to feel as if you are putting your talents to the best use." Dalheim adds that having the resources of the National Geographic Society at her fingertips is an incredible opportunity. As for the future, there is the possibility of other classroom magazines, says Dalheim. "We have had requests from teachers for both younger and older editions of *Kids*," she explains. "But for the time being, we are focusing on making *Kids* the best magazine it can be."

News of the Year

By Maureen Garry

Anniversaries in Children's Publishing

■ Penguin Putnam Books for Young Readers is celebrating the hundredth anniversary of Beatrix Potter's *Peter Rabbit*. More than 200 companies currently license Beatrix Potter merchandise.

■ A.A. Milne's *Winnie the Pooh* celebrated its seventy-fifth anniversary.

■ Ten Speed Press, the company best known for its job-hunting guide, *What Color Is Your Parachute?*, is turning 30. The company, founded by Phil Wood from his Berkeley apartment, is celebrating by publishing what it calls Ten Speed's *30 + 1* list of titles, which features the best books published by Ten Speed over the years. Of the titles, four are from Tricycle Press, the children's book division started five years ago. *What Color Is Your Parachute?* is listed by the Library of Congress as one of the most important books of the past 50 years. It has sold eight million copies; 1,000 copies are still shipped daily after 27 years in print.

■ *Working Woman* celebrated its twenty-fifth anniversary, but then went on hiatus. Its future is uncertain.

Awards

■ Virginia Euwer Wolff won the National Book Award for Young Literature for her novel *True Believer*, published by Atheneum Books.

■ The American Library Association (ALA) awarded the John Newbery Medal to Richard Peck, author of *A Year Down Yonder* (Dial Books for Young Readers). David Small, illustrator of *So You Want to Be President?* (Philomel), received the Caldecott Medal.

■ The ALA's Coretta Scott King Award was presented to Jacqueline Woodson for *Miracle's Boys* (G.P. Putnam's Sons).

■ The Association for Library Service to Children/Robert F. Sibert Informational Book Award was presented to Marc Aronson for his book, *Sir Walter Ralegh and the Quest for El Dorado* (Clarion Books).

- Author David Almond received the Michael L. Printz Award for excellence in literature for young adults for *Kit's Wilderness* (Delacorte Press).

- The Scott O'Dell Award for Historical Fiction was awarded to Janet Taylor Lisle's World War II-era novel, *The Art of Keeping Cool*. The book is a Richard Jackson Books, an imprint of Atheneum Books for Young Readers, in turn a division of Simon & Schuster Books for Young Readers.

- The Américas Award for Children's and Young Adult Literature, sponsored by the Consortium of Latin American Studies Programs (CLASP), was presented to author Antonio Skarmeta and illustrator Alfonso Ruano for *The Composition* (Groundwood Press); and to Lynn Joseph for *The Color of My Words* (HarperCollins).

- The Margaret A. Edwards Award for books for teens was awarded to David Almond for *Kit's Wilderness* (Delacorte).

- Prince Charles presented author J.K. Rowling, creator of the Harry Potter books, with the Order of the British Empire for her work in children's literature.

- The winner of the Aesop Prize, sponsored by the American Folklore Society, was *The Day the Rabbi Disappeared: Jewish Holiday Tales of Magic*, by Howard Schwartz, illustrations by Monique Passicot (Viking).

- The Jane Addams Children's Book Award went to *Through My Eyes*, by Ruby Bridges (Scholastic). Alice McGill received the picture book award for *Molly Bannaky* (Houghton Mifflin), illustrated by Chris K. Soentpiet.

- Jacqueline Woodson won the Los Angeles Book Prize for Young Adult Fiction for *Miracle's Boys* (G.P. Putnam's).

- Golden Kite awards were presented to Kathleen Karr for *The Boxer* (Farrar, Straus & Giroux), for fiction; to Ellen Levine for the nonfiction *Darkness Over Denmark* (Holiday House); to Jane Kurtz, *River Friendly, River Wild* (Simon & Schuster), for picture book text; and to David Shannon, *The Rain Came Down* (Blue Sky Press), for picture book illustration.

- The National Book Award has added e-books to its universe, but not as a separate category. They will be eligible within the already existing award genres of fiction, nonfiction, poetry, and young people's literature. The National Book Foundation's Executive Director, Neil Baldwin, said at his announcement at BookExpo America, "Our decision ensures that all important published literary work—whatever the format—will be part of the playing field" and evaluated on literary merit. Submissions for consideration, however, must be hard copy.

Mergers, Acquisitions, & Reorganizations

Books

■ In January, the FCC approved the merger of America Online (AOL) and Time Warner. AOL Time Warner packages together access to digital music, high-speed Internet access, interactive television, cable networks, magazines, movies, and a vast system of cable lines.

■ Random House and Classic Media purchased the financially troubled children's book publisher Golden Books Family Entertainment and shortly after began to announce layoffs. Golden is being integrated into Random House under the direction of Random House's President of Publishing Development, Joerg Pfuhl. Golden's Chief Operating Officer, Richard Collins, will work with Pfuhl.

The man who made splashy headlines for years trying to remake Golden, Richard Snyder, has left the company, his contract bought out. Pfuhl said at the time of the purchase that Random House wants to "stabilize and strengthen the great Golden Books brand." Golden Books library includes over 500,000 book titles, plus movies, television specials, cartoons, and an extensive comic book collection.

■ French media company Vivendi Universal acquired the fourth largest U.S. educational publisher, Houghton Mifflin, for $2.2 billion. Founded in 1832, Houghton Mifflin is expected to boost Vivendi's worldwide position to the number two spot in educational publishing. In addition to school publishing, Houghton Mifflin publishes juvenile fiction and nonfiction, and reference books for adults. After the acquisition, about 60 executives were laid off at the Boston offices.

■ Reed Elsevier acquired Harcourt and immediately sold that company's higher education division to Canada's Thomson Corp., which placed it in the Thomson Learning division. Reed Elsevier kept Harcourt's K-12 education group. Harcourt's trade division is also part of the school group.

Reed later merged its publisher of supplemental educational materials, Rigby, with Steck-Vaughn, Harcourt's supplemental line. It also closed Harcourt offices in Newton, MA.

■ Reed next invested in Riverdeep Group through the Harcourt Education Group. Riverdeep, based in Ireland and Massachusetts, produces K-12 instructional programs on the Web. Harcourt and Riverdeep are collaborating on electronic basal instructional products that will be sold under the Harcourt name. Riverdeep will receive royalties. The relationship with Riverdeep is boosting Harcourt's so far minor presence in online education.

Riverdeep acquired Edmark from IBM two years ago and recently purchased The Learning Company (TLC). from Gores Technology Group.

■ McGraw-Hill Companies purchased Frank Schaffer Publications from Torstar Corp. Frank Schaffer publishes elementary school and early childhood teacher resource materials, including

Good Apple Newspaper, Educational Oasis, Totline, Schooldays, Lollipops, Shining Star, and *Challenge.* McGraw-Hill later decided to end publication of *Shining Star* and *Challenge.*

Ira, Larry, and Frank Schaffer started an educational venture targeting teachers, www.TeachNow. com.

■ The Wicks Group of Companies purchased Delta Education from Torstar Corp. Delta is a publisher of math and science for kindergarten to grade 12.

■ Down East Books purchased Countrysport Press and its backlist of 30 books on fishing, hunting, and shooting. Down East, located in Rockport, Maine, has been a regional company focused on the East Coast. This acquisition will help the company broaden its sales nationally. Countrysport had been located in Michigan and moved to Alabama. Down East's imprint of outdoor titles, Silver Quill, will fold into the acquired list. Down East also publishes children's books, and regional craft, cooking, gardening, and art books. Plans are to publish at least 30 titles a year.

■ Scholastic acquired the rights to Pfeifer-Hamilton's children's books, including the best-selling *Old Turtle* and *The Quiltmaker's Gift.* Scholastic now publishes all nine of Pfeifer-Hamilton's children's backlist, but Pfeifer-Hamilton continues to publish adult titles.

■ F & W Publications sold the children's unit of its U.K. division, David & Charles Group, to Gullane Entertainment. Formerly known as Britt Allcroft, Gullane owns the rights to the popular Thomas the Tank Engine series. It produces TV shows and films and has been acquiring rights to a number of children's characters. The sale includes 150 backlist titles that will now be published under the Gullane Children's Book imprint.

■ Disney Publishing reorganized its children's book division into two groups: Hyperion Books for Children, with Andrea Pinkney as Editorial Director, and Disney Global Children's Books, headed by Jackie Carter, which focuses on licensed characters.

■ Penguin Putnam reorganized various units, including Dorling Kindersley in the U.S. Skip Fisher is overseeing the changes in American operations. The U.K. and U.S. editorial, sales, and marketing departments continue to function independently.

■ Advanced Marketing Services now has a 25 percent interest in the U.K. children's book packager and publisher Templar Co. Templar produces pop-up picture books and a wildlife series that Advanced Marketing's imprint, Silver Dolphin, publishes in the U.S.

■ John Wiley & Sons acquired Hungry Minds, originally named IDG Books, which publishes the For Dummies series, Frommer's travel guides, Cliffs-Notes, and *Webster's New World Dictionary,* among other titles. Wiley has long been well known as a publisher of business and professional books, and also does educational titles and children's books.

■ Scholastic Inc. purchased the book fairs segment of Troll Communications, making Scholastic the only operator of book fairs in North America. Troll is the second largest publisher of books for school fairs. Troll continues its children's book club business.

■ Guideposts Publishing acquired Ideals Publications and reunited the company's children's and adult divisions, separated almost a decade ago. Ideals Children's Books has about 260 titles on its backlist. Guideposts has another children's imprint, Candy Cane, which will continue to do board books while Ideals publishes other children's titles.

Magazines

■ In an attempt to salvage *Working Mother* and *Working Woman*, Carol Evans and MCG Capital combined to create Working Mother Media, but at *Children's Writer Guide* presstime, the viability of both magazines was unclear.

■ *Wee Ones Magazine* is a new monthly online magazine for children three to eight. The e-zine features entertaining stories, arts and crafts, science, math, and cooking for kids, and a parents' section, called The Big Ones.

■ Scholastic has introduced a magazine for new teachers, a spin-off of *Instructor* magazine. *Instructor New Teacher* will be published twice a year, and distributed free to new teachers.

■ Achieve Communications has released a new publication for school administrators and school business managers. *Inside Education* covers technology, financial management, curriculum, and staff development. The magazine will start as a bimonthly but plans are to go monthly by the end of the year.

■ Bertelsmann's Gruner + Jahr USA bought the teen fitness title *Jump* from Weider Publications and added its 400,000 rate base to *YM's* 2.2 million.

Multimedia

■ Right Start acquired the assets of Zany Brainy toy stores. Zany Brainy has sold multimedia products for children 4 to 12 for a decade. Right Start sells educational toys for children from birth to age four. Zany Brainy had filed for Chapter 11 bankruptcy protection and managed to continue to operate during the bankruptcy. Zany Brainy had acquired Noodle Kidoodle in 2000.

■ Zonderkidz, the children's publishing arm of Zondervan, signed a deal with Big Idea Productions to publish products for three Big Idea's projects: the VeggieTales series, the 3-2-1 Penguins series, and the film *Jonah—A VeggieTales Movie*. Big Ideas looked for a company, says Chief Creative Officer Phil Visher, that shared its vision: "We are thrilled to have our innovative storytelling and wacky sense of humor come to life through books produced by Zonderkidz." Future products will help parents "make a significant impact on the spiritual and developmental growth of their children," says Zondervan President and Chief Executive Officer Bruce Ryskamp.

■ The Walt Disney Company purchased the children's cable network, Fox Family Worldwide. The Fox Family Channel, which Disney plans to rename ABC Family, reaches about 81 million subscribers in the U.S.

Disney also agreed to buy outright the rights to Winnie the Pooh for a reported $350 million. Disney has licensed the Pooh characters since the 1960s, paying royalties twice a year. The rights had been owned by Clare Milne, granddaughter of creator A.A. Milne, and by other organizations, including publishers. Clare Milne will receive a lump sum of $40 million.

Launches & Ventures

Books

■ Random House launched a children's imprint, Wendy Lamb Books. Lamb is a Random House Vice President and Publishing Director of her imprint, which will publish 10 to 18 books annually.

■ Scholastic Inc. is launching a teen-book imprint, Push. It will publish first-time authors of fiction, poetry, and memoirs for ages 13 and up, with an emphasis on high school readers. The plans are to release 6 to 10 books a year.

■ Simon & Schuster Book for Young Readers is restructuring its paperback division and collapsing five paperback imprints into two. It will phase out Archway and Minstrel, which had been part of Pocket Books for Young Readers. Under the new organization, Aladdin Books will publish books for preschool through middle-grade readers, and Pulse will be a teen-focused paperback imprint. Pulse will take over Aladdin and Archway teen titles, and will do some original paperbacks. The Simon Spotlight imprint will continue to publish media tie-ins and novelty books, in hardcover and paperback.

■ OshKosh B'Gosh, the children's apparel maker, teamed up with Little Simon, an imprint of Simon & Schuster Books for Young Readers, to produce a line of OshKosh children's books. Simon & Schuster will publish a line of interactive books for newborns through age five, many featuring cloth elements that reflect the look of OshKosh clothing. The books will be sold at book retailers, online, and at OshKosh B'Gosh stores.

■ U.K.-based Bloomsbury Children's Books plans to open an office in New York City. Sarah Oedina, Editorial Director of Bloomsbury Children's Books in the U.K., will head the new office, which will publish hardcover titles and license paperback rights. The new list will include almost all the titles published by Bloomsbury in the U.K., and add American authors. The company plans to publish about 40 books a year in the U.S.

■ The Millbrook Press has dubbed its new children's trade imprint Roaring Brook Press. Millbrook plans for the imprint to publish about 40 picture books and novels annually.

■ Random House announced the creation of Random House Children's Books, a new division that combines

Random House and Transworld. Random House imprints include Jonathan Cape, Hutchinson, and Bodley Head, the Doubleday list, and newly acquired David Fickling Books.

David Fickling Books has become the first bicontinental children's publisher, allowing authors and illustrators to publish simultaneously in the U.S. and U.K.

■ Random House launched a series of children's books under its newly established Disney Books for Young Readers imprint. The spring list featured 66 frontlist and 70 backlist titles, which were previously published by Disney Mouseworks and Golden Books.

■ Key Porter Books, an independent Canadian publisher, formed a new imprint called Sarasota Press. Sarasota focuses on parenting and child development, general health, and alternative medicine titles.

■ For those who can't get enough of the bespectacled boy wizard, Scholastic published two spin-off books based on the Harry Potter series, and written by J.K. Rowling. The two books, *Quidditch Through the Ages* and *Fantastic Beasts and Where to Find Them,* are referred to in the original series. Proceeds from the sale of the books will go to a children's charity established by Comic Relief U.K.

■ Harry Potter has gone 3-D. Intervisual Books Inc. signed a contract with Scholastic, Inc., to produce two pop-up books based on the Harry Potter series. The books were released to co-incide with the release of the Warner Bros. movie, *Harry Potter and the Sorcerer's Stone.* Scholastic will market the 3-D books in the U.S. and Canada.

■ *Artemis Fowl,* by Eoin Colfer, was released internationally and touted as the next Harry Potter. It features an adolescent boy, Artemis Fowl, who kidnaps a leprechaun and then battles a band trying to rescue him.

■ Jesse Ventura, wrestler and Minnesota governor, is throwing his author's hat into the children's book ring. The outspoken celebrity has a deal with independent Minnesota publisher Lerner Publishing Group to write a children's book that describes the inner workings of government to children. Licensing and royalty fees from the book will be donated to Ventura for Minnesota Inc., a charitable foundation. Ventura's two adult books were best-sellers for Villard and Pocket Books.

■ Smallfellow Press is a new children's imprint of Tallfellow Press. It was begun by Lois Sarkisian, who owns a children's book illustration art gallery in Los Angeles called Every Picture Tells a Story. Veteran publishers Leonard Stern and Larry Sloan, of Price Stern Sloan, began Tallfellow. Smallfellow has four books in production and plans to publish its first title this fall. It will display the illustrations from its books at the gallery and in travelling art shows.

■ Marcato, the new book imprint established by Carus Publishing, has released its first list. Marc Aronson left his position as Senior Editor at Holt Books for Young Readers to become the publisher of the imprint, which he named. The first book published by Marcato, *Seek,* was written by Newbery Medalist Paul Fleischman.

■ Sesame Workshop Books will not launch a new children's book imprint, which it had planned for fall 2002. The imprint was to publish 10 to 12 fiction and nonfiction works for ages two to five, and picture books for ages four to eight. The imprint may simply be delayed a year, but no final decision has been made.

■ NorthWord Press is focusing more attention on the children's book business, expanding its trade line but even more dramatically increasing its production of products for institutional markets. NorthWord named Aimee Jackson to the newly formed position as Executive Editor of Books for Young Readers. The trade line of picture books and nature nonfiction will grow to 17 books, from 10. The school and library market is projected to grow to 70 percent of NorthWord's business, up from 39 percent.

■ Julie Andrews will write three books for the children's division of Harper-Collins, and will have her own imprint called the Julie Andrews Collection with her daughter, Emma Walton Hamilton. The three-book deal signed with HarperCollins will include two more Little Bo books.

■ The National Geographic Society has developed two series of readers, focusing on science and social studies, to help children hone their nonfiction reading skills. The Windows on Literacy series is written for kindergarten to grade two, and Reading Expeditions for grades three to six.

Magazines

■ National Geographic Society has also launched a nonfiction classroom magazine, *National Geographic Kids,* directed at grades three to six.

■ Pinatubo Press based in Asheville, NC, has launched *Explore!* magazine, which encourages children to think critically about how the world works. The title, published 10 times a year, is aimed at children 9 to 14. It has a circulation of 29,000.

■ *Becoming Family* is a new quarterly published by Family Ventures. The magazine is dedicated to celebrating and strengthening family life in America. Its audience includes parents, grandparents, teens, and children.

■ Primedia, the publisher of more than 100 specialty magazines, acquired the U.S. magazine business of Emap, the British publisher. The deal makes Primedia the second largest publisher in the U.S. in number of magazines, after the publishing division of AOL Time Warner. Emap has more than 60 consumer titles in the U.S., from *Guns & Ammo* to *Teen.*

■ Primedia and Steven Brill, who had teamed up to buy the media news website Inside.com, ended their partnership. Inside.com shut down as a separate news entity, and became a portal for Primedia's Media Central business publications, such as *Folio*. Brill also closed his media watchdog magazine, *Brill's Content*. Rumors are that financier Harry Kravis will take the media company private and sell each of the titles. Primedia titles include *Seventeen, Modern Bride*, and *New York Magazine*.

■ A number of changes have taken place in Primedia's Youth Entertainment Group also. Tommi Lewis Tilden, *Teen* Editor in Chief, says *Teen Beat* and *Tiger Beat* changed from monthly to quarterly frequency. The magazines moved their operations to Primedia's Los Angeles office.

■ *SportingKid* is a magazine for parents with kids who play team sports. The publication acts as a guide for instructing children in such valuable lessons as sportsmanship and teamwork, and provides articles that analyze sports trends and products. The magazine also has an online edition that publishes material distinct from the print title.

■ *FringeGolf* is a lifestyle magazine for young golfers, 18 and up, who don't fit the traditional mold. The bimonthly aims to cover golf "with all the spit and spirit it promised when Tiger walked off with the coat." It describes itself as having a "modern voice and irreverent style in vivid Technicolor." The website is www. fringegolf.com.

■ *American Cheerleader Junior* is a new bimonthly for 7-to-12-year old girls, a younger version of *American Cheerleader*. It will appear quarterly with a circulation of 50,000. It is published by Lifestyle Ventures and the Editorial Director is Julie Davis.

■ *Surfing Girl* is a new title aimed at teen girls. The bimonthly is published by McMullen-Argus Publishing. In addition to surfing, it covers shopping, travel, and music.

■ *GameNow* is a new video game magazine published by Ziff Davis Media Game Group. The monthly, aimed at ages 10 to 16, launched with a circulation of 150,000. *GameNow* features articles that spotlight PlayStation 2, GameCube, Xbox, and Gameboy Advance and also covers new products, game strategies, and reviews.

■ The publisher of *Girls' Life* is launching *Adam,* a title for young men in college and beginning careers. The bimonthly will spotlight such topics as personal finance, education, sports, pop culture, relationships, and health from an intellectual perspective.

■ *Kid Zone* features articles about crafts and stories for children ages 4 to 12, but focuses even more specifically on ages 7 to 10. The magazine is used in daycare centers, by parents, and by educators.

■ Talk show host Rosie O'Donnell followed in the footsteps of Oprah Winfrey and Martha Stewart by lending her name to a magazine. Gruner + Jahr relaunched its established but ailing *McCall's* magazine as *Rosie*. O'Donnell was named the title's Editorial Director.

■ *Sports Illustrated For Kids* is sporting a more contemporary look and some editorial changes: The magazine for ages 8 to 14 will focus more on action and inside information in its sports coverage and will add five new departments.

■ Time, Inc. acquired *Sesame Street Magazine,* along with its production, marketing, and distribution operations. The 1.1 million-circulation title has become part of Time's Parenting Group and will be delivered in the same polybag as *Parenting. Sesame Street Parents, Contact Kids,* and *Kid City* magazines were closed as part of the deal.

■ Scholastic Inc. has announced a geography education program for grades four to six. The program will include a geography feature in each issue of *Scholastic News,* for fourth graders, plus a special map skills book, *MAPMAN'S Map Skills,* for grades four to six. It is written by Jim McMahon, who is featured as MAPMAN.

■ Hachette Filipacchi has tapped into the popular teen market with *ElleGirl,* a younger sibling for the women's title, *Elle. ElleGirl* aims at girls 14 to 17. The magazine will focus more on fashion and style, and less on boybands and celebrities.

■ Condé Nast's *Glamour* changed its editorial coverage. The magazine began to place more emphasis on health, money and careers, and cover relationships in a new way. The announcement came in the aftermath of the September 11 terrorist attacks.

■ *BBW,* the only magazine left covering the plus-size market following the demise of *Mode,* is in trouble. At presstime, *BBW* was seeking backing to publish another issue, after cancelling one for lack of funds.

Multimedia

■ Teachers have access to a new line of teacher-created, classroom-tested materials for preschool to grade 12 that can be downloaded and printed out. They are made available by TeachNow, started by Ira and Larry Schaffer, sons of the founder of Frank Schaffer Publications. TeachNow's own products are found on the website (www. TeachNow.com). Materials from 10 other publishers, including J. Weston Walch and Teaching and Learning Company, will also be available.

■ The Supreme Court ruled 7 to 2 in favor of freelance writers in Tasini v. the *New York Times*, which was originally filed in 1993. The decision bans the digital reuse of freelancers' articles without their permission, leaving publishers potentially liable for fines for infringement. The case is more likely to affect articles, photographs, and illustrations produced 10 years ago, when contracts contained no clauses concerning electronic use.

The Court's ruling upholds a 1999 Federal Appeals Court decision that found that the *New York Times* and its codefendants, *Newsday*, Lexis-Nexis, University Microfilms International (now called ProQuest), and AOL Time Warner, had violated the copyrights of Jonathan Tasini and five other writers by reproducing their work on the publishers' websites and in such databases as Lexis-Nexis. Tasini is President of the National Writers Union and was lead plaintiff in the suit.

■ North-South Books launched a new novelty and merchandise division called Night Sky Books. Its publishing program includes original projects plus books based on best-selling titles and characters from the North-South and SeaStar list, such as Marcus Pfister's *Rainbow Fish*. Other plans include a movie tie-in program based on *Little Polar Bear,* by Hans De Beer. At that time, Warner Bros. plans to release an animated feature film in the U.S. Night Sky will publish 15 to 20 titles a year.

■ Amazon.com and Toys 'R' Us launched an online specialty and learning toy store called Imaginarium. The site allows users to search for toys that will enable children to exercise specific skills.

■ Houghton Mifflin has U.S. rights to publish books related to the release of the three-part film adaptation of J.R.R. Tolkien's *The Lord of the Rings* trilogy; the first film was released at the end of last year. The multibook deal includes at least six titles, two released each year to correspond with the film releases.

■ HIT Entertainment, a British licensing agent, added to its list of children's characters with its purchase of Lyrick Studios. HIT already owned the popular characters Bob the Builder and Kipper. Lyrick's book licensing properties include Barney and Friends and Freddi Fish. At the same time, Scholas.... a deal with Lyrick to be the U.S. publisher of all Barney hardcover, paperback, coloring and activity books.

■ Disney Publishing Worldwide and The Baby Einstein Company, which produces developmental media products for young children, will publish a series of books based on Baby Einstein's award-winning interactive videos that introduce babies to the arts. The series is part of a multi-year licensing agreement between Disney and Baby Einstein.

■ ReadingMonster.com is a new online resource for parents and others to help children with their reading skills. It features a free 10-question Monster Test to track a child's or student's reading progress.

■ AOL Time Warner, Random House, and Simon & Schuster are all releasing e-books for children and teenagers. The companies tackled the adult segment first, before trying it out on a generation that has grown up with computers. Time Warner affiliate ipicturebooks.com, which launched in February, already has about 200 e-books available for children ages 6 months to 10. Random House has teamed up with Sesame Street to release 10 picture e-books; Simon & Schuster is venturing into the young adult e-book market by releasing winners of the Newbery Medal for children's literature from its backlist, plus 30 other titles.

■ Hulabee Entertainment has previewed a new sports website for children,

SportsSquad.com. Hulabee is a digital media company created by Humongous Entertainment co-founders, Shelley Day and Ron Gilbert.

■ A television version of *A Wrinkle in Time,* the Madeleine L'Engle classic, will air on ABC as a four-hour miniseries.

■ Penguin has launched a new e-publishing imprint called ePenguin. The imprint will feature more than 200 Penguin titles from its catalogue, as well as e-book versions of children and teen titles, in Microsoft Reader and Adobe Acrobat eBook Reader formats. The ePenguin titles are also available from other online retailers.

■ *Inside,* published by Achieve Communications, has launched an online edition at www.insideeducation.net. The website features editorial from the print magazine and material written exclusively for the site. It offers Q&A interviews with school adminstrators, online columnists, and education-related resources.

■ *CosmoGirl!* magazine's website, Cosmogirl.com, has been made over through a deal with Alloy Online, a Generation Y media and direct marketing company. Alloy created the site's design, offers technology tools, hosts the magazine's online destination, and offers advertising and marketing services.

■ The electronic rights war between Random House and Rosetta Books rages on. Random House wants to prevent RosettaBooks from publishing electronic versions of its books and has sought a preliminary injunction against them. If the court agrees to the injunction, Rosetta Books would have to suspend publishing the e-books until the case is decided.

RosettaBooks argues that it owns the electronic rights to the books through contracts it signed with the authors last year and that Random House did not contract for those electronic rights. Random House asserts that the agreements it has with authors do cover electronic rights, even though such rights did not exist when the contracts were originally signed. The argument is that Random House's original author contracts allows it to "print, publish, and sell in book form" the author's work and that electronic form comes under that definition.

The Authors Guild and the Association of Author's Representatives have sided with RosettaBooks. Not surprisingly, other major publishers—Penguin Putnam, Perseus Books, Simon & Schuster, and Time Warner Trade Publishing—are siding with Random House in the case.

■ iUniverse.com has reached a milestone in printing and selling 500,000 books. Through iUniverse's e-publishing services, authors can self-publish their books in print-on-demand and e-book formats. The company also declared that almost 10,000 titles have been published by authors using iUniverse.com's e-publishing services. The company's self-publishing services are also available through Barnes&Noble.com, BooksAMillion.com, and Education World. iUniverse.com also has a business-to-business division and has developed custom publishing programs with Microsoft Press and Hungry Minds.

■ Simon Spotlight, an imprint of Simon & Schuster Children's Publishing, will publish five books based on Fox Family channel's Emmy-nominated animated show, *Angela Anaconda*.

People

Books

■ Dominic Barth was named Senior Editor at Charlesbridge Publishing. He was formerly at The Millbrook Press.

■ Deborah Brodie is the Executive Editor at Roaring Brook Press, the new children's trade imprint at The Millbrook Press.

■ Penguin Putnam appointed Debra Dorfman as President and Publisher of its Grosset & Dunlap children's imprint. She had been Director of Editorial Administration for book clubs at Scholastic.

■ Vincent F. Douglas has been named President of McGraw-Hill's Publishing Division.

■ Susan Hirschman, founder and publisher of Greenwillow Books, retired after 50 years. Hirschman began her publishing career at Alfred A. Knopf's children's department, followed by 10 years at Harper & Row. She became Editor in Chief of Macmillan's children's department in 1964. Hirschman founded Greenwillow Books in

1974 at William Morrow & Co., which was later acquired by HarperCollins.

■ Marcia Marshall retired after 25 years with Atheneum Books for Young Readers. Marshall produced many distinguished children's titles, including Natalie Bober's *Abigail Adams,* winner of the *Boston Globe-Horn Book* Award.

■ Kristina Peterson, formerly President of the Random House Children's Media Group, was named President and Publisher of the Simon & Schuster Children's Book Division.

■ John Rudolph was promoted to Associate Editor, Simon & Schuster's Children's Publishing.

■ Dina Rubin joined the staff of Franklin Watts and Children's Press as Managing Editor. Previously, she held editorial positions with Reader's Digest Children's Publishing and Scholastic.

■ Ginee Seo was named Vice President and Associate Publisher of Atheneum Books for Young Readers, part of Simon & Schuster's Children's Publishing.

■ Harold Underdown, formerly with Charlesbridge Books, was named to head up the editorial department at e-book publisher ipicturebooks.com.

Magazines

■ Julie Davis is Editorial Director of the new *American Cheerleader Junior*.

■ Ziff Davis Media Game Group has appointed John Davison the overall Editorial Director of the Game Group, and Simon Cox, Launch Editor and Creative Director.

■ Bill Lindsay took over as Editor in Chief of United Parenting Publications, which publishes 28 regional parenting publications across the country.

■ *Click*'s new Editor is Lonnie Plecha.

■ Rosanne Tolin was appointed Managing Editor of *Guideposts for Kids.*

■ Mortimer Adler, who developed the Great Books program, died at 98. Adler was also an editor of the *Encyclopedia Britannica* and the founder and compiler of Britannica's Great Books for the Western World series, first published in 1952. He was an educational reformer who based his philosophy on the works of Aristotle and St. Thomas Aquinas. Adler wrote and co-wrote moer than 45 books.

Closings

■ *Mademoiselle,* the women's magazine published by Condé Nast for 66 years, has ceased publication. The company blames the poor economic climate for the monthly's demise.

■ *Family Money,* published by the Meredith Corporation, has ceased publication after four years. Meredith says it will publish the magazine periodically as a special interest title sold on newsstands.

■ The Hispanic teen title *Latingirl* has ceased publication after two and a half years.

■ H & S Media shut down a number of magazines, including celebrity-teen magazine *hot* and *Pojo's Pokemon,* and the newly launched *Scooby-Doo Scooby Snacks,* before it filed for bankruptcy. It is also the publisher of *Mary-Kate and Ashley, Teen Style,* and *Rapup* magazines.

■ *Teen Girl Power* is no longer being published.

■ Primedia's Youth Entertainment Group closed *Entertainmenteen, Bop,* and *All About You. Tiger Beat* and *Teen Beat* changed from monthlies to quarterlies.

■ *Brill's Content,* a magazine that covered the media, closed.

■ *Offspring* is no longer publishing.

■ *dads* ceased publication. Gruner + Jahr USA, publisher of *Parents,* acquired the *dads* subscriber list and domain name from Dads Media, Inc. Effective with the May issue, *dads* subscribers started receiving *Parents.*

■ The *Teen People* Book Club has closed its operations as a result of the AOL Time Warner merger. The book club was a co-venture between Bookspan and Time Inc.'s *Teen People* magazine.

■ Ziff Davis Media announced magazine closings. The company stopped publishing *Family PC Magazine,* suspending plans to revive the title under the new name *Family Internet Life.* The company also announced that it would fold one of its consumer titles,

Expedia Travel, after four years and is rumored to have *Yahoo Internet Life* up for sale.

■ Rodale Press closed the young man's title, *MH-18*, after five issues of the quarterly.

■ AOL Time Warner announced the closing of *Family Life*.

Style & Technique

Move It: Pacing Your Fiction

By Darcy Pattison

"Pacing is highly underrated: It can make or break a story," says Andrea Weiss, Senior Editor at Pleasant Company, publisher of American Girl books. Pacing is the way that writing pulls a reader through the events of a story without a pause; the reader anxiously turns the pages and absolutely can't put down a story or book. It causes readers to keep reading into the wee hours of the morning.

To achieve the right pace for your story, says Cecile Goyette, Senior Editor at Dial Books for Young Readers, "Every single thing should be absolutely crucial to the theme." If the theme is about telling lies, then every element of the story should relate to lies and truth: plot, subplots, character, foreshadowing, exposition, emotional response, scene breaks, language.

Plot and Character

When every plot point relates to the theme, then the story moves. Weiss identifies two types of plot. "In most of the fiction we publish at American Girl, the protagonist is the instrument of change. That is, her actions drive the plot, and her own growth and change are a result of those actions and their consequences." For an action-oriented story, the character's arc—or "character's projectile," as Weiss calls it—has to keep pace with plot. "There should be a tight correlation between plot and character development," Weiss insists.

"The second type of plot is when a character changes or grows in response to events that are happening to or around him or her, and the emphasis is on what the character is experiencing emotionally rather than on the action itself," Weiss says. "Character development rather than plot moves us through the story. If you go this route, then pacing is even more important or the story, and the character, will feel contrived. The character development needs to be dead-on, not trite, with the character showing a gradual and believable change."

Goyette says, "If you have rote or stock characters, then it's harder to construct varied pace. You don't have enough color or dimension. Well-rounded characters offer more possibilities for narrative and emotional content and, as such, they can help serve pace."

Caitlyn Dlouhy, Senior Editor at Atheneum Books for Young Readers, says, "A reader will follow a great character for a while, but eventually something has to happen. Plot and character development determine the pacing of a novel."

Regardless of whether the character drives the events or the events drive the character, the character arc is critical to pacing. One tip is to develop that arc or projectile by defining the starting and ending positions. For example, at the beginning of the story about telling lies, the protagonist lies to the antagonist; by the end, the protagonist reveals the truth to the antagonist. What happens between the beginning and the ending to change the character's ideas, emotions, and actions about lies?

"Identify your crucial theme and the climax. When you know these, you can add the proper building blocks to lead up to that moment," Goyette says.

"You don't want a story arc where the character doesn't get it, doesn't get it, doesn't get it—and then suddenly gets it. Getting from point A to C in the plot isn't necessarily a straight line through B," says Weiss. "Instead, the character's behavior and understanding move forward a step, then maybe backward two steps, and so on. The story should be about the character trying different things." Proper development of this roundabout character projectile develops a rhythm fundamental to the story pacing.

Plot & Subplots

Weiss also emphasizes the need for subplots to support the main plot and theme. "Pacing has a lot to do with hierarchy of theme, how the subplots support a theme and build to one conclusion. Each subplot should be resolved individually, but should still move the story along and bring the whole to closure."

Weiss points to the Pleasant Company title, *Smoke Screen,* by Amy Goldman Koss. The book addresses the theme of honesty—the line between making up harmless stories, stretching the truth, and flat-out lying. One subplot is about the protagonist's, Mitzi's, mother trying to stop smoking, another is about Mitzi's crush on a boy, and the third is about problems with her best friend. Subplots like this can't move parallel to each other; instead, they must support each other. This means the order in which each is resolved is crucial.

Mitzi has lied to the boy at school, telling him that her mother is dying of a serious disease. Meanwhile, Mitzi and her best friend are growing apart. The lie about her mom snowballs until Mitzi finds herself in way over her head at school, without the support of her best friend. The first subplot is resolved when she loses interest in the boy; she realizes he's a jerk and her crush is obliterated. But there is still the lie to deal with, as well as her mother's smoking, and Mitzi needs an ally. She clears the air with her best friend, thus wrapping up another subplot. Finally, Mitzi's parents catch her in the lie, which has grown to epic proportions. They tell her that she must apologize to her class for lying. Mitzi strikes a deal: If Mom quits smoking before the end of school, she will apologize to the class. The last section of the book is a race to the finish to see if Mom will quit smoking or whether Mitzi will be spared public humiliation.

If the best friend subplot had been resolved last, the focus of the story would have changed and Mitzi wouldn't have an ally when facing her parents. Each subplot must support the main plot and must be resolved in a way that adds to the suspense.

Mary Pearson, author of *Scribbler of Dreams* (Harcourt Brace), created subplots that revolve around secondary relationships, too, but also support or echo the theme. She says, "It gives the reader a change of pace and the author another way to deepen the main theme. This resonance builds expectation, which will always keep the pages turning."

Story Points: Micro-pacing

In *Writing the Blockbuster Novel*, Albert Zuckerman says that pacing is "constantly repositioning the characters and posing ever new dramatic questions in the reader's mind. . . . [In] each scene and each chapter, take care to keep developing the plot, twisting it, spinning it in fresh directions and thus advancing the action. And on a

lesser scale, [the author] must develop and twist and spin even within each scene in small units of action that endure for a page or two or even less."

Zuckerman says that the big plot points are easy for authors to figure out. But the small *story points*, or *micro-pacing,* are more difficult. As an example, he analyzes the plot of chapter 45 of *Gone With the Wind*, identifying 24 small changes in dynamics in 21 pages.

The changes are in small actions, small emotional setbacks, awareness, intensity of emotions, information provided. This has also been called the *density* of a story. If only one action occurs in a chapter, the story doesn't move forward, and pacing is poor. For an example of a very dense story, read the first chapter of *Wings of a Falcon*, by Cynthia Voigt, and count the number of changes.

Details that support actions are related to micro-pacing. Linda Murray, Senior Editor at Troll Books, says, "Details help develop the action of a chapter, lead up to a key moment, and add depth to a story. But there is a fine line between details and overkill. It may take you three or four reads to identify details that can be edited out."

Foreshadowing

Foreshadowing is the technique of mentioning something early in a story that will become crucial later. "Foreshadowing is a way to strengthen pace, to lead you toward a more climactic moment," says Goyette.

Pearson uses foreshadowing in two different ways in *Scribbler of Dreams:* "I had a flash of blue whiz past the protagonist, which she shrugged off, but it leaves the readers with the expectation that this is significant. They can worry for the protagonist because they do indeed suspect that it's the truck of the antagonist speeding past her. In that case, the reader possesses the foreshadowing knowledge, not the character. In another part of the story, it is reversed: The protagonist drops clues as to what is to come"— that is, she is an instigator of the fore-shadowing—"but leaves the reader to wonder at the significance. When you develop a trust with the reader that these foreshadowing events will pay off, it keeps them enthusiastically turning the pages."

Exposition versus Emotion?

"Proper pacing will cut out unneeded exposition," Goyette says. Some people over-write and add too much explanation or detail. Whatever does not relate to the theme should be cut, regardless of how artfully conveyed that information is.

Arthur Levine, who has an eponymous imprint at Scholastic, says, "Exposition shouldn't be extra material that you couldn't find room to put anywhere else. An author shouldn't think of exposition as a separate component at all. Focus on storytelling; all the information should come from the storytelling. If you actually, consciously stopped and are indulging in exposition, it's a sign that you've lagged in the storytelling. You've fallen into the trap of telling instead of showing."

Instead, tell your story in the most dramatic and gripping way possible. "What about flashbacks?" asks Levine.

"You don't fill in the reader with a flashback. Think of a flashback as a narrative choice: It's just a piece of the narrative that you are telling out of chronological order. The author should have chosen the most dramatic point to tell that incident."

"Keep in mind the emotional pace of the book," Goyette says. "Give readers time to think, reflect, to cool down from an emotionally charged passage." It doesn't mean that the story needs to stop still, but the author needs to find a quieter place as a balance. For example, after that emotional passage, it may be the place to switch to a subplot with a quieter emotional arc.

Emotional pacing varies with different genres. "For a light, funny book," Murray says, "emotional pacing isn't so key as for, say, a mystery." She recommends *Holes*, by Louis Sachar, as a book with great emotional pacing.

Openers & Cliffhangers

Pacing is influenced by how you start a story, and how you end its many parts, whether scenes or chapters. To pace your story well, the opening sets the stage.

"One problem I often run across is a story line that takes too long to develop," Dlouhy says. "A reader will only give the story so much energy and if something doesn't happen, if the reader doesn't feel invested in the story because they don't see any development, you'll lose them. Kurt Vonnegut once said, have your characters do something immediately, even if it is to drink a glass of water.

"You can start with a disaster on the first page," Dlouhy continues, "or you can build and lead up to a disaster. There's no right or wrong here. It's subjective as to how the writer chooses to tell their story." Either way works, but the choice affects the pacing of the entire novel. You must look at the overall effect of the opening to judge its appropriateness.

Murray finds that some authors get bogged down in character description at the start of a novel. "Let the character unfold; the unfolding itself should have a certain rhythm of pacing. If the reader knows everything at the beginning, what will compel him to continue to the end?" she asks.

Endings of scenes and chapters may have even more variables than openings and writers should resist taking easy ways out. "Chapter breaks have to do with knowing what can take place offstage," Weiss says. You don't have to have a cliffhanger to end each chapter, but the reader must be left wanting to turn the page to find out what happens next. "Learn to know what needs to take place on stage and what the reader can assume. If a chapter ends with a conversation in which one person is revealing something, then end with the revelation, not with the immediate reaction to it."

Think in terms of scene cuts in a movie. A time gap is assumed by the reader, who also makes assumptions about what happened in that gap. If a chapter ends with a child failing to turn in a math page and the next chapter starts with the child sitting at the kitchen table at home crying and working on a math sheet, then the reader will assume that the teacher contacted the parent to report the child's laziness.

Smooth or Staccato Talker

"The least obvious thing about pacing is the importance of language," Weiss says. "Of course you need scenes that move—that's a basic of Writing 101. But the flow of language itself, the importance of sentence variety and having a good ear for rhythm and pacing, is underrated."

One typical suggestion in writing how-to books is to use short sentences, paragraphs, or chapters to speed up pacing. Goyette, however, says that isn't necessarily true. "You must allow for style and voice. If a section is too clipped and fractured in style, it may be hard to keep a flow going. An entire music composition in staccato isn't pleasing and it won't work in writing, either."

Weiss says, "Even words in a sentence have to be paced. It's a matter of timing." She suggests that when you reread a section to yourself, do it silently because a reader doesn't read out loud. "It's a visual test, not an oral test. You have to see how the words read off the page to someone coming to it without the benefit of vocal cues such as intonation and stress."

Dlouhy distinguishes dialogue, suggesting that writers read it aloud. "You can get used to seeing your dialogue written down, but when you read it aloud, you may realize that no one would construct a sentence like that when actually speaking to another person."

Either way, Weiss advises writers not to revise a sentence until it has been read in relation to the entirety. "Read from the top of the page, all the way down. You must check changes in context. Check to see if the rhythm of the preceding narrative sets it up."

Murray emphasizes the importance of considering your audience. "Use a vocabulary that kids can easily identify with. If you use very long words, or language that kids don't understand, that will bog down the story."

Hope for the Pace-Challenged

Dlouhy says that while pace is important, it's not the most important consideration in a story. "For me, the characterization and plot are most essential. If the plot is working properly, the pacing is working or at least is close to working. It's harder to give a writer suggestions on how to create or fix a character's voice. But you can help pacing."

Weiss agrees: "I look for a highly original premise and for voice. But when I find those, the author and I often have to work the most on pacing. That's okay. I can fix pacing, but I can't come up with the premise and voice."

It isn't all in the pacing. Premise, plot, character are all at least as important. But pacing is a web, a force, a vehicle to make all of the parts of a good story move together and move a reader.

Creative Nonfiction: Dancing the High Wire

By Ruth Sachs

Those days, Stefan Zweig's works were banned. School children had read his account of the laying of the first transatlantic telegraph lines and were awed by the innovative technology. In the 1920s and 1930s, Zweig wrote words that jumped off the page. History breathed, pedantry and preaching were banished. Zweig's readers saw Georg Händel, quill in hand as he composed *Messiah*.

Decades later, Tom Wolfe injected fictional technique into staid reporting in works as diverse as *The Right Stuff* and *The Electric Kool Aid Acid Test*. Before long, Wolfe's books became favorites among young adult and adult readers of the 1960s and 1970s, for their novelty, topics, and "kool."

Patricia Hersh broke out of her journalism mold with her 1999 nonfiction novel on teen life in America, *A Tribe Apart: A Journey into the Heart of American Adolescence*. She spent three years getting to know eight teenagers well, then told, or rather, allowed them to tell their stories. Some reviewers mistakenly thought the novel was directed to adults, to make them understand the serious issues teens face, but Hersh wanted teens to read her book, so they would feel known by an adult. "I know firsthand the comfort, personal confirmation, and insight I have gleaned from my own reading, and wish to create that experience for others."

Zweig's works found their way into the Nazi bonfires of the 1930s, certainly because he was Jewish but also because he broke boundaries with his writing. Wolfe and other authors of the new journalism were labeled *gonzo*, with its connotation of not quite legitimate. As Hersh's experience attests, creative nonfiction is still not universally understood or valued. It remains controversial in adult writing, and perhaps more so in young adult books.

Drama & Due Diligence

So why does creative nonfiction remain so hotly contested? Several major universities offer courses in the genre. Most undergraduate classes focus on the extant literature; in other classes, professors appear to treat it as a legitimate mode of expression with a how-to syllabus on the craft.

Yet a writer who approaches the average publishing house or literary agent with a nonfiction novel is likely to face an initial and unexpected obstacle: Justifying the choice of what some still consider a non-genre. The publisher may eventually accept the work, the agent may ask to read sample chapters, but that first hurdle remains high for all writers, and perhaps even higher for YA authors.

Both Spring Hermann and Mordicai Gerstein have managed to clear the editorial hurdle and publish books that truly qualify as nonfiction novels. Hermann did so in choosing the story of Abigail Carter and the Perkins Institution for the Blind in Boston, while Gerstein took on the story of Victor, the wild boy of Aveyron whose story had been told either as straight historical fiction or scholarly nonfiction before his work made it accessible to middle school readers. The work of Hermann and Gerstein illustrate some of the qualities and distinctions of creative nonfiction.

Lee Gutkind, Editor and founder of *Creative Nonfiction Journal,* speaks of the creative nonfiction writer's "immersion techniques." He describes the genre as "[d]ramatic, true stories using scenes, dialogue, close, detailed descriptions and other techniques usually employed by poets and fiction writers about important subjects." The author, Gutkind writes, can use "the diligence of a reporter, the shifting voices and viewpoints of a novelist, the refined wordplay of a poet and the analytical modes of the essayist."

Gutkind defines the *five Rs* of writing creative nonfiction as real life experience, reflection, research, reading, and 'riting. It is worth noting that of the five, real life experience is the least necessary, since a nonfiction novel can deal with a subject a writer could not possibly have experienced, such as life in a medieval town. And of the five, research is the one that is most indispensable, though without a good feel for the personalities involved (real life experience or reflection), the research should be left in the standard nonfiction genre without venturing across the threshold into creative nonfiction.

For her middle-grade book, *Seeing Lessons, The Story of Abigail Carter and America's First School for Blind People* (Henry Holt), Hermann did extraordinary research into the beginnings of the Perkins Institution for the Blind, an experimental school for the blind, a risky undertaking by Dr. Samuel Howe. The school eventually became known for graduating Annie Sullivan, Helen Keller's teacher. Abigail and Sophia Carter were two of the first six students when the school opened in 1832. Hermann's novel recreates the birth of the Perkins Institution through Abby's voice and deals with the character's homesickness for the Andover farm she left behind.

Seeing Lessons is the only middle-grade or YA book of any category, fiction or nonfiction, that turns up in a search for "Perkins Institution" or "Abigail Carter" on Yahoo.com or Amazon.com. The origins of the school appear in biographies of Julia Ward Howe, composer of the "Battle Hymn of the Republic," since Dr. Samuel Howe was her husband. Yet it is unlikely that young adult—much less younger—readers would be moved by the more objectively impersonal, impassionate approach of these biographies.

Seeing Lessons instead inspires its readers to do the impossible. As Abby learns to survive and triumph over homesickness and a physical handicap, she can teach children facing similar difficulties that they too can attain almost any goal. Hermann's research into the characters and the Perkins Institution for the Blind is considered high-quality writing by almost every reviewer; however, the author herself has difficulty attaching the label *nonfiction* to her work, preferring to call it "a bio-historical novel." While this book is one of the few current examples of a nonfiction novel for YA readers, Amazon.com lumps it in with historical fiction—not a satisfactory pigeonhole.

A Rare Thing

If it's any comfort to Hermann, the online bookseller does the same to Mordicai Gerstein's *Victor* (Farrar, Straus & Giroux). Gerstein's approach to creative nonfiction is even more rigorous, more along the lines of what must be deemed creative nonfiction or nonfiction novel. In *Victor*, he relies heavily on firsthand accounts of the well-intentioned rescue of the wild boy from the forest of Aveyron.

The story of the young boy abandoned by assassins in a forest near Paris, living on his own in the wild until hunters capture him and bring him to the city as a trophy, has been told many times in the two hundred years it has been known. Jean-Marc Itard, the teacher entrusted with the education of the boy who came to be called Victor, wrote a first-person account of the case. Countless child development texts recite Victor's educational development under Itard's tutelage, especially Montessori educators. Francois Truffaut's 1970 docudrama *The Wild Child* gave adults tremendous intellectual insight into the cultural and philosophical controversies of supposedly liberating a child from the freedoms inherent in living like a beast, to teach him speech and make him part of civilization.

Gerstein's nonfiction novel represented the first attempt of telling the story to YA readers. Kathryn Harrison, in a November 1998 review of the book for the *New York Times*, noted that Gerstein's "novel succeeds as a rare thing, a novel of ideas for adolescents." He introduces high school students to troubling questions, such as why anyone should want a society that requires forks and alphabets. If our natural tendencies are toward food and freedom, why should we compel another who has both without our strictures to adopt our rules and regulations? Gerstein succeeds at initiating this debate in a manner that a straight nonfiction book never could—by personalizing the battle and making the story live.

Almost as if to demonstrate why nonfiction novels remain the province of YA (and adult) literature, Gerstein also penned a picture book version of the story. *The Wild Boy* (Farrar, Straus & Giroux) may allow very young children to know the story. But it is stripped of all meaning, condensed into a fairy tale devoid of connection to reality. There are no bruises or lasting hurts in the version for younger children.

This phenomenon can also be seen in John Cech's picture book, *My Grandmother's Journey* (Aladdin Paperbacks). Cech tells the true story of his mother-in-law's journey from Russia to America at the end of World War II. Since the target audience is young children, he leaves out the gruesome details that could give them nightmares, thereby diluting the power of that grandmother's real life journey. There may be a place for such storytelling, but if a writer takes the time to research and understand a specific chronicle of events, a YA nonfiction novel would better serve his purposes.

The Creative Nonfiction Debate

Creative nonfiction can be the literary equivalent of gun control. People can feel so strongly about it that it colors their perception of everything else a person may attempt as a writer.

A historian participating in a "virtual conference" sponsored by the University of Albany/SUNY exhibited precisely this reflex. He had extolled the virtue of using historical fiction as a means of making new worlds meaningful. A colleague asked about the use of nonfiction novels for the same goal. His vitriolic response: "Per the question about the so-called *nonfictional novel*, I personally feel very strongly that I would not assign, would not purchase, nor would I read one." A third professor jumped feet first into the discussion, conceding the latent problems with historical accuracy, then defending his own use of creative nonfiction in history classes. He made this point: In 1863, a hundred years before Tom Wolfe, Louisa May Alcott penned a nonfiction novel, *Hospital Sketches*, whose worst failing was the changing of names.

In the mid-twentieth century days of creative nonfiction, it did emerge with no standards, no rules for what constituted good research. Editors and historians alike protested the "new" genre for its lack of public verifiability. *New journalism* suffered major setbacks in the 1990s at the hands of Janet Cooke who had to give back her Pulitzer Prize for inventing information about a 12-year-old addict, and Janet Malcolm who massaged a psychiatrist's quotes.

Despite the positive developments in creative nonfiction, we have not come nearly far enough in our understanding of this relatively new genre. Recently, an editor cast about for recommendations of nonfiction novels/creative nonfiction to include in a reading list. Almost without exception, the books that were mentioned were historical fiction, not nonfiction novels.

By way of contrast to the nonfiction novels mentioned above, consider Barbara Greenwood's historical fiction novels for YA readers. *The Last Safe House* takes the reality of the underground railroad during the Civil War, and fictionalizes it. Greenwood combines factual information with a story about a fictional escaped slave named Eliza Jackson. She blends real maps and factual passages with her fiction, adding to the authentic feel of

the tale. But without historically accurate actors, her book cannot be deemed creative nonfiction, no matter how deeply it moves her readers.

Greenwood's popular Pioneer stories also belong firmly in the historical fiction genre. *A Pioneer Thanksgiving: A Story of Harvest Celebrations in 1841* and *A Pioneer Sampler: The Daily Life of a Pioneer Family in 1840* both explore life on the frontier, by means of a fictional family named Robertson.

The books may be valuable teaching tools, and she may strike a note of reality due to the thorough research and fascinating minutiae (such as the advent of postage stamps). Yet like *The Last Safe House*, these are examples of high-quality historical fiction, not creative nonfiction.

Joe Cottonwood's middle-grade *Quake!* (Apple) comes even closer to the fine line separating historical fiction from creative nonfiction, while remaining firmly in the fictional category. He did indeed personally experience the 1989 earthquake in California, and the details of his experience enliven the story. But by choosing to narrate the event in the voice of a 14-year-old girl responsible for her bratty brother and a visiting friend, his highly acclaimed novel must be categorized as fiction, albeit fiction based on something he was intimately acquainted with!

As creative nonfiction has matured, standards and terms are still not uniform. Barbara Chase-Riboud describes her books as nonfiction novels. But her own recounting of the writing of *Echo of Lions*, a supposedly nonfiction novel about the rebellion aboard the Amistad by Africans illegally brought to Cuba as slaves, contains countless references to changing the historical record. "Another way I weave fact with fiction is by taking actual historical documents, such as letters, and changing them in some way through creative expression." She admits to inventing major characters, consciously leaving out parts of the historical record depending on narrative purposes, and "imagining" other aspects of history where she felt the historical record was not accurate.

Critics do not always help the cause of creative nonfiction. Some have identified Peter Landesman's historical fiction, *The Raven,* as a nonfiction novel, while he makes no such claim. He merely found an interesting unsolved mystery and wrote a fascinating novel based on the tale. Landesman never pretended that his invented ending was historically correct.

A magazine assignment in Haiti provided Madison Smartt Bell with his initial foray into writing creative nonfiction, exemplified by *All Souls' Rising.* He intended to churn out the requisite pieces about the country, its culture, and political situation for a paying assignment. That moment of identification with his subject changed the development of the articles, as he saw straight reporting becoming the distortion of the facts, not the new journalism approach.

With all these factors working against the still developing-genre known by so many names, it remains one of the most effective types of literary composition available to writers of history, social observers, even writers in the sciences.

Flesh & Blood

Before television brought us celebrities in place of heroes, publishers regularly turned out series that genuinely qualified as nonfiction novels.

Years ago, Edward Jablonski authored an anthology of short stories about World War I, *The Great War,* that highlights the honor of common soldiers who fought in the trenches in that bloody conflict. When I read Robert N. Webb's nonfiction novel about Florence Nightingale, a book in Grosset & Dunlap's We Were There series, I wanted to be a doctor with all my heart. Margaret Cousins's tales about Benjamin Franklin stirred my interest in science and politics and exploring the world around me. *Robinson Crusoe* was based on a true story. Hemingway wrote many stories and novels more true to his experiences than imagined. Walter Lord's *A Night to Remember* stunned readers with the powerful facts, but even more, with the story of the sinking of the *Titanic.*

If we can be both writers and historians or journalists or sociologists, not straying from the truth, but breathing flesh and blood onto the skeleton of that truth, we can present a reality to our young readers that may just stir their imagination and cause them to change the world.

Bibliography

- **Madison Smartt Bell:** *All Souls' Rising,* (Viking Penguin, 1996).
- **John Cech:** *My Grandmother's Journey,* illustrated by Sharon McGinley-Nally and Ian Wallace (Aladdin Paperbacks, 1998).
- **Barbara Chase-Riboud:** *Echo of Lions* (William Morrow, 1989).
- **Joe Cottonwood:** *Quake!* (reprint, Apple, 1996).
- **Margaret Cousins:** *Ben Franklin of Old Philadelphia* (reissue, Random House, 1987).
- **Daniel Defoe:** *Robinson Crusoe* (Modern Library Classics, 2001).
- **Mordicai Gerstein:** *Victor: A Novel Based on the Life of Victor, the Savage of Aveyron* (Farrar, Straus & Giroux, 1998); *The Wild Boy* (Farrar, Straus & Giroux, 1998).
- **Barbara Greenwood:** *A Pioneer Sampler: The Daily Life of a Pioneer Family in 1840* (reprint, Houghton Mifflin, 1998); *A Pioneer Thanksgiving: A Story of Harvest Celebrations in 1841* (Kids Can Press, 1999); *The Last Safe House: A Story of the Underground Railroad* (Kids Can Press, 1998).
- **Patricia Hersh:** *A Tribe Apart, A Journey into the Heart of American Adolescence* (Ballantine Books, 1999).
- **Spring Hermann:** *Seeing Lessons, The Story of Abigail Carter and America's First School for Blind People,* illustrated by Ib Ohlsson (Henry Holt & Company, 1998).
- **Edward Jablonski:** *The Great War* (Whitman Publishing Co., 1965).
- **Peter Landesman:** *The Raven* (Viking Penguin, 1997).
- **Walter Lord:** *A Night to Remember* (reprint, Bantam Doubleday Dell, 1976).
- **Robert N. Webb:** *We Were There with Florence Nightingale in the Crimea,* historical consultant, Louis L. Snyder (Grosset & Dunlap, 1958).
- **Tom Wolfe:** *The Electric Kool Aid Acid Test* (reprint, Bantam Doubleday Dell, 1999); *The Right Stuff* (reissue, Bantam Books, 1983).
- **Stefan Zweig:** *The Tide of Fortune,* out of print (1928; originally published in English in 1940; currently available in German on Amazon.de as *Sternstunden der Menschheit: Zwoelf historische Miniaturen*).

Online
- *Creative Nonfiction Journal,* Lee Gutkind, Editor (creativenonfiction.org/the journal).

Tone: The Essence of Story

By Darcy Pattison

"Tone is the glue that holds the various components of a story together," says Alix Reid, Editorial Director at Harper-Collins. "It underpins the narrative, the setting, the characters, the dialogue. It shapes the reader's response. If an author is writing a gothic mystery, and the setting is a dank and deserted castle, the heroine is a shrinking violet, and full moons and storms abound, then the tone has to be appropriately romantic, mysterious, and above all, respectful of the genre."

Humor, irony, satire, pleasantness, excitement, righteous indignation—the audience's anticipated reaction is what determines the tone in which a book or story is written. *Goodnight Moon,* by Margaret Wise Brown, has a soothing tone; *Captain Underpants,* by Dav Pilkey, has an irreverent, comical tone; *Out of the Dust,* by Karen Hesse, has a spare, restrained tone that matches the mood of the Dust Bowl.

Jeannette Larson, Senior Editor at Harcourt, Inc., says, "Tone helps the reader feel what the author is trying to communicate. It can give the author a more effective, subtle way to communicate their intention, to communicate an emotional element or mood that can't be told in words."

Can't be told in words? Tone is determined by word choices and yet a tone can't be told in words? Understand the distinction and you've got a strong grasp on the glue, the essence, of story. Tone isn't told. Tone is created.

The Way a Story Is Told

Tone is the way words are used. When you are listening to someone, the person's voice combines with nonverbal cues to convey an attitude.

Diana Capriotti, Senior Editor at Delacorte Books for Young Readers, says, "You put the story in the reader's head with clues about how to interpret it, but without a physical voice. You have to rely on setting, mood, and context to create the tone."

Because we commonly use the phrase *tone of voice,* it's easy to confuse *tone* and *voice.* Voice is the way a story is told. Elaine Marie Alphin, author of *Counterfeit Son* (Harcourt), which won the Edgar Award for the best young adult mystery, says, "The voice of a book comes from the main character, not from the writer. The voice plunges the reader into Cameron's mind and heart."

That's exactly where you want readers to be, not in the writer's mind and heart, but in the character's. Tone might even be called the *attitude* created by the words. Alphin created a tone that is a curious combination of hope and despair that echoes Cameron's voice. In this case, the voice and tone support each other.

On HarperCollins's spring list is Sara Nickerson's *How to Disappear Completely and Never Be Found*, in which, says Reid, contrasting voices form a unified tone. The novel switches back and forth between male and female characters with distinctive voices, and through them creates a tone of mystery and adventure.

Adverbs and adjectives might seem the obvious tools to define story tone, but they are not usually the most effective. Tone can be cued by words such as *quiet, angrily, sadly, joyful*. But relying on descriptive words is the most simplistic, least compelling way of setting tone. "The more experienced and better writer can get by without adverbs," says Capriotti. Quiet, anger, sadness, joy, confusion, bitterness, hope are better communicated by "every tool in the writer's arsenal," she says.

Before you begin writing, have a tone in mind. "It is essential to writing a story that has consistent tone that an author understand what sort of book he or she is writing, and understand who the characters are," Reid says. "Otherwise, you can end up with a story where the plot and characters are doing one thing, and the author is doing another."

Wendy McClure, Editor at Albert Whitman & Company, emphasizes the importance of this: "Tone should have been shaping the story all along." Know the tone before writing, and begin the story with the right one. "When it comes to novels, you need to structure the beginning of the story so the tone comes through right away," says McClure. "The most memorable stories I know start with a simple declarative sentence by the main character, saying exactly what she thinks about her predicament, or how a certain event affected her. That immediately sets the tone: 'This is how it feels to be me.'"

Organic Growth

Once what you have written captures the tone you intend, then learn to see it and stay with it.

"The key is to recognize a successful chapter or section, or learn to recognize a weak chapter or section," Capriotti says. Put the work aside for as long as you can stand it, then read it with an eye toward where the tone is working or not working. "Read it out loud. Look at how much explaining is done around dialogue. How is the information coming across? Are you forcing explanations into dialogue that shouldn't be there? Are you trying to make characters something they are not? See if you can reimagine a new way for the characters to present information. If you've created the right tone once, you can do it again."

Editors look for tonal consonance throughout a story. Larson says, "Look for every opportunity to make the tone consistent. Changing mood is important, so the reader's experience isn't flat. But changing the tone would bring in incongruity."

On a very simple level, this means that you can't start a story as a dreamy, stream-of-consciousness epistle and end as an action-packed thriller with short, sharp imperatives.

"This is not to say that a character always has to be exactly the same or have the same reactions to everything for the tone to be consistent," says Reid. "Obviously, in the course of a novel a character has to grow, change, and develop in some way. Nonetheless, that character needs to become something that grows out of what he or she is like at the beginning of the novel. I think about it like a tree, which adds rings around rings as it grows and matures. So, too, should tone, as it changes and matures through a novel, grow organically from the beginning of a novel, so that it's always recognizable, yet stronger, more solid, more powerful."

Consistency of tone is important even when a story has multiple points of view. Reid again points to Nickerson's *How to Disappear Completely and Never be Found* as an example of a novel with consistent tone despite a structure with alternating points of view.

Concrete Crafting

While much of the discussion about tone revolves around abstract issues, some concrete tasks can carry a writer far in establishing and maintaining tone. McClure says that the choice of details can do much of the work.

"Remember to show instead of tell. We don't want platitudes, but we do want details that are an extension of the character and the character's outlook."

Plot and organization synthesize with tone as well. McClure points to picture book stories that have simple refrains. The refrains provide a reassuring tone by suggesting that there is order in the world. The organization of the text always returns to a phrase that is important; the child knows that point in the story will come again and feels the ordering of events, which reinforces the tone.

The language and vocabulary used must also support the tone of a story. McClure says, "The vocabulary has to do the work of tone without being intrusive. If I'm conscious of the language, then I'm not sure the tone is working. You want the story to be seamless." After reading a story, McClure sometimes analyzes what worked and discovers that alliteration and assonance make certain words resonate, contributing to tone. But the technique should be subtle enough to work without calling attention to itself.

Story Tone: Titles to Study

Editors find it hard to talk about tone of voice in abstractions. They prefer to give examples of stories where tone works well. Here are some of their favorites to study.

■ Humorous Angst

Alix Reid, Editorial Director of HarperCollins, cites *Angus, Thongs and Full-Frontal Snogging,* by Louise Rennison. The story is told from the point of view of a young teenager, Georgia Nicolson, who is going through the very typical angst of a very typical teenager (makeup, acne, dating, girlfriends). Georgia sees the world through a comic lens. Even as she encounters some crises—her boyfriend dumps her, her best friend ignores her—and she is genuinely distraught, nonetheless she maintains her comic tone to deal with the events. Were she to go into a deep depression and become mute, or were she to become cynical and bitter as a result of these events, the tone would no longer be consistent and the story would fall apart.

■ Mystery, Adventure, Danger

Reid also refers to *How to Disappear Completely and Never be Found,* by Sara Nickerson. The story alternates two main points of view, that of a 12-year-old girl, Margaret, and a 12-year-old boy, Boyd. The novel moves between the characters and yet, while the voices and quests of the characters are very different, the overall tone remains cohesive. This is because the author was very conscious of the kind of story she was writing—a mystery. The tone of mystery and adventure and danger underpins the narrative of both characters.

■ Surprise

Jeannette Larson, Senior Editor of Harcourt, Inc., edits picture books and finds that for these, rhythm and sentence construction can convey tone and reinforce the word choices. *To Market, To Market,* written by Anne Miranda and illustrated by Janet Stevens, has surprises and humor. The story is told in a regular rhythm that is based on an old rhyme. The third line interrupts the traditional lines with an "uh-oh" refrain and something unexpected happens. Surprise is reinforced by the interruption to the regularity of the text.

■ Tradition and Poetry

The Trip Back Home, written by Janet S. Wong and illustrated by Bo Jia, is about a child going back to visit her mother's relatives in rural Korea. The characters step into an old world where they fill their days with traditions and chores. Larson cites the book because the poetic text has a gentle rhythmic pattern with repetitions of phrases; the text itself takes on the

Story Tone: Titles to Study

The running side tab "Style"

movement of what people have been doing for centuries in this place. One of the repeated phrases is "always every evening." Another pattern is a set of response phrases: "They gave us _____; we gave them_____."

■ Coming-of-Age: Tonal Varieties

Delacorte Press Editor Diana Capriotti offers several examples of books for middle-graders and young adults that use very different tones. *Night Flying,* by Rita Murphy, is a coming-of-age story with spare prose that captures the isolation of characters, especially of a young girl on the verge of womanhood who faces life with both confidence and doubt.

Sights, by Susanna Vance, is a very quirky, offbeat story about a character called Baby Girl who is also on the verge of womanhood. She must confront her self-image after her confidence is shattered by the switch to high school. The tone here is honest, vulnerable, yet with emerging strength.

Jacqueline Wilson's middle-grade novels are yet a different take on coming-of-age. Preteen girls need humor to face their teenage years. Wilson takes their needs seriously by being true to the heroines and supportive of the pains they are going through.

■ Honest Fears

Wendy McClure, Editor at Albert Whitman & Company, points to the Spider Storch books, by Gina Willner-Pardo, as books that have just the right humorous tone for younger readers facing their growing-up problems. Joey "Spider" Storch loves spiders and has plenty of insights about third-grade life. On field trips, it's best to avoid getting in trouble with the chaperones: "Mrs. Arkens made you hold her hand if you weren't behaving. Nobody wanted to touch the skin of someone else's mom." Spider gives voice to many of the feelings of kids at this age—unspoken rules and secret fears—but the books accomplish this with a mixed tone of youthful concern and humor.

Many of Albert Whitman's titles are concept books for children with special needs. Tone of voice can make or break the story, fiction or nonfiction. McClure says, "We try to present a kid who is not angry, not ecstatic, but with a tone of voice that acknowledges that there are both good and bad times in life. We don't sugarcoat; we tell it straight." *Sugar Was My Best Food: Diabetes and Me,* by Carol Antoinette Peacock, Kyle Carney Gregory, and Adair Gregory is an example. A diagnosis of diabetes is a frightening experience for a child, and the message in this book is "I've been there, too." Rather than just talking about bravery and optimism, nine-year-old Adair shares his disappointments and anger over the changes in his life. The tone helps kids know that, ultimately, the challenge can be met.

Dialogue can carry tone, too. Capriotti particularly dislikes the false dialogue that she calls *Dawson Creek* dialogue. "It's that self-aware teen voice with an elevated vocabulary. I don't know kids who talk like that. Don't fall into this trap, because it creates the worst sort of tone."

Individuality

Even these specifics leave some writers wondering about how to create a consistent tone; editors and writing teachers find it difficult to be more specific. "It depends. . . ," they say. Tone always depends on the story itself, on the makeup of the characters, the setting, the author's intent, and so many other minor and major elements of a story.

"The tone is the end result, but it is also the beginning," Capriotti says. "It's what's in the back of readers' minds as they encounter the work." It must also be in the back of the author's mind throughout the writing process. The author must solve the problem of tone in different ways for each story told. You have an arsenal of weapons: setting, characterization, language, rhythm, vocabulary, plot, organization. In the end, there are no right or wrong answers; there are only stories that work or don't work.

Capriotti offers a final suggestion: "Tone is the core of the manuscript. If it's right, it's great; if it's wrong, it's hard to correct. Move on to something else and come back with a fresh eye. Salvage what you can and begin again if you have to."

It's Drafty in Here

By Patricia Curtis Pfitsch

"When I was first starting out," admits author Jane Kurtz, "I was a one-draft writer. I assumed that the whole point was that you shouldn't have to revise. If I had to revise, I thought I wasn't doing my job right." Now, however, she understands it differently. "I revise tirelessly. It's not at all unusual for me to revise something a hundred times at one level or another."

Anyone who's been in the writing business for very long has, like Kurtz, learned that revision is perhaps the most important part of the process. "Some people can write a brilliant first draft," says Rebecca Davis, Senior Editor at Greenwillow Books, "but I've never heard of anyone who didn't have to revise." But how does a writer, working alone, with a critique group, or with an editor, move from a rough draft to something extraordinary? The answer varies from author to author and from manuscript to manuscript. The ingredients include a little magic, a lot of trust, and hard work.

Re-Vision

Jane Kurtz's first novel, *The Storyteller's Beads,* was originally two stories set in Ethiopia, where she had spent her childhood. One was a novel about a girl and her family escaping Ethiopia into the Sudan. The other story was about an Ethiopian Jewish girl and her grandmother. "They were written for different age groups," Kurtz explains. "To me they were quite different stories even though they were both about Ethiopia." She submitted them both to Harcourt, Inc.

"When I read these two pieces of writing," Elizabeth Van Doren, Editorial Director at Gulliver Books, an imprint of Harcourt, says, "what came to me was that they were telling the same story from two very different points of view. It was really a rather chilling moment—when inspiration strikes. It was very exciting."

Van Doren suggested Kurtz have the two girls meet and deal with all the issues of danger and prejudice together as they escape from Ethiopia.

"It was very complicated," Van Doren says, "to take two very different pieces of writing not intended to be novels and written for different purposes and make a novel of them."

Kurtz admits that the suggestion troubled her at first. "One reason was that I was in love with the original version." She found first one excuse and then another for not starting the revision. "But I know that the only way to deal with a daunting revision is to sit down and start messing with it. When I did, I saw that it wouldn't be as bad as I thought."

Kurtz and Van Doren talked about the form the new work would take. "What if it's told in one point of view?" asked Van Doren. "How do we differentiate between the two stories? What if it's told in two different voices, how will that work when the stories come together? It was a structural problem."

Kurtz decided to tell the two stories from alternating points of view. At first, she wrote two chapters from each girl's viewpoint before switching to the other viewpoint. After the girls meet, she switched viewpoints for every chapter. "I was taking chapters from Sahay's viewpoint in the old book and putting them in Rahel's viewpoint. Rahel is blind, so that was more of a challenge. I had to change the details she'd be noticing."

Van Doren also cautioned Kurtz not to cover the same action from two viewpoints. "So I had to keep the story moving forward, even though I was switching from one girl's experience to the other's."

Although Kurtz loves revising her work, some parts of the process are harder than others. "I admit I'm still hugely intimidated when I have to *re-vision* a work, go back and see it in an entirely new way. I come to the point where I think I absolutely cannot do it. I walk away from my desk. I call that point 'hitting the wall.' Somehow I manage to push on, and it's then that I often have a breakthrough moment; I see how I can do it."

For Van Doren's part, she never gave up hope. "It was very clear to me that this was going to work," she says. "An editor plays many roles. One is to be the bearer of that hope when the writer begins to lose it. Writers are all alone. They need someone to help remind them that there is a light at the end of the tunnel.

"It's like an architect who has a vision for the structure of a building. He has to work with the contractor to figure out how it's going to be realized. An editor takes both roles: You have a creative vision and then you and the author have to roll up your sleeves and figure out how it's going to work. Part of my job is to ask the right questions."

Inspiration & Magic

Asking the right questions helped Deborah Wiles totally re-vision her novel, *Love, Ruby Lavender*. Wiles had submitted the story to Van Doren as a picture book. "It was based on my memories of when my grandmother came to visit Hawaii," Wiles says. Van Doren loved the character but found the book too quiet. "She kept telling me, 'let go of your memories and write me a story.'"

Wiles, at Van Doren's suggestion, began expanding the book into a novel. "I made up several things. I introduced another little girl." Van Doren worked with Wiles on the chronology of the novel, and asked for a map of the imaginary town, which was eventually incorporated as an illustration in the novel. They worked on structure. "I had to toss out the second half twice," Wiles remembers. "There's a very distinct first and second half and my job was to make it seamless. There's a point where the grandmother leaves and the novel changes. That's okay, but the voice shouldn't change; the whole atmosphere should remain the same."

Author and editor spent five years on the book. "It was really hard," Wiles says. "I would get frustrated and put it down for a while and then I'd pick it up because I really loved the little girl." Finally, Van Doren asked Wiles, "Where is the grandfather?"

"The more I thought about it, the more I pictured Ruby and her grandmother missing the grandfather," Wiles said. "I saw there was more going on in Ruby's heart than I'd realized." Wiles realized there was a mystery surrounding the grandfather's death. "It was a big jolt. The mystery about the grandfather is the core of the book—it's why everything happens. I couldn't make the second half live up to the first half until I knew why." As Wiles began to understand Ruby's motivation, she asked herself questions. What did Ruby's heart tell her? How did she feel about her world, her mother, what was going on in her life? "The book changed under my hands as I began to weave this piece of the story in and out."

This is what Wiles loves about revision. "A lot of inspiration comes to you in the first draft, but when you get to revision, that's where the magic is. You can look back and see patterns and connections you never saw before. You can take those things and deepen and richen the story."

Not Just *Anygirls*

Sometimes a small change can make all the difference. It certainly did in the revision of *Dovey Coe,* the story of a 12-year-old girl on trial for murder. When Caitlyn Dlouhy, Senior Editor at Atheneum Books, started reading the book, she says, "The character Dovey was so spectacular that within three paragraphs I had my office door closed to read this manuscript. She was feisty and very protective of her brother and kind of a tomboy. But her sister, Caroline, was blonde and blue-eyed and very gentle and next to Dovey she came across as a cliché."

The author, Frances O'Roark Dowell, did several revisions of the book for Dlouhy both before and after the book was under contract. "She worked on the other characters," Dlouhy remembers, "and made changes to Caroline as well, but Caroline remained very much a blonde, blue-eyed *anygirl.*"

Dlouhy was certain Dowell could create a believable character for Caroline because "every other character in the book was so vivid and memorable." She suggested to Dowell that she change Caroline's physical appearance. "Change her hair color, or make

Advice to Writers

You're not working with an editor or a critique group. You don't have a children's writer friend who can help you revise. What can you do? The editors and writers who talked about revision for Children's Writer Guide to 2002 *have these suggestions for writers to consider in revising their work prior to submission.*

■ **Frances O'Roark Dowell,** author of *Dovey Coe*

"I read over what I did the day before and I find myself thinking, 'that doesn't sound right,' or 'I'm heading in the wrong direction here.' There's something very liberating about that. You can just cross out a chapter. It's the feeling that it's not set in stone. I haven't failed yet."

■ **Deborah Wiles,** author of *Love, Ruby Lavender*

"Have a little distance between revisions." Wiles explains that it helps to wait some time—a week, a month, or even longer—before tackling a draft. "Ask yourself questions: Why does this happen? Why doesn't that happen? And be willing to go through as many times as it takes. Writing is 90 percent persistence."

■ **Jane Kurtz,** author of *The Storyteller's Beads* and *Water Hole Waiting*

"I really believe in the notion of not trying to solve problems in your head. Sit down and play with it on paper." Kurtz also suggests that if a solution is not coming, it can help to put it in the back of your mind. "Keep your eyes and ears open to real life. Be willing to tuck it away and let something bubble up. You may stumble on something you didn't expect."

■ **Eleanora Tate,** author of *The Minstrel's Melody* and *The Secret of Gumbo Grove*

"Read every sentence in your manuscript aloud to yourself. When you *hear* what you've written, you pick up missing words or phrases, smooth out rough sentences." Tate also reminds writers to follow their own instincts. "If your gut feeling says 'Delete that page' then delete it, no matter how great the prose. When that same feeling says, 'you're not done,' then you aren't. Keep working."

■ **Caitlyn Dlouhy,** Senior Editor, Atheneum Books

"Show rather than tell. Give us scenes rather than recap what happens. Put your characters into those scenes. This is so basic, yet people don't do it." When it comes to character, Dlouhy suggests letting the reader see the character through what they say and do rather than what they look like. "If your character needs to be a cheerleader, don't let us know that right off. Let us see who she is as a singular person before you put the label on her."

Advice to Writers

■ **Rebecca Davis,** Senior Editor, Greenwillow Books

"Ask yourself, are my characters behaving consistently? They might act differently at the end of the manuscript, but it should be because they've grown to a different place. If they act differently in two scenes close together because it's convenient for the plot, then it's a problem."

■ **Marion Dane Bauer,** author of *On My Honor,* a Newbery Honor book

"One of the biggest pitfalls for a writer is trying too hard to keep the words you already have down. Sometimes the most freeing thing you can do is print the piece off so you'll have it there in hard copy. Turn it over so you aren't looking at it. Pull up a blank screen and hit that chapter again. If you find a scene and think, 'I did that well the last time,' then turn over your paper and let yourself copy back in again. But be very careful not to turn it into a typing exercise." Bauer also says this: "I have learned from experience that the problem is never right where I'm stuck—it's somewhere farther back. I have to go back and find where the problem begins and build toward the moment where I'm stuck. Then I can move forward." Bauer also notes that hearing the same comments from different people makes the point more meaningful.

■ **Elizabeth Van Doren,** Editorial Director at Gulliver Books

"One of the really important things about revision is being patient with the process. It involves taking backward steps, going astray, moving forward. One book might be easier—you get there really fast—and the next book might be a nightmare. You think you'll never get there. And then you do. You have to know when you're done. And there's a difference between being done and being perfect. You're reaching for perfection, not expecting to get there."

■ **Patricia Reilly Giff,** author of *Nory Ryan's Song*

"Even after 80 books, I am still unsure of myself. Writers should know that maybe that uncertainty never goes away. People say they keep revising until they can't figure out what to do next, and I think that's really true. You just revise as much as you can, until you don't know what to do next, and then it's time to send it out."

■ **Franny Billingsley,** author of *The Folk Keeper*

"Persist. Try to be as true to what your vision brings you as you can. Know that nothing you write is ever wasted. It was all those words that no one will see that brought me to the final draft of *The Folk Keeper.* I hope that gives people courage. Because it is an act of courage to write a novel."

her eyes green. Make her a redhead."

Dowell remembers the moment well. "I thought, that's easy enough to change. But once she changed to brunette, she really did change a lot. She went from being a fairly benign kind of person—events just washed over her—to someone who's aware of her looks and what kind of effect she has on people, and who plays with that a little bit. She's basically a good person, but she's bright and a little bored and has some fun."

How did Dlouhy know this small change would make such a difference? "Partially because one of my obsessions as an editor is character development," explains Dlouhy. "I find there are certain types of descriptions that become very limiting. If you mention that someone's a cheerleader in the very beginning of the book, the reader already has an idea of what that character is like, and more often than not, the writer creates a character you'd expect to come from a cheerleader."

Helping writers revise is Dlouhy's favorite editorial role. "I often take on novels that need a lot of work, but they all have some aspect that's very special. I know the author can make the whole novel just as special, just as strong. I love helping them bring the work up to that level."

Dlouhy believes that Dowell is one of the best revisionists she's ever worked with. "Some people revise by slicing in, inserting something, and coming out again. Frances sees how her change affects everything else. She goes through the whole manuscript paying attention to how that change affects the balance or the tension."

"Once you change a character," says Dowell, "you have to start rewriting scenes because she's acting in a very different way. I had to come up with things that would show Caroline, her ambitions and how she got involved with Parnell [a murdered character]. When I changed Caroline it wasn't just changing here and there; it was starting from scratch."

Dowell has a master of fine arts degree in poetry and feels that background influences the way she revises. "I do a lot of sentence revision. I have a hard time if a paragraph sounds terrible. I can't go on; it bothers me too much." During the first draft stage, she tries not to think about the story when she's not writing. "That's from my poetry, too. I let my subconscious go to work."

But during the revision stage, she allows herself to think about it all the time. "I carry paper around with me." For Dowell, revision is exciting. "When I'm revising, I realize that I haven't closed the door on the story yet. I still have the opportunity to make it great. You don't always achieve greatness, but there's a world of possibilities."

Center of the Wheel

"A novel is like a line of dominoes," says fantasy writer Franny Billingsley. If you push the first domino, all the others should fall over because everything should be connected." If connections are missing, the novel won't work, the dominos don't fall in the proper patterns. That's what happened with early drafts of Billingsley's second novel, *The Folk Keeper*.

Billingsley made a number of attempts at starting the novel, a story about a girl who doesn't know she is half-human and half-selkie (the sealfolk of many Celtic stories), but the dominos just wouldn't fall. "The first draft had a lot of language and no action. After a while I abandoned the beginning and started in the middle, but I had the same problem. There was no action, nothing for my character to do."

Her editor at Atheneum, the late Jean Karl, thought the basic problem was that the reader doesn't know what the character really wants. At the same time, Billingsley read a quote by author Ray Bradbury in *The Art & Craft of Novel Writing,* by Oakley Hall. Give your character a "compulsion," Bradbury had said, "and turn him loose!" The quote spoke to Billingsley. "I gave my character a really dangerous job."

The job is that of Folk Keeper, feeding the fierce creatures who live underground in the fantasy world Billingsley created. The job is a powerful one and her character, Corinna, who is an orphan, wants the power associated with the position. "That's when she acquired a personality, a really distinctive voice," Billingsley explains. "I had struggled so hard to make her interesting and scrappy, but she just ended up sounding like a brat. When I gave her this raging need, then I didn't have to put words in her mouth. Her *want* directed everything she was going to say." It was the missing link in the chain of dominos. "It's only one thing, but it's the center of the wheel. It affects everything."

Like Dowell, Billingsley doesn't outline her books before writing them. "I have an idea for my story and I don't know anything about it. Writing the first draft is so hard. My heroine turns the door handle and opens the door and what's on the other side? I don't know! It's like digging in a quarry with a teaspoon."

After she's done a few drafts and has a sense of what her story is about, she analyzes it. "I ask myself, what do I have here? What elements relate to other elements? What works and what doesn't work? Then I'll make a rough outline, really a series of cards on which I've written notes. I hang them on the bulletin board in front of me so I can remind myself."

The further into the revision process Billingsley gets, the more she likes it. "I got the letter from Jean Karl saying that I should give Corinna something she wants. The light bulb went off. I thought: Folk! I put the Folk in and things started to connect. The Folk, the caverns, everything was new. Even my character's name was different, but I got the finished manuscript to Jean in less than a year. That's like sprinting for me."

No Maps, but a Compass

Patricia Reilly Giff is another writer who does not outline before she writes. "I think it was Lois Duncan who said she could not think of *not* using an outline because it was like going across the country without using a map. I have to go across the country without a map. I can't outline."

Giff usually has a very rough idea of the book. "For example, before I wrote *Nory Ryan's Song* I told my editor I wanted to write a book about a girl in Ireland who lives through the Great Hunger in the 1840s. All I know when I begin is the main character, the setting, and the problem. Sometimes that's not very clearly defined."

Giff begins writing and may get seven or eight chapters finished. "I'll think this needs revision already. The boy may have become a girl, or vice versa. And so I begin again. I use the pages I have as an outline. Maybe I'll get to the tenth chapter the next time. On the book I'm working on now, I'm on the fourth revision. I still have about four chapters before I finish the book. Until I revise completely I won't do those last chapters."

Even after she's working with her editor Giff still begins over. "I don't remember clearly enough what is in the book to do it piece by piece. With the editor's remarks in front of me, I start to read the whole thing again." Sometimes something her editor says will spark a new idea. "She might not have meant to do that," Giff says, "but I'll think, 'If she's finding this, then maybe the whole book will need strengthening,' so I'll go through the whole book again."

Giff writes on a computer but prints using different colored paper to help her differentiate among drafts. "The first time I write I use green. When I revise, I change the color of the paper, print whatever the new work is in blue or yellow, so I can see very clearly where I am. The process I use is torturous, but it works for me."

Giff also goes through her manuscript looking for specific things. In her new book, *Pictures of Hollis Avenue*, the character Hollis is an artist and someone gives her a box of colored pencils. "I wanted to relate colors in the setting to the colors of the pencils—evergreen, sky blue, metallic gray. So I went through the book and added that, just that one little thing all the way through."

If she's writing in the first person, Giff goes through the manuscript looking at the beginning of each paragraph. "I make sure I haven't started too many paragraphs with the word *I*. For some reason, this doesn't happen in the third person; you don't start with *she* every time. But when I'm doing first person, it's a problem for me."

Another pass might be devoted to setting. "Writers are so hard-pressed juggling the character and the situation, they forget that a few sentences will create the world."

The Golden Kernel

For writers who can outline, does that preliminary work cut down on revision time? Eleanora Tate, author of nine books for children, says for her it does. "I'm not a writer who approaches revision with open arms," says Tate. "Frankly, I'd rather vacuum the carpet, do the laundry—almost any other work than do revision. Getting it down in the initial draft gives me the flush of accomplishment and a lot of relief. With revision I know I'm really not done. I have to face the hard work. But, like vacuuming, it's got to be done if you want that beautiful carpet to show through."

Tate begins a book by writing what she calls *the golden kernel*. "It's one or two paragraphs of what the whole story is about. Then I expand my kernel into one or two pages, adding more details." She can turn almost every sentence into a chapter-by-chapter book outline. "Of course, if a strong scene comes to me, I'll write it. With that summary and outline already in place, I can stick that scene wherever I think it should go."

Tate's outline helps her stay on track. "I have an idea of what happens in the beginning, the middle, the end," she says, though she may change the outline if necessary. "It's not set in stone. By the time I'm through, the book may not actually follow the outline exactly, but at least I'm headed in the right direction."

Even with the outline, Tate does a minimum of 10 to 12 drafts for each story or book. "The first three or four drafts are devoted to getting the story into shape. In *The Minstrel's Melody*, an American Girl History Mystery, I had a lot of back story that needed to be cut. The other drafts more fully develop my characters, examine the setting for authenticity and vividness, make sure my words set the appropriate mood for each scene, follow the theme and plot so my characters stay on the path, and check spelling and punctuation."

Picture Perfect

Is the revision process different for picture books? Davis of Greenwillow doesn't think so. "The issues that authors and editors are dealing with in novels and picture books are often the same," she says. "But the particulars are different, because the forms are so different. The pacing that is right for a novel would be far too slow for a picture book. A few deft sentences can develop a character in a picture book, but it will take more than just a few sentences to create depth of character development in a novel."

Davis worked with Kurtz on *Water Hole Waiting*, a picture book about monkeys waiting for their turn to drink at the water hole. "It was partly the writing that drew me first," Davis remembers. "Jane writes in a very lovely lyrical voice. It also had a really beautiful sense of anticipation. That was the something that would draw kids in: They know how hard it is to wait."

Kurtz's manuscript was on the borderline between fiction and nonfiction. "The monkeys spoke to each other in dialogue, but they weren't entirely anthropomorphic," says Davis. "They were behaving mostly as real monkeys do. They were waiting for the chance to drink, avoiding the more dangerous animals, munching on leaves to slake their thirst. They weren't going off and having human adventures, such as solving a mystery or playing in a playground."

Davis also saw the book as an excellent introduction to African wildlife, so she worked with Kurtz to move the book more toward nonfiction. "One of the first things we talked about was getting rid of the dialogue so the monkeys wouldn't actually be speaking." In some cases, Kurtz, who cowrote the book with her brother, simply had to remove quotes. "What had been written as dialogue could just as easily become narrative. Other parts had to be changed more because the monkeys were really having a conversation. We also had to work to make the monkeys' actions and personalities come out more in the text," explains Kurtz. Davis "coaxed us into writing more of a story."

Davis sees her role in the editing process as that of listener. "The editor needs to understand what the writer is trying to say, understand the piece, understand where the characters fit, and the style of writing. I need to challenge the writer to write more cohesively, more precisely." She rarely suggests specific ideas or even words to revise, even when something specific occurs to her. "I know it's likely that the author will come up with something better. And often, it's not what I expect. I like being surprised."

Davis and Kurtz also worked together on *Rain Romp*. "Some of the dialogue was the ordinary, everyday things people say to each other," Davis says. "It didn't establish who the characters were." So she asked Kurtz to think about how the dialogue could show more about the personalities. "She just changed it a little but suddenly, instead of just advancing the plot, the dialogue said a lot about the characters. It was fun to read aloud. I didn't know what she would do, and what she did come back with was marvelous."

Begin Again

A picture book may not be easier to revise, says Marion Dane Bauer, "but a preschool picture book is so short, it allows you to start over repeatedly in a way you couldn't with a novel."

Bauer cites a manuscript she just finished for Simon & Schuster. The publisher wanted a companion to *My Mother Is Mine,* a Mother's Day book they published last year. That book features delicate lines of verse in which a child talks about her mother. The artist illustrated each line with an animal mother and only showed the human child at the end. "I thought anything I tried to do in the same vein would feel like milk toast," explains Bauer.

Nevertheless, she tried something similar. "It had lots of shifts of tone and the editor said, 'too many shifts of tone.' So I revised my concept." She researched animals. "There aren't a lot of creature dads, especially not mammals," Bauer says. "Insect and fish dads are more involved." She wrote an informational Father's Day book. "There were a couple of brief lines for the very young child. Then in brackets I did a totally informational thing, adding facts."

But her editor wasn't happy with it. "He said it wasn't lyrical like my other books. So I dropped all the informational content and reworked the lines to make them more lyrical. I also managed to add some of the information."

Her editor thought that version was more lyrical, but said it wouldn't work for them. "The animals I had used were odd," Bauer explains, "and he didn't think the problem was fixable." He was willing to let Bauer submit the Father's Day book to another publisher. "But no other publisher was out there thinking they wanted a Father's Day book from me," Bauer says. "I thought I'd be foolish to try to sell this somewhere else when I have this publisher interested."

So she began again. "I put everything aside and kept only some of the animals in my mind. I ended up with something more like what I'd done for *My Mother Is Mine*—simple little verses referring to what my father does for me without naming the animals. Then the animal could appear in the picture. It could even be a more unusual animal because you weren't having to say the name in the text."

Her editor liked this version. "I'd used a couple of off-rhymes and he didn't let me get by with that. The rhythm wasn't quite right, either. So at that point I went to polishing."

Bauer thinks that sometimes it's the better writers who never learn to revise successfully. "They don't have the ability to let go. They know what they've done is good. They'll polish but they won't truly revise. People who have more humility about their process are more apt to be able to look at it in a fundamental way. They will change the concept if it needs changing instead of just taking what went down the first time and polishing it."

When to Say 'Stop'

Are there times when a writer should say no to a change? Eleanora Tate says yes. "Sometime we authors have to stand our ground, because after that book is published, it's kind of late to take back the words." Tate finds that sometimes editors don't know about the cultural or racial situations she writes about. "But my fiction books celebrate neighborhoods and communities and the families who live there, so I don't want anything added to my books that is not culturally or racially authentic—nor removed if it is authentic."

Tate will send extra documentation to her editors to justify her words, and her editors sometimes document changes they've requested her to make. "Jeanne Vestal actually came to Myrtle Beach, South Carolina, where I lived while writing *The Secret of Gumbo Grove*, so she could visually see the culture from which I was drawing my story. Cheryl Hudson at Just Us Books would explain why she required certain sensitive changes when she edited *Just an Overnight Guest* for reprinting, and that was very helpful."

What about critique groups? How should a writer process other people's opinions? "It's absolutely essential that you always keep a very solid awareness that it's your piece," says Bauer. "You listen, take notes and then decide what's right for your work. If you find that you're ignoring everything that everybody says, either you're in the wrong group, or you're too well defended; you aren't getting any benefit from the group you're with." Bauer also notes that hearing the same comments from different people makes the point more meaningful. "By the time I get the same response from totally unrelated people who haven't fed one another by sitting in the same group, it has a different kind of impact."

"I think you should be very careful about choosing who you want to read your work," cautions Tate. "Some people know what they're talking about and others just like to hear themselves talk down your work!" Tate occasionally calls a friend who's also a children's literature scholar. "We talk over one or another aspect of my work-in- progress. When writers specifically ask for advice, they should mentally prepare themselves to receive it."

Giff agrees. "If you trust your editor, you have to pay attention to what she says. If you're going to change it, you'd better have a good reason, not just, 'Oh, I like it.' You'd better be able to say, this part of the book needs this particular scene or structure. If you don't, the book may be published, but it might not be as good as it might be. Publication isn't the only goal."

Whether they love or hate revision, whether they revise alone or with the help of an editor or critique group, whether they outline or just jump in and write, most writers agree on one thing that Giff says clearly: "Revision is the shading, the texture, the deepening of your story. It's at the heart of your writing."

"Revision is a process with no fixed beginning or end," says Van Doren. "It's an incredibly complicated winding road. If you keep your eye on the fact that you're creating something wonderful, that can be your inspiration as you navigate that difficult road."

Bibliography

■ **Marion Dane Bauer:** *If You Had a Nose Like an Elephant's Trunk* (Holiday House, 2001); *My Mother Is Mine* (Simon & Schuster, 2001); *Jason's Bears* (Hyperion, 2000); *An Early Winter* (Clarion, 1999); *Sleep, Little One Sleep* (Simon & Schuster, 1999); *If You Were Born a Kitten* (Simon & Schuster, 1997); *Turtle Dreams* (Holiday House, 1997); *Am I Blue? Coming out from the Silence* (HarperTrophy, 1994); *What's Your Story? A Young Person's Guide to Writing Fiction* (Clarion, 1992).

■ **Franny Billingsley:** *The Folk Keeper* (Atheneum, 1999); *Well Wished* (Atheneum, 1997).

■ **Frances O'Roark Dowell:** *Dovey Coe* (Atheneum, 2000).

■ **Patricia Reilly Giff:** *All The Way Home* (Delacorte, 2001); *Nory Ryan's Song* (Bantam Doubleday Dell, 2000); *The Gift of the Pirate Queen* (Yearling, 1998); *Lily's Crossing* (Delacorte, 1997); Fourth Grade Celebrity Series (Yearling); The Kids of the Polk Street School Series (Yearling).

■ **Jane Kurtz:** *Water Hole Waiting* (Greenwillow, 2002); *Jakarta Missing* (Greenwillow, 2001); *Faraway Home* (Harcourt, 2000); *River Friendly, River Wild* (Simon & Schuster, 2000); *I'm Sorry Almira Ann* (Henry Holt, 1999); *Terrific Connections with Authors, Illustrators and Storytellers,* co-authored with Toni Buzzeo (Libraries Unlimited, 1999); *Fire on the Mountain* (Aladdin, 1998); *The Storyteller's Beads* (Harcourt, 1998); *Trouble* (Gulliver, 1997); *Pulling the Lion's Tail* (Simon & Schuster 1995).

■ **Eleanora Tate:** *The Minstrel's Melody* (Pleasant Company, 2001); *African American Musicians* (John Wiley, 2000); *Don't Split the Pole: Tales of Down-Home Folk Wisdom* (Yearling, 1999); *Thank You Dr. Martin Luther King, Jr!* (Yearling, 1998); *A Blessing in Disguise* (Bantam Doubleday Dell Books for Young Readers, 1996); *The Secret of Gumbo Grove* (Yearling, 1996); *Front Porch Stories: At the One-Room School* (Yearling, 1993).

■ **Deborah Wiles:** *Freedom Summer* (Atheneum, 2001); *Love, Ruby Lavender* (Harcourt, 2001).

Style

Exercise Your Writing

By Sandy Fox

"I view writing exercises as *magic*," says Julie Williams, poet and creative writing instructor. "Every single time we do them in a group, magic happens." Even exercises done in the privacy of your own home can create personal magic.

I became acquainted with writing exercises at a conference where Julie was leading a group. I tried to resist. I wasn't interested. I didn't need them. But I found myself in a circle of fellow writers scribbling madly, almost without thought. Suddenly I discovered insights, depths to my character, and emotional connections that brought me to tears. Take a surprising journey of discovery by delving into writing exercises.

Discover Depth

It is said that all writing is autobiographical, more or less. Certainly the passions and desires you give your characters resonate within yourself. The fears and concerns they voice find echo in some of your own past fears. Being a logical writer, I needed to connect with these deep emotions in a roundabout way. Exercises helped me do that. In Julie's group, I chose to work on *Gina*. I'd written three chapters and an outline of the novel to be conjured around her.

When Julie instructed us to begin with: "At ___ _age_ ___ _character's name_ didn't know _____," I wrote:

At 12, Gina didn't know:
- ✔ She couldn't change the world.
- ✔ Sometimes injustice doesn't go away.
- ✔ Some fears are stronger than friendship.
- ✔ You could be scared of your neighbors.
- ✔ People don't live true to their beliefs.
- ✔ People could hate for no reason.
- ✔ It could be incredibly hard to do the right thing.
- ✔ Sometimes parents are scared.
- ✔ Working together in a bad situation can build bonds.

The words on the paper helped me see the depth of betrayal, the growing up, and some of the conflicts and events Gina would experience in the

Writers' Favorite Exercises

■ **Lists:** "List unusual places you know, occupations/skills/hobbies, and interesting people," recommends **Sharon Addy**, author of *Right Here on This Spot*. Use the lists as the basis of story location or characterization. List things you were interested in as a child and list things you'd like to find out more about today, as possibilities for nonfiction topics.

■ **Emotions:** "*It isn't fair.* Think back to a time in your life when something happened to you that wasn't fair," suggests **Joan Broerman**, creator of "We Love to Write Wordshops" for schools and libraries. Remember the scents, the sights and textures. Remember events that led up to it and the emotions you felt.

■ **Scenes:** "When I travel, I always try to take time to describe a scene," says **Pamela Greenwood**, co-author of *Take Off!* under the pen name Ryan Ann Hunter. "If I'm looking for details for a character I'm working on, I'll watch a child and describe him or her." Use the five senses to bring the scene to life. Put into words the facial expressions, body language, and attitudes as well as the physical description. From an objective perspective, what kind of personality does the child have?

■ **Characterization:** "Every person does things a little differently." Use those differences, says **Emily Rhoads Johnson**, author of *Write Me If You Dare*. Describe three people, or characters, doing these ordinary activities. Reveal their personality through their actions: getting up in the morning; making and eating a sandwich; getting the mail; reading a book; watching television.

■ **Draw on your past:** "Use the prompt '*I remember*,' or even more provocative, '*I don't remember*,'" suggests poet **Julie Williams**, to produce writing of depth and feeling. Use this with a character you want to learn more about.

■ **Fill in the blanks:** Author of *There Goes Lowell's Party!*, **Esther Hershenhorn** offers this exercise:
  – My name is _____.
  – I just hate it when _____.
  – I wish more than anything in the world that _____.
  – I'm so sorry that _____.

Exercises on the Move

When you are away from your office or computer, you can still do writing exercises.

■ **Eavesdrop**. Listen to conversations at the mall, park, fast food restaurant, or other public place. Seek to capture the voice or voices speaking. Write down their dialogue word-for-word. Spend 10 minutes creating a character from that voice. Listen for problems or conflicts. Use one to create a plot. ("Ever since the snake crawled up my leg, I hate going there.")

■ **Sit someplace**. Feel the mood and describe it, using as many evocative words as you can. Then describe the place as if you were setting a scene for a romance novel, a Western, a mystery, science fiction, or a detective story.

■ **Pick up interesting or unusual objects.** They might be stones, shells, seed pods, fern fronds, charcoal. Write about them. You might want to attach an emotion to each one (shocked shell, cautious geode). Become your character and write from his or her point of view.

■ **Look at a stranger.** Imagine what looking into the person's eyes would reveal. What does he or she want most? What will they do to get it? Outline the conflict to help with plotting, or write down their thoughts as they seek to achieve their goals.

novel. I realized Gina was leaving behind much of childhood. While I knew she would choose to befriend an African-American girl in a town with many bigots, I had not internalized the depth of the impact this decision would have on her. Without this writing exercise, I wouldn't have been able to identify consciously the issues Gina would face—issues that helped me with plotting and with understanding dimensions of my character.

Sometimes we discover similarities between ourselves and our characters as we examine these issues. Many writing exercises help us deal with our concerns as writers and people. Exercises in *The Writer as an Artist: A New Approach to Writing Alone and with Others,* by Pat Schneider, help writers deal with fears of failure, of insecurities in their writing that may have originated with early school writing. She leads writers through exercises to help them free their creativity and be able to take risks in writing. I wonder sometimes if those who choose to write and create don't share a common imagination, vivid enough to explore the universe and give us wild, passionate reflections—and rejections—far beyond the mere words

A Circuit of Writing Exercises

■ What other characters say about a person can reveal the person's character to readers before that character even comes into view. Write dialogue using one speaker to reveal a second character's personality. Then write dialogue that reflects not only the character's personality, but that of the speaker. Examples:
   "Sure he's tough, but he doesn't scare me."
   "He's so cute. What a bod! And he knows it."

■ Choose something edible (spearmint leaf, strawberry, apple) and describe it using the five senses. How does it look, feel, sound, smell, taste?

■ The bravest thing I ever did (or saw someone do) was _____ because _____ .

■ When I was _____ years old, I loved/hated my brother/sister/cousin/other child when they _____, so I _____ .

■ Pull out a photograph or drawing from a magazine or a family album. Write about it. In writing groups, each person brings a family photo. First write about someone else's family. Then write about your own.

■ List things you've lost. Write about one and how its loss affected you.

■ Take characters from two different books or stories you're working on. Have them meet. Record their actions and conversations.

■ Stop and feel, see, hear. Record the sensations around you right now—the sounds, textures, smells, sights. Use specific details.

written on a page. Exercises can help us gain courage to go on.

A Tool for All Writing

Are you at a point where you need to understand your character better?

Carry on an interview with your character. Ask questions and type the character's answers. Somehow, writing exercises free the unconscious mind to soar, explore, and discover.

As we delve into the minds of our characters and learn their fears, passions, needs, and wants, we come to understand information that helps with plotting. Revealed fears and weaknesses become stumbling blocks in the progress of the story. Passions help them persist in the face of adversity. Strengths move them to discover ways to resolve their conflict. As you craft a story you might ask: What does

A Circuit of Writing Exercises

■ Examine the setting of a story of yours. What would happen if it were set instead in New York City? Minnesota? A ranch in Texas? A small town in the deep South? How would things change? Choose one setting and write about it.

■ How are you feeling now? Anxious, excited, angry, lethargic, hopeful, or delighted? Create that mood in your writing. Set a scene that reflects that mood. (Anxious: "The startled sparrow flitted and turned, then perched on a thin wire. Its tail flickered in an uncertain breeze.") Show mannerisms that reflect that mood, or write dialogue conveying a mood without using the word.

■ Choose a powerful passage in a favorite story or book. Type it, word-for-word. Look for the effective literary devices the author used to build the emotional content and strengthen characterization. Incorporate those techniques into your stories.

■ Listen to the sounds of words. Categorize them—based only on the sound, not the meaning—into categories such as sharp, soothing, rural, urban, or any other categories you select. (Perhaps *Seattle* sounds soothing, while *catsup* sounds sharp.) Make lists of words that sound young, old, short, skinny, and so on. (For more word exercises, see the sidebar "The Word Box," page 139.)

■ Write the jacket cover copy for your story. (Your editor will love you if you do this well.)

your character want most right now? After you learn that, ask: What stands in the character's way? Use writing exercises to help plot your stories.

Other writing exercises can be more general, taking us back to our childhood and helping us to view the world through the eyes of a child again. Let your mind reflect back to a vivid time in your childhood, say, maybe fourth grade. Visualize the classroom, the smell, the texture of the desk, the noises. Can you remember your friends or other kids in the classroom? Describe them. What was important to you then? As you send your mind back in time, you can recreate the feelings and the world-view of a child that age.

At times, we want to improve our writing techniques. Can we explore the poetry, rhythm, and music of

Shooting Sparks

Writing exercises shoot creative sparks in all directions. The same exercise can lead to dozens of different results. So use exercises time and again. Each time let the exercise spark your writing toward the end you want that particular day. For example, suppose your exercise was to write about an object—a bowl decorated with zebras. Look at a few possible outcomes:

■ **Character**: Think about who created the bowl.

    The bent woman swayed in to the rhythm of the potter's wheel. She hummed a familiar African melody as her fingers prodded and pressed the slick clay. Feast night for Jabda in two weeks. Her boy would soon be a man.

■ **Plot development:** How would your story's character feel about the bowl?

    Darcy hoped for in-line skates for her birthday, but Aunt Sophie's package seemed oddly heavy. And her mysterious smile. Aunt Sophie liked voodoo dolls and bones. Darcy shivered. Maybe she didn't want to open the package after all.

■ **Setting:** Delve into mood, scenery, and/or imagery.

    Moonlit sky touches the white stripes with an iridescence that makes the zebras seem half there. The rest melt into dark mystery. Shadows, bending grasses. Slithering, swishing, stomping. A gadfly bites. Tail swats. A head shakes. The cloying scent of night-blooming jasmine mingles with the fresh odor of urine.

■ **Story Ideas:**

Follow Arizona writer Dawn Dixon as she explores the bowl.

    A bowl full of zebras? The Zebra Bowl—a zebra sports stadium?

    Bowling for Zebras—or zebras that bowl? A herd of zebras.

    Zebra herding. I heard a zebra. A bowl made of zebra hide.

    Hiding zebras—hey, that might work. What if a zebra herd broke out of a zoo and a child decides to hide them? What about a child hiding zebras could be fresh or original? Where? A fabric shop? A wallpaper store? An art gallery?

■ **Language:** Play with words. Create new ones.

    Zebras galleaped over the nightdusky shimmerface of the urn. Lions slurithered past withered oncewater craters and watchly waited for yum-sucklings.

The Word Box

Gather a collection of words. They may be emotions (rancor, delight, trepidation, zest), opposites (diligent/slothful, faded/bright, silence/cacophony), adjectives (forceful, green, sinuous, shimmery), verbs (attack, slip, jingle, giggle), specific or proper nouns (eucalyptus, Mohawk, love seat, symphony, Reebok), even made-up words (Jabberwocky, zlipthr, cumolt)—any words that you find delicious, provocative, enticing. Do you like the way a word sounds? The thoughts or feelings it evokes? Own it by putting it in your word box.

Use tickets, cardboard, or index cards and write your words on them in bold letters. Or cut out words or phrases from magazines and tape them on the cards. Put them in a box, bowl, or container. Use these words as springboards to a myriad of exercises.

■ Pull out several random words and write about them, or create a story or poem from them.

■ Randomly, or thoughtfully, put words with household objects like *sinuous* on a rock, *Fancy Mama* on a grater, *anger* on a high-heeled shoe. See what creativity it sparks.

■ Choose a single word and write from it for three minutes.

■ Pair up several nouns and verbs (minister lopes, vaporize snow, marble dash). Write about one or more of them.

■ Use colors and attach them to ideals, abstractions, or emotions (puce envy, caramel jealousy, peppermint love). How does it feel? Who feels this? Write about them.

writing? Sure. A good source of writing exercises is *Poemcrazy: Freeing Your Life with Words*, by Susan Goldsmith Wooldridge. Or create a *word box* or *pool*, a group of unrelated words and work with them. (See sidebar above.) Pull out a few and write from them for 10 minutes.

Do give yourself a time limit when you write. Williams says, "I think it's the juxtaposing of two seemingly disparate elements that makes writing exercises work." She's referring to the notion of *free writing* placed within the tight constraints of a *timed* writing exercise. To write without stopping, without editing, without judging, for 3 minutes, 5, 7, or 10 minutes, throws on a creative switch in us. Then to read it out loud to an audience prepared to listen, really listen, without stopping, without editing, without judging, brings it to the realm of *voicing*. Voila! Magic.

Find the amount of time that works for you. Begin with a short time, three to five minutes. That seems to discourage dawdling, but encourage the ideas. Some exercises may need more time. Remember all the exercises suggested here and in the sidebars are for you. If you finish early with what you need to say, keep thinking for the rest of the time limit. Sometimes greater insights come. When working alone, if you're in the middle of a brilliant idea, don't stop when the time is up. Keep creating.

At those times when your writing demands depth, encouragement, freshness, direction, or impulsion, look to writing exercises to recharge.

Submissions

Submission Samples

Peeking into Proposal Packages

By Susan Tierney

Want to take a look? Sure you do. Every writer, from novices to the old hand with dozens of credits, is at least curious about how others put together submissions. New writers may feel they're being let in on secret rites, and in a way they are, by such peeking. While there are no absolute rules about structuring submissions, the *secret* is in the skill that creates a professional offering. That skill is developed. Even experienced writers may pick up a tip or two by looking at how others put together a proposal package.

In the spirit of sharing secrets, here is a sampling of proposals—not simply queries, the relatively brief letters that, standing alone, are perfectly appropriate for many projects. Here we offer examples that have worked when more was called for. One of the secrets of good proposals is to provide enough information, but not too much. Another is to give the true flavor of the project. A third is to meet the audience need—direct the proposal to the specific editor and specific company as if you were having a personal (but always professional) conversation.

How this is done is illustrated in the sampling that follows. The collection offers a variety of approaches, but even these can be mixed and matched to optimize the presentation of your project. Before each submission package is a discussion of the format, contents, and approach, and the merits of each. Peeking at these successful proposals can help you create a proposal of your own, packaged to sell.

The Packages

■ *Submission 1.* Nonfiction article: history or profile query, outline/synopsis, bibliography.

■ *Submission 2:* For nonfiction theme publications: article query and outline.

■ *Submission 3:* Picture book: query, nonfiction; résumé.

■ *Submission 4:* Fiction series proposal: Religious adventure query; synopsis and outline; character list; résumé.

■ *Submission 5:* Nonfiction proposal, two-book set: overview; outline; author information.

■ *Submission 6:* Nonfiction series proposal: outline/synopsis; sales points; author information; sample chapters.

Submission 1
Article, History or Profile

Query: The query directed to *Cobblestone* is for a history magazine that is theme-based, but one of the strongest qualities of this query letter is the real enthusiasm the author exhibits for his subject. This is not an author responding solely to an interesting subject and warming up to the topic in the process of developing the idea. This is a writer who has a slant on his subject, and makes it clear from the very first paragraph. Note that the author chose to begin his submissions package with a query—including an "argument" for the piece, with details, rather than a polite, brief cover letter that simply indicates what else is attached. The cover letter is an option for many submissions packages, but here, the strength of the package is in the query.

The letter's lead paragraph turns a view on its head, and is engaging because of it. This author disagrees with a traditionally accepted view, and makes a wonderful case for another perspective. The boy behind the man, Francis Marion, did not lead an uneventful life as some historians may have said, and this query is a strong argument for offering a profile of a historical figure as a child and young man—overcoming physical limitations, setting off on adventures and standing up to all challenges, setting a direction to his life. The writer makes it clear why such a subject would be of interest to young readers.

The query is, again, effective in the author's knowledge of his subject and exhibits the ability to find the resources to put together an article of high quality. The author includes a brief but clear statement of his qualifications, and is direct and professional in tone throughout. The suggestion for a title, "Living Beside the Santee," is always a plus. Editors may have other ideas, but they always welcome an appealing title suggestion.

Outline/Synopsis: A hybrid of an outline and synopsis accompanies the query. The numeric listing of subjects—family, at sea, war—indicates how the 750-word article might be constructed, but rather than using brief phrases and a formal outline, this proposal takes shape as a brief narrative. It's a small step for an editor to see how the article will come together from this proposal format.

Bibliography: To many children's magazines, but particularly to those that focus on history or science, the article sources are crucially important. The bibliography here includes important adult biographies of the main subject, Francis Marion, written over many years; some were written close in time to Marion's life—one in 1821, when people who knew Marion might still be alive and so might serve as a primary source, an important consideration for a history magazine. It also includes sources on large topics of background importance, such as the history of the British West Indies; and a children's book written on the colony of South Carolina. The bibliography is a significant coda to a well-composed submissions package.

The article was published in the December 2001 *Cobblestone*.

Submission 1
Article Query
History or Profile

Meg Chorlian, Editor
Cobblestone
30 Grove Street, Suite C
Peterborough, NH 03458

Re: Scheduled theme issue on Francis Marion, the Swamp Fox

Dear Ms. Chorlian:

Hugh Rankin, in his fine biography of Francis Marion, declares that Marion's life before and after the American Revolution was boring and scarcely worth writing about. Rankin devotes only 5 of his 300 pages to the first 43 years of Marion's life.

But what an amazing five pages they are! The future military hero is born undersized, with malformed ankles and knees (and he will always be undersized and have ankle and knee problems). Marion grows up in the lush countryside of colonial South Carolina, spending much of his time hunting and fishing. He learns farming, but receives only a little home schooling and probably no formal education. At 15, he tries life at sea and sails away to the romantic West Indies. On the return voyage, his boat is sunk by a whale and he survives seven days in an open boat by drinking the blood and eating the raw flesh of a dog who had been the ship's mascot. At 18, he takes over the management of his father's plantation. In his twenties, he serves in two campaigns against the Cherokee, winning one horrifyingly bloody battle that makes him a local legend. Rankin sums up Marion's life to this point as "rather mundane."

Strangely, other biographers agree with Rankin. I don't. I think children especially will find the early part of Marion's life fascinating. From birth through the Cherokee campaign to the establishment of his own plantation, Marion's life would make an exciting narrative of about 750 words for *Cobblestone*, tentatively titled "Living Beside the Santee."

I am a former teacher of English, former radio music host, and former Peace Corps volunteer who, it happens, once spent two days on the ocean in an 18-foot open boat. The experience was anything but mundane. I have had articles accepted by *Highlights for Children* and the *Christian Science Monitor,* copies of which are enclosed, along with an outline/synopsis for "Living Beside the Santee." Thank you for your consideration.

Sincerely,
Jerry Miller

Submission 1
Article Outline/Synopsis
History or Profile

Outline/Synopsis for "Living Beside the Santee"

1. Family: All four of Francis Marion's grandparents were Huguenots who fled from France to South Carolina's Indian country to escape religious persecution. They were pioneers along the Santee River. By the time Marion's father was grown, the former frontier had become a place of rice and indigo plantations.

2. Youth: Marion was born undersized, with malformed ankles and knees that would plague him throughout his life. Despite his small size, he always had remarkable endurance and determination. The hunting and fishing in the lush countryside in which he grew up were excellent and he became a dedicated hunter and fisher among the moss-hung cypresses, lazy rivers, marshes, and forests of oak and sweet gum.

3. At sea: At 15, Marion sailed to the West Indies to try life at sea. The beautiful tropical islands were bustling trade centers. On the return voyage, Marion's boat was rammed and sunk by a whale. Seven crew members escaped in a small open boat and endured only by killing a dog for nourishment. Five survived. Marion returned home.

4. Plantation: When Marion was 18, his father died. Although he was the youngest child, Marion took over management of his father's plantation.

5. War: South Carolina had little involvement in the French and Indian War, but near the end of that long struggle, the Cherokee joined the French and attacked the South Carolina frontier. At 25, Marion joined the first of two campaigns. During the second, he led a troop of 30 men as the spearhead of an attack. Twenty-one were killed or wounded in the fierce battle, but his success made possible the success of the entire campaign. Marion became a local legend, but was sickened by the cruelty he saw. The experience set the stage for his part in the Revolutionary War.

6. Temporary Peace: Marion returned to his family and a peaceful life of hunting, fishing, and farming. He had his fill of war. Shortly before the Revolution, he established his own 200-acre plantation near Eutaw Springs.

Submission 1
Article Bibliography
History or Profile

Bibliography for "Living Beside the Santee"

■ Bass, Robert D. *Swamp Fox: The Life and Campaigns of General Francis Marion* (Holt: New York, 1959).

■ Burns, Alan. *History of the British West Indies,* revised (Allen & Unwin: London, 1959).

■ Fradin, Dennis Brindell. *The South Carolina Colony (Thirteen Colonies)* (Children's Press: Danbury, CT, 1992). Ages 9-12.

■ c. *A Sketch of the Life of Brigadier General Francis Marion, etc.* (Charleston, 1821; new edition, 1948).

■ Rankin, Hugh F. *Francis Marion: The Swamp Fox* (Crowell: New York, 1973).

■ Rogozinski, Jan. *A Brief History of the Caribbean: From the Arawak and the Carib to the Present,* revised (Facts on File: New York, 1999).

■ Savage, Henry. *Rivers of the Carolinas: The Santee* (University of North Carolina, 1968).

■ Simms, William Gilmore. *The Life of Francis Marion* (New York, 1844).

■ Williams, Beryl and Epstein, Samuel. *Francis Marion: Swamp Fox of the Revolution* (Messner: New York, 1959).

Submissions

Submission 2
Themed Issues, Nonfiction

Query: The simplicity of this two-piece proposal could mask how well it is marked by clarity, directness, and appropriate level of detail. The query letter succinctly directs itself to a specific editorial need:

(1) by responding to an announcement in a trade publication (*SCBWI Bulletin*);

(2) for articles for a themed issue on New Zealand;

(3) by briefly defining the article slant (origins and use of *kiwi* words);

(4) by indicating the author's specific qualifications for writing on this subject (while the author isn't herself a New Zealander, she has traveled there, lived in a similar culture, and remains in touch with New Zealanders);

(5) by including broader qualifications as a writer (publishing credits and teaching experience).

The query also nicely indicates the author's receptivity to redirection if the subject is appealing.

Outline: The outline is a model of the traditional annotated outline form and for an article of this kind is particularly effective. The suggested title "Grab Your Cossies and Jandals for a Cracker Day" is a "grabber" (pun intended). It uses the imperative grab, perhaps the strongest of verb forms in English. The title is a bit of a riddle or mystery of the kind that would definitely appeal to kids because it has the feel of being in on a secret if you know the meanings: what exactly is a cossie or a jandal or a cracker day?

The outline's introductory paragraph neatly offers several more examples of words spoken in an English dialect that the average American wouldn't know. The outline shows that the article will set up the origins of such words, taking a complex subject to a basic, but informative level, and with the appeal of story: arriving in canoes to settle islands, and sea travel and new settlers hundreds of years later. The author then distinguishes between different categories of words, and draws the entire article together with a summarizing conclusion, but one that will also draw young readers into their own creativity and involvement with language.

This query led to publication in the New Zealand *Faces*, January 2001.

Submission 2
Article Query
Themed Issues, Nonfiction

Elizabeth Crocker Carpentiere, Editor
Faces
30 Grove Street
Peterborough, NH 03458

Re: New Zealand issue

Dear Ms. Carpentiere:

    I read in a recent *SCBWI Bulletin* that you are reviewing proposals for an upcoming issue on New Zealand. I am a writer and poet and I teach with the California Poets in the Schools program. Some of my recent work has appeared in *Hip Mama, New Moon,* and a variety of anthologies. I also have three articles forthcoming in the May *AppleSeeds.*

    Enclosed please find an outline for a proposed article for *Faces.* "Grab Your Cossies and Jandals for a Cracker Day" details the origins and use of typical "kiwi" words and phrases.

    I believe that I am especially qualified to write these articles because of my background in languages of the world; because I have traveled to New Zealand three times, and lived for nearly a year in Australia, which shares a heritage similar to New Zealand's; and because of my potential sources: the neighbors and close friends I maintain who are native to New Zealand and who have introduced me to their flavorful language and foods. I also have a longstanding friendship with a school librarian on the North Island.

    Please let me know if you would like to pursue this article or if I can slant it in a direction that suits your editorial needs. Thank you for considering these ideas.

Sincerely,
Karen Lewis

encl: résumé, query

Submission 2
Article Outline
Themed Issues, Nonfiction

Faces Issue: New Zealand
Proposal: Nonfiction article, about 800 words

"Grab Your Cossies and Jandals for a Cracker Day"

You might be confused if you visit New Zealand. Although the spoken language is English, someone might ask you if you'd like a *hokianga* or a *vegemite* sandwich for *tucker*. They might let you know that their parent is a cow spanker or a coastie. These and other words are examples of how language adapts to a unique place and time.

I. Brief History of New Zealand Settlement.

    A. *Aotearoa* or Land of the Long White Cloud: name given the islands when Polynesian Maori people first arrived in their canoes some time between 800 and 1300 A.D.

    B. *Maori*: the original settlers. The word means *native*. Some Maori words are commonly used today in New Zealand.

    C. *Nieww Zeeland*: name given to the islands in 1642 when the Dutch sea captain Abel Tasman "discovered" the land of the Maori. It was named after the Zeeland province in Tasman's native Netherlands. Waves of European settlers arrived in the 1800s, most speaking British English. These settlers, and their Australian neighbors, also invented unique words.

II. Current Kiwi Expressions and Their True Meanings

    A. Terms with European roots: cossie; jandal; flea taxi; cracker; throw a wobbly; go for a skate; greenie; hook your mutton; marmite; hen cackle; cow spanker.

    B. Terms with Maori roots: Kia or a; give jaro; Pakeha; kumara; kiwi; hokianga.

    C. New Zealand place names reflect a delicate balance between Maori and European roots. Include colorful and descriptive examples.

III. Conclusion

    Languages always evolve to include new cultures and ideas. Can you imagine how some of the unique words in your own region came to be? Create your own dictionary of slang. Imagine some new words to express current styles, emotions, or special places in your life.

Submission 3
Picture Book

Query: The query for a nonfiction picture book may share much with an article query, as in the preceding submission package, but here's another way to go about it, without an outline. Be sure you know your market when you make your choice about a submission approach. Does the magazine publisher or book company want a query only or do they want an outline? Of course, this picture book query is arguing for the merits of the attached manuscript; it is not simply a cover letter.

Without an outline or synopsis, more information must be conveyed in the query itself. In the picture book example, that is done efficiently in about 100 words more than in the preceding article query. In the picture book query, the first paragraph places the title right up front, and attractively and succinctly synopsizes the subject.

Like every good query or proposal, the picture book description highlights a core idea or underlying theme that focuses the project. In this case, it is family involvement and continuity in work that often delights children—the making of apple cider in the autumn. The potential charm of the story comes through: the range of ages; the old family business, now at risk; the universal appeal of the seasonal, especially for children; the making of something that lends itself to activities.

A very strong point is the author's declaration that the book was conceived to fill a market gap. That's music to an editor's ears. The author bolsters her statement by naming, and distinguishing, titles that could be thought to be on the same topic. The query follows up with clarification of the ages targeted, and because the author has classroom experience, she speaks to how the book might be used in schools. The Millbrook Press's primary markets have long been the institutional market—schools and libraries—so the author tailors the query to the company. Yet another marketing point is the author's availability for what she characterizes as "many opportunities for school visits," which marketing and publicity departments at book publishers like to hear.

Résumé: In the query, the author strikes the right balance between detailing a good subject and her experience and ability to follow through, from composing to contributing to the selling of the book. Her specific writing experience is reinforced with the somewhat informal, brief, sufficient résumé. (Compare the résumé on page 158.) She highlights the range of writing, and writing-related work, she has done, and provides a sampling of her published pieces. While no picture books are listed, the author clearly makes a good case for herself in this proposal package. She has more than "worked up" to the potential for writing a picture book. *Apple Cider Making Days* is to be published for readers in kindergarten to grade three this fall by Millbrook.

A note on the author: Her résumé indicates she was a nurse, but does not say she was a pediatric psychiatric nurse, working with children and young adults. That's something she might consider adding. Her second children's book is to be published by Random House in spring 2003.

Submission 3
Picture Book Query
Nonfiction

Jean Reynolds, Vice President and Editorial Director
The Millbrook Press
2 Old New Milford Road
Brookfield, CT 06804

Dear Ms. Reynolds:

I am pleased to submit my manuscript with the working title of *Apple Cider Making Days*. It is based on the workings of the Meckley orchard and cider mill near Jackson, Michigan. The participation of the extended family, including the very youngest members, is critical to the continuity of the operation. Ray Meckley, age 73, believes most of the family-owned cider mills in the U.S. will disappear in the coming years.

I wrote this manuscript to fill a gap among children's books. There are books available about apples, such as *The Seasons of Arnold's Apple Tree,* by Gail Gibbons, and *How to Make an Apple Pie and Travel Around the World,* by Marjorie Priceman. But I could not find any books in print that give children the experience of being on a working farm and making cider.

Through my experience in elementary school classrooms, I know that teachers and librarians look every fall for books related to apples. This is especially true as fewer classes take field trips to real orchards. Teachers want a book such as *Apple Cider Making Days* to read aloud to classes before seasonal lessons and activities. I see this picture book as a readaloud book for kindergarten and first- and second-grades, and as a book for independent readers in grades three, four, and five. The book will give me many opportunities for school visits.

While I have indicated page breaks on the attached manuscript, there are a variety of ways the sections could be handled. I would be happy to write to the specifications of the editor and needs of the illustrator.

It would please me very much to have The Millbrook Press publish *Apple Cider-Making Days*. I have submitted the manuscript to other editors, but sincerely hope that you will find the book is a good fit for your list. I look forward to hearing from you.

Sincerely,
Ann Purmell

encl: publishing and professional credentials

Submission 3
Picture Book Résumé
Nonfiction

Ann Purmell . . . At a Glance
Address, Telephone, E-mail

Experience
■ Writer of inspirational and children's literature.
■ Freelance journalist and feature writer for *Jackson Citizen Patriot* (Michigan), a Booth Communications daily. Affiliate newspapers throughout Michigan carry my articles.
■ Freelance writer for *Jackson Magazine,* a monthly business publication.
■ Guest lecturer for Children's Literature and Creative Writing classes at Spring Arbor College, Spring Arbor, Michigan.
■ Performs school presentations for all grade levels.

Articles
Published numerous articles, including:
■ "Prayers to the Dead," *In Other Words: An American Poetry Anthology* (Western Reading Services, 1998).
■ "Promises Never Die," *Guideposts for Teens* (June/July 1999). Ghost-written, first-person, true story.
■ "Teaching Kids the Financial Facts of Life," *Jackson Citizen Patriot* (July 20, 1999). An interview with Jayne A. Pearl, author of *Kids and Money.*
■ "New Rules for Cider? Small Presses Might Be Put Out of Business," *Jackson Citizen Patriot* (December 12, 1999).
■ "Jackson Public Schools Prepare for Change: Technology, Ideas Shaping Education," *Jackson Magazine* (December 1999). An interview with Dan Evans, Superintendent of Jackson Public Schools.

Education
■ B.S., Nursing, Eastern Michigan University.
■ Post-B.A. work, elementary education, Spring Arbor College.
■ *Highlights for Children* Chautauqua Conference, summer 1999.

Submission 4
Fiction Book Proposal, Religious Adventure Series

Query/Cover letter: Here is the essence of many a writer's wonderings. What exactly is the difference between a query letter and a cover letter? Well, sorry to say, it depends. Most of the time, a cover letter is a simple statement: Here it is—my manuscript for a picture book, my article, my proposal for a multivolume series. But sometimes a cover letter is interchangeable with a query letter, giving a quick summation of the subject, hook, author credentials and serving as the introduction to a larger proposal package. But it's fair to say, if not universally acceded, that a cover letter doesn't go into detail and a query does.

In the example of the fiction series proposal package, it would be easy enough to say that the first element is a cover letter introducing the details of the other elements of the proposal package for an adventure series proposal. But in many ways, the letter is a query. It's not just a polite, professional note saying, "Please consider the attached." Beyond that request, the letter provides specific information about a series concept and author experience and viewpoint.

The tone of this letter is professional, but warm. It has personal undertones, which are sometimes appropriate. The *sometimes* carries an enormous caveat. In most cases, the overly personal in a query will not meet with a positive response. Be enthusiastic, share a unique but eminently defensible point of view, but do not become overtly personal. Always remain professional, even when sharing personal connections to a subject. For a religious publisher, to whom a personal faith commitment is requisite, a sincere voice that conveys the truth of that faithfulness is merited. In any other case, such personal information crosses professional boundaries.

Synopsis & outline: The combination of an overall synopsis and an outline offered by the author of the Artemus Anderson series is one option of series proposals. If it's a choice that is right for your project, make sure the synopsis touches on overall theme, voice, age, and distinctions, whatever the genre. The chapter-by-chapter outline/synopsis should be more specific about events and characters, without going into lengthy detail.

Character list: In this proposal, the author divides events from characters to some degree. That can be useful. The outline/synopsis indicates the story arc, while the character list begins to give a sense of how characters will be shaped and interact, and what motivates them.

Résumé: The résumé in this proposal package is not unlike the résumé on page 153, although it is slightly different in form. It is efficient, complete (although for space reasons, we have limited the number of published articles listed on the author's actual résumé).

Note that we have not included synopses for additional books in the series, which the author did include in the proposal package. The first book, *Arty Goes West,* has been published by Sword of the Lord and the second book in the series is scheduled for publication in the next year.

Fiction Series Proposal, Query
Adventure, Religious Publishing

Guy King, Director of Publishing Operations
Sword of the Lord
P.O. Box 1099
Murfreesboro, TN 37133-1099

Dear Mr. King:

I have written a Western adventure that I believe will appeal to readers from 8 to 12, and have enclosed a synopsis and samples for your review. The story is the tale of 12-year-old Artemus Anderson and his mother, who leave Ohio and head west to take over a ranch, after the death of Arty's father. *Arty Goes West* is the first of a projected series of six books.

From the time Arty and his mother step into the stagecoach, they experience the adventures of everyday life and perils. Without an overlay of preachiness, these adventures allow young readers to witness the benefits, even the practicality, of living the Bible on a daily basis. I hope to make the books similar to the Moody Press's Sugar Creek Gang series, by Paul Hutchens. My books will differ in setting, time period, and voice, but the Biblical values will be the same.

I have been a junior high and high school English teacher for 15 years. During that time, my wide reading among books for young people and for adults has led me to the realization that the fictional characters who most influence young readers are those rich and developed enough to appear in more than one book. I have completed the second book and am working on the third in the Arty series.

Please find attached a simple chapter-by-chapter outline of the first book, a brief synopsis, a list of characters, synopses for three more projected books in the series, and my résumé.

Thank you for taking time to consider my proposal for *The Adventures of Artemus Anderson,* which I am also submitting to other publishers. I know that Sword of the Lord already publishes fine books for young readers, and I would be honored to add my work to your list. I believe you will find it to be in harmony with the Sword's doctrinal positions.

Sincerely,
Mark L. Redmond

encl: synopsis and outline for book one, character list, series synopses, résumé

Fiction Series Proposal, Synopsis & Outline
Adventure, Religious Publishing

Synopsis: The Artemus Anderson Series

Set primarily in the small Texas town of White Rock and the surrounding area, this series covers events in the life of Artemus Anderson at ages 12 and 13. The time is the mid-1870s. Arty and his mother travel from Ohio to take possession of a cattle ranch that Mr. Anderson purchased shortly before his death in a fire. Arty and his mother struggle to overcome the heartache that accompanies their loss. Arty has a personal battle with anger and bitterness toward God. Meanwhile, he faces numerous daily struggles as he finds that life in the West rapidly pushes a boy toward manhood.

As he makes friends, Arty learns about responsibility, sorrow, love, relationship to God, joy. As readers follow Arty through the series, they will learn what life was like in the "Wild West," how kids were much the same as they are today, and that Biblical living, then and now, is rewarding both practically in the world and spiritually.

Outline: The Adventures of Artemus Anderson, Book 1

Chapter 1: Arty and his mother, Mrs. Anderson, are on their way by stagecoach to claim their Texas ranch. They are confronted by two villains, whom they manage to defeat by using their wits.

Chapter 2: Arty and Mrs. Anderson arrive in White Rock, Texas, the town closest to their ranch. They have a misunderstanding with the marshal.

Chapter 3: They spend the night in town. The following morning, Arty and his mother go to the ranch, escorted by the marshal and ranch foreman, who has ridden into town to meet them.

Chapter 4: Before they leave town, they are again confronted by the two villains from the stagecoach, but the marshal and foreman intervene and the villains land in jail. At the ranch, the Andersons meet several cowboys, and the old cook, who is the focal point of a funny incident.

Chapter 5: Two months have passed. Arty witnesses to the cook, who is bitter toward God because of past events. Although the cook doesn't share Arty's beliefs, he likes the boy. The cowboys present Arty with a pony, and more humor follows, mixed with a spiritual lesson.

. . .

[The outline continues through Chapter 12. A synopsis for each additional book in the series is included in the proposal package.]

Submission 4
Fiction Series Proposal, Character List
Adventure, Religious Publishing

Artemus Anderson, called Arty, is a typical 12-year-old boy, full of energy and mischief. Because of the death of his father, Arty is closer to his mother than the average boy his age would be. His mind is as active as his body, and he finds abundant fuel for his imagination in the books that his mother makes available to him. Arty struggles with sorrow and bitterness over the loss of his father.

Elizabeth Anderson, Arty's mother, also battles sorrow over the loss of her husband. She tries to be strong for Arty, but has brief lapses. She is kind, loving, patient, and displays a good sense of humor. She also shows courage, determination, and faith as she carries out her husband's dream of running a ranch, the Circle A. She is in her twenties.

Luke Bodie is a U.S. marshal who lives in White Rock, the closest town to the Circle A. A widower, he is dedicated to his work. He likes people in general and, while he is a laid-back personality with a ready smile, he is also a serious man. He is in his early thirties.

Tom Green appears in the second book in the series. He attends school with Arty. The boys become friends and share adventures.

Chad Harte is a tough, wiry cowboy of average height and top hand at the Circle A ranch. Although only in his mid-twenties, he has had many experiences and gladly shares his "savvy" with Arty. Chad enjoys a good practical joke.

Bill Munson was the Circle A foreman for the previous owners and has agreed to stay on to work for Mrs. Anderson. He is a gentle, pleasant, soft-spoken man wrapped in a short, powerful body. He has a cowboy's sense of humor but is hard-working and knows how to manage other cowboys. He is in his late twenties.

Miss Ross, the schoolteacher, is a lovely young redhead who captures Arty's heart on the first day of school. Although she is strict, she is dedicated, patient, kind, and truly concerned about her students.

Bo Smith is a gigantic, powerful, 18-year-old ranch hand whom Bill and Chad have helped make into a first-class cowboy.

Esther Travis is already beautiful at 12. She is the oldest of three sisters and becomes one of Arty's closest friends. She is mature and level-headed for her age and always encourages Arty to do what is right and honest.

Submission 4
Fiction Series Proposal, Résumé
Adventure, Religious Publishing

Address, Telephone, E-mail

Teaching Experience
- Secondary English, Granger Christian School, Granger, IN,1978 - present
- Seventh Grade, Calvary Christian School, Kingston, TN, 1975 - 1976

Education
- Tennessee Temple College, Chattanooga, TN, 1971 - 1975
B.S., Secondary Education, English Proficiency

Stories and Articles Published
- "Randy's Right Attitude," *Kidz Ch@t* (June 2001)
- "The Switch," *Grit* (December 2000)
- "Nevertheless," *Power Station* (April 2000)
- "No Other Way," *Counselor* (February 2000)
- "The Rescue of Robyn," *Counselor* (February 2000)
- "Laying Up Treasure," *Guide* (January 2000)
- "Anna's ID Blues," *Guide* (Winter 1999)
- "The Hedge Helper," *Story Friends* (Summer 1999)
- "A Real Friend," *Bread for God's Children* (June 1999)
- "The Reward," *Western Digest* (September 1999)
- "Something in Common," *Guide* (Winter 1998)
- "The Toad," *R-A-D-A-R* (Winter 1998)
- "People Repair," *Discoveries* (October 1998)
- "The Outing," *Guide* (Summer 1998)
- "The Perfect Size," *Junior Trails* (Summer 1998)
- "The Same God," *R-A-D-A-R* (Summer 1998)
- "The Offering," *Teens on Target* (June 1998)

Editing Experience
- *Financial Freedom Starting Today,* Mark Royer, Ph.D (Morris Pub., 1998)

Submission 5
Nonfiction Book Proposal, Two-Book Set

Overview: "Young readers. Everything they need to know. Fun. Facts. Behind the scenes. Surprising. Inspiring. Record-breakers."

What editor could resist? And those are the words used just in the overview of this submission. The enthusiasm, solid examples, and wonderfully clear form of the proposals for a two-book set and an eight-book series (see Submission 6, page 162) show clearly why this is an author who has had great success.

Outline: The chapter by chapter outline is specific and substantive— no vague or passive "the ancient Olympics will be covered" or "the modern Olympics start up again" or "Olympic controversies." Rather, the outlined description of the contents reads, "what happens to facilities after the Olympics are over"; "famous 'doping' incidents; what can be done to stop drug use."

The outline projects the levels of research and accuracy the editor can expect—high—and, equally important in children's books, responds to problems discussed in the books. For children, surely, problems cannot simply be presented. Solutions, and the security of answers that adults can *help* them find in the world, are essential. That may seem a subtle point to extract from this sample proposal, but it is a very important one.

Author information: Like the entire proposal, the author biography is compact but thorough. It indicates the writer's extensive experience without needing to go on and on, and it includes titles and publishers that reflect the author's experience writing works of the kind now proposed—nonfiction, educational but entertaining.

Perfection Learning Company is publishing the set on the Olympics this year.

-159-

Submission 5
Nonfiction Book Proposal, Overview, Outline, Author Information
Two-Book Set

Joanne Mattern   *Address, Telephone, E-mail*

Proposal for
<u>BEHIND THE SCENES AT THE OLYMPICS</u>
<u>GREAT MOMENTS AT THE OLYMPICS</u>

<u>Overview:</u> This two-book set provides young readers with everything they need to know about the Olympic Games, including the history of the games; inspiring athletes and record-breakers; historic moments behind the scenes; surprising trivia and fun facts; and why the Olympics continue to inspire and interest people around the world. Each book will be set up as follows:

<u>Format:</u>   48 pages, full-color photos
<u>Age Level:</u>   9 to 14
<u>Reading Level:</u> fourth grade

<u>Contents:</u>   <u>BOOK ONE: BEHIND THE SCENES AT THE OLYMPICS</u>
- *Chapter 1* The History of the Olympics: Information about the ancient Olympics and how the games were recreated in the modern era.
- *Chapter 2* Making the Team: How athletes are chosen for the competition.
- *Chapter 3* When the Olympics Come to Town: How host cities are selected; preparations for the events; what happens to the facilities after the Olympics are over.
- *Chapter 4* The Darker Side of the Olympics: Controversies and tragedies, including the terrorist attack in Munich in 1972; boycotts, wars, and political demonstrations; the terrorist bombing in Atlanta in 1996.
- *Chapter 5* The Shadow of Drugs: How and why athletes use performance-enhancing drugs; famous "doping" incidents; what can be done to stop drug use.
- *Chapter 6* The Future of the Olympics: Can the Olympics overcome recent controversies and world politics?; what the Olympics mean to athletes, nations, and people around the world.

<u>Contents:</u>   <u>BOOK TWO: GREAT MOMENTS AT THE OLYMPICS</u>
- *Chapter 1* Record Breakers: A look at some of the most incredible athletic performances, including:

Nonfiction Book Proposal, Overview, Outline, Author Information
Two-Book Set

- Bob Beamon, who shattered the men's high jump record in 1968.
- Nadia Comaneci's seven perfect scores in gymnastics in 1976.
- Swimmer Mark Spitz's seven gold medals in 1972.
- Torvill and Dean's astounding perfection in pairs figure skating in 1984.
- Florence Griffith-Joyner's stunning victories in track and field in 1984.

- *Chapter 2* Surprises: Profiles of athletes who were not expected to win, including:
  - Rulon Gardner, who defeated the "unbeatable" Russian champ in weight lifting in 2000.
  - The U.S. hockey team's stunning victories in 1980.
  - Billy Mills, a Native American who came out of nowhere to win the 10,000-meter race in 1964.

- *Chapter 3* Inspiring Athletes:
  - Cathy Freeman, an Aborigine who united Australia as she competed in track and field in 2000.
  - Marla Runyan, a blind runner who competed in the 2000 Olympics.
  - Dan Jansen, who overcame personal tragedy and disappointment to win a gold medal in speed skating in 1994.
  - Wilma Rudolph, who could barely walk as a child, yet went on to win gold at the 1960 Olympics.
  - Akinori Nakayama, a gymnast who competed despite a broken foot in 1972.

- *Chapter 4* Trivia: Fun facts, such as:
  - The only person to win gold medals at both summer and winter Olympics.
  - The youngest and oldest gold medalists.
  - The person who won the most gold medals.
  - Odd sports that were once part of the Olympics.

About the Author: Joanne Mattern has written more than 125 books for children, including the World's Weirdest Animals series (Troll Communications); *Coming to America: The Story of Immigration* (Perfection Learning); *Going, Going, Gone? Saving Endangered Animals; Crazy Creatures of the World; Crazy Creatures of Australia; and The Outrageous Animal Record Book* (all published by Perfection Learning); and many classroom readers for Macmillan, McGraw-Hill, and Scott Foresman.

Submission 6
Nonfiction Series Proposal, Outline/Synopsis, Sales Points, Sample Chapters

Outline/Synopsis: The point in including the two-book set and eight-book series proposal packages by the same author—although the formats for the two proposals are parallel—is to highlight the differences in level of detail, and to show this very experienced author's grasp of project scope.

Would it be possible to do an eight-book series on the Olympics? Perhaps. Does such a scope really meet the needs of the target age range? Probably not. Does a series on each of the continents and the widely variant animal life make for interesting reading for children? Almost certainly. That is clear throughout the proposals. And that is perhaps the most important lesson of a proposal for nonfiction: The project must have an inherent integrity, interest for children, and individuality—it must not duplicate other books on the market.

The overviews in the two proposals are similar in approach and content type. The outlines differ in level of detail: The two-book set outline indicates chapter contents; the series proposal outlines content by book. Both indicate the *ruling passion*, if it may be termed that, the core subject in that section of the writing project and how it will be presented. The eight-book series proposal is, naturally, considerably longer. The proposal follows the form, function, and length of the writing venture.

A paragraph introduces the contents by referring to range ("all types of wildlife, from mammals to insects") and focus ("habitat" and "special fea-

tures"). Each following paragraph details one of the volumes and selects especially intriguing creatures, range, or distinctions, such as "the strange lungfish, which can survive buried in the mud during the desert's long dry season" or animals on the same continent, from "the snow leopard of the Himalayas's frozen peaks" to "the Komodo dragon of the tropics."

Sales points and author information: A look at the competition in the marketplace and an argument for placement of this particular proposal go a long way with editors. This one distinguishes the series from the myriad other children's books on animals through ease of use, the continent-by-continent perspective, and the style, which is supported on the following pages of the proposal with excerpts from sample chapters. The author information is really a sales point, too, for this and any series. The "About the author" paragraph here focuses on the author's background in writing about nature. In Submissions 5 and 6, her ability to slant books, provide interesting hooks and useful contexts is made evident.

Sample Chapters: No matter how much you say you write in a kid-friendly style, nothing proves it so much as writing samples. After all, in the proposal the audience is an adult but the book will address some age range of children. In this proposal, the sample chapters also show the depth of coverage and each volume's organization is made even clearer.

Part of the Animal Geography series appeared in 2001, and the remainder is being published this year by Perfection Learning Company.

Submission 6
Nonfiction Series Proposal, Outline/Synopsis

Joanne Mattern   *Address, Telephone, E-mail*

Proposal for
ANADE="underline">ANIMAL GEOGRAPHY
an eight-book series

Our world has seven continents, plus a vast expanse of ocean, and each area features its own unique geography and animal population. Each title in the eight-book Animal Geography series will focus on a different continent, or the ocean world, and provide an in-depth look at some of the animals that live there. Each book will be set up as follows:

Format: 48 pages, full-color photos
Age Level: 9 to 14
Reading Level: fourth grade

Contents: Each book will focus on the continent's animal life. Examples will include all types of wildlife, from mammals to insects. Special attention will be given to the animal's habitat—the special features that make the animal suited for life in this particular place. Full-color illustrations and photos will bring the text to life.

AFRICA: Home of savannah creatures such as the lion, the zebra, and the speedy cheetah; the strange lungfish, which can survive buried in the mud during the desert's long dry season; the tiny but vicious army ant; the armor-plated pangolin; and the weaver bird, builder of unusual nests. This book will also include a section on Madagascar, home of the lemur and the aye-aye, animals found nowhere else in the world.

ANTARCTICA: This frozen land and its cold seas support a surprising variety of life, including krill, the tiny creature on which all other Antarctic life depends; the emperor penguin; the albatross, a long-distance flyer; the orca (killer whale); and the springtail and Antarctic mite, two of the most unusual insects in the world.

ASIA: The world's largest continent is home to the snow leopard of the Himalayas's frozen peaks; the Komodo dragon of the tropics; the magnificent but endangered tiger; the stunningly beautiful peacock; the giant panda; and the stick insect, master of camouflage.

[The outline continues with the continents and oceans and then moves on, as on the next page, to Sales Points.]

Submission 6
Nonfiction Series Proposal, Sales Points

<u>Sales Points:</u> There are other "animal atlases" on the market, but all of them cram the whole world into one unwieldy reference book. Several of these books focus more on regions (woodland creatures from all over the world are grouped together, for example) rather than on specific continents, making it hard for the reader to isolate a particular part of the world. By presenting each continent in a separate book, the ANIMAL GEOGRAPHY series can provide more detailed and accessible information to readers.

The writing will also set this series apart from other animal books. Lively, kid-friendly text will keep readers turning the pages in search of more fascinating facts. At the same time, meticulous attention to facts will make this series a valuable reference source and a must-have for both school and public libraries.

<u>About the Author:</u> Joanne Mattern has written more than 125 books for children. Many of her books focus on animals and nature, including the World's Weirdest Animals series (Troll Communications) and Smart Thinking! Clever Ways Animals Make Their Lives Easier (Macmillan/McGraw-Hill).

Submission 6
Nonfiction Series Proposal, Sample Chapters

Sample Chapter for
ANImAL GEOGRAPHY series

VOLUME 6: NORTH AMERICA
THE DESERT

Deserts are dry places. Hardly any rain falls there, and the land is hot, arid, and empty.

In North America, large areas of the southwestern United States and Northern Mexico are covered by deserts. The largest desert is called the Great Basin. It lies between the Rocky Mountains and the Sierras. The mountains block the rain that comes from the Pacific Ocean. This makes the Great Basin a hot, dry, place. More deserts lie to the south of the Great Basin. These are called the Mojave and the Sonoran.

The desert is home to a very special plant, called the cactus. A cactus sucks up every bit of rainwater and moisture it can and stores it in its fat trunk. Many animals depend on the cactus for food and water.

You would think that no animals could live in such a hot, dry climate. But all sorts of animals do live in the desert. Special features on their bodies and special ways of behaving help them survive in this harsh place. The desert is full of life!

Reptiles and Amphibians

The Western Rattlesnake: The rattlesnake is one of the deadliest creatures in the desert. Its long front teeth, called fangs, are connected to special sacs filled with a poisonous venom. If the snake sinks its fangs into a small animal, the poison will kill its victim very quickly. Even bigger animals and people can die from a rattlesnake's bite. Food is often hard to find in the desert, but that doesn't bother the rattlesnake. Once the snake eats a big meal, such as a mouse, it will not have to eat again for many days.

The rattlesnake gets its name from the rattle on the end of its tail. This rattle is made of rings of hard, dry skin. When a rattlesnake wants to scare away an enemy, it shakes its tail. The rattling noise warns enemies to stay far away.

The Sidewinder: All that hot sand in the desert can be pretty painful to crawl on. But the sidewinder snake has developed a clear way to travel without getting burned. . . .

[The sample chapter on the desert continues through other desert animals, mammals, birds, and insects and spiders.]

Rules of the Game

By Mary Northrup

What is short, well-organized, packed with information—and too often ignored? Writers' guidelines. In a page or two, publisher guidelines provide the clues new and established writers need to focus submissions for the best possible chance of acceptance. Guidelines can have an enormous payoff, but only when writers read them for the details of content, format, and procedure.

Even published writers sometimes become cavalier about guidelines, not paying close enough attention to distinctions and clues to optimize their chances of acceptance. From beginner to expert, writers benefit from checking in regularly on magazines' changing specifications in their guidelines and re-analyzing current needs.

On Purpose

Typically, writers' guidelines include a description of the magazine and its readership. Sometimes the information is very broad, very basic, and yet can reveal a tone, voice, or worldview the author should recognize.

Boys' Life's guidelines, for example, open: "*Boys' Life* is a general interest, four-color monthly, circulation 1.3 million, published by the Boy Scouts of America since 1911." *American Girl* guidelines declare: "The mission is to celebrate girls, yesterday and today." *Pockets* includes its *editorial philosophy*: The primary purpose of *Pockets* is to help children grow in their relationship with God and to claim the good news of the gospel and apply it to their daily lives." The *Creative Classroom* guidelines remind authors that manuscripts should be "geared toward kindergarten through eighth-grade teachers." *FamilyFun* guidelines explain, "Our goal is to inspire families to spend time together by providing the surefire ideas and activities that will make that time a success. In other words, we take fun seriously."

Something for Everyone

A unique sentence or two from selected writers' guidelines:

■ **AppleSeeds:** "Please include a completed copy of the query form found on the back of this sheet."

■ **Babybug:** "Before attempting to write for *Babybug*, be sure to familiarize yourself with this age child."

■ **Children's Better Health Institute:** "Each manuscript is carefully considered for possible use in all magazines, not only the one to which it was originally addressed." Manuscripts are to be sent to a particular title, not to the whole group, as "this aids us in tracking your manuscript."

■ **Click:** "*Click* prefers a more informal, conversational style to a formal, textbook style. The best articles tackle one idea or concept in depth rather than several ideas superficially."

■ **Cobblestone:** "Historical accuracy and lively, original approaches to the subject are the primary concerns of the editors in choosing material."

■ **Columbus Parent:** "For pre-written articles, please include a query letter with your submission along with ideas on how you intend to incorporate a 'local angle.'"

■ **Connecticut's County Kids:** "Use bullets and subheads to separate thoughts, especially in feature articles."

■ **Creative Classroom:** "Be aware that we cannot print previously published material, articles or ideas."

Learning the goal of the publication and the audience it hopes to reach is the first, critical step toward knowing if the piece you are proposing or have written will be a match for a magazine.

Attention to Detail

Every publication's guidelines include the types of articles and other submissions it seeks, including genres and subjects. The Children's Better Health Institute (CBHI) magazines (*Turtle, Humpty Dumpty, Children's Playmate, Jack And Jill, Child Life, Children's Digest, U*S*Kids*) accept fiction and non-fiction, poems, recipes, and puzzles, all with a health-related message. Further

explanation comes with a listing of topics CBHI considers health-related, such as sports, safety, and nutrition. With this emphasis, CBHI guidelines even remind writers what foods should be avoided in recipes.

Cobblestone Publishing titles (*Cobblestone, Calliope, Faces, Odyssey, AppleSeeds, Footsteps*) include guidelines for each type of article the magazines accept: feature articles, supplemental nonfiction, fiction, activities, poetry, and puzzles and games. A variety of suggestions is given for each category; for example, fiction suggests "authentic historical and biographical fiction, adventure, retold legends . . .."

FamilyFun's ideas for features and

Something for Everyone

■ **FamilyFun:** "Since we receive many queries on the same topics, please be as specific as possible about what makes your idea unique and your qualifications to write it."

■ **Girls' Life:** "Every story should have a headline, by-line, introduction, lead, body and conclusion."

■ **Good Apple Newspaper:** "Sample illustrations are welcome if they lend themselves to the explanation of the ideas. However, please note that all illustrations for the publication will be done by freelance artists. Therefore, submitted illustrations are only for editorial purposes."

■ **Highlights for Children:** "Writers with extensive background in a particular field are encouraged to share their experiences and personal research."

■ **Hopscotch** and **Boys' Quest:** "We will entertain simultaneous submissions as long as that fact is noted on the manuscript."

■ **Ladybug, Cricket,** and **Cicada:** "An exact word count should be noted on each manuscript submitted. Word count includes every word, but does not include the title of the manuscript or the author's name."

■ **Muse:** "Please note that because of the unique mission of *Muse*, extensive rewrites are often necessary."

■ **Odyssey:** "The inclusion of primary research (interviews with scientists focusing on current research) are of primary interest to the magazine."

■ **Scientific American Explorations:** "Please say where in the magazine you feel your proposed article will fit best."

departments describe what is needed and the tone they seek. For example, the Family Almanac section, which includes activities and projects and is perhaps the most open to freelancers, is described as "direct and cheerful."

Highlights for Children's guidelines supply descriptions and needs for fiction, rebus stories, nonfiction, crafts, finger plays/action rhymes, party plans, and verse. A careful reading under *fiction* reveals that both stories for younger readers (3 to 7) and older readers (8 to 12) are accepted, but those for older readers have an extra criterion: They "should be appealing to younger readers if read aloud."

Sometimes knowing what was successful in previous issues helps. *American Girl* provides examples of past articles that might get a potential author thinking in the right direction.

Many magazines state their special or specific needs, which can be a big clue that they are not getting enough to meet those needs. *Pockets* continues "to need articles about real children involved in environmental efforts, peacemaking, and helping others." The guidelines also specifically state the need for games and activities for ages five to seven. *Highlights* declares

Sources for Guidelines

<u>Books</u>

■ **The American Directory of Writer's Guidelines: A Compilation of Information for Freelancers from More Than 1,500 Magazine Editors and Book Publishers,** 3rd edition. Compiled and edited by John C. Mutchler (Quill Driver Books, 2001).

■ **Children's Writer's & Illustrator's Market.** (Writer's Digest Books, annual).

■ **Christian Writers' Market Guide.** Sally E. Stuart (WaterBrook, 2001).

■ **The International Directory of Little Magazines & Small Presses.** Paradise, CA: Dustbooks, annual.

■ **Magazines for Libraries.** 10th edition. (Bowker, 2000).

■ **The Writer's Handbook.** (Writer, Inc., annual).

■ **The Writer's Market.** (Writer's Digest Books, annual).

<u>Websites</u>

■ **Writer's Digest:** www.writersdigest.com/guidelines.

A drop-down menu includes Children's under Books and Child Care, Parental Guidance, Juvenile, and Teen & Young Adult under the broad category of Consumer Magazines.

■ **Writers Guidelines Database:** mav.net/guidelines/index.html

From the drop-down menu under Publications, choose Children's or Family & Parenting.

■ **Writers Write:** www.writerswrite.com/guidelines

Enter a keyword, such as children or parenting, to find magazines. You can specify paying or nonpaying, fiction or nonfiction or poetry.

its "frequent needs" of humor, mystery, sports, adventure, traditional tales, urban settings, and world cultures. CBHI wants more holiday stories, articles, and activities.

Some magazine guidelines indicate when to send in seasonal material. CBHI wants to see it "at least eight months in advance." *American Girl* recommends at least six months. *Highlights* takes seasonal material at any time of the year.

Writers do well to note the types of articles or subjects they should *not* sub-

mit. *Girls' Life* "does not accept unpublished fiction or poetry from adults." *Highlights*: "Suggestions of crime and violence are taboo" and "rhyming stories are seldom purchased." *Cobblestone* and *Calliope* guidelines specifically state "no word finds," although authors may send in other types of word puzzles, mazes, or picture puzzles. *Scientific American Explorations* is a parents' magazine, and therefore does not accept articles written for children. The same goes for *Creative Classroom*, which targets teachers, not students.

Amounts

Almost all guidelines indicate the desired lengths for submissions. The Cobblestone Publishing magazines provide a word count for each of their types of articles; some are a range, such as 300-to-600 words for supplemental nonfiction or up to 700 words for activities. A word count for stories and articles and a line count for poems are specified by Cricket magazines, except for *Babybug*, which gives a sentence or line count for their very simple stories.

Hopscotch and *Boys' Quest* state that the "ideal length" of a piece is 500 words. *Hopscotch* does go on to assure writers that longer pieces will be considered. *Surprises* gives a range of 200-to-350 words and makes clear that one to three activities should also be included with the article.

Payment information is generally, though not always, included in the guidelines. *Ladybug* pays up to 25¢ a word for stories and articles and up to $3 a line for poems, with a $25 minimum for each. *Highlights* pays $100 and up for fiction and nonfiction, and $25 and up for crafts, finger plays, and verse. *AppleSeeds* pays $50 per page, with 100-to-150 words figured per page. Other publications, such as *Creative Classroom,* state that "payment will be negotiated prior to publication."

The types of rights purchased may be indicated. *Boys' Quest* and *Hopscotch* buy first American serial rights. *Highlights* and CBHI buy all rights. The Cricket Group purchases various rights, depending on the magazine and a piece's publishing history.

Sending and Receiving

The surest way to please an editor from the very beginning is to follow the preferences for submission format exactly. In some ways, these are the heart of guidelines. Whatever your topic, your tone—and they are critically important—editors can be peevish if they get manuscripts when their work procedures only accommodate queries, when they get a disk, but they only review hard copy or prefer e-mail.

Meg Chorlian, Editor of *Cobblestone*, says, "A good query shows that the author has taken the time to follow our procedures, and that always makes the editor's job easier."

Guidelines almost invariably give specific instructions about submission form. All provide a mailing address; some provide e-mail addresses, although *Boys' Life* states "e-mail queries will not be read." Other publications, such as *Yes Mag,* welcome e-mail. If submissions are accepted on disk or in specific word processing formats, those are noted.

The eternal question for freelancers is "query or manuscript?" It does matter. *Highlights*, the Cricket Magazine Group (except *Muse*), and CBHI magazines want to see manuscripts. *Boys' Quest* and *Hopscotch* prefer manuscripts, although "we do not rule out query letters." *American Girl* wants to "receive ideas in query form rather than finished manuscripts." *Scientific American Explorations* prefers "queries, rather than completed articles. That way we can work with potential authors to develop articles that best fit our needs." *FamilyFun, Girls' Life,* and *Yes Mag* also want queries. *Yes Mag* even contains helpful hints in the guidelines asking leading questions that the query should answer about the lead or *hook,* the focus, and the approach for the article. *FamilyFun* won't accept manuscripts at all for features. Cobblestone Publishing magazines require queries.

The form of the query or manuscript is important, and clues to what the editors want can be found in some guidelines. The *Good Apple Newspaper,* which publishes teaching units and activities, reminds writers to include their name and address "on the manuscript itself and not just on the cover letter" and to include the grade level of the activity. Atypically, they also accept a handwritten manuscript, "if it is not possible for the ideas to be typed."

Hopscotch and *Boys' Quest* include the reminder to send an SASE with sufficient postage, while *Babybug* and *Ladybug* bluntly state. "Submissions without an SASE will be discarded." CBHI gives instructions on spacing, what must appear on the first page of the manuscript, and adds "Title pages are not necessary." At *Girls' Life,* a manuscript must arrive with "a complete list of sources, telephone numbers, and reference materials." Cobblestone Publishing magazines give a complete how-to for submitting a query, including contents of the cover letter, an outline, bibliography, and writing sample for those new to the magazine.

Some publications adhere to style manuals, listed in the guidelines. *Multicultural Review* prefers *The Chicago Manual of Style* and *Webster's Ninth New Collegiate Dictionary,* but will ac-

cept other standard sources. *Girls' Life* uses *The Associated Press Stylebook and Libel Manual,* while *Boys' Life* follows *Manual of Style and Usage* of the *New York Times.*

Some magazines note their response times in the guidelines. Cobblestone assures writers that "queries sent well in advance of deadline may not be answered for several months" and positive responses "are usually sent five months prior to publication date." *Girls' Life* states a 90-day turnaround time, although the manuscript may be "placed in a file for possible future consideration." *Babybug* and *Ladybug* recommend allowing six to eight weeks for a response to a manuscript; *Spider, Cricket,* and *Cicada,* 12 weeks; *Click,* 3 to 4 months; and *Muse,* 16 weeks. *American Girl's* response time is 12 weeks. *FamilyFun* takes four to eight weeks. *Multicultural Review* asks that you allow four to six weeks, while *The Horn Book Magazine* requires four months.

A Theme

Some magazine issues are based on themes, and either every article or most of the articles in that issue must relate to it. Theme lists, like guidelines, are available by mail or at websites.

Cobblestone Publishing magazines require that all articles relate to a designated topic. Their theme lists state the subject, issue date, and query deadline date. *Yes Mag* has a theme section, but also has departments that are not theme related. *Pockets* lists themes, issue dates, and due dates, and the guidelines expound on each theme with questions and statements to encourage ideas. *Hopscotch* and *Boys' Quest* list their open themes several years in advance. They also welcome articles that do not follow the theme list, as "we may consider it for a future issue."

Regional parenting publications often work with monthly themes. Request an editorial calendar or check to see if they are provided on the publication's website.

Even Better Than Guidelines

Of course, reading the guidelines while examining the actual magazine is the best way to get an idea of how your writing will fit in.

Krista West, Assistant Editor of *Scientific American Explorations*, says, "There's nothing more valuable than getting story ideas from a writer who has obviously taken the time to peruse our back issues and really understand *Explorations'* mission. We are very interested in serving the needs of concerned, educated parents who want to get their kids pumped on science. This may not come through in the writers' guidelines, but it does become apparent in the magazine, and we need writers who understand that mission."

CBHI guidelines suggest that looking at current issues "will acquaint writers with each title's 'personality,' various departments, and regular features." At *Creative Classroom*, "we highly suggest that you familiarize yourself with *Creative Classroom's* general writing style, tone, and topics by reading some of our previous articles." The editors of the *Horn Book* want authors to "have a solid familiarity with the *Horn Book* before submitting manuscripts."

Writers can and should order sample copies; guidelines generally include instructions for mail purchase. *Good Apple* provides an 800 number for requesting copies. Several publications note that some content of the publications is available on their websites, but order samples for a broader, deeper view.

Origins

Guidelines don't, like Athena, spring fully formed from the head of each publication. Magazines take various paths to pull them together. Donna Borst, Editor of *Good Apple* (and also *Schooldays, Oasis, Lollipops,* and *Holidays & Seasonal Celebrations*), says, "I, as the editor, write the guidelines."

At *Scientific American Explorations*, West says, "Our writers' guidelines are written by the editorial staff at the magazine. One person writes a draft and it is passed around for changes/comments. The final product ends up being a group effort."

Guidelines seem to be fairly stable, with updating taking place only if changes are made at the publication, and not for the ebb and flow of current needs. Chorlian of *Cobblestone* observes, "When we began receiving quite a few queries or articles on disk, we incorporated that into our guidelines."

Writers save wasted time and effort when they give guidelines the proper attention. Editors endlessly report receiving material that a careful reading of the guidelines could have avoided. Borst says, "The basis for our guidelines is that I want people to understand that we do not publish informational articles. Our units, activities, etc., must

Guidelines on the Web

While writers can always use the time-honored tradition of writing to an editor with an SASE for guidelines, increasing numbers of publishers are placing writers' guidelines on their websites. Because the sites are usually designed to attract subscribers, tracking down the guidelines can be a hunt. Here are a few, with directions:

■ **American Girl:** www.americangirl.com
    Click on About Pleasant Company, then the starred Writer Guidelines. At this point, you have a choice: Click on either Books or Magazines.
■ **Boys' Life:** www.scouting.org/mags/boyslife
    Click on Contact Us, then Read the *Boys' Life* writers' guidelines.
■ **Children's Better Health Institute:** www.cbhi.org
    This one makes it easy. For *Turtle, Humpty Dumpty, Children's Playmate, Jack And Jill, Child Life, Children's Digest, U*S*Kids*, click on Submit Work.
■ **Cobblestone Publishing:** www.cobblestonepub.com
    Click on Magazines for *Cobblestone, Calliope, Faces, Odyssey, Footsteps, AppleSeeds*. Select the title you wish to see and click on Tell Me More!, then Writers' Guidelines.
■ **Cricket Magazine Group:** www.cricketmag.com
    From the home page, click on Submission Guidelines for *Babybug, Ladybug, Spider, Cricket, Cicada, Click, Muse*.
■ **FamilyFun:** www.familyfun.com
    Click on About Us, then Writer's Guidelines.

have some sort of teacher or student activity to accompany them. Many times I get material that is more like a report than a unit."

"While we are clear on what we expect in a query, we still get incomplete queries," says Chorlian. "We feel that if the guidelines are read carefully, most mistakes will be avoided in the query process."

Explaining some of the details of a magazine's audience, content, and preferred submissions style, writers' guidelines are a link to the editor. Guidelines are there to guide you to publishing success. Use them to succeed!

Guidelines on the Web

■ **Girls' Life:** www.girlslife.com

Click on Contact Us. Then scroll down to the Freelance Writing box. Select Writers' Guidelines.

■ **Guideposts for Kids:** www.gp4k.com

Go to Parents' Place. Click on GP4K Writers' Guidelines to have them e-mailed.

■ **Highlights for Children:** www.highlightsforchildren.com

Click on the starred Parents Click Here!, then on About Us, then Contributor Guidelines.

■ **The Horn Book:** www.hbook.com

From the home page, click on Magazine, then Submissions Guidelines, then How to Send Article Submissions to *The Horn Book Magazine*.

■ **MultiCultural Review:** www.mcreview.com

From the home page, click on Authors' Guidelines.

■ **Parenting Publications of America:** www.parentingpublications.org/parent

Click on search our current member list, then on the button Find All Publications. From the over 150 titles, click on the one you want, then on the web link. Each is different from there.

■ **Yes Mag:** www.yesmag.bc.ca

From the home page, click on Writers' Guidelines.

Working All the Article Angles

By Vicki Hambleton

At some point, we all hear from our own mouths or from fellow writers the comment, "I love what I do, but I'll never get rich writing for children!" Well, *some* children's writers get rich, but plenty of others could be making more than they do, if they only started working all the angles. If you're interested in making a good living from writing, it requires seeing all the possibilities your writing can afford you, like turning a $50 article into something worth several times that amount.

Selling an article or an idea more than once fattens your wallet, but even more important, it widens the circle of editors who may be interested in future work from you. Many writers never think about recycling work, but the ones who do often have tricks of the trade they're willing to share: how they take one idea and recast it for different markets, resell an existing article to a variety of noncompetitive markets, make the most of reprints. Some of the writers interviewed here work full-time at their writing, while others have other careers and write in their spare time.

Same Article, Multiple Markets

Writer Susan Taylor Brown tells the story of how a single article became almost a cottage industry. Her secret: reprint rights. Brown, who holds down a 40-hours-a-week job as an engineering coordinator, in addition to writing and teaching, has sold the reprint rights to a single article about 150 times. "I'll probably average $50 a sale, and from that one piece, I've made about $7,500. Mind you, that is over a four-to-five-year period, but I wrote the piece once and there was no reworking at all. I sold it as is, as a reprint."

Many publications buy reprint rights, especially regional parenting magazines. "The first parenting article I wrote," says Brown, "has been reprinted more than one hundred times." Selling reprint rights is no problem if you have originally sold only one-time rights. But what about if you have sold all rights? Even then, you are not totally out of luck.

Author Karen O'Connor says she has sometimes asked for rights to be returned. "I had a stellar opportunity to do just this with *Reader's Digest*. However, this publication buys all

rights so I wasn't sure what to expect," explains O'Connor. "I had sold *Reader's Digest* an article in 1987 on a topic that I consider to be evergreen. I had used the piece as a tearsheet to send to editors and a couple of them asked about using the article. I called *Reader's Digest* and because the piece was so old, the company returned all rights to me." O'Connor cautions writers to make sure you get that permission in writing from an editor, and keep the correspondence in your files.

O'Connor encourages writers to ask questions. She recalls one editor, speaking at a writers' conference, who said to his audience, "I can't make a go of publishing if you don't write. I am no different than you are. I have kids, I pay a mortgage, and I take out the garbage. The point is, I need you to come to me with ideas. I'll let you know if the ideas work for me or not."

"There is a reticence," says O'Connor, "on the part of some writers to contact editors, a feeling that you can't disturb them. But publishing changes and editors change. Don't be afraid to take a chance."

If the idea of selling reprint rights is new to you, Brown suggests making a list of editors who might be interested in a particular article. "I periodically send out a letter to editors letting them know what articles I have available for reprinting. They may or may not be interested, but that letter usually gets me on their list for writers to contact when they are looking for material."

O'Connor suggests contacting editors even if you are not sure whether or not they buy reprints. "I got this idea from a fellow writer: Send an introductory e-mail to editors that includes a numbered list of article titles and a one- or two-sentence summary of each piece. Then I add a line asking editors who are interested to e-mail the *numbers* of the articles that interest them. Then I send the complete pieces." Brown goes one step further

Reeling in Your Angles

Gordon Burgett is the author of numerous books on the business of reselling your writing. His titles include *Sell and Resell Your Magazine Articles* and *How to Sell 75% of Your Travel Writing*. His next book will be *How to Sell 75% of Your Freelance Writing, Then Sell It Again and Again*.

Most writers don't know that they can sell an idea or even the exact same piece time and again, and if they've heard about the concept, they simply don't know how to do it. It all starts with the initial planning and querying. Newcomers wear blinders and want to sell one very narrow subject to one editor, then start again. That's exhausting. Think wide at the outset and gather for several pieces at once, then resell every one of them, if you can, again and again.

The best way is to approach each article as if the topic could be divided into several segments, or parts of a circle. If you are doing a piece for kids about, say, "Your First Trip to Yosemite," gather information, experiences, and interviews for many articles at once:

- The trip itself.
- Having fun in the car getting there and driving home.
- Specific parts of the site: trails, stable, famous old hotel, bears.
- Special things for kids to do at Yosemite.
- How to use your camera at Yosemite.
- What to avoid: poisonous snakes, oak, ivy, cliff edges, bears, etc.
- Visiting during the four seasons (one article each).

Each of these becomes a separate query. Editor responses to the queries will tell you where to focus your attention in writing the article. The best part is that information gathered for one article can be used in every other article, as long as the overall slant, structure, and the lead of each is clearly different.

Then take every one of those first-rights articles and sell the second or reprint rights to any other editor who will buy it, since second and reprint rights are nonexclusive.

First rights are more common than all rights, but if a publication buys all rights, your rewrite for another market must be significantly different—all but unrecognizable. Rewrite the piece from a distinctly new angle or slant it to sell to a special audience, then sell the reprints from that secondary sale. Try to achieve an average of three reprints for every original, but you'll still run into the odd piece that only one editor finds sufficiently worthy!

by posting her list on her own website and sending editors to it.

One Idea, Many Articles

Reprints are certainly the easiest way to get extra mileage out of your writing, but not the only way. Many writers take a subject and refocus the topic to meet the needs of different audiences. The essentials of the piece remain the same, but the angle changes.

"I've found I can take my core message in a given piece and present it for different audiences," says O'Connor. She cites an article called "What Do Teenagers Need (and Want) from Their Parents?" The answer was comfort, connection, and consistency. As she thought about it, O'Connor realized the same principles applied to her relationship with her aging mother. She retooled the piece and named it "What Do Our Parents Really Want (and Need) from Us?" She took it one step further and applied the same ideas to the office: "What Do Our Co-Workers Really Need and Want from Us?"

"I sold those pieces very quickly," O'Connor says. "It was a great way to take a very solid idea and turn it into several articles." This technique works particularly well with how-to articles, she says, and O'Connor finds that how-to's usually sell very well.

From Magazine to Book & Back

Book projects can spawn articles as well. Brown recently published a picture book, *Can I Pray With My Eyes Open?* "I wanted to figure out a way to promote the book," she says, "so I came up with the idea of doing a tearsheet I called 'Ten Things Your Child Should Know About Prayer,' and sent it out as a press release. Then I thought to myself, wait a minute, this is an article!"

Brown turned the tips into a piece that she sold, and resold, to parenting publications. She then repositioned the piece to sell in the adult market, calling it "Ten Things You Should Know About Prayer." Next, she applied the idea to friends, coming up with "Ten Tips for Making Friends," which sold to parenting and children's magazines, each about 20 times over.

O'Connor followed the same route, but in reverse, by turning articles into books. "I wrote an article for a young adult magazine on working with horses, a roundup of careers in the equestrian industry. Then I reworked the topic and sold it to a children's magazine. It occurred to me that each of the sections of the article could be expanded into a chapter of a book."

She did more research and the resulting book, *Working With Horses: A Roundup of Careers*, won her the National Press Woman's Award. Along the way, O'Connor interviewed a young woman who, at the time, was one of a very few female farriers. This became the source for an article for a magazine doing a series on careers for girls.

The Angle of Pitch

While it's all very well to take a piece and reshape it to meet the needs of different audiences, some writers would call the technique the equivalent of putting the cart before the horse. They prefer to do their research up front, considering possible angles before an article is ever written.

"When I am going to do an interview," says author Sandy Fox, "I usually like to think about the angles, first. That way, my research is most effective."

Fox recalls a trip to an elephant sanctuary run by a man who takes in the animals when they are not wanted. "I was originally assigned an article on elephants in North America," says Fox, "but in my research I discovered that this man also trains people from all over the world to work with elephants. That became my second article—a piece for teens on how to become an elephant caretaker. I thought an article on how domestic elephants can help cure diseases in wild elephants would appeal to *Ranger Rick*." Another angle she considered was one that would meet the needs of Boy Scouts earning merit badges, which she would market to *Boys' Life*.

It helps, explains Fox, to study different magazines to get a sense of the approach that will interest their readers. "If a magazine is all about fun, then pitch them a fun story, not something serious about the plight of elephants in the wild. If you are pitching a religious publication, you might figure a way to do a story about how God works in nature."

As you look at different markets, don't forget that you can often pitch the same piece to religious and secular magazines. "I sold an article to a fraternal organization magazine about how to study less but learn more," says O'Connor. "I also thought it might work for some of the small Christian publications for children. If I were writing for a spiritual magazine,

I might have a scripture addition with some reference to God's plan for our life, so that the piece would appeal to families who are churchgoers."

Like Fox, writer Kelly Milner Halls is a strong advocate of doing research first. "Any time you endeavor to interview an expert for a single article, do your homework first. Find out who this person is, where they come from. Read all you can about their work and personal life before you interview them. It betters your odds of discovering multiple angles."

Hall almost never resells an article. She finds it much easier and much more interesting to write a unique piece for each editor. "I interviewed a scientist working with the native peoples of the Amazon region of South America. I sold three articles based on that interview: one on how Amazon kids go to school; one on how rain forests help kids stay cool in a humid climate; and one that was a travel diary from the scientist's daughters about their first trip to the Amazon with Dad. I got three very different pieces, each with unique quotes and artwork, for three very different publications."

No matter how you do it, using your talent to take your work to the biggest audience is always rewarding. As Brown puts it, "Getting published isn't always about the money. Many times it's about self-esteem. It's a wonderful validation of your ability as a writer to see your name in print again and again."

Personally Speaking: Writing from Your Life

By Marnie Brooks

Ever experience something hilarious or hair-raising? How about heartbreaking or profound? Sure you have. Writing about it can generate income, bylines, and satisfaction.

Magazines for ages two to six don't often use personal experiences because the articles don't appeal to their young readers, but older juvenile markets—from beginning readers through the middle grades and into young adult markets—look for personal experience articles. They can take the form of essays, as-told-to interviews, profiles of adults or children, depictions of recent events. Personal experience can be turned into activities, career articles, travel and recreation pieces, humor, even history or science articles based on personal experience. The market is wide open—like a skydiver's parachute or a child's mind.

The Real Deal

It has been said that all writing is autobiographical, that every work depends in some measure on the writer's own experience. Personal experience pieces do that overtly, unlike fiction and other forms of nonfiction that ultimately disguise the writer to some degree. Much of the appeal of personal experience pieces is in the open connection between the writer—who is saying "this really happened to me" or "I did this"—and the reader who wants to empathize, experience the same, or learn from another's experiences. That's why personal experience lends itself to articles about growing up, whether into adolescence or adulthood.

Deborah Vetter, Executive Editor of *Cicada*, looks for personal experience with a coming-of-age feel. "The best way to see what works for us is to read some of our recently published pieces. In 'That Bright Land,' by Susan Yoder Ackerman (March/April 2000), the author details her experiences as a youth volunteer in Appalachia. Hans Sebald's 'My First American' (November/December 2001) relates his experiences as a teenager in Hitler's Germany."

Cicada is a literary magazine for teens, established in 1998 by the Carus Publishing Group, which also publishes *Babybug, Ladybug,* and *Click* for younger readers and *Spider, Cricket, Muse,* and *Cobblestone* for middle readers. *Cicada* works with experienced and new writers, Vetter says. "We are always willing to consider new authors. Photos are useful but not necessary. If I could offer some advice, it would be 'don't write down to your audience.' *Cicada* readers are sophisticated and can appreciate complexity and shades of gray. Write at an adult level and let the reader come away with something to think about."

"Realism, teen-friendliness, honesty, and a full-circle journey from story to strategies work well for us," says CollegeBound Network Editor in Chief Gina LaGuardia. The College-Bound Network includes *College Bound,* in print and electronic versions; *SUCCEED;* and various online sites and newsletters. Opportunities abound in the Network and can be investigated at www.collegebound.net. "We not only want articles that tell a story, but that also teach, and not in a condescending manner, but rather as an older sibling or friend speaking to a peer," says LaGuardia. "We want to hear advice from experts interspersed with the *real-deal* narrative. The challenge for the writer is how to supplement such information within the main body of the piece, or present it as an entertaining, educational sidebar."

Career-related experiences can provide interesting material for kids from elementary school to college. Curiosity is the nature of childhood. Even before adolescence, however, young audiences like to read about others' real experiences of all kinds.

For ages 6 to 12, *Hopscotch* and *Boys' Quest* want personal experience pieces on myriad subjects ranging from outer space to horses. "Personal experience or nonfiction with good supporting photos is a plus for us," says Editor Marilyn Edwards. "Basically, we are interested in anything that goes with our themes."

The magazines are open to experience pieces in a variety of forms, including profiles, interviews, or as-told-to stories. First-person accounts can be taken from a childhood experience of the author or an adult experience that stems from a career, hobby, or a subject of interest to kids—as long as it coincides with a theme. Both publications have theme lists available for issues as far in advance as 2005.

Edwards also cites articles that might help writers see what works for her and how these articles fit in with the theme format. "In the August 2001 issue of *Hopscotch,* which is about different kinds of schools, someone wrote about a young girl who visited a school in England. Another wrote about girls who go to school in China, and another wrote 'A Summer School for Skaters.' In all cases, the writer furnished good photo support."

For writers interested in *Boys' Quest,* Edwards recommends pieces in the August 2001 issue on flying. "An article called, 'Grandpa in Space' is about John Glenn's most recent flight into space. We also included an interview with a pilot of a special Air Force plane. Another author wrote a story about an experience she and her children had in flying on the blimp, the *Spirit of Akron.* Again, all had good photo support."

Hopscotch and *Boys' Quest* are new-writer friendly. "We publish material

Why & How

The reasons writers share their personal experiences are as numerous as the subjects they cover. For some it's catharsis for a trauma coupled with a desire to help another going through something similar. Others write about joys, memories, or accomplishments.

Series author Marcia Thornton Jones says, "I write about experiences and people that stand out for some reason. Most of my pieces center on my parents because I'm convinced I had the best. I also write about school and friendships to stay connected to experiences that define who I am."

Personal experiences are written in the first or third person, but Jones finds writing in the first person works best for her. "It seems the most natural and honest way. My first draft is a free-write exercise, with everything I can remember as fast as I can. I imagine I am that child again—seeing things unfold. After the first draft, I go back and look for places where I can explore more deeply including details of what it was like, and how I felt."

Author Jennifer E. Bowman often finds inspiration based on her life growing up biracial in a white family. "I am half-black, and was adopted into a white family. It seems to be en vogue to adopt across the races nowadays. It's a great thing, but I also think prospective adoptive families need to be careful that they understand what they're getting into, to make sure they approach the situation with the best interest of the children being adopted."

"I love essays—to read, and write," says author Linda Zapczynski. "I buy books of essays and books about essay writing. My family inspires me and I've found it's a relief to see that others have similar wishes, heartbreak, and weirdness. It's great to get paid for writing about something I love."

Zapczynski writes in both the first and third person. "It depends on the tone. A more serious essay may warrant first person, to get closer to the reader. I've found omniscient works great for humor, but I don't follow a format . . . I evolve constantly."

that fits our needs," says Edwards. "The writer may have written a few children's books or never have been published. We consider all material sent to us."

Edwards reports that their new magazine, *Fun for Kidz,* appears six times a year and is targeted equally at boys and girls 6 to 12. Themes will include helping others, pets, camping, and food fun. Articles should have activities such as puzzles, crafts, nature activities, recipes, or community service ideas.

"Our issue on recycling has all kinds of activities that relate to the subject," says Edwards. "Depending on the theme, we might be interested in articles about someone involved in an activity, if it includes ways the reader can also become involved. Photo support is important."

Fiction related to the theme could be accompanied by a sidebar to show how the reader can become involved in that same activity, suggests Edwards. "In the latest issue, we had fiction about a city boy and girl who visit their uncle in the country. The uncle takes them on a walk through the woods and the boy thinks this is going to be really boring. They look for animal tracks and both of the kids get into this. The story is followed by a detailed article on how to make plaster of Paris animal tracks from tracks in your backyard or the woods. This is *exactly* the type of thing that we would snatch up."

Do Something

Parenting, child care, and family magazines are fertile grounds for writers with activities and other articles based on personal experience. If you're a parent, grandparent, or have worked with children as a teacher or a volunteer, you may have an extra key to selling personal experience pieces.

Jennifer E. Bowman's first two personal experience pieces were for *American Baby.* "One was on pregnancy and the other was on newborns," she says. "The first was rejected a couple of times before the editor from *American Baby* expressed an interest. The second I wrote after querying the same editor with a follow-up idea."

Although national magazines like *American Baby, Child,* and *Parents* sometimes prefer to work with established writers, many welcome freelancers and new writers as well. A great way for newer writers to catch an editor's attention is with shorter pieces or anecdotes for a magazine's regular columns, such as *American Baby'*s Personal Experience and Crib Notes, and *Child'*s First Person and Lesson Learned. Bowman didn't let the rejections before *American Baby* daunt her. "The lesson I learned was that often it's not the writing that causes rejection, but that you've tried the wrong market, or had bad timing for a subject. I studied *American Baby* and it paid off."

Victoria J. Coe had a similar experience with *Parents.* "Although I had published a nonfiction book based on personal experience, the piece for *Parents* was my first personal experience article for a magazine. My query was rejected twice before *Parents.* I was familiar with the magazine's departments and targeted my article for As They Grow . . .. I followed their format for word length, style, sidebars, etc. *Parents* paid me well, then again for reprint rights when the article appeared in its Spanish edition."

Coe found that activities with her children led to contracts. "I enjoyed writing stories with my first child, so when my second was about four, I wrote with him. His stories were completely unlike his brother's at the same age, so I decided to investigate why. I contacted a preschool teacher at a university child development center and a psychology professor and asked for their insights. I soon realized I'd tapped into an interesting topic for an article. Additionally, I received 'free' expert advice about my own kids' development . . . one of the best perks of the experience."

Robin Hansen has had personal experience articles accepted in *FamilyFun*. "I'd written a book, *Sunny's Mittens*, about a girl learning to knit from her grandmother," in the third person, says Hansen. "I queried *FamilyFun* to run the book with its knitting patterns, but they wanted a first-person account. Since the book was a fiction flip on my teaching my daughter to knit, I just rewrote it."

Hansen made herself familiar with *FamilyFun*'s format. "It was exactly the kind of magazine I would have loved to have had when my kids were little," she says. "The ideas, tone, and stories were who we are as a family. I also did a piece on theme vacations

that they liked, so they asked me to write about our family's Native American theme trip to Arizona."

Besides parenting publications, Hansen has used her experiences for articles and projects for children's magazines including *Hopscotch, Cobblestone,* and *Highlights for Children.* "I love to write about doing things and learning with my kids. With children's magazines, I usually push a craft or similar project."

Close to Home
Another option is to submit to regional family publications that look for experience pieces from local writers familiar with topics specific to their readers.

Writer Linda Zapczynski, mother of three, found opportunities with the regional magazines *Family Times, Big Apple Parent,* and *MetroParent.* "The beauty of experience essays is that they concern anything and everything. I've written about the hilarity of kids, differences in religion, family estrangements, relationships and growth—like families, no topic is untouched."

Regional publications worked for Hansen too. "I've been a journalist for years and have written experience pieces for our local newspaper, *Yankee Magazine, Down East Magazine,* and others. Regionals are a great market and enjoyable to write for."

Writing for Peers

While the majority of writers for teens and children are adults, there are also openings for aspiring young writers of personal experience pieces.

Free Spirit Publishing, specializing in nonfiction for children and teens, parents, educators and counselors, publishes materials to help young people and to promote self-esteem.

"We do invite people, especially teens, to submit stories for books about specific issues," says Nancy Robinson, Communications Director at Free Spirit. "For example, we recently put out a call for teen comments and experiences about the use of labels (*jocks, preps, goths, abercrombie zombies,* etc.) for a book to be published this year called *More Than a Label: Why What You Wear and Who You're With Doesn't Define Who You Are,* written by teen author Aisha Muharrar. The best way to find out about such calls is to check the Free Spirit website at www.freespirit.com."

Gina LaGuardia, CollegeBound Network Editor in Chief, encourages high school and college students to submit articles. "What we find most captivates our readers—ambitious and intelligent college-bound high school juniors and seniors—are real life stories that convey unique, yet relatable tales of teen trials and triumphs."

She cautions against tired or passé subjects. "Like our readers, we are so 'over' sagas such as 'I got hazed' or 'I had the roommate from hell' or 'I left my small town home for big city college life.' Instead, we search for specific, yet adaptable stories of student struggle and success: 'How I coped with missing my mom' or 'My grades spun out of control.'"

Newspapers are also excellent targets for selling personal experience pieces. Along with bylines and money, they offer rewards of file clips and speedy publication, but many writers overlook them. While living in Saudi Arabia, writer Lisa Greenberg spun her personal experience pieces into a five-year stint writing a weekly parenting column for *The Riyadh Daily.* "I had already established my credentials with feature articles on local culture and knew the newspaper wanted to start a home and family section, so I proposed the column."

Formats for personal experience writing can be flexible; articles don't have to use the first person. Greenberg used the third person jazzed up with personal stories from her own family. "I'd often begin with a we've-all-been-there incident, add research from education, psychology, or child development, and end with an upbeat suggestion for practical use."

Author/illustrator Ann Fearrington found a niche for her experiences in the *Raleigh News & Observer.* Her first article appeared in the travel section as an interview of her kids and their friends on how to survive a week at the beach with their parents.

"That piece was tiny, only about four inches by six inches." The article was a hit and Fearrington parlayed its popularity into a column that blossomed into full-page articles. "When you're a new writer, you don't get to see much in print, you don't get much, if any money, and you get tons of no's," she says. In contrast, "I found newspaper work was an immediate gratification. I got published and paid quickly."

Fearrington learned lessons about writing as well. "My editor had autonomy. I turned the article in and only saw the edited version in print. I watched what she did and gave her what she needed. She loved it. Newspaper and magazine editors work under constant pressure. If you can write what they want, in their eyes, you're golden."

Illustration skills added to Fearrington's saleability, but even writers without artistic talent can provide visuals. "Most writers are not artists and editors are happy with photographs," she says. "If you go out with your Brownie 101, take pictures and submit them with the article, it can make a difference. We're a visual generation. Not only do readers want pictures, but editors are enticed by them too."

Booking It

Another publishing vehicle for personal experience articles can be found in essay collections and the anthology series that have exploded since the success of the *Chicken Soup for the Soul* books.

Rebecca Kraft Rector, author of *Tria and the Great Star Rescue,* had her first personal experience piece appear in *Money: Save it, Manage it, Spend It,* by Mary Bowman-Kruhm. The book, part of Enslow Publishers' Teen Issue Series, is about how people handle their money. "I wrote about something I did after I started my first real job," Rector says. "I took money from my retirement account and bought a horse. I wanted to share my experience and offer kids an alternative view to the idea that you should always save your money for the future. I showed how having a horse has enriched my life."

Naturally Curious

Magazines targeted at kids interested in the natural world and the environment need good experience pieces that inform as well as entertain their readers. *North Carolina WILD Notebook* is the young reader's section in *Wildlife in North Carolina Magazine,* published by the North Carolina Wildlife Resources Commission. "The commission wanted to get kids interested in natural history while also providing materials that could be used by teachers and parents," says *Notebook* Editor Consie Powell. "What began as a simple environmental education newsletter in the 1980s evolved into a four-color magazine feature. Our articles have subjects from bears to bats and grasses to underwater habitats."

Powell notes that their best pieces come from an author's personal experiences with a particular flora or fauna. "Writers with a close connection to their subject can combine personal passion with the facts and research necessary for a good nonfiction piece. We work with one subject per issue and while our pieces are assigned, we are open to those who have experiences with the natural world."

Anne Marshall Runyon, natural science illustrator and nonfiction author, loves sharing her experiences with kids. "After researching for some habitat paintings, I realized how much there was to learn about grasses. I wrote a piece for the *Notebook*'s readers to give a quick and accurate look at some of our native species." She added a nature activity about grassy look-alikes.

Roger Powell, a zoology professor at North Carolina State University, has studied black bears for 20 years and used experiences with his child to write an article on black bear cubs for the *Notebook*. "My daughter Virginia has participated in my research in Pisgah National Forest for most of her life. The experience of handling bears with her help was my inspiration for 'Mountain Cub.'"

Funny Bones

Along with innate curiosity, kids are born with a sense of humor. They love anything that tickles their funny bones from creepy weird to wacky. Editors want humor too.

Vetter says *Cicada* likes humor, but only when it's interesting and relevant to teens. She suggests prospective writers read "The Possible Poisoning of Mrs. Downing," by Susan Yoder Ackerman, in the January/February 2001 *Cicada*. "It's a humorous reminiscence of the author's teenage experiences taking care of an aristocratic old lady."

Humorous pieces are a staple at *Hopscotch* and *Boys' Quest*. They want lively writing that is wholesome and unusual. "We are always looking for humor and often need items for Ticklers and Teasers," says Edwards.

Bowman's pieces for *American Baby* were *light*. "When I originally submitted the first piece about pregnancy, I included everything—the good, the bad, and the ugly. My editor asked me to revise, to be upbeat and positive. Since they prefer this style, I've repeated it with the subsequent articles I've written for them."

Humor works with parents as well. Zapczynski's first experience essay was on the "joys" of family ironing. "It was tongue-in-cheek about a taboo chore, avoided at all costs and usually mastered by one family member who is christened as *chief ironer*. I included the importance of a well-ironed shirt and, the master manipulation of the ironer by iron manufactuers and family members. I had fun!"

Beyond the Experience

Personal experience writing can also lead to lucrative projects such as book deals, features, and other forms that keep ideas going out and money coming in.

Hansen's pieces further her book publishing goals. "Sometimes responses to an article can pump a book—either boosting sales or encouraging a publisher to accept it." Her first book, *Fox & Geese & Fences* (Down East Books), was accepted and published only because *Down East Magazine* had received over 2,000 letters in response to her personal experience article for them on Maine mittens.

Greenberg serialized children's mysteries set in Saudi Arabia. They were collected, published in a book, and used as reading material in local schools. "I also wrote many traveling parents/family articles for hotel magazines and more than 30 features for airline magazines using our family's experiences as travelers in Europe and the Middle East."

Traveling with her kids launched Fearrington's idea for her second picture book, *Who Sees the Lighthouse?* (G.P. Putnam's Sons). "I'd always had my sights on books," she says, "but writing for the newspaper put my name out there and gave me experience."

Children's series author Marcia Thornton Jones (*Barkley's School for Dogs, The Adventures of the Bailey School Kids*) has also published personal experience and likes to focus on childhood events. The memoirs help with her fictional characters. "Many times something in one of my books reminds me of a childhood event. Writing about the memory helps me connect to the story and, hopefully, makes my characters more realistic."

Zapczynski feels any publication is encouraging and motivates work on new projects. "In my case, features for a regional parenting paper followed publication of some of my personal experience pieces."

Runyon now regularly creates and illustrates puzzles and nature activities for *WILD Notebook*'s youngest readers.

Life is rich with experiences. No one's life is ordinary or lacking in experiences to share. Understanding how to use yours can bring personal and financial rewards—and make you an expert in a field all your own.

Personal Experience Markets

Elementary and Middle-Grade
■ **Boys' Quest:** 103 North Main, P.O. Box 227, Bluffton, OH 45817. www.boysquest.com. Ages 6 to 13. Lively writing from a young boy's viewpoint to inspire boys to read.
■ **Chickadee:** 179 John Street, Suite 500, Toronto, Ontario M5T 3G5 Canada. www. owlkids.com. Ages 6 to 9. Real kids in true life; aim to entertain and interest kids in the world around them.
■ **Girls' Life:** 4517 Harford Road, Baltimore, MD 21214. www.girlslife.com. Ages 10-14. Essays, interviews and profiles; know the audience's voice.
■ **Hopscotch, The Magazine for Girls:** P.O. Box 164, Bluffton, OH 45817-0164. www.hopscotchmagazine.com. Ages 6 to 12. Basic subjects of interest to young girls.
■ **New Moon: The Magazine for Girls & Their Dreams:** P.O. Box 3620, Duluth, MN 55803-3620. www.newmoon.org. Edited and written by girls 8 to 14. Adult writers for Herstory and other columns.
■ **North Carolina WILD Notebook:** 5208 Olive Road, Raleigh, NC 27606. Ages 6 to 12. Personal experiences with flora and fauna.
■ **Owl Magazine:** 179 John Street, Suite 500, Toronto, Ontario M5T 3G5 Canada. www.owlkids.com. Ages 8 to 14. Science/nature/environment; kids in real situations.

Young Adult
■ **Cicada:** P.O. Box 300, Peru, IL 61354. www.cicadamag.com. Ages 13+; Coming-of-age; humor.
■ **Seventeen:** 850 Third Avenue, New York, NY 10022. www.seventeen.com. Ages 13 to 19. Study the personal essay column.
■ **Twist:** 270 Sylvan Avenue, Englewood Cliffs, NJ 07632. www.twistmagazine. com. Girls 14 to 19. Freelancers for Real Life column only: Spotlights a teen overcoming obstacles or challenges; recent stories covered anorexia, panic disorder, narcolepsy, drunk driving.
■ **YM:** 375 Lexington Avenue, 8th Floor, New York, NY 10017-5514. www. ym.com. Teen girls; dating, relationships, personal triumphs

College
■ **The Black Collegian:** 909 Poydras Street, New Orleans, LA 70112. www.black-collegian.com. African-American college/graduate students; careers/jobs.
■ **Campus Life:** 465 Gundersen Drive, Carol Stream, IL 60188. Ages 13 to 19. "Message" stories; break-in with first person/as-told-to. Christian slant.

Personal Experience Markets

■ **College Bound Magazine, SUCCEED Magazine:** 2017 Clove Road, Suite 206, Staten Island, NY 10304. www.collegeboundmag.com. Queries acceptable by e- or regular mail. E-queries: editorial@collegebound.net The CollegeBound Network includes:
  - *College Bound Magazine Online*: www.CollegeBoundMag.com
  - *CollegeSurfing*: www.CollegeSurfing.com
  - *Student Rewards*: www.StudentRewards.com
  - *Inside Edge*: www. insideedgenewsletter.com

■ **College Preview:** 3100 Broadway, Suite 600, Kansas City, MO 64110. Ages 16 to 21. Motivates Black and Hispanic youth toward college and careers.

■ **Equal Opportunity:** 1160 E. Jericho Turnpike, Suite 200, Huntington, NY 11743-5405. www.eop.com. For college juniors and seniors. Career guidance for multi-ethnic minorities.

■ **Journey:** 3100 Broadway, Suite 600, Kansas City, MO 64110. Ages 16 to 25. Educational and career source guide for Asian-American students.

Parenting/Childcare

■ **American Baby:** 249 West 17th Street, New York, NY 10011-5300. www.americanbaby.com. Monthly. Small number of new writers. Know the style and what's been published recently.

■ **At-Home-Mother:** 406 E. Buchanan Avenue, Fairfield, IA 52556-3810. www.athomemothers.com. Quarterly. Upbeat. Mostly freelance-written.

■ **Child:** 375 Lexington Avenue, New York, NY 10017-4024. www.childmagazine.com. Monthly. Check website for ideas.

■ **Family Digest, The Black Mom's Best Friend:** P.O. Box 3368, Danville, CA 94526. Quarterly. Targets issues for black moms and heads-of-home.

■ **FamilyFun:** 244 Main Street, Northampton, MA 01060-3107. www.familyfun.com. Appears 10 times a year. Published by Disney. See the Family Almanac, Family Ties, and My Great Idea columns.

■ **Parenting Magazine:** 4th floor, 530 Fifth Avenue, New York, NY 10036. www.parenting.com. Appears 10 times a year. Parents of ages birth to six. See the Family Reporter and Ages and Stages departments.

■ **Parents:** 375 Lexington Avenue, New York, NY 10017. www.parents.com. Monthly. Query. Stories appeal to a wide variety of parents.

■ **Twins:** 5350 S. Roslyn Street, Suite 400, Englewood, CO 80111-2125. www.twinsmagazine.com. Bimonthly. Covers parenting of multiples. Upbeat. See Growing Stages, On Being Parents, Special Miracles columns.

Personal Experience Markets

Regional Parenting/Family

■ **Big Apple Parent/Queens Parent:** 9 East 38th Street, 4th Floor, New York, NY 10016. www.parentsknow.com. Monthly. New York City family life. Keep up on current events.

■ **Chicago Parent:** 141 South Oak Park Avenue, Chicago, IL 60302. www.chicagoparent.com. Monthly tabloid. Personal essays must be compelling.

■ **Metro Parent Magazine:** 24567 Northwestern Hwy., Suite 150, Southfield, MI 48075. www.metroparent.com. Monthly. Issues of interest to Detroit-area parents.

■ **Northwest Family Magazine:** Suite B-1, 2275 Lake Whatcom Boulevard, Bellingham, WA 98225. www.nwfamily.com. Monthly items of interest in northwest and western Washington state.

■ **South Florida Parenting:** 5555 Nob Hill Road, Sunrise Hill, FL 33351. www. sfparenting.com. Monthly. Information and events for parents in southeast Florida.

■ **Tidewater Parent:** 5700 Thurston Avenue, Virginia Beach, VA 23455. www.tidewaterparent.com. Monthly tabloid. Conversational tone. Parents of ages birth to 11.

■ **Western New York Family:** P.O. Box 265, 287 Parkside Avenue, Buffalo, NY 14215-0265. www.westernnewyork.com. Monthly. Covers western New York state parents of ages birth to 12. Family-oriented events. Conversational style.

Business
& Career

The Writer & the IRS

By Veda Boyd Jones

An author parked her car in the elementary school's parking lot and opened her trunk. She unloaded a four-legged stool, a suitcase with wheels, two easels, and poster-sized blowups of her book covers. She had deducted all these items as writing expenses on her income tax form. Standing all day for school presentations took its toll, so she had invested in the stool. Sitting in a chair would have made her too low, but a stool allowed her to maintain a professional presence. Carrying her books and other props in tote bags became unwieldy. The pull-along suitcase solved that problem. Her publisher had not given her a promotional budget, so she took pictures of her covers and had them blown up for display on the easels.

This author was knowledgeable about tax laws, and you should be, too. Supplies and equipment for your writing business, whether for the putting-words-on-paper side or the publicity side, may be income tax deductions—if you keep solid records.

Maintaining a writing business isn't only typing at a keyboard and printing pages, speaking to groups, and signing books. Those are income producers, but many expenses must be subtracted before you know if there is a profit or a loss for your business. Solid records will show whether the ink on the bottom line is red or black, and that's important to you and the Internal Revenue Service (IRS).

Changing Tax Regulations

Instructions for Schedule C, Profit or Loss from Business, state: "An activity qualifies as a business if your primary purpose for engaging in the activity is for income or profit and you are involved in the activity with continuity and regularity. For example, a sporadic activity or a hobby does not qualify as a business."

One guideline the IRS uses to determine if your writing is a business or a hobby is that you must make a profit in three out of five consecutive years. If you have been writing for years without much success, the IRS may decide your writing is a hobby, and you may only deduct expenses to equal your income from selling your work. "The IRS has been successfully

Tracking Submissions & Income

Article: _"The Writer & the IRS"_

Date: September 2001

Submitted to: _Children's Writer Guide to 2002_

Postage: $1.35

Rejected by:

Accepted by: _Children's Writer Guide to 2002_

Fee: $XXX

Date paid: June 15, 2002

Article:

Date:

Submitted to:

Postage:

Rejected by:

Accepted by:

Fee:

Date paid:

challenged on the three-year rule, however, so you might want to consult a tax expert if you've been writing longer and haven't yet made a profit."

Tax laws change annually, and this article is not an official tax guide. It is the taxpayer's responsibility to keep up with the changes or hire someone who knows current tax laws to fill out those income tax forms. By the way, an accountant's fee is a tax deduction.

Solid Records

■ *Submissions record:* You don't need a fancy computer accounting program to keep track of income and expenses. A simple ledger book will do, and you should develop an individual system that works for you. On the income side, keep track of each submission: the date, where it was sent, and the cost of postage to send the manuscript and the self-addressed stamped envelope for the editor's decision. When the editor replies, record the acceptance or rejection. This submissions record will show the IRS that you are a serious writer.

■ *Receipts:* Keep a file for receipts, and keep them all, no matter if you think one is a deductible expense or not. It's much easier to throw out a receipt at tax time than conjure one up months after the expense was incurred. You may want to set up a monthly record sheet for each area of deductions: supplies, home office, telephone, equipment, etc. On this sheet, record the expenses as they occur. Or you can wait until the end of the year and make a day of sorting the receipts and adding up totals.

■ *Checking account:* Set up a separate checking account for your writing business. This will keep your personal life and your writing life separate and will be an additional record of income and expenses. If the check paid to you does not have an attached stub, make a copy of the check to put in an income file before you deposit it.

Deductions

With a creative business like writing, deductions can range from paper clips to airplane tickets. A survey of writers reveals an array of deductions they took and why the items qualified as deductions.

■ *Ideas sources:* Ideas come from everywhere around us: real life, TV, newspapers, magazines, radio, and books. Real life doesn't come with a deduction, but you may deduct the cost of newspapers, magazines, and books. One writer's accountant told her that a percentage of her cable television bill was deductible since programs provided ideas she had turned into published articles. Check with your own accountant on that one.

■ *Market research:* If you want to sell to a particular magazine, you must study it first to determine the editorial mix of the magazine and the type of articles and stories the editor prefers. This is one more reason for buying those magazines and deducting the costs. If you're marketing a nonfiction book, you need to know what books have already been published on your topic, and you may use those in your bibliography. You should also read books by your targeted fiction or nonfiction publisher to analyze the style the publisher likes. Again, keep all receipts. Even if you bought a magazine or book at the grocery store, keep that long tab and circle the cost of the publication for use at tax time.

■ *Topic research:* Often you can find books you need for research at your library. Public libraries are free to those who live in the library district, but if you use one out of your district, you may have to buy a library card. Universities often charge non-students a fee for using the library. The cost of the cards is deductible. If the library doesn't have the book you need, you can usually find it through interlibrary loan. If there is a fee for this service, file the receipt. If you keep the book too long and must pay a fine, make a note of it.

If you photocopy an article at the library, keep a record of how much it costs. If you must pay a per-page charge for printed material from special library computers, note the date and the amount of money you spent and put it in your expenses file.

There are occasions when you will need to watch a video as research. Write down the title of the video and the title of the article or book you're writing that requires that you rent the movie. The IRS would frown on a long list of deductions for films watched for pleasure.

■ *Travel:* The mileage of every writing-related trip in your car should be written down in a little notebook you keep in your vehicle. A trip to the library or museum for research, a trip to a bookstore, the post office, a writing class, a writers' meeting, a confer-ence—any writing-related trip should be recorded. You need exact mileage to multiply by the per/mile deduction set each year by the IRS. An alternative method is to keep track of actual expenses (oil, gas, repairs, etc.) but that means much more bookkeeping.

Transportation expenses, including airplane tickets, are fully deductible even if you mix a little pleasure on a business trip. If you fly to California for the SCBWI conference and stay an extra few days as a tourist, the airfare is covered, but the meals and lodging for your vacation days are not deductible. If a trip is primarily for pleasure with a little business mixed in, you may deduct only expenses directly attributed to your business.

Can you deduct that 10-day trip to England if you sell a magazine article on the history of Big Ben? Foreign trips have different regulations. As a general rule, you can calculate the percentage of time you spent on research and writing and deduct that percentage of the trip. Learn about foreign travel tax laws before planning your trip and you may qualify for more deductions.

Hotel accommodations while on a research trip, a speaking engagement (if not covered by the group you're speaking to), or a conference are deductible.

■ *Home Office:* The IRS has tightened requirements for a home office. If you have a room or area that is used "regularly" and "exclusively" as a writing office, you may deduct a percentage of home costs. If your home has 1,500 square feet and your office has 100 square feet, you may deduct one-fifteenth of the mortgage interest, utilities, real estate taxes, depreciation, and repairs. Similar deductions apply to renters.

You may convert an extra bedroom into a home office, but you can't leave the bed in there. That shows there is another use for that room, and an overnight guest sleeping in your office disqualifies this deduction.

■ *Equipment:* In the past, you could depreciate the cost of equipment such as a typewriter, computer, copier, camera, fax machine, office furniture, etc. Recent tax laws allow you to deduct the cost of equipment up to thousands of dollars a year (for example, $20,000). This number changes annually, but this way of deducting equipment means less record keeping than the depreciation route. Maintenance costs on your equipment are also deductible.

■ *Telephone:* Writing-related long-distance calls are tax deductible, but not your home phone's base rate. A

second phone line that is used for your writing business or your Internet connection is deductible. That Internet service is also a deduction. If family members use it half the time, then you'd better deduct only half.

■ *Office Supplies:* An office supply store is a candy store to writers. Paper, envelopes, disks, files, pens, rubber bands, even those little colored flags to use as bookmarks can be deducted if they are used in your writing business. Keep the receipt for a new software program or upgrade for your word processing program. The costs of printing stationery, envelopes, brochures, bookmarks, and stickers are also deductions. Just be careful not to get too carried away or your writing profit will be eaten up with fancy goods that really aren't necessary.

■ *Postage:* Keep the mailing/shipping receipts and maintain your ledger of submissions to show exactly how much it cost to mail your manuscripts. Postage for sending books to reviewers, paying your professional organization dues, sending published copies of articles to the people you interviewed for the article—mailing/shipping anything relating to your writing business is a deduction.

■ *Networking:* Part of the writing business is networking with other writers. Costs of writing conferences, writing courses to refresh your skills, and memberships in professional organizations are deductions. Fees for entering your manuscripts in writing contests are also deductible. Networking is an important part of writing. From other writers you can learn about markets, new editors, and writing techniques.

And of course, there are more magazines to deduct—those dealing with the profession, so you can keep on top of what's happening in the business. Don't neglect this networking area; just be sure to take the deductions.

■ *Meals:* When you are on the road speaking or researching or if you are networking with other writers, you can deduct a portion of the cost of your meals. Currently, that amount is one-half, but that is always subject to change. Instead of taking a percentage of the cost of the meal while traveling on business, you can opt for the standard daily allowance.

Your meal at a writing group that meets for lunch every Wednesday to swap markets would be an allowable expense. If you interview a person over lunch, you probably should pick up the tab and deduct both meals.

■ *Publicity:* An author may want to make sure kids leave a school talk with something in their hands if they can't buy the author's book. Bookmarks listing the author's books and signed by the author are the favorite giveaway, and the cost can be deducted. The cost of an author's books that are donated to libraries, charity auctions, and sent to reviewers is also deductible.

Need a professional photo for press releases or brochures? Hire a good photographer and deduct the cost. Of course, the postage for sending the press releases and the printing cost of brochures should be subtracted from your income.

■ *Consultants:* In a broad sense, a typist, book doctor, publicist, and photographer qualify as consultants, and their fees are deductible.

■ *Photographs:* If you are responsible for photos that accompany a writing project and you take the pictures yourself, film and film development are deductible expenses. If you buy stock photos from a supplier, that cost would also be a deduction.

■ *Miscellaneous Expenses:* If an expense pertains to your writing business, there's a way to deduct at least a portion of the cost. Stay on top of what are legitimate deductions by reading finance magazines, tax guides for the current year, and books on self-employment.

■ *Filing Those Forms:* Many writers pay their taxes quarterly. The amount is based on what they paid the year before plus or minus their projected earnings and deductions. Because there is no employer paying half the social security taxes for freelance writers, the burden of paying the entire social security tax rests on the writer. Allow for this when you are estimating your taxes.

Writing is an odd business. You start with nothing but an invisible idea and develop it into something tangible like a novel. But that's a romantic notion of writing. Even in the old days before income taxes, it took a pencil and paper to create a manuscript, and those old tools of the trade are tax deductible today—if you keep solid records.

We Hereby *Grant* You . . . Money

By Sandy Stiefer

Most writers have a hard time asking for money. It's bad enough trying to collect on unpaid contracted or published manuscripts; searching for other funds may never even come to some authors', or potential authors', minds. But money earmarked for writers is out there just waiting to be requested, from organizations whose sole purpose is to give out money. You have only to find them and apply for a grant.

A grant is, in a way, free money. You don't have to pay it back, but it may require certain commitments, such as matching the funds the grantor (or funder) gives you, detailed financial reports on how money was spent, and reporting on the results of the project that was funded. Some grant applications are very involved, requiring a huge amount of detailed paperwork describing the project, who will benefit, and how each dollar will be spent.

Grants to individuals are usually less than $2,000 and allow you to spend the money without any follow-up. Other grants go to organizations or projects, but involve commission-

ing writers. A high percentage of these organizations with full coffers just waiting to be tapped are foundations, small or large. Others are government agencies and still others, nonprofits and corporations.

When I lived in LaCrosse, Wisconsin, the LaCrosse Community Foundation was a local funder for community projects. I was a member of the Friends of the Library and we needed additional hours from our part-time librarian. The library did not have enough money in the budget, so I wrote a grant application to the foundation for funds. The foundation's mission was betterment of the community; funding the librarian certainly met the specifications.

"Foundations exist purely to raise, manage, and give away money for good causes," says Hope Clark in her e-book, *Funds for Writers: The Book*. Clark is a freelance writer who edits three funding newsletters. Foundations "range from local small foundations to the state-focused, the regionally-based, and the nationally broad." By day, Clark works in a federal lending agency that assists public entities and nonprofits find

What Is a Fellowship?

Hope Clark's definition of *fellowship* is *a grant for advancement of career.* She writes in her e-book, *Funds for Writers: The Book,* "Fellowships can come in the simple form of registration for a writers' conference to full expenses paid including monthly stipend to study in Europe or at a major university. They usually have a theme, mission, or purpose."

In 2000, the National Endowment for the Arts provided fellowships worth $20,000 each to 41 American fiction writers, creative nonfiction writers, and translators.

A look at the fellowship announcements of the Writer's Colony at Dairy Hollow in Eureka Springs, Arkansas, illuminates who receives fellowships and what the fellowships can do for writers. Leigh Buchanan Bienen from Evanston, Illinois, is a lawyer and teacher of law. She has published law-related articles in scholarly journals and has published a book of short fiction. The residency will allow her time off from her day job(s) to work on a fiction project. Brenda K. Lewis of Ravenwood, Missouri, has extensive experience in nonfiction, journalism, and professional newsletters. While at the colony she will work on her first novel.

Clark notes in *Funds for Writers,* "Fellowships are quite generous if you are free enough to take advantage of the opportunities they present. The learning experiences obtained through these gifts can be the catalyst you need to reach your goals. Open your mind and see if you can make a fellowship work into your writing goals."

funds. *Funds for Writers: The Book* and her website (www.fundsforwriters) help writers find grants, fellowships, and awards.

What Grants Do for a Career

Grants are given for works-in-progress or projected works. Earning one is not unlike achieving a "please send sample chapters" letter from an editor, except a grant puts money in the bank upfront. *Awards,* often accompanied by money, are given for completed works on merit and often for addressing a particular subject, region, or audience—multicultural stories, a book on the Southwest, early reader literacy.

Government agencies give grants to individuals and organizations. Grants to schools, for example, can benefit writers. Corporate grants are made mostly to local communities, promoting the corporation's reputation in their home base, but community projects may need writers. Many foundations are funded by corporations, such as the Kellogg Foundation, the Ford Foundation, and the Sprint Foundation. The Sprint Foundation's major areas of interest include education, community improvement, youth development, and the arts and culture—

all with possibilities for writing jobs in the organizations that receive the foundation's grants. For example, funding may go to a nonprofit cultural arts center, which then hires an author to teach writing or illustrating classes or a poet to give readings.

Nonprofit groups give grants to each other, to other organizations, but not often to individuals. Writers benefit because the nonprofit organizations hire writers for grant writing itself and for a variety of writing projects.

While the first way a grant helps is by putting cash in your bank account, at $2,000 or less they won't give you the financial freedom to quit or take a leave from your day job to stay home and write. They can allow you to travel to do research, or pay for writing classes, a conference, or other expenses.

These smaller grants are achievable for many, but some writers dream of the golden ring—a *fellowship* that can establish or advance your writing career. A National Endowment for the Arts (NEA) fellowship will fund a literature experience worth $20,000 by allowing you to take extended travel time for research, return to school for a graduate degree in writing, go to a writer's colony for an extended stay, or to just stay home and write that ground-breaking novel. A fellowship can also put you on the map. An NEA award is prestigious; publishers and editors can't help but notice that you were considered worthy of this highly competitive award.

As a federal agency, the NEA's mission is to encourage American creativity and excellence in art. Since 1967, it has awarded more than $35 million to 2,378 writers, and sponsored work resulting in more than 2,200 books that have included *The Color Purple,* by Alice Walker, William Kennedy's *Ironweed,* and *A Map of the World,* by Jane Hamilton. According to the NEA, more than 70 percent of the recipients of the Pulitzer Prize, the National Book Critics Circle Award, and the National Book Award in Poetry and Fiction during the 1990s had been Arts Endowment Fellowship winners, often 10 to 20 years before they won the major national award.

At the University of Wisconsin, the Institute for Creative Writing Fellowships offers a stipend of $22,000 and an academic year in residence at the Institute. The Vermont Studio Center offers month-long residencies valued at $3,000 each. Many universities and colleges with creative writing programs offer fellowships—begin by searching in your own state.

Where They Are

The NEA offers the top prize for writers. With the competition so fierce, excellence in literature is definitely needed. But what about writers who aren't quite to that point? Where is the middle ground and how can they still get money to help their careers?

Since most publishing emphasizes commercial success rather than literary merit, many fine stories languish for lack of a publisher. Writers whose goal is artistic excellence rather than best-seller lists should keep their day jobs. *Literary* writers may find publication with small or university presses or journals, which usually do not have the budgets for

Grant Information Sources

Websites
- **Donors Forum of Chicago:** www.donorsforum.org
- **The Foundation Center:** www.fdn.org
- **Funds For Writers:** www.fundsforwriters.com
- **Library Spot:** www.libraryspot.com/features/grantsfeature.htm
- **National Endowment for the Arts:** http://arts.endow.gov
- **National Endowment for the Humanities:** http://humanities.endow.gov
- **Society of Children's Book Writers and Illustrators (SCBWI):** www.scbwi.org
- Also search for a website for your own state's arts and humanities council.

Books

Directories to grants tend to be big, expensive books; find them in the reference section of libraries. More reasonably sized and priced books are available, however, to give you information on grant opportunities and processes.

- *The Foundation Directory,* 23rd edition. (Foundation Center, April 2001).
- *The Foundation Grants Index,* 29th edition. (Foundation Center, December 2000).
- *Foundation Grants to Individuals* (Foundation Center, June 2001).
- *Grant Writing for Dummies,* Beverly A. Browning (Hungry Minds, February 2001).
- *I'll Grant You That: A Step-By-Step Guide to Finding Funds, Designing Winning Projects, and Writing Powerful Proposals,* Jim Burke, Carol Ann Prater (Heinneman, May 2000).

healthy advances, expansive book promotion, or even payment for a short story. Grants and fellowships can help writers toward financial independence.

Published writers can need money just as much as beginners. But when it comes to grants, the decisions are tipped in favor of the published writer. "To be frank, beginners have a more difficult time obtaining grants," says Clark. "Grants for writers are by definition for *writers*. Funding sources, whether government agency, foundation, endowment, or nonprofit, have missions and visions clearly defined. They have a board and members and public donors to answer to. If their mission is to promote writing in the community, they want to know they invested well. With a beginner, the track record isn't there and funders are skeptical. To get a writing grant, one must have proven one's ability to write. For new writers, I recommend writing, gathering some clips, and then pursuing the grant. Acquiring a grant is no different than acquiring a choice writing assignment. Without clips, an editor doesn't want to give you the assignment."

Successful freelancers may not need the many smaller grants out there. For beginners, or intermediate writers who have published a few stories but don't have extra money for career-building activities, a grant can take you to a conference or a writing class when you might not otherwise be able to. It can also help put food on the table, buy that new computer you need, pay a babysitter so you can write your book, or finance a research trip to gather information for your book.

What's a Writer to Do?

Before targeting those choice Endowment for the Arts fellowships, aim your pen at the smaller and more local sources of money. There are plenty.

Perhaps the best known among children's writers are the grants from the Society of Children's Book Writers and Illustrators (SCBWI). SCBWI has been making grants to members since 1977 and awards grants to both published and unpublished writers and illustrators. There are several categories: The Don Freeman Memorial Grant-In-Aid for picture book artists, Barbara Karlin Grant for picture book texts, and four Work-In-Progress Grants— the General, the Grant for an Unpublished Writer (for a writer who has not published a children's book), Grant for a Contemporary Novel for Young People, and the Nonfiction Research Grant. The grants award $1,500 to the winner, and $500 to the runner-up in each category.

Since SCBWI has grown in prominence over the years, so has the impact of the grant. Karen Wojtyla, Publishing Director of Random House Books for Young Readers, says, "I think if the grant is from a well-known and respected organization like SCBWI that is a signal that tells me that experienced children's book people saw good things in the work."

In the early 1990s, SCBWI commissioned a survey to find out what the impact to the recipients of its grants had been. There were 26 responses from the 36 recipients contacted. Twelve of them reported that their work-in-progress that had won the grant went on to be published. Of the 14 whose grant projects had not been published, six had gone on to publish other books, stories, or articles.

Winning the grants certainly helps the writers. In 1985, Mary Jane Auch says she was becoming discouraged in her publication attempts. "I had written four mid-grade novels and had quite a collection of rejections. The grant gave me validation, although I probably would have kept going anyway." According to the SCBWI survey, validation and the sense of self-confidence winning a grant gives is perhaps even more important than the money. Auch was the runner-up that year in the work-in-progress category. Later, she says, "I sold two books in the same week to two different publishers. One was *Cry Uncle,* the book that won the SCBWI grant." Since then, Auch has racked up dozens of published books.

Winning the grant also makes an impression on editors. Pamela Todd applied for a 1997 work-in-progress grant. She had already submitted several picture book manuscripts, had gotten "good" rejections and positive critiques, but no sales. "I was already well along with *Pig and the Shrink,* a middle-grade novel that I had been working on for three years," she says. She submitted her application and continued working on the manuscript. After winning the grant, she later received a letter from Random House's Wojtyla, who had served on the grants panel and told Todd she had liked the book and would like to see it when it was finished.

"In judging manuscripts, I was look-ing for quality of writing," says Wojtyla, who read the completed manuscript and told Todd that she'd like to make an offer to purchase it if she would be willing to revise the book. *Pig and the Shrink* was published in 1999. Since then, Todd has contracted to publish a picture book with Wojtyla and is at work on another novel.

Jonathan Soloman won the 2000 work-in-progress grant for a writer who has not published a novel. He had not done any children's writing. He was encouraged by Judy Blume one day when interviewing her on an NBC Saturday morning show for kids. He worked on his novel for several years in between his other jobs. Of winning the grant, he says, "The money is nice, but better than that is that the submission of the book gets noticed because of the grant. It encouraged me to finish the book." He then submitted it to a publisher. It came back with notes for improvement and an invitation to resubmit.

There are approximately 15,000 SCBWI members. In last year's grants competition, there were only 200 entries. Susan Achorn Burgess, Work-In-Progress Grant Coordinator for SCBWI, says there may be a reason for this: "It's so much work! The work-in-progress grant application requires the same steps a writer would take to submit a book proposal and only a small portion of the membership has both the interest in applying and the skills to do so. As an aside, although the grants are open to all members, the applicants are mostly unpublished, so the skill levels are wide-ranging."

Howdy, Pardner

There is yet another way to optimize grants. Hope Clark, author of the e-book *Funds for Writers: The Book,* says, "Partnerships I absolutely preach! Schools are just one avenue. Any group can be a partner. And the project and genre determine the partner." Clark suggests looking at the project you want to write. Many of us don't think beyond the mainstream book and magazine publishers. But she says, "What if a writer wants to write about child abuse—fiction or nonfiction. Team with a child abuse charity or nonprofit for several reasons: background information, professional support, advertising, and access to grant funds that are restricted to nonprofit entities. A child abuse nonprofit can make a grant proposal for an informative book to be developed to better inform the public about identifying signs of abuse. Or a writer could prepare educational material, advertising, brochures, whatever."

Author Wendie Old found work in this way. "My first big paid writing job was through a grant that Johns Hopkins University got to revise their Success For All program. I was hired to write the stories for beginning readers. It paid my daughter's way through school."

Think of your own pet project interests and the possible partners you could team up with. There are times when a commercial publisher won't touch a book deemed not commercial enough, inappropriate for its list or readers, or too focused or controversial, yet a nonprofit would gladly work with you because of shared views and vision. "Either way is access to the funds," adds Clark. "Network with those that have the dollars."

As if that were not enough to get you thinking about all of the work to be had out there, Clark has yet another suggestion: form your own nonprofit group to obtain grants. Clark says a *nonprofit* means no more than "a club with a focus." Your writing group could become a nonprofit organization with the mission of providing published authors to read to school children. Setting up a nonprofit takes research and paperwork, but it can lead to a whole other side to your writing career as well as help the careers of many writers in your own community. Clark cites Carolina Romance Writers Association as an example of a group of writers who formed their own nonprofit organization. The SCBWI is another. The Internal Revenue Service (IRS) website, www.irs. gov, can help you find out more about becoming a nonprofit organization.

Grant writing itself is another job—after all, someone has to write them. Applications are explicit and can be demanding, often needing some creative wording to be sure your project is in line with the granting organization's goals and vision. Grant applications require analysis of the grantor's mission so that you can put into words just what the project you are seeking funds for will do for the community and for the funder. If you like nonfiction writing, grant writing can be another avenue to explore in your writing career.

The application process for any granting organization can be time-consuming. Connie Goldsmith, who was the SCBWI work-in-progress grant runner-up in 1998, says, "Although the application process was very explicit, I didn't find the instructions difficult to follow." Writers can increase their chances by being as meticulous as Goldsmith was.

Burgess adds, "The directions need to be followed to the letter." She says a tip sheet comes with the application to help writers, but "it's ironic that writers simply do not read carefully." If grant applications to any granting organization are not done according to the instructions, they are rejected.

Profit from the Nonprofits

Don't think just in terms of cash in your pocket, although that's certainly pleasant. There are other sources of money for writers. Nonprofit organizations receive grants for a number of projects. Libraries are nonprofits; schools are too and frequently apply for grants. Those grants can include providing author fees for school talks, bringing writers into classrooms for a one-day writing course, and paying to have a writer-in-residence at the school for a certain period of time. Author Susan Rottman gave a school talk that was paid for by a Michael Jordan grant to the school.

Also look beyond schools. A local, regional, or state arts center or council may be a source of cash grants or work paid for by grants. Giving writing workshops to adults or children is a popularly funded project. As an example of this type of work, I taught writing classes to children through our cultural center for the arts. My fee was paid through a grant to the center for fostering creativity and literary arts in children. I taught classes at the center for two years and had a blast doing it. That work led to other jobs. The local Girl Scouts asked me to teach creative writing at summer camp. Then I was asked to be the writer-in-residence at the middle school, which had obtained a grant to pay me. So the money doesn't always come directly to your pocket as a cash grant, but grants will pay you for your expertise in the form of fees.

To find this type of work, Clark has some advice. "I suggest contacting your state or local humanities and arts councils. That is always a good starting place for the less than seasoned writer. Every state is different, but each state has small grants to aid artists. There are some grants available out there for small goals such as conferences, career development, emergency need, or just general all-purpose use. In any case, one has to have a project in mind to even qualify for a $500 grant from a humanities commission. Having a clear focus is everything." A Yellow Pages or Internet search can help you get started.

Not all arts councils make grants to individuals. The Missouri Arts Council (MAC), under state law, cannot fund individual artists. To be eligible to apply for MAC funding, an organization must be Missouri-based and tax exempt, and incorporated as a Missouri not-for-profit corporation. MAC does fund, however, several literature organizations that produce publications, readings, and so on. My own Missouri Writer's Guild is a nonprofit educational association that receives funding from the state arts council. That would be a good place to start looking for funds if you live in Missouri. Other states have their own arts councils and writers' organizations.

Where's the money? It's all around you. It's not going to drop into your hands without some effort, but with a little mining you can pursue your interest in writing and add facets to your career. Many good writers out there just never quite hit the best-seller list—but there is still a good living to be made by pursuing writing interests. Now get your pick and start mining a new vein of gold for your career.

Business

Revise Your Life

By Joan Broerman

Writers know how to revise. Cut the scene that doesn't reveal something about character or move the story forward. Build the drama in a pivotal scene. Substitute a stronger, more specific verb for a lazy one. Add sensory details where they can be most effective. No smells? Where can they lure the reader into the story?

Writers learn to be creative and revise until their work fits within a set of guidelines. If the word count is 900, the serious writer knows better than to send 1,500. If an editor says no talking animals, the wise writer turns an adorable bunny rabbit into a human character that can tell the story just as beautifully. If the publisher advises, "*Read* what we do!" that writer knows it is not a call to imitate, but to get an idea of the publisher's tastes, the scope of the company's materials, and how the writer's manuscript could augment an existing body of books or magazines.

The determined writer revises again to use this specialized knowledge.

Every writer has the same amount of time in every day. 24 hours. 1,440 minutes. Time creates boundaries, just like guidelines. Some writers are more creative within those boundaries and their lists of credits stir admiration in some and the oft-heard comment "I'm going to write someday, when I have time" in others. How do writers who really want to write create within the boundaries of those 1,440 minutes? How do writers revise their lives to include their writing?

Minutes Are Like Calories: They Add Up

Many weight loss plans begin with a direction to the dieter: List every morsel or crumb that passes your lips in a day. The prospective dieter who tastes for the seasonings in the soup simmering on the stove or samples the filling to be spread on a child's sandwich is exhorted to write that down. At the end of the day, the dieter counts the calories in all those tiny tastes and is horrified. The rainbow in this discovery is that the dieter can skip those tastes that sabotage the waistline and lop calories from the diet plan immediately. No strategizing about how many ounces of this or that for each meal is needed—yet.

Time is the same way. Where do you spend yours? Do you pick up the phone to chat for five minutes but find you are saying good-bye half an hour later? Do you sneak a peak at your e-mail and an hour goes by before you return to your writing? How long does it take you to pet the dog, water the plants, sort the mail, make a list? All these daily tasks are part of your time diet. To see where the time goes, carry paper and pen around and jot down what you do throughout one day. Yes, breaks count. If you don't take breaks, you should. More about that later.

Minutes are the close-up focus on a writer's day. Consider the big picture, too. In a class for new writers given about eight years ago, author Kerstin Hamilton asked attendees to rank how each spent the five greatest blocks of time. One student could have made this list: family, church, day job, volunteer work, writing. Hamilton cautioned that if anyone listed the number-one time block as writing, it was her considered opinion that that writer needed to "get a life." After all, writers need something to write about!

Next, Hamilton asked the students to use the same five time blocks and rank them according to the way the writer wished they ranked. The writer of the above list may have switched the rankings for writing and volunteer work. Finally, Hamilton challenged each person: "What are you willing to give up to change group one to group two?" Could the writer of the two sample lists reduce volunteer activities from six to four? This would become a goal. This was not to be a sudden stop, like giving up coffee or chocolate forever, but a shifting of priorities. Interestingly, all the members of that writing class are published authors today, and Hamilton continues to publish, too. Her latest book is *This Is the Ocean* (Boyds Mills Press).

Goals and Dreams

Author Debbie Sanders gave each member of her critique group a small notebook with *Goals and Dreams* written on the cover. A dream can come true—but only in fairy tales do they come true with no effort on the part of the dreamer.

Writers must set goals to make dreams come true. The wisdom behind Sanders's gift to her writing friends was this: When the dream is recorded on the page, it reminds the writer of why she strives. The goals, also written down, become a set of reasonable steps. The writer can see achieving the goal, on paper and goal by goal, getting closer to realizing the dream. A writer who dreams of a publishing career, as Sanders does, can get there credit by credit. When Sanders's life revolved around driving two busy teenaged daughters to gymnastics meets, she wrote an article on gymnastics and sold it to a children's magazine. Write what you know? Write where you go! That article is one goal met.

Dieters are told not to hang their heads in shame if they splurge on a chocolate sundae. They can get back on the diet the next day and continue to move toward their goals. Time dieters can do the same thing. What if your time diet is upset when your march toward a goal is interrupted by the sudden appearance of a long lost friend or relative? So you drop everything for that day and sit up half the night talking and then you are too tired the next day to pull your thoughts together and get back to work. You don't have time or energy to lecture yourself. Guilt, shame, and regret are the visitors who should be turned away. Live in the moment with that surprise visitor and let the present nurture you. If it takes getting up early a few days to catch up, wasn't that surprise worth it? The writer raises her hand and says, "I can do that!"

Dessert First

Most diets seem to be about foods that taste like the real thing but aren't. A discerning eater knows the difference. So too does a discerning reader sense that the writer had little enthusiasm for work written while tired or stressed. Fatigue is difficult to disguise. The writer's pressures can seep through in the work.

A few years ago I wrote an article entitled "Dessert First" for a professional newsletter. The gist was that writers should choose their best time of day, whether it's early morning, the lunch hour, or late night—whenever creativity is at its height, and do the most valued writing then. What? Take time for fiction that might never sell but was begging to be written? Instead of meeting that deadline for an article under contract? Yes.

If you have something inside you that wants desperately to tumble across the page, it isn't going to leave you alone. You will fight against it to satisfy your contract and fatigue will settle into your writing bones. Energy is more desirable. Let your writing energize you. Grab time or make time, but do it. Try an hour of writing what you love each day for a week and see if you don't feel better at the end of each day, just knowing that you paid heed to those voices crying for your attention.

Grab time? Make time? Author Kathi Appelt has a story: "Years ago, I discovered that I could find time for anything—cleaning closets, running the PTA, making Halloween costumes, organizing the church rummage sale—anything except writing. Here I was, someone who called myself a writer, and yet I could never find time to write. And of course, being a good mom, a responsible citizen, and a homemaker were important too, but it seemed as if I put everything ahead of my writing.

"Then one day I was complaining to a friend of mine about never having time to write, and she urged me to make a daily time commitment. She asked how much time I could commit each day, and after mulling it over, I said, 'Thirty minutes! I can set aside 30 minutes a day.'

"My friend laughed and said, 'No, that's far too long. You'll never find 30 minutes a day.'

"Puzzled, I responded, 'Okay, how about 15?'

"Her response was the same. 'No, that's still too long.'

"Beginning to feel belittled, I said, 'Okay, I'm going to write for five minutes every day!'

"Expecting her stock answer, I was surprised when she said, 'Fine! Five minutes a day works.'"

Appelt says that was 11 years ago and she hasn't broken or changed that commitment. "I always find five minutes a day to write, and I count things like making out my grocery list or balancing my checkbook. As long as my pen is hitting the paper, I'm happy that I'm satisfying the commitment. The truth is, it's not the length of time. It's the *sitting down*. Getting started is the hard part. Once you sit down, the 5 minutes turns into 10, then 20, and so on. Anyone can find five minutes."

Appelt's list of starred reviews, including *Down Cut Shin Creek: Kentucky's Pack Horse Librarians,* grows and her books land on "best" lists consistently. *Kissing Tennessee* is an American Library Association Best Book for Young Adults and a Quick Pick for Reluctant Readers. Readers will be treated to four new picture books from Appelt this year. Her five-minute system obviously puts her where she needs to be, pen and paper in hand, to do the writing she loves.

Who's in Charge?

Who controls your time? What if your daily schedule is destroyed by hours spent at the doctor's office or in a traffic jam or waiting for an appointment that never takes place? No one has control over other people. A writer who carries a good book or a marketing newsletter or even a bag with notebook, pens, and a manuscript to edit uses those found moments to inform, educate, or move projects forward.

What if other people attempt to control your time? Kristi Holl, author of 24 juvenile novels and more than 150 articles for children and adults, is also Web editor for the Institute of Children's Literature. One of the sections under Rx for Writers is the Writer's Support Room. Holl's article "Return to Sender" says that writers often face pressure to quit writing from family and friends who trigger guilt or evoke fears, making the writer feel obligated to stop writing and attend to their needs instead. But Holl cautions writers not to see this as a sign that the writer isn't meant to write. "It's a mark of insecurity in your loved ones." Holl recommends reassuring loved ones of their importance, but encourages the writer to continue writing regularly. Eventually, family and friends will adjust.

In her article "Enforcing Boundaries," Holl cautions those who seek to carve out time for their writing: "We look for hidden pockets of time to write. We set aside time alone to think, to do research, to journal. All the planning in the world, however, won't do a bit of good unless you set and enforce boundaries with those who (for whatever reasons) feel they own your time." Holl emphasizes that the writers must believe in themselves. Respect yourself and respect will come from others.

Is There Such a Thing as a Writeaholic?

According to Workaholics Anonymous, answering yes to three or more of the following questions could mean you are a workaholic or well on the way to becoming one. What if you substituted the word writing *for* work*?*

1. Do you get more excited about your work than about family or anything else?

2. Are there times when you can charge through your work and other times when you can't?

3. Do you take work with you to bed? on weekends? on vacation?

4. Is work the activity you like to do best and talk about most?

5. Do you work more than 40 hours a week?

6. Do you turn your hobbies into money-making ventures?

7. Do you take complete responsibility for the outcome of your work efforts?

8. Have your family or friends given up expecting you on time?

9. Do you take on extra work because you are concerned that it won't otherwise get done?

10. Do you underestimate how long a project will take and then rush to complete it?

11. Do you believe that it is okay to work long hours if you love what you are doing?

12. Do you get impatient with people who have other priorities besides work?

13. Are you afraid that if you don't work hard you will lose your job or be a failure?

14. Is the future a constant worry for you even when things are going very well?

15. Do you do things energetically and competitively including play?

16. Do you get irritated when people ask you to stop doing your work in order to do something else?

17. Have your long hours hurt your family or other relationships?

18. Do you think about your work while driving, falling asleep, or when others are talking?

19. Do you work or read during meals?

20. Do you believe that more money will solve the other problems in your life?

Workaholics Anonymous offers "Tools of Recovery" and writers can make use of them. See the website http://people.ne.mediaone.net/wa2/tools.html.

One of Holl's "favorite recovery writers" is Julia Cameron. Mine, too. *The Right to Write* is more recent than my well-thumbed copy of *The Artist's Way*. Holl quotes from the newer book in her article "Where's the Drama?" and discusses personal dramas, those intrusions of life that the writer could write through *if* the dramas weren't allowed to jackhammer thoughts into chunks. Your teens are at war with your rules? Your mother employs guilt to sabotage writing time? Your spouse interrupts your momentum toward the deadline by deciding to bring the boss home to dinner? To keep going despite the crisis at home when there is an editorial deadline on the calendar, the writer must "close the door to your turbulent mind," says Holl, not just your office, or "We'll just bring the turmoil with us into our writing space."

Holl's strategy for reconnecting with her writerly self is to visit a collection of reminders of who she is. She touches each item, her first children's book, snapshots of her children, a letter from her dad written nearly 20 years ago, a chocolate candy wrapper, and relives the memory associated with each treasure. The drama that upset her fades into a perspective that allows her to return to her writing.

My favorite Cameron book, *The Artist's Way*, gives permission to the driven writer to take breaks, play, recreate. Cameron tells her readers, "Spending time in solitude with your artist child is essential to self-nurturing." She urges those who would create to recreate: "A little fun can go a long way toward making your work feel more like play."

Personally, I've found that rewarding myself with a break at reasonable stopping points, after a chapter is completed in rough or revised form, or after half an hour of researching a topic, not only refreshes me, but the production total is greater at the end of the day. *Not* taking breaks from my desk is hard on the brain as well as the back.

Work Smart

Sandra Markle, author of more than 60 books for kids, including the popular Outside and Inside series (*Outside and Inside Dinosaurs, Outside and Inside Alligators*, and others) considers information-gathering to be so time-consuming that she strives to use what she collects in at least three ways. She might write a book, a magazine article, and a talk, all derived from the same research materials.

When Susan Campbell Bartoletti, author of award-winning books such as *Growing Up in Coal Country* and *Kids on Strike!*, sold her first magazine article, she took the money and invested it—in herself. She recalls joining the Society of Children's Book Writers and Illustrators (SCBWI) and paying the membership dues as "the first step that made me a pro." When she attended her first SCBWI conference in 1989, it was also her first plane ride. "I cried. It was the first time I'd been away from my husband and two small children." Bartoletti continued investing her writing earnings in memberships, courses, classes, and conference materials, all carefully selected to help her cut down on what she calls "the apprenticeship time" in this challenging field of writing. Since that first SCBWI conference, Bartoletti has sold more than a dozen picture books, novels, and nonfiction titles.

Multi-tasking is a buzzword for the person who manages to do many things at the same time. "I was multi-tasking before I knew there was such a word. I called it *juggling*," says wife and mother Lin Oliver, who also heads her own film production company, is completing her dissertation for a Ph.D. in educational psychology, and is co-founder and Executive Director of SCBWI, now beginning its fourth decade. Although her sons are not children anymore (Theo is 21, Oliver Baker is 18, and Cole is 12), Oliver says her boys need a different kind of parenting today, one that takes more time and energy since her advice is likely to factor into life-changing decisions. Deciding which shirt to wear is a little different from choosing a college.

Through Lin Oliver Productions, Oliver writes and produces film for children and families based mostly, although not always, on children's books. E. B. White's *Trumpet of the Swan* was produced as an animated feature cowritten by Oliver, and her television production of Alfred Slote's *Finding Buck McHenry* received an Emmy nomination. At the time of this interview, she was writing a series based on the *Wayside School Stories,* by Louis Sachar.

Countless children's writers and readers of children's books have been touched by the organization Oliver, and fellow writer Stephen Mooser, founded, SCBWI. At a recent celebration of the organization's thirtieth anniversary, the two were deluged with notes, cards, and letters of appreciation. "There might not have been a *me* if there had not been a *you*" wrote one grateful published author.

Thirty years of books created by thousands of members results in quite a stack. It would take a museum to give those endeavors their due, and Oliver is busy developing another project close to her heart, the Museum and Foundation for Children's Books.

Continuing to multi-task, Oliver's dissertation is about contemporary children's authors. "How do they access their own childhoods in their writing?" Oliver asks. "What is unique about writing for children?"

What is unique about Oliver's busy life? She doesn't get tired. Why? The clue lies in one word that connects all the dots of her minutes and hours: *children.* "Everything I do comes from the thing I most care about and these things are interchangeable." She counts them: "children and families, raising my own, my profession—writing and producing children's films and scripts for TV and movies, SCBWI." The list continues with writing about children's authors and building a museum to showcase children's books.

"We all have a life we want to fill with what is meaningful," says Oliver. "The search can be exhausting. When the pieces fit, this brings us meaning and pleasure." For Oliver, the pieces fit, and her energy flows.

Revise your life to show that you love what you do. Love the work. Love the writer. Time will take care of itself.

Self-Publishing's New Aura: Respectability

By Josephine "Joi" Nobisso

For the past few decades, writers and illustrators who self-published wore scarlet letters—*A* for *amateur*—and *D* for *desperate*, while the review media maintained them in frosty exile. Today, as new technologies and access to professional consultation make producing superb books ever easier, and as children's corporate publishing consolidates into ever larger machines with more formulaic tastes, self-publishers are enjoying new red-letter days. They brandish *S* for *savvy* and *I* for *independent* while smart and powerful review venues give their titles just notice.

Quality, Not Vanity

More and more authors are self-producing books that out-perform titles from established publishing houses, only to have the bigger houses then acquire the projects for sizeable sums. With that, the old taboos connected to self-publication are evaporating.

The picture book *The Jester Has Lost His Jingle* had been rejected by many big publishers, but the parents of the author, a spirited young college man who had died of Hodgkin's disease at the age of 22, published it themselves in 1995. The next year, it was on the best-seller lists of three major newspapers, and a year later the book had sold almost a quarter of a million copies. Many thousands had also been donated to youngsters with cancer and other special needs.

"Create wonderful things, be good, have fun." That's the mission statement of Klutz Press, another spectacular self-publishing success story. In 1977, when three college friends sold juggling lessons and bean bags on the sidewalk, they grossed $35 the first week. Realizing that they'd reach a larger audience with a book, they put their juggling tips into *Juggling for the Complete Klutz*. The rest is publishing history. Klutz titles regularly appear on book and toy best-seller lists, and are available in 19 countries. In 2000, Klutz expanded by partnering with Nelvana Communications, home to animated Babar, Little Bear, Franklin the Turtle, and other characters from children's books.

This is not to say that every self-published book is professional or even interesting. It continues to be true that far too many independent projects are unprofessionally conceived, executed, and presented.

The motives that drive authors and illustrators, aspiring or established, to produce their own children's books are absolutely opposed to the practices of vanity publishing. Professionals who go it alone are often already too frustrated with the vagaries of traditional children's book publishing to tolerate the larger ills inherent in vanity or subsidy publishing. Disappointed with the "big house" decision wheels that turn too slowly, or with a book's design or positioning and marketing, children's book professionals can make the worst candidates for vanity publishing.

Instead, the professionals who self-publish today succeed by demonstrating a powerful commitment to established publishing conventions. This kind of self-publisher wants to be in the running. The writer creates the best project possible, presents it through capable channels, and supplies the demand of a studied market.

Two Self-Publishing Candidates

The first rule in self-publishing is to choose a worthy project. Self-publishing is perfect for two kinds of writers and writer/illustrators: the unpublished creator with an especially appealing project and the published one whose book was put out of print prematurely.

If you have an unpublished manuscript, have done all your homework, paid your dues, studied the field, objectively analyzed your text, presented it to professionals such as those you find in a no-nonsense critique group, and still know it to be a wonderful and unique book that cannot find a publisher, your project may make a good self-publishing candidate. Much work is involved in the steps outlined below and in the Epitome Tips List sidebar (see pages 226-232), but yours is certainly a possible dream.

Good as that formerly unpublished project may be, however, it is the published author with an out-of-print book who is even more advantageously positioned to make that first foray into self-publishing. Perhaps you had a published project that was not only an excellent book, but that also had not been promoted thoroughly by its first publisher. If you know where to find a strong market for that book, you can reissue it without having to see to the attendant editing, design, and preproduction elements the first-timer faces. This will ease your transition into self-publishing, allowing you to concentrate on the business end of the process, an aspect with at least as many details to it as the creative aspect. (See "Something Old: Resurrecting the Out of Print," on the opposite page.)

Gone, the Venerable Old Practices

Despite recent changes, residual false assumptions persist that self-published books that have never been in print are not "good enough" to be acquired by the traditional houses.

Also abroad is the prevailing myth that every house's list has its own particular and idiosyncratic bent. That was true for many years, but is much, much

Something Old: Resurrecting the Out of Print

Assuming you have retained the copyright to your now out-of-print work, and assuming that your contract with your original, "big" publisher allows for it, you can begin the process of bringing an out-of-print book back by sending a letter requesting reversion of rights from the book's former publisher. If you are not also the illustrator of the project, you will have already discussed your plans to publish independently—and will have negotiated an agreement—with the artist, who should also request reversion. If the illustrator is not interested in having an author bring the book back, most standard contracts treat the creators separately, so that an author would then be free to pursue illustrations from a different artist. Or, an author/illustrator team may even decide on another path: They may want to split the duties and expenses of self-publishing. Whichever course your project takes, be sure to have a publishing attorney draft equitable agreements between you, the creators of the project.

If indeed the original artist on the project agrees to have the book released again, your next step is simply to inform your former publisher that you are applying to obtain the book's printing films. Your contract probably calls for their acquisition at a fee "no higher than the cost of manufacture." It is easier to pay for the films, plates, or disks at this stage than to have them created by the printer. If you do not have access to the original films, you have two options for printing. The first and best is to have the printer reshoot from the original art. If the illustrator no longer has access to all the pieces, however, you may have the film shot directly from existing books. This second option may have you facing quality control concerns, but these can be overcome with care and patience during the proof stages of the printing process.

less so today, as the tastes of "traveling" editors are diffused through the industry. For a dozen years now, I have suggested that every editor be given a byline on the copyright page of a book, to maintain their association with a book as well as acknowledge their work and their taste. More and more editors are being lifted from their desks to play publishing's version of musical chairs. In my 30 years of publishing, no two of my books were ever acquired by the same editor.

The consolidation among big publishers has forced authors and illustrators to create ever new relationships and seek publication from many different houses. Writers may follow editors on their migrations. They may find that a house that has published their work rejects some or all subsequent projects because they don't fit the house's new needs, so they move on to another house. A company's editor or art director might pursue writers or illustrators who have appeared on the lists of other houses. The professional voices of these creators are therefore diffused as well. On both sides of the publishing desk, fidelity to one house is largely passé.

The fact that publishing is subject to so many arbitrary and fluctuating elements has reconfigured its dynamics until it no longer resembles the field it once was. Often, one house's list resembles another's. For readers, this has left gaps that self-publishers, with their specific visions and voices, may fill neatly.

That good news gets even better. As houses merge, they also purge, or downsize. The experienced and talented staff members they release—editors, copyeditors, designers, art directors, indexers, and prepress production people—often work at large, setting up shop from their homes. A serious independent publisher has no problem using the same professional services the big houses always used. I have said it before: Publishing shot itself in the foot when it let all that talent go.

By necessity, as self-publishing widens and improves, reviewers are driven to take individual titles more seriously. While it's true that established publishers' imprints carry weight with certain review media and industry insiders, those reviewers can't undermine their own positions by ignoring worthy projects, regardless of imprint. When review space is allotted to unknown authors and smaller presses, review media sustain their credibility. The public, after all, doesn't choose books by the publisher's imprint; it chooses according to a book's appeal and usefulness.

It is no longer "the house" alone that arbitrates publishing tastes. Two organic factors contribute more today to the course of the industry: readers' needs and creators' impulses. This has opened up infinite possibilities for the self-publisher.

Go Figure: Income & Visibility

Among the many reasons for self-publishing is the financial one. The same day on which I received a royalty statement from a large house reporting that they had sold only 62 copies of my picture book with them in 6 months, I was lugging that day's orders from my self-publishing company, Gingerbread House, onto the deck for a pick-up: 236 units. In that same 6-month period the big house had lost 750 of my author-generated school orders because of their inability to deliver on time, misunderstandings over discounts, and a general disorganization.

Self-publishing does not preclude your publishing with the more established houses. In fact, if you do it with professionalism, you are entitled entry into the very ranks of the other houses. You may join the same professional organizations, pursue the same awards, compete for the same markets, and so on. After all, just as any writer who was now published was once unpublished, any house that is now big was once small.

Since having launched Gingerbread House, I have had several books acquired by other houses. I'm still being published by mainstream editors at companies that include Houghton Mifflin, Scholastic/Orchard, Pauline

Books & Media, and Richard C. Owen. More professional journals and books than ever are featuring my essays on writing, publishing, and teaching. Self-publishing has not diminished my consulting work, either: I still conduct about 100 workshops a year on the craft of writing.

If you have ever been frustrated by the sluggishness of your progress in children's books, self-publishing can give your efforts a boost that can sky-rocket your career. Before launching Gingerbread House, an Internet search on my name turned up 7 matches, and this was after I had been an author of award-winning, respected books, many of which had gone into several printings. A year later, because of the free rein in getting Gingerbread's books into the hands of reviewers and opinion-makers, a search turned up 255 dedicated matches on Google. That's an enormous relief for me as an author, and a happy vindication for the venture. Gingerbread House has placed more copies of my three books in one year than did the books' two previous publishers over the course of a dozen years.

Recently, my print brokers e-mailed the guest list for a dinner party they were giving for their East Coast clients. Many of the guests—authors and illustrators—were friends who, encouraged by the success of Ginger-bread House, are making plans to self-publish. The mood at that dinner was high and happy. And why wouldn't it be? Professionals who had always felt restrained by the constraints of dodg-ing the grinding gears of publishing's big machines were passionately dis-cussing special markets, niche readers, and creative ideas for printing and production—all in the new spirit of self-publishing: respectability.

Epitome Tips: What It Takes to Self-Publish

Once you have your most professional and promising project in hand, the work has only just begun. Here is an outline of the steps to take to bring your children's book into the light of day. The list offers "Epitome Tips" that pinpoint the single most effective strategy I have found connected to each item. You will perform many of these tasks concurrently, of course, so this list serves only as a guide of what to expect.

Planning & Preparation

- **Over-the-Top Tip:** Do not attempt self-publishing unless you are passionate about your project and convinced of its unique value. The hardest book to market successfully is the one that is "just another pretty face."
- **Overview Tip:** Study *Literary Marketplace* (LMP), a two-volume reference book available at your library and updated annually, to get a grasp of the magnitude and scope of the field. Read guidebooks like *The Self-Publishing Manual* (805-968-7277, http://ParaPublishing.com), and marketing books like *1001 Ways to Market Your Book* (Open Horizons Publishing). Peruse the Library of Congress site (http://lcweb.loc.gov) and learn the services offered to publishers, including Cataloguing in Publication (CIP); the site will orient you to the publishing process. Do the same with the site for R.R. Bowker, and the ISBN U.S. Agency, which issues standard book identification numbers (http://www.isbn.org/standards/home/isbn/us/isbnus.html).
- **Business Plan Tip:** For free, the Small Business Administration (www.sba.gov) can direct you to the conferences and seminars about running a business, and offers workshops in drawing up business plans.
- **Market Scoping Tip:** Visit every niche site that might have a possible connection to your book's theme, and determine whether you have a chance of hooking up with the sponsor. Bookmark the site. Later, offer them review copies.
- **Editorial Services Tip:** The Editorial Freelancers Association (EFA) (www.the-efa.org) is a national, nonprofit, professional organization of self-employed editors, writers, indexers, proofreaders, researchers, desktop publishers, and translators. After the EFA screens your request for service, it posts your job to their list so that you can find a match between your needs and the skills of the responding professionals.
- **Company Name Tip:** Don't name your self-publishing press after yourself.
- **Professional Organizations Tip:** Join the Publishers Marketing Association (PMA) (www.pma-online.org) and the Small Publishers Association of North America (SPAN) (www.spannet.org). You will save money with discount programs with freight shippers, office supplies, and more.
- ***Publishers Weekly* Tip:** Membership in SPAN will make you eligible for a greatly reduced subscription rate to *PW*.

Epitome Tips: What It Takes to Self-Publish

Legal & Business

- **Another Company Name Tip:** Before deciding on a company name, have your attorney do a search to be sure that another business does not already use it. Check with a domain name provider to be sure that the name is available.

- **The Don't Do It Yourself Unless You're a Lawyer Tip:** Don't set up a Limited Liability Company or Corporation (LLC), and get a Federal Tax I.D. number, without the advice of a lawyer familiar with publishing.

- **Internal Revenue Service (IRS) Tip:** When you apply for an IRS SS-4 Employer Identification Number, as you set up your small company, ask for the free disk about small businesses and the IRS.

- **The Checking Account Connection Tip:** Opening a business checking account allows you to process checks immediately and, eventually, to accept charge cards.

- **Copyright Tip:** Do not apply for copyright until after your book is printed. Simply print the necessary copyright information on the copyright page of the book, citing the year of publication, not the year of the printing. This will afford you some leeway in time, making it possible to obtain more reviews and awards, the eligibility for which is predicated by a book's copyright year. It's common in publishing to refer to a book's release date as "a fiction," in that publishers must decide the copyright date based not necessarily on the actual year in which it is printed, but by the amount of lead time a book needs to get into the hands of reviewers and award personnel.

Office & Equipment

- **Computer Tip:** Invest in a good computer system now, with a scanner and printer that will handle promotional print work for signs, boards, etc., later.

- **Technology Tip:** Connect to the best, fastest online service available.

- **Stationery Tip:** Include your website address on *all* stationery.

- **Office Supplies Tip:** Don't skimp on packing materials. If books are damaged in transit, they are returned to the publisher for a full credit.

- **Mailing Tip:** You can save on Priority Shipping through the U.S. Post Office in two ways: either save on packaging materials' costs by using their preprinted boxes, or save on postage by using your own mailer with their Priority label affixed.

- **Credit Card Tip:** You don't have to go through the expense of setting up a merchant account if you will be taking credit card orders only from your site. Sign up with CCNow, or another such company, which allows small businesses to sell online without charging the fees normally associated with

Epitome Tips: What It Takes to Self-Publish

acquiring *merchant status*. These avoidable fees include application or set-up charges, the leasing or buying of credit card terminals, and paying monthly minimums, regardless of sales. Services like CCNow charge a heftier interest rate—in the area of nine percent—but no other fees and no monthly minimums. They conduct secure credit card transactions for you, from your site, and make twice-monthly deposits into the bank account of your choice.

- **Another Credit Card Tip:** If you'll need to accept credit card orders over the phone or "back of the room" at speaking engagements, consider the favorable deal from Costco, or other discount warehouses. Through their member services desk, they can provide you with merchant status at competitive rates, ones that, often, are better than those from your bank.

Production & Distribution

- **Art Direction Tip:** Be generous in your dealings with your illustrator. Work with a contract from the beginning. Offer a kill fee for the first illustration, in case your visions cannot be reconciled.
- **Design Tip:** Discuss the book's trim size—the actual dimensions of the pages and cover—and other design considerations with the artist before any artwork is started. To keep costs down, keep sizes standard.
- **Software Tip:** Invest in good, inexpensive back-room publishing software, like PUB123 from www.support@adams-blake.com, or Publishers' Assistant from www2.upperaccess.com/upperaccess/software.htm.
- **Printer Tip:** If you'd like your books printed by the same firm that printed your books for other, established houses, look on your copyright page. Some publishers give attribution. If it's not there, drag out that carton that held books you bought to help your publisher with promotion. Emblazoned on its side should be the name of the printing firm.
- **Printing Tip:** Full-color printing is less expensive in Asia. Work through a broker if you are printing overseas. This does not increase your costs and it yields many benefits: They pay the air shipping; they vet the project; they answer every question, etc. Gingerbread House uses Regent Publishing Services, and we are very satisfied with them. Get quotes from several printers, which you can find listed in *LMP*. You might locate *PW*'s report "Printing in Asia," which is updated every summer. If you attend trade shows like BookExpo America (BEA), many printers—both onshore and off—take booth space there and will be happy to show you finished books they have produced.
- **Another Printing Tip:** Text-only books, such as young adult novels, and

Epitome Tips: What It Takes to Self-Publish

those books using only black-and-white art are priced very well in the U.S. and Canada. Get several quotes, again, from printers listed in *LMP*.

- **Another Printing Tip:** Get both hardcover and softcovers of picture books printed at the same time. Softcovers will open up opportunities unavailable to hardcover only, such as sales through book clubs and quantity buyers, like warehouse clubs.
- **Distribution Tip:** Interest a distributor in your project by showing him as nearly completed a dummy as you can, before going to print. You will be going through a submissions process not unlike the one you go through for manuscripts. It's a speculative, and subjective, process. Under each distributor's listing in *LMP* you will find a listing of the publishers represented. Study these carefully to decide if there is a market match between your books and those the distributor already represents. Your books need to go down a well-beaten path into appropriate and fertile markets.
- **Another Distribution Tip:** If a distributor does not take you on, don't worry: you can create affiliate relationships yourself with online booksellers like Amazon.com and Barnes & Noble, and set up accounts with the major wholesalers, like Baker & Taylor and Ingram, yourself. That is, of course, if you are willing and able to do the order fulfillment, process returns, and invoicing. Ingram recently announced that it would require every press with fewer than 10 titles to establish a relationship with a distributor. They are referring small publishers to the distributor Biblio.
- **Fulfillment Tip:** If you do not interest a distributor and you are not interested in doing all the nitty-gritty of fulfilling orders, hire a fulfillment house.
- **Storage Facilities Tip:** Even if you interest a distributor, it will not take all your stock all at once. Make sure that your books are stored in the kind of comfortable atmosphere where you would put a baby down for a nap. (And make sure the floor is sturdy enough to hold the weight of the loaded pallets!)

Promotion & Sales

- **Retail Pricing Tip:** You must be able to price your book realistically at 8 to 10 times its printing cost to make any money. This is not an exaggeration. If you're going to sell a book for $15, the printing cost should be $1.50 or less.
- **Blurb Tips:** Early in the project, create book blurbs of 10, 25, and 100 words. These will serve you well as you apply for listings and pitch your book to potential readers and markets. These can serve as book flap and catalogue copy. Websites that offer to feature your book will sometimes

Epitome Tips: What It Takes to Self-Publish

need a short tag line about it. The Advance Book Information (ABI) form you will fill out to be listed in Bowker's *Books in Print* will ask for a 10-word description. Create 25- and 50-word biographies of the book's author and illustrator for similar purposes.

- **Photo Tips:** Be creative with the promotion photographs of the author and illustrator. No mug shots, fuzzy backyard party shots, or glamour poses—unless there's a humorous reason for choosing these. Make multiples of all photos available in both color and black-and-white. Magazines like the color; newspapers prefer the B&W.

- **Mailing Lists Tip:** Your most targeted mailing to children's bookstores will be to members of the Association of Booksellers for Children (ABC). The preprinted mailing labels you *rent*—or buy for one-time use or for a year—from ABC will save you lots of time and trouble in trying to accumulate all that targeted mailing information yourself.

- **Bookstore Tip:** You can look up 4,600 independent bookstores, with their URLs, e-mail addresses, and descriptions at www.bookweb.org/bookstores.

- **Press Release Tip:** If you cannot create a dynamite press release, or are tentative about how, hire it out to someone whose expertise is in press releases.

- **Advertising Tip:** Don't do it. Or, at least, don't do *much* of it. Or, don't do much of it until you have quotable reviews to cite. Readers believe reviews, but regard ads with reserve. Leave the bestowing of accolades to the professional reviewers. Instead, invest in having your printer produce F&G's, which are *folded and gathered* sheets of your book. The F&G's stage in printing comes just before your book is bound, and it shows the entire book in a kind of soft *dummy*. Four months before your publication date, send these to established trade publications, like *School Library Journal, PW, Kirkus Reviews, The Horn Book,* and others. Send finished books to other venues like magazines that may have subscribers in your book's niche, or to website owners who review children's books, like About.com. Four months later, send finished books to those same reviewers, to show that the book is indeed ready.

- **Review Tip:** Send advance book announcements to *PW*, for use in their spring or fall Children's Book Issue. You yourself create the blurb for these announcements, thus giving a heads-up to potential book buyers.

- **Review Copies Tip:** Don't be skimpy. Send to every legitimate review medium.

- **Promotion Tip:** If you can't do it yourself, hire a promotion professional. You will find them through the Society of Children's Book Writers and Illustrators (SCBWI), and in listings in *LMP*.

- **Website Tip:** Keep it ever current.

Epitome Tips: What It Takes to Self-Publish

- **Trade Show Tip:** If you have a distributor, they will take your book to the fairs and represent you. This does not preclude your signing up for booth space, too, should you like. Apply early for advantageous booth positions so that you are not far from the action of the larger houses. BEA is the largest book trade show in the nation, and is held in various cities. The schedule for the next several years is May 3-5, 2002: New York City; May 30-June 1, 2003: Los Angeles; June 4-6, 2004: Chicago; June 3-5, 2005: New York City. Other important book fairs are sponsored by the American Library Association (ALA) and the International Reading Association (IRA). For a comprehensive list of the myriad trade shows—regional, national, and international—see the listings on the Association of American Publishers (AAP) website at www. publishers.org/home/aboutb/fairs.htm
- **International Trade Show Tip:** If you have a rhyming text, it does not have great potential for translation rights, so skip the Bologna Children's Book Fair, which is a foreign-rights-only event. Concentrate on participating in domestic shows. Apply early.
- **Book Club Tip:** Send softcovers to overseas book clubs. Gingerbread House has had five large orders from two of these, on the same title! Some were presold, which means that we never even saw thousands of books; our printer in Hong Kong sent them directly to their destinations.
- **Best Book-Selling Tip:** You are a children's book creator, with a special direct connection to your audience in the form of author and illustrator events and school visits. Do not make ordering books a prerequisite for a visit, but do create a professional and easy-to-follow book-ordering packet to bring to the events.
- **Book Signing Tip:** Have inexpensive, colorful stickers made by the companies that create return address labels. Mine say, "Personally Autographed by the Award-Winning Author."
- **Value Added Tip:** Offer free author autographing and personalized dedication from your website.

Publishing Industry

- **ISBN Tip:** Purchase only the block of ISBNs (International Standard Book Numbers) you will realistically need. These are obtained from R.R. Bowker, www.BowkerLink.com (1-877-310-7333).
- **Bar Code Tip:** Bar codes, and the comparable European Article Number (EAN) are available online. Get the information for one company, Bookland, at www.barcode-us.com/info_center/bookinfo.htm. Fotel also provides bar coding and label printing (www.fotel.com). Have the bar code e-mailed directly to the designer or the printer.

Epitome Tips: What It Takes to Self-Publish

■ **SAN Tip:** You'll obtain a Standard Address Number (SAN), an identification number for electronic (online) communication, from Bowker. Print it onto your stationery and program it into your invoicing software.

■ **Listings Tip:** Submit an Advance Book Information (ABI) form to R.R. Bowker early so that your book will be sure to be included in the appropriate edition of *Children's Books in Print.*

■ **CIP Tip:** You will not be eligible for the Library of Congress's Cataloguing in Publication (CIP) data block (which appears on your copyright page) until you are an established and proven publishing house. You can, however, obtain a P-CIP from Quality Books, a company that distributes small press books and other materials. You should, however, apply for a Library of Congress Catalog Card Number LC or LCCN, and incorporate this into your P-CIP data block. For explanations and details, see http://www.quality-books.com/qb_gloss.html.

■ **Awards Tip:** The Children's Book Council (CBC) is now updating and planning to reissue its out of print and very useful guide, *Children's Books: Awards and Prizes.* See pages 355-402 in this *Children's Writer's Guide* for a listing of awards and prizes, as well.

The processes that initiated you into writing and publishing have also given you on-the-job training. You know and love children's books; you have read, studied, and created them. You have attended the conferences, taken the classes, and undergone the experiences of submission, rejection, and, maybe, publication. All of these have given you knowledge and insight that contribute toward making you a good candidate for self-publishing. Good luck with your launch!

Writing for Children's Writers

Journals of the Trade

By Joan Broerman

Subscribe to one or two magazines about writing and suddenly advertisements for others fill your mailbox. Once you tap into the body of materials published for your information and career guidance, the problem becomes not where to look but what to choose. Any number of weekly, monthly, bimonthly, quarterly, and semiannual newsletters and magazines cover marketing as a craft, marketing and publishing news, book reviews, and business for writers. Similar Internet sources are multiplying exponentially. In addition to subscribing to wide-ranging trade publications, writers can join professional organizations that publish newsletters geared to memberships. When time and money are at a premium, choosing which publications to buy and read is an important decision for a writer.

The Review Media

Becoming knowledgeable about classic and current children's writing is essential to any children's writer's career, and a joy. Why write for children if you don't love the books and stories that children love, and learn to distinguish between truly good work and the rest? The trade publications that can be most useful in such discernment are the review media.

A review, says Roger Sutton, Editor of *The Horn Book Magazine*, is written for the reader, not the author or publisher. But a wise author learns from review journals what it is that readers want, the books that are being published, and the houses that publish them. Reading reviewed books broadens a writer's knowledge of what is current and considered review-worthy; it helps the reader/writer observe technique and pacing; it stirs the imagination. As Sutton observes, reading reviews allows authors to see what concerns those who recommend books for others.

The bimonthly *Horn Book* annually reviews 400 books in-depth and is the authoritative journal on children's literature and reading. It was founded in 1924 as the first magazine to concern itself exclusively with children's books. Named for an old-fashioned teaching device, a paddle-primer or *hornbook*, the publication's goal is "to blow the horn for fine books for boys and girls," wrote the founder, Bertha Mahony. Today, the reviews are joined by thought-provoking articles, editorials, and columns on the myriad aspects of children's literature. Accep- tance speeches by the Newbery and Caldecott winners are carried in the July/August issue each year.

Proudly cited by authors whose books garner a mention, *Kirkus Reviews* is another highly respected review journal, although it reviews adult and juvenile titles. Originally called the *Kirkus Book Service*, its evaluations were typed by Virginia Kirkus, who thought, in 1933, that people should know about books before they bought them. Karen Breen, Children's Book Review Editor of *Kirkus*, says today the publication focuses on how a book is put together. "One of the things we try to do is tell why a book works or doesn't." The reviewers look for how a book is presented to the reader. They might evaluate whether, for example, the voice and character development are appropriate for the age of the audience. Breen receives books from publishers in bound galleys or in the folded-and-gathered (F&G) stage before they are printed in final form. Eighty-nine percent of the readership consists of librarians, and those writers who read *Kirkus* are usually reading their own reviews. Breen thinks a writer can learn a great deal about technique from reading the bi-weekly *Kirkus*, each of which includes about 60 reviews.

The New York Times Book Review established its children's book section well after the *Review* had begun, and grew it slowly. In each weekly issue of the *Book Review*, only a few children's books may be reviewed, but it also periodically does longer pull-out sections on children's publishing. Because of the limited space it devotes to children's titles—although it has added children's best-seller lists in the wake of Harry Potter—the *Book Review* tends to focus on name authors and its coverage has never been that wide. But the quality of the reviews is high and the *Book Review* itself is a strong tool for writers who want to keep abreast of contemporary writing.

Riverbank Review founder and Editor Martha Davis Beck rediscovered children's books at the stage of life when many do, when she became a parent. Her new appreciation of the richness of children's literature fueled a determination to give the field more in-depth attention. She read scholarly journals that were insular and reviews written for parents that were more fluff than substance. She dreamed of offering a thoughtful but accessible perspective to parents, teachers, librarians, and writers—especially those who write for children.

In the summer of 1998, the *Riverbank Review* was established in partnership with the University of St. Thomas in St. Paul, Minnesota. Last summer, the review journal became independent of the university, but Beck reports that content and readership have not changed. A committee of five contributing editors selects books for review and screens the year's titles for the magazine's Children's Books of Distinction Awards. Ten finalists and then three winners are chosen in the categories of picture

Websites of Interest

- **Book Links:** www.ala.org/BookLinks
- **Booklist:** www.ala.org/booklist/index.html
- **The Boston Book Review:**
www.bookwire.com/bbr/children/children.html
- **Children's Book Council:** www.cbcbooks.org
- **Children's Book Insider:** www.write4kids.com
- **The Children's Literature Web Guide:** www.acs.ucalgary.ca/~dkbrown/index.html
- **Children's Writer:** www.institutechildrenslit.com
- **The Horn Book:** www.hbook.com
- **The Midwest Book Review:** www.execpc.com/~mbr/bookwatch/
- **The New York Times:** www.nytimes.com
- **Publishers Weekly:** www.publishersweekly.com
- **Riverbank Review of Books for Young Readers:** www.riverbankreview.com
- **The School Library Journal:** http://slj.reviewsnews.com
- **The Scoop Children's Book Reviews:** www.friend.ly.net/scoop/
- **Society of Children's Book Writers and Illustrators (SCBWI):** www.scbwi.org
- **Wooden Horse:** www.woodenhorsepub.com
- **The Writer:** www.writermag.com
- **Writer's Digest:** www.writersdigest.com

Also of Note:
- **The ALAN Review:** This journal for educators on young adult literature is published by the National Council of Teachers of English (NCTE). The archives can be found at the Digital Library and Archives site. http://scholar.lib.vt.edu/ ejournals/ALAN/alan-review.html. The ALAN, or Assembly on Literature for Adolescents, site itself is http://engfac.byu.edu/resources/alan/.
- **Parents' Choice Foundation:** www.parents-choice.org. This consumer group's "reviews" of products are of a different nature than those in the review media or scholarly journals, but they can be an extremely useful measure of what the nonlibrarian consumer—the parents who buy books for their children—will value. Parents' Choice Awards for books are given each spring and fall.

books, fiction, nonfiction, and poetry.

To designate a book of distinction, Beck explains, she and her editors look for exceptional writing and illustrations and choose books they think will become the classics of tomorrow. These titles have family appeal and may be good purchases for home, as well as school, use.

"So much is happening in picture books, for example," Beck says. "I like the idea of giving three awards with an exciting range rather than having to choose just one book as a general winner." The last three picture book winners—*Buttons*, by Brock Cole, *Dinosaurs!*, by Peter Sis, and *Yoshi's Feast*, by Kimiko Kajikawa and illustrated by Yumi Heo—demonstrate that range.

To grace other pages of the quarterly, Beck chooses articles and essays about creating the work, the art and craft of children's books. "We have pieces written by the writers regarding the aspects of their work. We hope to give a more filled-out picture about what goes into a children's book. Why does the author write? How?"

Riverbank Review is available at newsstands and by subscription. See www.riverbankreview.com for more information and a list of award recipients.

The People Who Know

One prestigious review journal is published by the American Library Association (ALA), one of many publications produced by the organization that is of interest to writers. *Booklist*, which is the ALA's flagship review journal and will celebrate its hundredth birthday in 2003, reviews books, videos, and reference materials for children, young adults, and adults. *Book Links: Connecting Books, Libraries, and Classrooms* is another ALA publication, whose importance to the writer is in showing how a book (or the writer's future book) can be used in the classroom.

Booklist is a "recommended-only journal." For the most part, a review in *Booklist* constitutes a qualified recommendation. On rare occasions, *Booklist* makes use of a special feature called Focus to alert subscribers to books that "we know will be highly promoted, but we feel cannot be recommended," says Stephanie Zvirin, who has been Books for Youth Editor at *Booklist* for two years and on the editorial staff for 26 years. She says they receive about 5,000 books annually and review about half in 22 issues, with 100 to 130 in each.

Zvirin says writers can get a sense of book trends from reading *Booklist*. "See if your idea is really new by seeing what the publisher is putting out there this season."

In an analysis of fewer than 200 words, the reviewers strive to present a balance of strengths and problems. Reviewers comprise a staff of four professional children's reviewers, who do half of the reviews, and contributing reviewers, who are consultants to schools, authors, teachers, children's librarians. These are people, says Zvirin, who "know the children's book world and children's literature, and they write very well." Zvirin's advice to writers is "Read, read, read before you write. Know what's out there. Read the journals. Go to the library and read as much as you can that is well written.

Read children's magazines, children's writing, and books about writing."

Why is it important for a writer also to know what is happening in a classroom? Laura Tillotson, Editor of *Book Links,* offers this insight: "*Book Links* gives writers an opportunity to see how books can be used in the K to 8 classroom, first and foremost. In each issue we tie a variety of trade books—from picture books to novels to poetry to nonfiction—to themes that relate to classroom curriculum. For instance, in recent issues we've published articles on how to teach the Bill of Rights using fiction, as well as how to inspire younger students to write their own poems using poetry from picture books. As a former trade books editor, it's been my impression that the typical beginning writer envisions his or her book as something that will be read by parents to children or by children independently. *Book Links* shows that there is great opportunity for trade titles beyond that scenario, that teachers can use books as jumping-off points for broader discussions in the classroom. Reading *Book Links* will help educate a writer about the many educational uses of trade books and the current climate in children's book publishing and will also provide a broad overview of the types of books being published. Not to mention that we regularly feature interviews with and essays by both well-known and up-and-coming authors."

Tillotson relies on in-house research to select books for articles, and *Book Links*'s freelance contributors are mostly school librarians, teachers, and children's literature professors who do extensive research before recommending a book in any given article. The book must tie into the theme of the article. Contributing authors must make sure that the titles they include have been tested in the classroom and work for that subject.

Big Picture, Little Picture

Cahners/Reed Elsevier publishes *The School Library Journal,* a monthly with a circulation of 41,000 that critiques materials for children only. Trevelyn Jones is the Book Review Editor. Last year, her staff reviewed 4,200 books to help its readership of purchasing librarians make informed acquisition decisions.

Jones says *The School Library Journal* gives writers a sense of what is being published in what area, and the quality of books for which schools will spend their often limited dollars. She explains to writers, "I think they could see a flooded field, but they'd get an overview of what is being published. Our reviews delve into the qualities of each book. Writers would get a sense of what librarians are looking for." When Jones reviews children's books, she says, she does not warm up to "preachy teachy."

Jones has two tips for writers: A librarian is a valuable resource for helping writers find materials, but don't plunk a manuscript in front of your librarian expecting it to be read. This isn't part of the job. Instead, if you let children's librarians know you are looking for other children's writers, they could help you connect with a meaningful network. Jones's second tip for writers is a book, *From Cover to*

Cover, Evaluating and Reviewing Children's Books, by Kathleen Horning, a children's librarian at the Madison Public Library in Madison, Wisconsin. From Horning, writers will learn what librarians consider to be important qualities in each genre.

Other Trade Groups

The National Council of Teachers of English (NCTE), the International Reading Association (IRA), and the Children's Book Council (CBC) are other professional associations for educators that publish their own journals and newsletters. These materials can inform the writer about changes in classroom teaching methods, concerns of the classroom teacher that a writer might help address, and how books and authors are being used to undergird curriculum.

According to the CBC, 8,000 juvenile titles are published each year. The CBC is a nonprofit trade organization concerned with literacy. Its members are trade book publishers and packagers, but it works with librarians and others who promote children's reading. The CBC's most high-profile event is National Children's Book Week; its colorful and original posters celebrating that week have long decorated the walls of libraries. The CBC publishes books and pamphlets of interest to writers, and a semiannual newsletter called *Features* that is directed at writers, publishers, educators, and librarians.

For Fellow Writers

As much as professional library journals can offer writers, professional writing publications open up another spectrum of information, on magazines as well as books, on career, and on the art of writing.

Whether you are just starting out, have been submitting consistently but with few results, or have a folder full of clips and are ready to expand your range of markets, membership in the Society of Children's Book Writers and Illustrators (SCBWI) will plunge you into an Olympic-size pool of information. SCBWI has more than 16,000 members around the world and two categories of membership: published (full membership) and unpublished (associate membership). Its newsletter, the *Bulletin*, is published six times a year. SCBWI President Stephen Mooser says the newsletter "keeps members up-to-date on the industry, provides educational advice and strategies, provides marketing information, and inspires them to keep going."

SCBWI is divided into more than 60 regions, and many of the regions have their own newsletters. Most are open to subscribers no matter where they live and whether they are SCBWI members or not. To find out about all existing regional newsletters, see the SCBWI website at www.scbwi.org.

SCBWI France Expression is an annual publication, but Editor Erzsi Deak, who is the SCBWI International Regional Advisor Chairperson, adds subscribers to her online list and sends out numerous updates on the international market via the Internet. Deak gleans her information from many sources, she says, including Internet "surfing, the *New York Times*, *PW Daily (Publishers Weekly)*, *The*

One Man's Opinions on Trade Journals

Many large professional organizations also hold regional and international conferences and Larry Dane Brimner, author of over 100 books for young people, is a popular speaker at these conferences. He keeps up-to-date on the times and places of future conferences through trade journals. He also gleans helpful information. Brimner encourages his fellow writers to consider the multiple audiences of a book: the children themselves, their parents, and their teachers. "Being familiar with educational trends and jargon enables you to 'slant' your pitch to teachers in their own language." Knowing that your latest book is covered in a state's social studies framework or that your book demonstrates a particular writing process or that its topic is one of concern to administrators simply makes it easier, Brimner says, to tailor your promotion to this important audience.

A personal example from Brimner: "When I pointed out that my book, *Cat on Wheels,* demonstrates the six traits of writing, it suddenly became appealing to teachers involved in the six-trait writing process." Brimner thinks the best way, aside from being a teacher, to figure out how your work fits in the curriculum is by staying abreast of teaching trends and the jargon that goes with them. The writer can do this by subscribing to one or more trade journals.

However, Brimner offers a caveat: "Subscribe to a few appropriate journals, but don't overdo it, and don't let your subscriptions detract from your main work—*writing.*" By "appropriate" Brimner means the readership of the particular publication. "If you write primarily for younger children, then a subscription to a journal that caters to secondary teachers is money down the drain."

Looking for inspiration? Brimner reads the "material wanted" or "what we need" sections common to many journals. He says these appear once a year, usually in January. "Often scribed by librarians, they'll let you know what is being requested by teachers and kids—and perhaps you'll find the seed for your next book there."

Business

For the Writer's Bookshelf

Every writer needs a library—those indispensable books that are there, no matter when the writer needs to consult them.

New Covers on the Shelves
- *The Complete Idiot's Guide to Publishing Children's Books,* Harold D. Underdown and Lynne Rominger (Alpha Books, 2001).
- *It's a Bunny Eat Bunny World,* Olga Litowinsky (Walker Publishing Co., 2001).

Old Standards
- *The Art of Writing for Children,* Connie Epstein (Archon Books, 1991).
- *From Cover to Cover, Evaluating and Reviewing Children's Books,* Kathleen T. Horning (HarperCollins, 1997).
- *How to Get Your Teaching Ideas Published,* Jean Stangl (Walker Publishing Co., 1994).
- *How to Write a Children's Book and Get It Published,* Barbara Seuling (Charles Scribner's Sons, 1991).
- *How to Write and Sell Children's Picture Books,* Jean Karl (Writer's Digest Books, 1994).
- *Writing Books for Young People,* James Cross Giblin (The Writer, Inc., 1995).

School Visits and Promotion
- *How to Promote Your Children's Book,* Evelyn Gallardo, third edition (Primate Productions, 2000).
- *Terrific Connections with Authors, Illustrators, and Storytellers,* Toni Buzzeo and Jane Kurtz (Libraries Unlimited, 1999).

Writer, *Achuka* (www.achuka.co.uk), publishing professionals, and Ricochet.Fr members." The France regional website is www.kidbookpros.com. These newsletters have an annual subscription cost of $10 to $15, and most regional newsletters are within this range.

Friendly Voices

Editor and Publisher Audrey Baird loves to write acceptances and saves 50 percent of *Once Upon a Time* for freelancers, many of whom get their first byline in this 32-page quarterly magazine. Launched in 1990, *OUAT* is considered a "back fence" for children's writers and illustrators. Its goal is for writers to get a sense of belonging to a writers' community and gain wisdom from others. Baird says, "We concentrate on what we do best and I believe we do it better than anyone else. We offer answers to those who ask and we

For the Writer's Bookshelf

For Recharging Batteries
■ *The Artist's Way: A Spiritual Path to Higher Creativity,* Julia Cameron (J.P. Tarcher, 1992)

Annual Guides for Children's Writers
■ *Children's Writer's & Illustrator's Market,* published by Writer's Digest, Inc., focuses entirely on the children's market. Editor Alice Pope notes that an established writer may have contacts through an agent. She hopes the unagented will find the directory helpful. Because Pope thinks writers should avail themselves of many sources of information, she includes not only an annual update of markets but a range of articles that give nuts-and-bolts advice, profile editors, and inspire. A standard feature is a section called First Books featuring interviews with first-time authors. "We get e-mail about First Books. People recognize me at conferences and tell me what they learned from it." Pope, a past Society of Children's Book Writers and Illustrators (SCBWI) Regional Advisor, thinks the First Books section builds a bridge to SCBWI and she lists upcoming SCBWI conferences in the book.
■ *Children's Writer Guide,* published by the Institute of Children's Literature, and which you are reading at this moment, is also produced annually. It covers the entire spectrum of the children's writing industry, reviewing the important news of the year and analyzing the possibilities for the year to come. Along with the monthly *Children's Writer* newsletter, it offers in-depth articles on technique, research, business, and all aspects of writing for children. Debuting in 1996, the *Guide* has grown in size and sales and the information gathered between its pages by published writers and publishing experts serves as documentation for those researching the field of children's magazines and books.

Business

give beginners a chance for that first byline."

Among the 11 well-published columnists are Barbara Seuling, Ann Tompert, Kristi Holl, Judy Delton, and Golden Kite winner Ellen Levine. Ron McCutchan, Senior Art Director of the Cricket Magazine Group, offers information for illustrators, and Joan Hyman, Book Editor at Boyds Mills Press, tells "What I've Learned So Far" in her informative column. Guest editors list submission tips and current needs, but marketing information is not a staple. All contributors are unpaid, but Baird says the payback is in the magazine's reputation and enthusiastic letters from the readership. Fan mail is forwarded and friendships spring up among contributors and readers. Baird thinks of *OUAT* as "our" magazine.

Editor and Publisher Laura Backes was a literary agent before founding the monthly *Children's Book Insider* (*CBI*). Backes distills basics in this 12-page how-to newsletter and allots about a quarter of the space to marketing information. The other pages cover career strategies, writing craft, and genres. Reading a Backes editorial is like jumping into a discussion with other writers and illustrators. *CBI* is available online and back issues are available on CD-ROM.

Children's Writer is a monthly marketing update that not only benefits the students and instructors of the many writing courses taught by its publisher, the Institute of Children's Literature, but many subscribers beyond the Institute family. The Institute also publishes this annual *Children's Writer Guide.*

Established more than 11 years ago, *Children's Writer* is a 12-page newsletter that packs detailed articles on craft, technique, style, and, above all, market trends and updates—all geared to the children's writer—into an easy-on-the-eyes blue-and-white format. Articles analyze categories of writing and give current market news, but also encourage and try to find a means to approach markets whether they are burgeoning, changing, or even in a downturn. The goal is to leave readers ready to write and prepared to sell. The first eight pages focus on two or three areas of children's publishing, in fiction or nonfiction, magazines and books, and on publishers specific to those areas. Editor Susan Tierney says the mission of the newsletter is "to provide writers at all levels of experience with news about children's publishing markets and to offer analyses of *currents*, trends, through the voices of the editors and writers themselves."

Award-winning author Elaine Marie Alphin contributes the Commentary column, which deals with important and sometimes controversial subjects for writers. *Children's Writer* also runs regular contests and publishes the winning entries and companion articles on the contest's genre, whether adventure for middle-graders, how-to's for early readers, or readaloud stories for preschoolers.

A separate four-page section, Marketplace, features two columns, The Craft and The Profession, on topics from grammar to rights to motivation. The newsletter also aspires to inspire, says Tierney, and to help writers improve skills and techniques, prompt ideas, and be a forum in a segment of publishing that has increasingly come into its own as the business and art of writing have combined.

General Industry Publications

While the publications above focus specifically on the needs of librarians or educators, or on writing for children, writers' magazines in general publish articles of interest to all writers.

Publishers Weekly (*PW*) is the most notable of industry publications, and reports on book publishing in all its dimensions. *PW* publishes two issues a year that concentrate on the children's market, but the section called Forecasts in every issue is also very helpful. These brief descriptions function purely as information about what's to be published, but also act as reviews. Writers study the market by browsing through libraries and bookstores, picking up catalogues at writers' conferences, and writing for guidelines—but the one piece of information that is hard to get is what is already in the pipeline and hasn't yet come out the other side. *PW*'s Forecasts decrease that knowledge gap. Many writers, and all publishers, crave starred reviews in *PW* almost as much as an award, since people across the publishing industry—including booksellers, editors, publishers—look on the magazine as their "Bible."

PW concentrates on the children's market in its Spring Announcement Issue and Fall Announcement Issue, published in February and July. These include a feature article on children's books, and a long list of publishers and titles to be published in the next season. These issues can be purchased as single copies for $15. (Contact Helene Checinski, Cahners Business Information, Circulation Department, 245 West 17th Street, New York, NY, 10011; e-mail: hchecinski@cahners. com).

Writers' Digest magazine publishes a bimonthly column for children's writers in addition to publishing an annual marketing guide, *Children's Writer's & Illustrator's Market (CWIM)*. The *Children's Book Insider* serves as a quarterly update for marketing information in the *CWIM*.

The Writer, established in 1887 and considered a staple in many writers' libraries, was purchased by the Kalmbach Publishing Company in the spring of 2000 and was redesigned the following year. The "new" magazine featured writing for children in its June 2001 cover story. Editor Elfrieda Abbe reports a good response to that issue and says every issue should have something of interest to children's writers. This magazine has a wide range of genres and markets to offer its readership and is available on newsstands as well as by subscription.

Only you, the writer, know where you are in your career at this moment and which trade publications will provide you with the information of most use to you. The good news is that there are journals and newsletters available to speed you on your way to the *next* level. An informed writer, a reading writer, is usually a productive writer.

Create Your Own Website

By Ruth Sachs

If you're a famous writer, say, a J. K. Rowling, this article will not interest you. Rowling doesn't have to worry about marketing her books. Her appearances are scheduled for her. Her publicist can ensure that interviews don't interfere with her writing time. Warner Brothers created her website, www.harrypotter.com.

We lesser mortals sometimes struggle to publicize our books and increase sales. Fortunately, the Internet can simplify the task. Before you hire a publicist, consider designing a website.

Enchantingly Personal

I ran across Carolyn Meyer's books on a recommended-reading list. I checked to see if she has a website. She does, www. readcarolyn.com, and it is enchanting.

Meyer's site accomplishes practically everything a writer could want. It's a great marketing tool, devoting an entire page to her books, with links to Amazon.com. The site provides a short biography and photographs children will like. Meyer reaches out to her audience—readers and teachers. Savvy kids will bookmark the Grammar Dragon page to use when writing reports. Meyer lets teachers know she is available to speak in schools, and is direct about her rates. She lets children peek over her shoulder in her journal, involving them in the creative process. She praises the teenage boy who is her Webmaster, giving him his own page.

Design elements on the site are worth noting. Meyer keeps the same banner, "Website of Carolyn Meyer," on every page. Her photographs load quickly, a critical part of design. If graphics are slow, visitors may hit the stop button and go somewhere else. The overall look of Meyer's site is clean, uncluttered, fun.

Meyer says she has had the most positive feedback about the journal page, which she keeps updated. She says, "I debated including my e-mail address, which has turned out to be both blessing and curse. I like the contact with the kids, but since I get at least half a dozen e-mails a week and I answer every one, I get really irritated by the requests for information for an assigned paper. Still, I think the dialogue with the kids is a good thing

In Admiration

One author website touches me deeply. I stumbled across it because *The View from Saturday* won the 1997 Newbery Medal. I had never read E. L. Konigsburg, even though she won the Newbery 20 years earlier for *From the Mixed-Up Files of Mrs. Basil E. Frankweiler* and though, every morning when I make coffee, I look out on the elementary school she attended.

Students in the School of Library and Information Studies program at Florida State University (FSU), near Konigsburg's current home, learned of her second Newbery, and decided to honor her by creating a website, with her permission. They interviewed her, obtained permissions to use magazine articles online, then designed the site. FSU allows the site to reside on the campus server. Fran Durrenberger, the Project Manager for the site, wrote the lesson plans included for Konigsburg's *A Proud Taste for Scarlet and Miniver*.

Konigsburg's site (http://slis-two.lis.fsu.edu/~5340f/index.html) pays tribute to a great writer of children's literature. The home page says, "This site was created with teacher and student needs in mind, but it is for anyone who enjoys the writing of an intelligent, witty, and creative author."

While the focus of the accompanying article has been the development of your own website, it seems appropriate to include the FSU effort as an example of a project that high school and college students could undertake. To embark on such a project, use a search engine to find a writer with connections to your area. If that writer does not have an author's website, create the initial official site in their honor (if they are still living, remember to get their permission first, especially since you will want to use their likeness).

Once the site is up, go to Yahoo.com and have it added to the appropriate category. Go to Arts & Humanities, then Literature, finally Authors, and choose the genre you write for most often. Down at the bottom, right-hand corner of your screen, you will see a link that takes you to "Suggest a Site." (Make sure you have written down any other categories you would like to belong to, since within the submission process, you can add several.) Once Yahoo lists you—three to four weeks—almost every other search engine will begin to include you too.

and I have no intention of pulling the e-dress." Neither will she pull the photograph of herself as a snaggle-toothed girl, despite the objections of a teacher, who felt it was inappropriate in this age when kids are so image-conscious.

Marketing Plus & Minus

Sharon Creech's website, www.sharoncreech.com, is beautifully laid out, extremely professional—and solely a marketing website. Its book pages have a structure perfect for a student looking for a *CliffsNotes* version of her portfolio. Once you click on a thumbnail of a book's cover, you see publication information, reviews, a summary, what inspired the book, tidbits (e.g., what's real and what's not), and the awards the book has won.

Creech's biography and Q&As also revolve around the books themselves, and some material duplicates that on the book pages. Creech uses hyperlinks extensively, linking one page to another. The single question "Are you going to write a sequel to *Walk Two Moons*?" links to four books.

The two pages that might have either a more personal touch or a hint of the outside world continue to shine the spotlight on the author and her books. Creech doesn't reach out to her audience as Meyer does. In "Photos and Family," you see where Creech writes, and pictures of family, as they relate to her work. The links to "Other Sites and Resources" connect to items about the author or her books only and not, as might be expected, to outside resources. Creech doesn't list an e-mail address (you should never put personal information such as your home address, telephone, or fax number on a site), and the only way to contact her is through her publisher.

Technically, this site is very pleasing. It is easy to navigate. It gives visitors a comprehensive view of Creech's work and a sense of who she is. Yet its emphasis on the author and her work, to the exclusion of the reader, violates a major tenet of marketing: Focus on the client, on the reader. You don't quite believe that Creech's Q&As come from questions people have asked; they feel like a list of things she wants you to know.

Thematic & Fun

If you haven't read one of her dark and scary books, you will immediately know Susan Price's specialty when you see "Here there be dragons" on her home page, www.susanprice.org.uk. A black cat named Nebukadneza does all the talking, an interesting way to get around the first- versus third-person quandary in writing website text.

Price keeps up delightful humor from page to page. She tells of a fall from a horse she took to help make a character in *The Sterkarm Handshake* real. Nebukadneza provides humor while also giving information about the books.

The site is stylish, fun, with just enough bells and whistles to be attractive to kids who have read Price's work. The style would be inappropriate for writers who tell contemporary stories or short nonfiction works, or picture books. But it is just right for Price. She says the site originally was very different, although it had the same atmosphere—a rambling old house, with a sinister housekeeper for a guide to various rooms. But it took too long to download, so she simplified.The site still loads comparatively slowly, but Price plans further revisions.

Like Meyer, Price wants contact with her readers and includes her e-mail address. "I suppose what brings me the most pleasure is when a reader contacts me through the site, but very few actually have." Now that she's won the Guardian Book Prize and has a new book, *The Wolf Sisters,* she will probably have a full inbox soon.

In Progress

To watch a website in development, bookmark www.joanbauer.com. Joan Bauer's husband is a computer scientist who is writing the code directly in HTML, using a Linux-based system, something few of us will do! He uses Netscape Communicator to preview and debug, and GIMP for the limited image manipulation.

Note how clean the site is. You don't have to overwhelm visitors with graphics to be effective, and the site loads quickly. Bauer includes excerpts from her writing that give a true sense of her voice and what to expect from her books. Her *Hope Was Here* was recently awarded a Newbery Honor.

The number of hits to the site has been increasing, which translates into a heavier e-mail load for Bauer, "more e-mail than any one person can handle right now," in her husband's opinion. She answers all of it. Bauer's site strives to be reader-focused. Friends in academia originally urged her to create the site as a resource for those who study a writer. But she and her husband also see it as an opportunity to provide information for fans.

As a footnote, Bauer's site has a useful tip for foiling spammers, the highly illegal marketing specialists who "harvest" e-mail addresses off websites, message boards, and chat rooms. The Bauers leave spaces in the e-mail address onscreen, but the hyperlink goes to the correctly spaced address. This can help, but isn't foolproof; some say a hyperlink isn't safe from spammers, either.

Mixed Reviews

Once you start, it's hard to stop reading Robin McKinley's site, www.sff.net/people/robin-mckinley because she sells her writing by making you feel part of her world.

The site's textual excellence is mitigated by two features. While the left frame is a navigation bar of sorts (unless you're an expert designer, avoid frames), essentially you do not navigate because the site is one long, continuous page with links.You scroll down and down. There's nothing sinful about that. It's only that Web users have come to expect a series of linked short pages, and not giving readers what they expect can upset their equilibrium and send them away impatient. Because McKinley's home page is far too long, it comes up too slowly as it copes with loading all those links.

McKinley also does not update her site very frequently. The most recent "update," at this writing, consists of indicating that her appearance dates are "TBA" and that you can put a banner

Help! How Do I Start to Create a Website?

You say it's all well and good to talk about creating a website, but your sibling doesn't know HTML and your spouse is an accountant? Never fear. The new generation of Web design software was created for newbies who don't know what URL and HTML stand for.

If you know absolutely nothing about Web design, the *wizard* in Microsoft's *Publisher 2000* will have your site completed in less than eight hours, provided you already have a general concept in your head and your portrait scanned.

Bill Gates and company made the Web design portion of *Publisher* as simple to use as the desktop publishing module you have likely mastered already. Use *Publisher* until you've got your sea legs, till you feel comfortable with basic terminology like navigation and banner, hyperlinks and uploading. It will give you a decent website, one you will not be ashamed of.

Be forewarned, however, that a *Publisher* site is likely to have 'errors' you cannot cure with that software. Fonts will change size in different browsers, and so will page width. It's not bad enough to rule out *Publisher 2000* for beginners, but you will eventually want your site to look better. Once that version of your site is finished, you can graduate to *Front Page 2000*. *Front Page* is less intuitive, and I do not recommend its so-called wizard, or templates. Customizing the template is harder than creating from scratch, so invest in a good how-to book, or simply work through the tutorial that comes with *Front Page* (and take notes). Set aside a quiet day for this project, and you will get it done. Be aware that *Front Page* can import neither your site nor your theme from *Publisher*, so you will be creating the site from the home page up.

The ultimate upgrade (unless you can pay a Web designer to write code for you) is *Dreamweaver*, but it is far more expensive than either *Publisher* or *Front Page*.

If you are a Macintosh user, sadly there are no really good, inexpensive options for you. *Page Mill 3.0*, the software that comes with the iMac, is very difficult to use, at least in comparison to *Front Page* and *Publisher* for Windows. Check out current recommendations on amazon.com for Web design software for the Mac, but be prepared to pay more and do less.

linking her website to yours. There is no new content.

She apologizes for a crash on her site that meant lost e-mail, but a message sent to her well after the crash date went unanswered. These flaws make you wonder if the author is no longer active, or is being distant. If you are like most authors and supplement your writing income with speaking engagements, you do not want the teacher audience to find you unavailable.

If you write as well as McKinley, you can get by with a one-page site like this. Her Q&As contain some very funny work. But if you would rather not invest much writing time on your website, stick to simple navigation tools.

Terry Trueman's site, www.terry-trueman.com, is remarkably comprehensive. The author gives short and long overviews and many details about his work. He includes an excerpt from *Stuck in Neutral* and gives specifics about his speaking appearances. Just as Price's website evokes a sense of her books, the strong look of Trueman's site couples with his passions for education, mental health, and family issues to give a feel for who he is.

The site, however, has drawbacks. The pages have different formats, making you think on occasion that you've left his site. While the banner always has "TT" and a bird image, the banner as a whole is never the same. It uses a variety of fonts, sometimes has subheads and sometimes doesn't. It's visually confusing. The index on the left of the site varies from page to page, too. On any website, elements must change from page to page, for content

or other reasons, but visual and organizational variations and lack of consistency are unsettling over time.

On my system, that "TT" appears to be in a font called EraserDust, so either the initials are a slow-loading graphic or show up in that style only on computers with the font. Be careful when using specialty typefaces in your website. No one else may see them the way you do.

Trueman lists many ways to contact him, but an e-mail to him never got a response. If your "customers" are not convinced of their value, the publicity off your website can backfire.

Think about how you intend to handle correspondence, and occasionally review your success. Avoid using auto-responses through your e-mail system; your readers may think you're a real snob! Your website is meant to be a place for your readers to connect—and want to connect again through your writing.

By the way, check out my website at www.ruthsachs.com and tear it to shreds—I mean, critique it in an e-mail to me, at the address found on the site.

Idea Generation

Hot Leads: Track Ideas from *Live* Sources

By Jackie Horsfall

The annual Kids' Bird Count presentation at your local nature center is electrifying. You're inspired to race home and write an upbeat article, seeing real sales potential. Unfortunately, mired in family obligations, you can't find time to pound out a draft until three days later. Sitting at the computer, you struggle to pull your thoughts together, but the information stored in your head has faded into vague facts and numbers. Was that 200 red-crested cockatoos facing extinction, or 2,000?

Coming up with ideas for articles and stories that are fresh, provocative, and fascinating is a real challenge for writers. Often the greater challenge lies not in finding great ideas, but in capturing and retaining available information, milking all the possible sales angles from one topic while it's still fresh in the mind. Take a tip from crime scene investigators tracking hot leads in homicide cases. Write it up on the spot, detailing all the pertinent facts while the evidence is fresh.

Get Out There

Sure you can find all kinds of topics on the Internet and in the library, but that's just the point—they're already published. Turn off the computer, get outside, and create the possibility of getting lost in an adventure in your own community. There's nothing happening, you say? The best writers find stories in every nook and cranny. Whether you live in a backwoods burg or a booming metropolis, ideas are everywhere, free for the taking—if you know where to look.

Check your local newspaper or radio station for listings of community programs and cultural events at museums, hospitals, nature centers, and service clubs. Read your school bulletin for news on class field trips, exchange students, and holiday celebrations. Scan grocery store flyers for free cooking demonstrations and nutrition classes. Take note of the bulletins from your home improvement center for how-to demonstrations, like container gardening, you could gear down to child level. Star those programs you think will lead to a fascinating article or story. Then grab a clipboard, arm yourself with a "Hot Leads Tracking Sheet" (see page 254), and track your great ideas.

Hot Leads Tracking Sheet

■ **What's It About?**
- Event _____
- Date _____
- Presenter _____
- Resource _____

■ **Key Words** _____
_____

■ **Wow! I Didn't Know That!**
_____
_____
_____
_____
_____

■ **Questions**
_____
_____

■ **Working Titles**
_____

■ **Sales Angles:**
- Story _____
- Article _____
- Recipe _____
- Activity _____
- Game _____
- Jokes _____
- Poem _____
- Seasonal _____

■ **Research**
_____
_____
_____
_____

Hot Leads Clues

Enter the headings on the "Hot Leads Tracking Sheet," on the opposite page, into your computer and print multiple copies, or type the headings on letter-size paper and photocopy.

Then, whenever you start following a lead, answer these questions:

What's It About?: Provide yourself with at-a-glance basic information for filing purposes and memory jogging if you can't work on your material immediately. Include the date; the presenter—speaker, event organizer, demonstration leader—and resources, such as the sponsoring organization. Since you'll be generating multiple sales angles and/or seasonal pieces, you'll find the basics at your fingertips when you begin each one—even if it's years later.

Key Words: What was the name of that snail the park ranger mentioned again? And what were those spiny things sticking out of its head called? Jot down those important theme words, scientific or technical terms and their definitions, the correct spelling of names, organizations, and locations.

Wow! I Didn't Know That!: Capture the information that grabs your attention, makes your pulse race, and stirs your curiosity. Italian caterpillars summoned to court in 1659 for damaging property! Doughnuts invented by a boy tired of eating mom's heavy cakes! If you didn't know it, most likely kids and editors won't either. Choose the most fascinating point for your pitch or selling point, the hook for your cover or query letter.

Questions: When it's time to raise your hand for Q&A after the presentation, don't be stricken by a temporary mind-fog. Jot down your questions as you think of them. If they haven't all been answered during the Q & A, approach the presenter after the program.

Working Titles: Possible titles can be silly or serious, as simple as overheard phrases incorporating key words, but will provide a head start when you sit down to compose.

Sales Angles: Brainstorm on the fly. Tap into your imagination to create possible slants for multiple pieces. On average, one topic can generate 5 to 10 different sales ideas, or combinations of ideas. Pair an article with a recipe or activity. A story with a game or joke.

Research: Do in-depth, post-presentation fact-finding at the library or on the Internet. Put that white space to good use. Use the margins and back of your Hot Leads sheet for additional facts, figures, diagrams, and quotes. If possible, get the presenter's telephone number or Internet address (ask for this information after the presentation) in case you need to verify facts or get a direct quote.

Take a few tips from busy freelance writers: Investigate your own backyard—and local library, civic associations, university, clubs, and more—and you'll find no shortage of timely topics. Get those fascinating details down on paper before they vanish. Think in multiples and try to spin more than one idea out of your initial research. You'll be a giant step ahead of the competition—and have an endless supply of great ideas.

Ideas

Tracking Sheet Idea 1: Soybean Festival

■ **What's It About?**
- Event   Local school bulletin announces lecture by exchange teacher who recently returned from a year in Japan
- Date   April 2, 2002
- Presenter   Gena Walker, teacher
- Resource   Edmond High School teacher-exchange program

■ **Key Words**   evil spirits, soybeans, oni (demons, monsters), Bean-Throwing Day (first week of February)

■ **Wow! I Didn't Know That!**
1. Teachers wear scary oni masks on Bean-Throwing Day.
2. They throw soybeans in classrooms.
3. Kids get packets of soybeans on their lunch trays.
4. Soybeans taste like dry-roasted peanuts.
5. Bean-throwing is a religious ceremony in shrines and temples.

■ **Questions**
1. How did the bean-throwing originate?
2. What is the religious significance?

■ **Working Titles**
"Bean-Throwing Day"; "Beans on My Jeans"; "Spirits and Soybeans"

■ **Sales Angles:**
- Story   American child, frightened of ghosts, learns to scare them.
- Article   Uses of soybeans around the world.
- Recipe   Soybean snacks.
- Activity   Making oni masks.
- Game   Soybean toss.
- Jokes   Soybeans are *stir-fright* vegetables.
- Poem   "Beans for Halloween"
- Seasonal   First week of February; possibly Halloween.

■ **Research**
Bean-throwing mythology.
Onis.
Japanese schools.

Tracking Sheet Idea 2: Junior Olympics

■ **What's It About?**
- Event   Local middle school bulletin announces Junior Olympics competition with area schools. Junior Olympics pre-games presentation.
- Date   May 5, 2002
- Presenter   Simcoe City Middle School
- Resource   school athletic staff

■ **Key Words**
Olympia, stade (length of a stadium), pentathlon (5-round elimination)

■ **Wow! I Didn't Know That!**
1. First recorded game in Greece was in 776 B.C.
2. First game was a foot race.
3. Gymnasiums were built for athletes to worship and train in.
4. Games purpose: religious & military (keep soldiers in shape for war).
5. Married women not allowed to watch or compete.

■ **Questions**
Why aren't Olympic games played every year?

■ **Working Titles**
"Go for the Gold"; "Honors on Olympia"; "Great Greek Games"

■ **Sales Angles:**
- Story   Child overcomes disability to participate in games.
- Article   How local girl used Olympic win to aid food pantry.
- Recipe   "Fast" food (play on words) for a healthy body.
- Activity   How to organize a neighborhood Olympics.
- Game   Discus Throw (using a Frisbee).
- Jokes   Why can't Cinderella throw a ball?
- Poem   "I Can Run, I Can Jump"
- Seasonal   Submit a year before next Olympics (winter/summer).

■ **Research**
History of the Olympic Games in classic and modern times; other Olympics—junior, special, for older athletes.

Tracking Sheet Idea 3: Sea Turtle Watch

■ **What's It About?**

- Event Local Rotary Club announces a community presentation
     by Earthwatch volunteer returning from sea-life study
     in Costa Rica.
- Date   August 18, 2002
- Presenter Walt Newcomb, volunteer researcher
- Resource Earthwatch; Costa Rica aquarium

■ **Key Words**

  leatherback nesting sites; sea turtle; Playas Grande;
  Langosta Beach

■ **Wow! I Didn't Know That!**

1. Populated beach areas are destroying ancient nesting grounds.
2. Many baby sea turtles are eaten by birds before they reach the water.
3. Eggs are often stolen by humans while the turtles are laying them.
4. Turtles drown in long nets used by fishing boats.
5. Turtles choke on floating plastic.

■ **Questions**

  What can kids do to help turtles breed and re-populate?

■ **Working Titles**

  "Here Today, Gone Tomorrow"; "Turtle Trials"; "Losing the
  Leatherbacks"

■ **Sales Angles:**

- Story   Kids stop tourists from taking eggs home as souvenirs.
- Article   How kids can help turtles or other endangered species.
- Recipe   "No Turtle" Green Pea Soup.
- Activity   Organize groups for beach cleanup, especially plastic bags.
- Game   Save the Turtle Tag.
- Jokes   Do turtles wear people-neck sweaters?
- Poem   "Turtle Tears"
- Seasonal Nesting season.

■ **Research**

  CTURTLE website
  Recent Endangered Species List from the Fish and Wildlife Service

Tracking Sheet Idea 4: One-Room Schools

■ **What's It About?**
- Event   Historical Society newsletter announces community Open House at preserved 1878 one-room schoolhouse.
- Date   October 10, 2002
- Presenter   President of Living History Program
- Resource   Hilltown Schoolhouse Living History Program

■ **Key Words**   spelling bee, copybook, privy, hornbook, recitation, elocution

■ **Wow! I Didn't Know That!**
1. One-room schoolhouses served grades 1 to 8.
2. Heated by wood or coal—teacher made hot lunch on stove.
3. Blackboards actually boards painted black.
4. Pump organs used instead of pianos (temperature & humidity effects).
5. Children called to school with hand-rung bell.

■ **Questions**
     How did classrooms get their water, books, paper, other supplies?

■ **Working Titles**
     "Historical Society Newsletter Announces Community Open House"; "Little Schoolhouse in the Woods"; "One Room for All"; "Reading, Writing, 'Rithmetic"

■ **Sales Angles:**
- Story   Historical: 1800s girl arranges chicken dinner to raise funds for slate blackboard.
- Article   Daily schedule of typical student in 1800s.
- Recipe   One-vegetable soup (based on original 1878 recipe).
- Activity   Make your own copybook.
- Game   Make your own copybook.
- Jokes   Why did the schoolhouse turn red?
- Poem   The No-grade School.
- Seasonal   School year tie-ins.

■ **Research**
     State historical records—how teachers were located, contracted, paid.

Tracking Sheet Idea 5: Mushroom Hunt

■ **What's It About?**
- Event — A local nature center newsletter announces a mushroom hunt led by an amateur mycologist.
- Date — September 2, 2002
- Presenter — Dr. William Grant, Biology Professor
- Resource — Central University biology dept.; Woodland Nature Center

■ **Key Words** — fungi; edible; poisonous; cap; spore; stem

■ **Wow! I Didn't Know That!**
1. A single fungus can cover 30 acres and weigh more than 10 tons.
2. Without fungi, we'd be up to our eyeballs in fallen trees and woods debris.
3. Never lick your fingers after handling; many are poisonous.
4. People who collect mushrooms are called shroomers.
5. Mushrooms pop up without warning—thought to be magical.

■ **Questions**
What are the symptoms of mushroom poisoning?

■ **Working Titles**
"Mushroom Madness"; "Falling for Fungi"; "Fungi Among Us"; "Fairy Rings and Dead Man's Fingers"

■ **Sales Angles:**
- Story — Junior high kids on a mushroom hunt find a real fairy ring and real fairies.
- Article — Avoiding poisonous mushrooms.
- Recipe — Mushroom soup.
- Activity — How to make spore prints.
- Game — Fungi forage.
- Jokes — What room do you never have to clean?
- Poem — "I'm a Little Umbrella"
- Seasonal — Spring or fall.

■ **Research**
Mushroom field guide.
State mushroom society
Cornell Center for Fungal Biology

Writer Anecdotes

Observe, Dream, Question

By Veda Boyd Jones

Where do you get your ideas? No matter if an author is speaking to a bunch of kids at school or a group of adults at a community event, that question is always asked. Each writer answers differently, but there's one definitive answer.

Ideas are "everywhere!" says Brenda Seabrooke, voicing the opinion of writers across the country. Seabrooke, who has written 16 books for young readers, gets ideas from "the air, the sky, driving down the road, malls, memories, but probably mostly from places and people."

Cheryl Harness, whose works include 16 American historical picture books that she wrote and illustrated, gets ideas from "Angels, the encyclopedia, PBS documentaries, or shooting the breeze with editors."

Gary Blackwood, author of *The Shakespeare Stealer* and *Shakespeare's Scribe,* says, "When you get really serious about writing, everything starts to look like an idea to you: historical markers, dreams, random thoughts, places you visit, people you meet, other books, etc. Though I make a note of some of them, it seems that the re-

ally good ones always come back unbidden, like one of those songs you can't get out of your head—except that the songs are usually the most mindless, annoying ones, while the ideas that keep coming back are usually the best ones."

Although she can sometimes trace what prompted an idea—a subject studied in college, a promise made in junior high, or a magazine article, Pamela Smith Hill, author of award-winning historical fiction and fantasy, says she doesn't know what transforms something so general into her own book idea. "I really can't say, and for me, that's part of the magic of writing. My best ideas come from somewhere so deep within myself that I'm surprised they come from me at all."

"I think you're juggling three balls called *observation, memory,* and *imagination* when you write, and your ideas come from a combination of those three places," says Vicki Grove, author of middle-grade and young adult novels and winner of the Society of Midland Authors 2001 Fiction Prize for Outstanding Contribution in the Field of Children's Literature.

Opening Minds

These writers don't have a private line to ideas; they practice the connection. "It's all in the eyes, keeping them open," Grove says. What the eyes see should be sent directly to the heart because emotions are what make good stories. "Pay attention to who's doing what to whom. Stories are about what people do to and for each other."

Blackwood advises, "Try to look at everything and everyone you see, and everything you read, as a potential story or article idea. After a while, your mind gets into that habit."

Lois Ruby, whose most recent book is *Soon Be Free*, a companion to her earlier, *Steal Away Home*, says writers should "be open to sensory input, diverse ideas, foreign travel, concepts that seem beyond our understanding, and ideas that are alien to our own value system." Be willing to feel uncomfortable. Don't write about what you know; write about what you want to know, and then go and find out about it. "Above all, read!" Ruby says. "I thank a librarian friend, Sally Hayes, for the sign I carry with me to all the schools I visit, and it's great advice for writers, too: 'You Don't Have to Read Every Day, Just on the Days You Eat.'"

Hill agrees that reading, "passionate reading on subjects that interest or inspire you" is key to opening yourself to ideas. "Listen to music. See a play or movie. Go to the art museum. I've found that other creative disciplines can sometimes trigger that mysterious part of my brain that generates ideas."

A three-step process for developing ideas works for Linda Joy Singleton, author of some 20 middle-grade and YA novels. First, daydream. "Daydreaming is a natural pastime for creative types; no training required."

Second, question everything. "If you're watching a show on TV, reading a book, or hear some interesting gossip, ask yourself how someone would feel in that situation. Maybe a main character is having a problem, but you wonder about his little brother. How would *that* character feel? Ask yourself different questions leading to conflicts and ideas."

Third, examine emotion. "If something makes you feel strongly, ask yourself how a character might feel in a similar situation. Or remember back to a pivotal moment in your life and use the feelings you experienced. Let your mind wander—which brings us back to daydreaming."

Harness advises writers to "develop the habit of *what-if?-ing*. If you do, imagining scenarios becomes second nature."

Marilyn D. Anderson, author of fiction and nonfiction books for children, says writers should "read everything they can get their hands on: magazines, newspapers, and books about history, science, current events. Listen to people around you, especially kids. They'll tell you what's important to them."

June Rae Wood, winner of the Mark Twain Award for *The Man Who Loved Clowns*, believes writers should eavesdrop. At a mall or a restaurant "you'll only hear snatches of conversation, but you can dream up scenarios to explain what you've heard. This is a great way to get the creative juices flowing."

Storage

Wood collects ideas for future projects. "My 'idea box' is a stack of papers about 18 inches high—newspaper clippings, a list of unusual character names, notes to myself, interview notes, tidbits of information on various subjects. The whole thing is a hodgepodge that I sift through to jog my memory or give me a direction when I'm ready to start a new project."

Grove is a bit more systematic. "I jot ideas down on whatever scrap of paper is handy, then tape all those scraps into blank notebooks. I call it laminating, because I use fat tape!"

Anderson uses sticky notes, which are stuck all over her office, and has a file called "Good Ideas." Blackwood says, "I just scrawl ideas on pieces of paper and cram them in a pigeonhole above my desk. Usually they stay there, but once in a while I dig out something and use it."

Singleton has a recipe box with ideas written on index cards. Although she keeps them, she has yet to use one for a book. The same applies to Hill. "I have a big, fat, ragged file labeled *Writing Ideas*. In it are scribbled notes and newspaper and magazine clippings on everything from Queen Elizabeth the First to Crazy Horse to Bob Gibson. Have I used any of the clippings I've saved so diligently year after year? No. But the file gives me peace of mind. If I run out of ideas, then maybe I'll find something in the file."

Idea Boulevards

Ruby jots down ideas in a notebook. Some of them work out, but others do not. "While outside sources are stimulating, ultimately, I think, ideas have to bubble up from within the writer. For me, they come from two roads that join and feed into a third, broader boulevard. One is a sense of time, place, and history. Is there a particular point in time that intrigues me? Is there a place that begs me to explore it? Is there a dramatic event in history that spurs my imagination and demands that I ask tough questions? And the toughest question: Is there some basic issue of justice involved in that moment in time? If the time/place captures my attention and merits further research, then I wait for the other, more important road to appear on the horizon, which is the character who will drive the story and humanize the time and place. If there's a good conjunction of time/place and person, then the boulevard spreads out before me, and a story begins to write itself."

Ruby's ruminations about idea development are shared by other writers. Blackwood says, "I used to start writing almost as soon as an idea hit me. Now I live with it for a while, taking voluminous notes, exploring the possibilities, coming up with names and personalities for the characters, planning out a story line, and trying mentally to compose a

Where Did You Get That Idea?

■ **Marilyn D. Anderson:** While waiting at the beauty shop one day, Anderson overheard some women talking about baseball cards. That reminded her that her cousin John used to collect them along with that awful bubble gum. He wouldn't chew the gum, but stacked it high on his dresser. "What if the room got very warm and the gum got really sticky? And what if things started sticking in the gum?" The result was *The Bubble Gum Monster* book series.

■ **Gary Blackwood:** "I've always liked survival stories of all kinds, so I started thinking about a situation in which a boy would have to fend for himself. Getting lost in the woods sounded like a natural." *Wild Timothy* was Blackwood's first young adult novel.

■ **Vicki Grove:** The author remembered an event in her life when a popular girl came up to her in the public library and stuck volume O of an encyclopedia under Grove's sweater. "She told me to walk out the back door with it and give it to her in the parking lot. After about 20 of the worst minutes of my life, I got up the courage or whatever to shove the encyclopedia back where it belonged, then ran crying all the way home." In *Crystal Garden,* Grove has the character actually steal the volume for the popular girl. "I often bring memory and imagination together in this way so I can see what would have happened had I taken a different fork in the wacky and angst-ridden road of adolescent life."

■ **Cheryl Harness:** While in Washington, D.C., Harness visited the big old house on Pennsylvania Avenue. Then on the plane to New York, she read a magazine article about the opera *The Ghosts of Versailles.* She put the two together and came up with *Ghosts of the White House.*

■ **Pamela Smith Hill:** "My idea for *The Last Grail Keeper* really began in 1976 when I took a graduate seminar in Arthurian myth and legend. As part of the seminar, I researched Glastonbury and its shadowy connections to the Holy Grail. Long after I graduated, I continued my research and readings. Somehow, literally over decades, the idea for the book took shape: magic in slow motion."

good opening paragraph before I start actually writing."

Hill also fleshes out an idea with notes about character, plot, setting, and even dialogue. "From there, I sketch out the story in a very loose outline. At this point, I may stop and do three to four months of intensive research. Or I may just dive in and start writing. I usually balance writing with ongoing research."

Outlining is a tried and true method of seeing if an idea is strong enough for a book. Seabrooke says, "I

Where Did You Get That Idea?

■ **Lois Ruby:** "In all my stories an ordinary person, nested in an extraordinary situation, is pushed to his or her moral limits." In *Soon Be Free,* time moves back and forth in alternating chapters between the 1850s and the present day, in and about a house that was a haven for runaway slaves on the Underground Railroad in Lawrence, Kansas. The protagonist James must make a choice "that will jeopardize either the Kentucky runaways he's come to love or the gentle Delaware Indians who have been his good neighbors in Kansas." Until the last page of the first draft, Ruby had no idea what the boy would decide "or how his heart could endure whatever choice he made. Believe me, that's one of the most frightening and exhilarating aspects of writing!"

■ **Brenda Seabrooke:** Seabrooke lets her mind mix separate elements in time and come up with unique ideas. "*The Haunting at Stratton Falls* was the result of childhood memories combined with a recent spooky experience and a dress I had in ninth grade."

■ **Linda Joy Singleton:** "On the Fourth of July 2000, I was watching the movie *Big* with Tom Hanks. At the end of the show, when Tom grew little again and returned home, I wondered, how will he explain about being gone for nearly two months? By that evening I had come up with an opening line: "When my best friend disappeared, I knew she'd be back in five weeks. Just like the others." Once I had this opening, I was excited and hooked. Seven months later, I finished a young adult suspense called *Vanishings.*"

■ **June Rae Wood:** "A few years ago, my sister's husband, a truck driver, was on the road when Janie went into labor on July fourth. Consequently, Mom and I drove her to the hospital and paced the floor waiting for her to deliver. When the baby arrived, I told Janie, 'If I had a little girl born on the Fourth of July, I'd have to name her Liberty or Freedom.' Janie's response was 'Yuk! Those are the worst names I've ever heard,' and she named her little girl Chelsey. But that conversation planted the seed. I created my own little girl named Freedom, age 13, born on the Fourth of July, and wrote a book around her. Her name and birth date are the keys to the mystery in *A Share of Freedom.*"

Ideas

always try to outline first and usually the outlines run about 12-plus pages, but once in a while a book eludes outlining, so I have to write it all the way through to find out how things happen. I always know what's going to happen, just not always exactly how."

Wood starts with a three-page, double-spaced outline. "This is basically a letter to myself, telling me who the characters are, what the conflict will be, and how it will be resolved. I have to know how a story will end before I start."

Because Harness writes and illustrates picture books, she makes a rough storyboard instead of an outline, then begins the research phase.

Series of Windows

An idea doesn't come with all the details filled in, and those details take research and lots of it. That research can generate even more ideas. Harness's research on *The Amazing Impossible Erie Canal* revealed that while the canal was being dug across New York state, "The Night Before Christmas" was being written in New York City. That fact sparked the idea for *Papa's Christmas Gift* about Clement C. Moore and the world of 1822.

"As for finding an idea while researching another project," says Lois Ruby, "oh, my, yes! Each question I answer opens the window on another question, the answer to which leaves me gasping because so many, many ideas pop up, and I haven't 'world enough, or time' to explore them all."

When Grove was researching white supremacy groups for *Reaching Dustin*, "I became interested in the big cheese, the KKK. So I got deeply into this particular group in my next book, *The Starplace*," which explores racial prejudice in the 1960s.

Since many writers have the same idea; it's a writer's perspective of the idea that makes it unique, and yet some writers feel they will jinx an idea when they share it with others. That the idea will be stolen by someone else isn't part of the fear.

"I keep my stories to myself until I have something down on paper," says Wood. "If I *talk* a story as opposed to writing it, I lose my steam."

Grove also keeps an idea to herself at first. "Then usually a group of kids that I'm talking with at a school will ask what I'm working on, and suddenly I'll find myself trying to tell them, figuring out what I'm actually doing as I go. Their reaction will have a lot to do with how I proceed, what I jettison and what I add."

Many writers bounce their ideas around with family members. Blackwood admits that sharing the idea with his wife and daughter "helps me firm it up, make it more concrete. Sometimes they point out possible holes or problem areas in the premise, which, though it rankles me a little, forces me to come up with a solution. As the idea takes shape, I do most of my thinking in a notebook, rather than out loud, because so many of the things I come up with are dead ends."

Ideas are everywhere, but writers must be open to the world around them to find ideas, and then they must incorporate their own experiences to give the ideas an individual slant. Develop a writer's eyes and ears so that you notice ideas, and let those ideas travel to your heart and your imagination. Get the idea?

People, Places, Things: Ideas Abound

Ideas always begin with people. Argue that events may be the germination of an idea, and take a step back to see the individuals at the heart. Even catastrophic events beyond human control—earthquakes and disease—may begin with an objective, apparently distant prime cause, but they in turn create human tales. What writer doesn't at some point recognize that every story is a human story? Here we present a list of people, and events with anonymous people behind the story, to inspire ideas for writing of every kind. Peruse, ruminate, develop. Have fun and meet success with the smallest germ of an idea, the briefest encounter with a person from the past or present.

The list is in no way comprehensive and in many ways arbitrary. Many of the most well-known historical figures—Plato, Cleopatra, Joan of Arc, Elizabeth I, Mozart, Lincoln, Shakespeare, Napoleon, Lindbergh—are not here, simply because they have been written about so much. Other famous names—Hippocrates, Hannibal, Columbus, da Vinci, Dracula—are included, with miscellaneous facts that may spur ideas for new slants on old names.

The Ancients
Dates B.C.E.

■ Ictinus and Callicrate: were the architects of the Parthenon. 5th c.

■ The Greek philosopher Empedocles theorized that everything is made of four elements—air, earth, fire, and water—and that the body is ruled by four humors—blood, bile, black pile, and phlegm. The nineteenth-century Matthew Arnold wrote a poem called "The Song of Empedocles." 5th c.

■ There is debate over the man known as Confucius, but tradition and some hard evidence indicate he was a Chinese moral and political reformer whose disciples gathered his writings, the *Analects*. Confucianism is a moral and social system based on human relationships, status, and kindness. 5th c.

■ Celtic art entered a new stage, integrating the classical and Eastern. It is exemplified by bronze wine flagons from the second half of the fifth century B.C.E. found in the Moselle.

■ Herodotus, the "Father of History," wrote the first comprehensive historical treatise, giving events perspective and critical analysis. His primary subject was the Persian Wars. 5th c.

- The Chinese developed cast iron around 400 B.C.E.
- Hippocrates still accepted the belief that four humors rule the body and that their imbalance causes illness. But he also stressed cleanliness and diet as essential to good health. He was the purported source of a code of medical ethics, although there is no proof the Hippocratic oath began with him. 4th c.
- His widow erected the Mausoleum for King Mausolus in Halicarnassus, in modern-day Turkey. It was one of the Seven Wonders of the Ancient World. 4th c.
- The Greek philosopher Epicurus taught that pleasure—peace that comes from the absence of pain—is the highest good. *Epicure* has come to denote the sensual. 4th to 3rd c.
- A Greek poet and dramatist known for humor, plots based on love stories, and for his characters, Menander was a prolific Athenian writer of New Comedy. 4th to 3rd c.
- Seleucus was a general of Alexander the Great who created an empire in Asia after Alexander's death. 4th to 3rd c.
- Chares of Lindus was the sculptor of the Colossus of Rhodes, a Wonder of the Ancient World. 3rd c.
- The King of Epirus, Pyrrhus's wars against Macedonia and Rome took such a toll that *Pyrrhic victory* came to mean a victory won at too high a cost. 3rd c.
- In China, the crossbow was invented. 3rd c.
- Scipio Africanus Major was the general who conquered Hannibal in the Punic Wars, in North Africa. He won the name "Africanus" for the victory. He was a member of a large patrician Roman family. 3rd to 2nd c.

- The Roman dramatists Plautus and Terence, renowned for comedies, imitated Menander. Plautus depicted daily life, and developed stock characters to great effect. Terence's work was more sophisticated. Both Romans influenced comedies of manners of the Renaissance and later. 3rd to 2nd c.
- Mattathias of Modin was one of the Maccabees, a family that rebelled against religious persecution of Jews in Syria. One of his sons was Judas— later called Maccabeus, or the Hammerer—whose rededication of the Temple in Jerusalem is celebrated at Hanukkah. 2nd to 1st c.

First Century A.D.
- Juvenal was a Roman satirist whose epigrammatic poetry denounced decadence, immorality, and tyranny.
- The famous Roman Coliseum, or Flavian Amphitheater, was finished and dedicated under the Roman Emperor Titus, around 80 A.D. Titus also destroyed Jerusalem, in 70 A.D.
- The emperor Trajan commissioned a forum in Rome, which became part of an extended meeting area built over centuries. Trajan was Spanish, the first non-Roman emperor. The architect of the Forum of Trajan was Apollodorus of Damascus.

Second Century
- Simon Bar-Kokhba and Rabbi Eleazar led a Judean revolt against Roman rule in reaction to the Emperor Hadrian's edicts restricting Jewish practices. The rebellion was not successful and is considered the beginning of the last Diaspora.
- Astronomer and geographer, Ptol-

emy wrote the *Almagest*, which was used for more than a millennium, until Copernicus questioned the placement of Earth at the center of the universe.

■ Apuleius was the author of *The Golden Ass,* a comical adventure about a man transformed into a donkey. The Latin poem was popular for centuries.

■ Marcus Aurelius was a Roman emperor but is known perhaps even more for his *Meditations*, a classic text on Stoic philosophy. Stoicism taught that the divine shapes reality, and man can become free by conforming—abandoning passion and excess and living in line with nature.

■ Greek physician to Roman emperors, Galen recognized that blood is carried in the arteries, and he made other important discoveries that influenced medicine for centuries.

Third Century

■ A Platonist who merged Christian belief, Scripture study, and Greek philosophy, Origen strongly and permanently influenced Christian theology.

■ Mani was a Persian who founded Manichaeism, a dualistic philosophy that used elements of Hellenistic Christianity, the mysteries of Gnosticism, and Eastern beliefs.

■ The king Ardashir I reunited Persia. He was the first of the Sassanid dynasty and named Zoroastrianism as the state religion.

■ Horse breeding advanced and flourished in the Roman empire.

Fourth Century

■ Samudra Gupta founded an Indian dynasty that ended the tribal system and moved toward a society based on caste.

■ Constantine the Great was the famous pagan emperor whose vision of a flaming cross before the Battle of Mulvian Bridge led eventually to Christianity's wide acceptance. His mother, St. Helen, was said to have found the "True Cross" on which Jesus was crucified.

■ Constantine's nephew and emperor, Julian the Apostate, was also a scholar who tried to turn Rome back to the ancient Gods.

■ The medieval empire of Ghana was founded in the fourth century and endured until the thirteenth. It was long supported by trade in gold and salt. The modern nation of Ghana took its name from the ancient empire.

■ Theodosius the Great allowed the Vandals to settle in Roman territories, opening the gates to the empire's end. It would be divided into Western and Eastern empires, represented for centuries by Rome and Constantinople (Byzantium). Under Theodosius, Christianity became the state religion.

■ The Chinese astronomer Yu Hai studied the equinoxes.

■ The Mayans advanced in their understanding of astronomy and developed a fairly sophisticated calendar.

The Middle Ages
Fifth Century

■ The Huns and Vandals attacked throughout Europe, including Gaul and the city of Rome.

■ Odoacer, a German chieftain, overthrew the last Roman emperor, Romulus Augustulus, and established his own kingdom in Italy. The year became the standard date given for the fall of the Roman empire: 476.

Ideas

■ Theodoric the Great established the Ostrogothic kingdom of Italy.

■ Clovis, ruler of the Franks, was converted by Bishop Remigius, or St. Remy, to Christianity.

■ North American natives used bows and arrows.

■ The first written Buddhism texts were collected.

■ Japanese developed in written form, based on Chinese writing.

■ The Jewish Haggadoth were compiled from legends and stories to illustrate the Torah's morality and theology.

■ Tradition says Bodhidharma travelled from India and founded Zen Buddhism in China. Meditation as the path to enlightenment was its driving principle.

Sixth Century

■ A Roman philosopher and politician who fought corruption, Boethius was thrown in prison where he wrote the influential *On the Consolation of Philosophy*.

■ Justinian the Great became Byzantine emperor, issued a code of civil laws, and conquered North Africa, Italy, and part of Spain. His reign saw the beginnings of the European silk industry when his missionaries smuggled silkworms out of China. His wife Theodora improved the legal rights of women. Justinian and Theodora are depicted in the famous Byzantine mosaics at Ravenna's Church of St. Vitale.

■ Belisarius was a Roman general who led Justinian's battles, and was among the last in the "imperial" tradition of ancient Rome.

■ Saint, Doctor of the Church, pope, Gregory the Great was a monk of St. Benedict, founder of monasticism. He sent missionaries to convert the Anglo-Saxons; legend says when he first saw natives of Britain, with fair complexions, he said they were truly "angels," playing on the name of the "Angles." Gregorian chant was named for him.

■ St. Patrick, St. Columba, and others represented a flourishing of Irish culture in the "dark ages" of Europe. Irish song, story, art, and spirituality spread to the continent with an impact that lasted more than a century.

■ The Indian astronomer Aryabhata discussed the Earth's rotation, planetary movement, and calculated pi.

■ The first version of the story of Siegfried and Brunhild, in oral tradition, dated from this time.

■ Buddhism grew in China, making inroads against Confucianism, and spread to Japan.

Seventh Century

■ Chao Yuan Fang classified more than 1,700 diseases in a Chinese treatise.

■ Caedmon authored the beautiful "Caedmon's Hymn," the oldest English Christian poem. It used pagan poetic forms about a Christian subject.

■ Mohammed founded Islam. Only decades after his death, disputes led to new sects: the Sunni, Shi'ite, and Khawariz Muslims. The Koran was completed. The Dome of the Rock was built. In the same century, Arabs conquered Jerusalem and Persia, and destroyed the great library at Alexandria.

■ Windmills were invented in Persia.

■ In England, what will be called the Sutton Hoo treasure when discovered centuries later, was buried with an Anglian king. It included exquisite examples of Anglo-Saxon metallurgy, including cloisonné.

■ The Japanese devised block printing.

■ Japan's great monastery of Horyu-ji was built.

Eighth Century

■ The T'ang Dynasty gave rise to a golden age of poetry in China. Among the most accomplished poets were Li Po, Tu Fu, and Wang Wei.

■ Mayan culture was at a peak, with advances in math and astronomy.

■ Irish manuscript illumination flourished and spread through the seventh century and into the eighth. Examples included the Book of Durrow, the Lindisfarne Gospels, and the Book of Kells.

■ Known as the Venerable, Bede wrote *The Ecclesiastical History of the English People,* a history covering the period from the Caesars to 731.

■ The leader of the Franks, Charles Martel, stopped the Arabs at Poitiers. Legends formed around this defeat of the Moors in Europe. Martel was the son of Pepin and his grandson was Charlemagne, who crowned himself Holy Roman Emperor on Christmas Day in the year 800.

■ Caliph Harun al-Rashid ruled in a golden age of Arabic culture. He is thought to be the caliph in the stories of the *Arabian Nights*. He negotiated with Charlemagne, even sending him an elephant and a water-clock. Music thrived under al-Rashid.

■ A society grew in size and influence in the Mississippi River Valley.

■ Saicho was a priest who started a Buddhist sect, T'ien-t'ai, and popularized tea in Japan.

■ The epic Anglo-Saxon poem *Beowulf*

was written as early as the eighth century. It is marked for its use of the vernacular, mixing pagan and Christian elements, and for adventure.

■ Bells and pipe organs originated.

■ A learned monk from Northumbria, Alcuin, traveled to the continent, met Charlemagne, and strongly influenced Carolingian culture and religion.

■ Gunpowder was first used in China for fireworks.

Ninth Century

■ King Alfred the Great, of Wessex, defended England against the Danes first by paying the Danegeld and eventually by defeating the Norse invaders. He supported learning, furthering vernacular poetry and written histories, including the Anglo-Saxon Chronicle. The scholar Asser wrote Alfred's biography.

■ The Vikings invaded far and wide in the ninth century, including Paris. They founded Russia under their own Prince Rurik, and made their capital at Novgorod. Rurik's line will continue as the ruling family until 1598.

■ Plainsong, a form of chant, evolved. It began a century earlier with the introduction of tropes—melodic passages sung in the liturgy.

■ Scientists and philosophers Al-Rhazi and Al-Khindi conducted scientific experiments to study motion and heat, and rejected many alchemical principles. Al-Rhazi was a renowned physician who headed a Baghdad hospital. He distinguished measles from smallpox and wrote medical texts.

■ The term algebra is first used in a work by Al-Khwarizmi.

■ The Moors introduced cotton and silk to Spain.

- Cyril and Methodius invented the Cyrillic alphabet.They were Christian missionaries to the Slavs.
- Mayans migrated in two waves to the Yucatan peninsula.

Tenth Century
- The Chinese Than Chhiao described four kinds of optical lens.
- Tai Zu founded the Sung Dynasty and initiated modernizations.
- An imperial Chinese painting academy was started, focusing on landscapes and the higher purposes of art.
- The Sufi form of Islam developed in reaction to Muslim orthodoxy. Sufi is mystical, philosophical, and stresses divine love.
- Arab Spain under Abd ar-Rahman III became a center of learning. Science continued to progress at a high level, particularly in Moorish Cordoba. Among other developments, the alembic, a distillation device, came into use.
- The building of the Great Mosque at Cordoba, spanning three centuries, continued.
- The astrolabe, predecessor of the sextant, was perfected and introduced into Europe, possibly by the French mathematician Gerbert, who became Pope Sylvester II. Gerbert may also have been responsibile for introducing Arabic numerals to Europeans.
- Uniting several territories, Miezko became the first king of Poland. He converted to Christianity and Poland turned toward the West culturally.
- Viking exploration and expansion —raiding—hit its height around the year 1000. The first colony in Greenland was started by Eric the Red.
- The European center of power, in Frankish lands under Charlemagne, shifted to Germany where Otto I became king and Holy Roman Emperor.
- The Benedictine Abbey of Cluny was founded as a monastic reform movement and fought church abuses. The second abbot of Cluny, Odo, answered only to the pope.
- Romanesque architecture came into full flower. Some of the finest examples include Vezelay in France, and the cathedral of Speyer in Germany, as well as the Cluniac churches in France and Compostela, Spain.
- In Northern Europe, the iron plow and a more efficient horse collar, for a horse's chest rather than neck, emerged.
- Organs were used in churches and monasteries, contributing to the development of polyphony from plainsong.

Eleventh Century
- A Chinese astronomer, mathematician, and government offical, Shen Kua, wrote of the magnetic compass, movable type, and the origin of fossils. Pi Sheng was the Chinese printer who used movable type.
- Chinese botanical and medical texts had important pharmacologies.
- Avicenna was a Muslim physician and philosopher who used Aristotelian thought expounded by Galen to develop medical theories and write the encyclopedic *Canon of Medicine.*
- Guido d'Arezzo developed the principles of modern musical theory and notation.
- Architecture and the arts continued to thrive in Europe, continuing on to the great Renaissance of the twelfth century. Examples include: Durham Cathedral; the cathedral at Pisa; West-

minster Abbey; St. Mark's Cathedral in Venice; the Bayeux Tapestry, the first poems and songs of the troubadours and the first chansons de geste.

■ Canute ruled Denmark and Norway and was England's first Viking king.

■ After England's conquest by the Norman William I, the Conqueror had the Domesday Book compiled, detailing land ownership and taxes.

■ The Tale of the Genji was written about Japanese court life by a woman named Murasak Shikibu. The Eiga, a history of 15 Japanese emperors, also belongs to this century.

■ In Chihuahua, Mexico, an underground irrigation system was built for crops and city water.

■ Burma became a country.

■ A supernova that became the Crab Nebula appeared after an explosion of a star in Taurus. It was visible for 23 days and 633 nights.

■ China cultivated tea and cotton.

■ The pueblos of the Chaco Canyon were built by the cliff-dwelling Anasazi. They will be given the name *pueblo* centuries later, by Spaniards. The Anasazi lived communally. They irrigated the land and farmed, but lived in the cliffs of the mesas.

■ The Maoris had occupied New Zealand by this period.

Twelfth Century

■ The European Renaissance of the Twelfth Century produced major people and events: Eleanor of Aquitaine, Henry Plantagenet, Thomas á Becket, Richard the Lionheart, John Lackland and the Magna Carta, the height of the Crusades, Abelard and Eloise, Bernard of Clairvaux, David I of Scotland, the founding of the Knights Templar, Frederick Barbarossa, Saladin, and Maimonides.

■ English moved from Anglo-Saxon to Middle English with the embrace of French, latinate, words. In France, two dialects vied: *langue d'oc*, the language of the troubadours and Eleanor of Aquitaine, and *langue d'oïl,* the language of Paris and the trouveres, and the ancestor of modern French.

■ In German, the vernacular *Nibelungenlied*, the epic of Siegfried was written. The epic influenced the French *chansons de geste*, especially those by Chretien de Troyes, author of the *Chanson de Roland*.

■ The first miracle plays were performed in Dunstable, England.

■ In architecture, the century gave rise to the cathedrals at Chartres, Bourgues, Canterbury, Durham, and Lincoln; London Bridge; the bridge at Avignon; Abbé Suger's Saint Denis, one of the great examples of High Gothic architecture; and in Edinburgh's Holyrood Abbey. Gothic architecture increasingly broke up the heavy walls of Romanesque building by glass, and the artistry of stained glass matured This was also the century of the flying buttress.

■ Oxford University was founded, as was the Univerity of Paris.

■ Anselm of Canterbury, an early Scholastic, argued the existence of God can be reached through reason, not just faith. Later, the great debates over reason and faith took place between Peter Abelard and Bernard of Clairvaux. The Spanish Muslim Averroes made similar arguments and wrote commentaries on Aristotle that remained influential into the Renaissance.

■ Welcher of Malvern, an Anglo-Saxon in an England ruled by the Normans, devised the degrees, minutes, and seconds of latitude and longitude.

■ Nicholas Brekspeare became the only English pope, as Adrian IV.

■ French monks Robert of Molesmes and Stephen Harding improved farming and animal breeding in England. At about the same time, rabbits were domesticated.

■ Pope Adrian IV granted Henry II of England sovereignty over Ireland. The imposed feudal system clashed with the independent Irish kingdoms.

■ Crusaders brought sugar to Europe where it began to replace honey.

■ Fire and plague insurance were issued in Iceland.

■ The Yellow River's path was changed several times by the Chinese.

■ The Shogunates began, lasting for seven centuries.

■ Japan's priest-poet Saigyo-hosi wrote *Senzaishu*, 31-syllable poems.

■ In India, the first great Hindi bards composed their epics; Omar Khayyam, mathematician and poet, wrote the *Rubaiyyat* and other works.

■ In Colombia's Andes, the Chibchas developed strong social and political structures. The tale of *El Dorado* probably began with a Chibcha religious ceremony that used gold dust.

■ The temple complex of Angkor Watt was built in Cambodia. It may be the world's largest religious structure and was marked by extensive sculpture depicting Vishnu and Krishna. Angkor Watt was attacked and ruined in the same century.

Thirteenth Century

■ Venice became Europe's commercial center. Its great galleys made longer voyages and larger cargoes possible. Venice moved its glass factories to the island of Murano, for safety.

■ Monk Matthew of Paris wrote a history of the world and of England.

■ Leonardo Fibonacci wrote a treatise on algebra, promoted the use of Arabic numerals, and studied geometry and trigonometry. The Fibonacci sequence, made of adding consecutive numbers was named for him.

■ The medical school at the University of Bologna was founded.

■ The Children's Crusade took place.

■ In London, an asylum for the insane called St. Mary of Bethlehem opened in England. Shortened to "Bethlehem," it was the origin of the word *bedlam*.

■ Count William II of Holland built a palace at the Hague, which became the capital of the Netherlands and is today the location of the International Court of Justice.

■ Covent Garden began as a London *convent* garden, a fruit and vegetable market. It later moved, expanded, and centuries later became the site of the Royal Opera House.

■ Bela IV built Buda to replace Pest, after Mongols destroyed the city

■ The German minnesingers began in the tradition of the French troubadours, but mixed lyrical poetry and epic. Among them were Walther von der Vogelweide, Gottfried von Strassburg, and Wolfram von Eschenbach, author of *Parsifal*.

■ Snorri Sturluson wrote the *Prose Edda* in a golden age of Icelandic literature. It is filled with the stories of Norse legend and myth.

■ Italian friar, bishop, and physician Theodoric of Lucca used soporific sponges soaked with opium and mandragora, as an anesthetic.

■ Genoa and Florence issued gold currencies.

■ Roger Bacon was a philosopher, natural scientist, teacher, and monk who brought scientific study to Oxford University. It is possible Bacon used a telescope to observe spiral nebulae, a microscope to see cells, and devised a magnetic needle and spectacles.

■ Rudolph was the first to rule the Austrian Hapsburg Dynasty that endured until the end of World War I.

■ Jacobus de Voragine compiled the lives of the saints in *The Golden Legend*, a popular and influential volume.

■ The spinning wheel was invented in Europe. Its use became widespread in the next century.

■ Noodles—pasta—were introduced into Europe by the invading Mongols.

■ William Wallace battled for Scottish sovereignty but he was ultimately defeated by the English longbow.

■ In Europe, sailors used navigational charts for the first time. Ships had rudders fashioned to their sterns.

■ Charcoal-burning furnaces first appeared in central Europe.

■ Sundiata Keita led the Battle of Kirina to defeat the Mali armies and establish a large, rich, African kingdom empire in sub-Saharan Africa.

■ The Ottoman Empire was founded in Anatolia by Turkish tribes, and endured until the end of World War I.

■ The Sufi lyrical poet Djeleddin Rumi wrote the Mathnawi and founded the dervishes, Islamic monks who came to be known for their mystical dance.

■ Raziya, the Sultanah of Delhi, ruled a Muslim empire in India.

■ Islam established itself in India during the Delhi kingdom.

■ Mongol leader Genghis Khan conquered Persia and Russia and invaded China, which first used gunpowder as a weapon against the Mongols—bullets fired through bamboo.

■ Chinese opera and theater flourished.

■ Zen Buddhism spread to Japan, where the simplicity of temple architecture changed to more elaborate, Chinese-influenced, halls with painting and sculpture.

■ Burial mound enclaves were constructed in what is today Moundsville, Alabama. At Natchez, Mississippi, at the very end of the century or beginning of the next, the eight-acre Emerald Mound was built.

Fourteenth Century

■ The English constructed a stanch, or weir, in the Thames to control water depth for ships. They were used in other rivers and canals in Europe.

■ The Hanseatic League encouraged commercial fishing. The league also standardized weights and measures; standardized currency; negotiated deals and settlements; and opened up many areas of trade.

■ The French Salic Law prevented inheritance of the throne through the female line.

■ The bubonic plague devastated a starving China and spread to Europe.

■ Germans in Mainz developed a paper industry that led to the use of paper money and vastly improved written communication. Paper replaced vellum, made with animal skins. The watermark developed in Italy.

■ The Aztecs established Tenochtitlan, which became Mexico City.

■ During a civil war, Kitabatake Chikafusa wrote *Jinno-shotoki*, a history of Japan.

■ Surgeon to the popes at Avignon, Guy de Chauliac wrote the *Chirurgia Magna*, covering ophthalmology, surgery, fractures, growths, hernias, and more.

■ A political writer, philosopher, and logician, William of Occam wrote of concepts that led to the modern separation of church and state. Occam's Razor, or the principle of parsimony, said that the most obvious explanation for an event is the likely one, that it is better to do with less than more.

■ Giotto's frescoes and paintings point toward the emphasis on perspective and natural representation that will mark Renaissance art.

■ Geoffrey Chaucer wrote his poems and plays and died in 1400, leaving *The Canterbury Tales* unfinished. Chaucer also may have acted as a spy, because of ties to the royal family. He certainly held government positions.

■ Other important writers and works were Dante, Petrarch, Boccaccio, *Piers Plowman,* and *Sir Gawain and the Green Knight.*

■ Guillaume de Machaut wrote music in the liturgical tradition and about courtly love. His work is particularly known for its counterpoint.

■ The Dutch developed windmills for drainage and locks for canals.

■ Iron guns and cannons were developed and deployed.

■ The Alhambra Palace of Moorish kings, and their courts' chambers were finished in Granada.

■ The Buddhist monk Chu Yüan-chang fought the Mongols and became the first emperor of China's Ming Dynasty. Ming armies conquered Korea.

■ Taillevent wrote the first French cookbook, at the behest of Charles V.

■ Noh plays, credited to Kanami Kiyotsugu and his son Zeami Motokiyo, emerged in Japan. Male performers wore masks and acted on bare wooden stages in stylized dramas.

The Renaissance
Fifteenth Century

■ First references to playing cards were made in Europe. Paris had a law prohibiting card games on work days.

■ One of the earliest banks opened in Genoa, the Casa di San Giorgio.

■ Nicholas of Cusa posited that the Earth revolves daily.

■ Thomas à Kempis wrote the Imitation of Christ, among the most widely read books for centuries.

■ The Welsh Mabinogian were collected, full of ancient Celtic myths.

■ The age of exploration and expansion began. Henry the Navigator, a Portuguese prince, established a naval base, observatory, and school to study navigation and geography. Bartolomeo Dias sailed around the Cape of Good Hope. Portuguese explorers discovered bananas in Africa.

■ Portugal imported and sold its first African slaves.

■ Henry V's English archers won the day in one of the great battles of the 100 Years War with France in the Battle of Agincourt.

■ The first major Reformation figures

wrote and took action: John Wycliffe in England, Jan Hus in Bohemia.

■ Henry VI founded Eton.

■ The Flemish Limbourg brothers created exquisite illuminated manuscripts such as *Très Riches Heures* and *Les Belles Heures* for the Duc de Berry.

■ Jan van Eyck made his mark on Flemish painting with his depth and detail, especially in his portraits. Other major Flemish artists to follow were Hieronymus Bosch and the next century's Pieter Bruegel.

■ Michelozzo Michelozzi built Florence's Medici Palace.

■ Polyphony developed and matured.

■ During the Quattrocento, Brunelleschi first used perspective in painting; Massaccio, Botticelli, Fra Angelico, Fra Filippo Lippi painted; Ghiberti, Donatello, and Verrocchio sculpted, all preceding the masters of the High Renaissance, da Vinci, Michelangelo, Raphael.

■ King Dracula of Walachia massacred 20,000 Turks and was deposed.

■ At the Feast of the Pheasant, 28 musicians hid inside a huge pie for the Duke of Burgundy. The event is the basis for "Four and twenty blackbirds baked in a pie."

■ The Dutch devised drift nets for fishing and Archimedian screws for dams.

■ Rifles were first made.

■ As an ally of the Medici, the Vatican excommunicated anyone who imported alum, used to fix colors in cloth, from the Turks.

■ In an effort to promote archery for the national defense, Scotland forbid the playing of *futeball* and *golfe*.

■ Louis XI commissioned France's national postal service, Poste Royale.

■ The first Paris printing shop opened. William Caxton was the first English printer, producing about 100 titles, including Thomas Malory's *Morte d'Arthur*.

■ The Malleus Maleficarum, a witch-hunting manual, was written.

■ Ivan the Great called himself *czar*, or caesar, of Muscovy.

■ Prince Ulugh-Beg of Timurid composed a catalogue of stars and planetary motion.

■ Coffee came to Constantinople, via the Turks. The first coffee house was named Kiva Han.

■ Songhai was a large empire in the Sudan, expanded by Sonni Ali and Askia Muhammad I.

■ Zara Yaqub ruled Ethiopia and protected Coptic Christians.

■ The Golden Pavilion in Kyoto was completed.

■ Cheng Ho, a Muslim originally named Ma, took many maritime voyages to explore and conquer for the Chinese emperor. From one he brought back giraffes and zebras.

■ Vietnam became independent of China.

■ Yoshimasa, a shogun, brought the tea ceremony to Japan.

■ Under King Sejong, Korea established an alphabet, which led to a combination of letters and ideographs.

■ Pachacuti founded a dynasty that eventually extended Incan rule to its widest boundaries, until the next century, when Spanish conquest began.

■ The Incas created farm land by digging terraces into the Andes and adding top soil from the valleys.

■ The Aztec Calendar Stone, or Sun Stone, was erected.

Ideas

Sixteenth Century

- In England's Star Chamber, where judicial precedings had taken place for centuries, legal rights were severely restricted under Henry VIII's chancellor Thomas Wolsey. There, Thomas More, author of *Utopia*, was brought to trial.
- Martin Frobisher and John Davis rediscovered Greenland.
- Spanish settlers brought African slaves to Hispaniola. John Hawkins began the English slave trade. Pope Leo X condemned slavery. Pope Paul III excommunicated Catholic slave traders.
- In Venice, music was printed with movable type for the first time.
- Niccolò Machiavelli formed Italy's first national army.
- Rio de Janeiro was founded by the Portuguese.
- Martin Waldseemuller was a German mapmaker who named America after Amerigo Vespucci.
- Francois I became a patron of Renaissance culture and the arts. He and Henry VIII met with great fanfare and cost on the Field of the Cloth of Gold.
- Nearly 2,000 workers took 15 years to finish the chateau of Chambord.
- Renaissance artists and architects included Bramante, Titian, Correggio, Holbein, Vasari.
- The Mannerist style of art and architecture was a reaction against perspective and proportion. It exaggerated, even distorted, figures. El Greco Tintoretto, and Cellini created its most successful examples.
- *Everyman*, the most famous of English morality plays, was written.
- Gemma Frisius used standard time measurements in connection with longitude to improve navigation.
- Georgius Agricola established mineralogy as a science.
- Francois Viete, the "father of algebra," introduced letters into math. Simon Stevin introduced decimals.
- In *De Humani Corporis Fabrica*, the Flemish anatomist Andreas Vesalius illustrated the human body, based on cadaver dissections.
- Gerardus Mercator developed a projection map to depict latitude and longitude in two dimensions.
- A honey shortage resulted when Henry VIII closed England's monasteries—and their honey farms.
- The Italians made ice cream.
- The sweating sickness repeatedly struck England. Physician John Caius designated its cause—"filth."
- John Heywood published a book of proverbs such as "better late than never" and "beggars can't be choosers."
- Atahualpa was the last Incan leader, executed by Spanish conquistadors.
- Shipwrecked Portuguese explorers were the first Europeans, and their muskets the first guns, in Japan. Nagasaki opened to foreign trade.
- Hugh Roe O'Donnell and Hugh O'Neill asked Spain's Philip II for aid in obtaining Irish independence.
- English actor James Burbage opened the first playhouse.
- Thomas Gresham conceived of the London Royal Exchange, leading to the city's centrality in world trade.
- European porcelain was first made in Tuscany.
- Tycho Brahe saw a supernova and questioned whether the heavens were always the same. His assistant Johannes Kepler calculated planetary orbits.

- Siberia was explored and settled.
- A life insurance policy was first sold in England.
- William Lee invented the knitting machine.
- Zacharias Janssen invented the compound microscope, allowing micro-organisms to be studied.
- Edmund Spenser wrote *The Faerie Queene*.
- Paracelsus dismissed many old medical notions, such as the humors, and used chemicals like laudanum, iron, and sulfur in medicines. He mixed science and the occult.
- German hymns and chorales arose and matured.
- The lute was a popular instrument.
- The coach was invented in Hungary.
- In China, crop rotation with corn and sweet potatoes improved health leading to an increased population.
- Ten-year-old Wan Li ruled China under the name Shen Zong.
- Zahir-ud-din Babar conquered the sultan of Delhi and formed India's Mogul Empire.
- Muslim armies conquered the Hindu Empire at the Battle of Talikota.
- Akbar was the greatest Mogul Emperor of India when measured in conquest, administrative efficiency, and promotion of learning and the arts.
- Japanese rice riots took place in reaction to heavy taxes.
- Toyotomi Hideyoshi united Japan; made Edo the capital; invaded Korea, but had his navy destroyed by an ironclad Chinese ship; and built Hideyoshi castle with 30,000 workers.
- The Japanese first ate tempura, after missionaries taught them to deep-fry.

Seventeenth Century

- Religious issues led to regicide in England where Charles I was executed. Oliver Cromwell ruled.
- In France, religious wars threatened to re-erupt with the murder of Henry IV.
- The French began settlements in the West Indies, including Martinique.
- James Lancaster of the East India Company prevented scurvy by giving his crew lemon juice.
- An imposter posed as the Russian czar for months after Boris Godunov died. The Romanov dynasty began with Czar Mikhail Romanov.
- The *Mary Margaret* was the first English whaling ship.
- Rob Roy became Highland chief of the MacGregors.
- Paul de Chomedey founded Montreal.
- London's stock exchange started.
- Manhattan's Wall Street was named for the Dutch wall built to defend the city against the English.
- *Corante*, the first newspaper in London, launched.
- Blaise Pascal invented an adding machine, formed the theory of probability, and preached mysticism.
- Architect Jacques Lemercier built Versailles and added to the Louvre.
- Sugar and tooth decay were linked by a German traveler who saw the black teeth of England's Queen Elizabeth, who loved sugar.
- Lemonade was concocted, as sugar prices dropped in Paris.
- Tea came to England. The first coffee house opened, and 75 years later, the city boasted 2,000. They were social, trade, and political centers.
- Honeybees were brought to North America.

■ William Harvey's *Essay on the Motion of the Heart and the Blood* said the heart is a muscle that pumps blood.

■ Theophrase Renaudot opened the first medical clinic for the poor, in Paris.

■ Francis Bacon began formalizing the scientific method, using inductive reasoning to posit and test hypotheses. Bacon died of pneumonia after stuffing chickens with snow to freeze them.

■ Evangelista Torricelli invented the barometer.

■ Rene Descartes applied algebra to geometry, laying the groundwork for modern math. He said that knowledge results when doubt is systematized.

■ Johann Glauber discovered nitric acid, used in explosives, and many other chemical compounds.

■ Mathematician Christian Huygens devised the pendulum and transformed clockmaking.

■ Isaac Newton developed calculus by discovering rules for using algebraic figures that have a rate of change.

■ New techniques for working with wood led to cuckoo clocks.

■ Robert Boyle distinguished the principles of chemistry from alchemy. He defined element, reaction, analysis.

■ Jan Swammerdam, a naturalist, described red blood cells.

■ Robert Hooke showed that respiration depends on blood changes. In France, blood was transfused from a lamb to a boy.

■ Anton von Leeuwenhoek made 247 microscopes and saw microorganisms.

■ John Napier used logarithms.

■ The first pawn shop opened, in Brussels.

■ Bank checks were first used in London. They simplified foreign trade.

■ Catherine de Vivonne held the first French intellectual salon.

■ Spain's Philip IV responded to accusations of social decadence by banning the ruff.

■ The German passion play, the *Oberammergau*, was first performed.

■ Ben Jonson, a contemporary of Shakespeare and a bricklayer turned playwright, wrote *Every Man in His Humour, The Alchemist,* and *Volpone*.

■ John Donne wrote his intense love poems and religious devotions.

■ John Milton composed his epic poetry, including *Paradise Lost*, and mixed in politics.

■ John Dryden was England's first English poet laureate.

■ Inigo Jones incorporated Palladian design principles in London's Banqueting House and Covent Garden Church. Jones also built sets for masques.

■ Christopher Wren was an astronomer and mathematician who won fame as a Baroque architect, and especially for St. Paul's Cathedral and Piccadilly Circus.

■ William Kidd turned from English naval captain to pirate.

■ Miguel de Cervantes wrote *Don Quixote de la Mancha*.

■ The Spanish dramatists Lope de Vega and Pedro Calderon wrote their classic works. In France, the great playwrights were Jean Racine and Jean Moliere.

■ The picaresque novel was first written in Spain, and influenced French stories into the next century.

■ Madame de la Fayette wrote an early form of the psychological novel, *The Princess of Cleves*.

■ "Three Blind Mice" was published.

■ Claudio Monteverdi was the first great composer of opera. Heinrich

Schutz wrote the first German opera.

■ Orchestral music added the French horn.

■ Among the great artists of the century were Bernini, Rubens, Van Dyke, Vermeer, Hals, Lorrain, Poussin, Velasquez, Murillo.

■ Ballet originated.

■ Pierre-Paul Riquet constructed the Languedoc Canal, connecting the Mediterranean and Atlantic via the Garonne.

■ Jan van Riebeck founded Cape Town, South Africa.

■ Chinese playwright Tan Xiansu wrote *The Peony Pavilian.*

■ Tokugawa Ieyasu founded a shogunate that improved Japan's industry and economy.

■ Inns were built from Edo to Osaka, to improve travel.

■ Kikkoman, the soy sauce company, opened near Edo.

■ Kabuki theater originated.

■ Englishman Will Adams was shipwrecked in Japan, married, renamed himself Anshin Miura, and advised the shogunate.

■ Shunsai Hayashi wrote a Japanese history, *O-Dia-khi-Ran.*

■ China conquered Taiwan.

■ Abel Tasman, a Dutch navigator, landed in New Zealand.

The Enlightenment
Eighteenth Century

■ The *News-Letter,* the Colonies' first ongoing newspaper, launched in Boston.

■ Jethro Tull invented a seed-planting drill.

■ Peter the Great founded St. Petersburg. Bartolomeo Rastrelli built its Winter Palace

■ The English take Jebel-al-Tarik, which became Gibraltar.

■ Denmark became the first to stop the slave trade.

■ In Poland, Thaddeus Kosciusko championed independence after fighting in the American Revolution.

■ First Chancellor of New York state and scion of an influential family, Robert Livingston administered the presidential oath to George Washington.

■ As the French Revolution progressed, the places in which politicians sat in the Assembly—right, left, and center—came to represent their political affiliations, with radicals on the left.

■ The Spanish amputated an English sailor's ear and the War of Jenkins's Ear began.

■ North Carolina slaves rebelled in the Cato Conspiracy.

■ Benjamin Franklin started the first city police force in Philadelphia, where streets were also first lit, with globe lamps.

■ Abraham Darby discovered how to smelt coke, made from coal.

■ In London and Boston, smallpox inoculations worked.

■ John Hadley invented the reflecting quadrant, to determine latitude at any hour. John Harrison invented the marine chronometer, to determine longitude with more precision.

■ John Kay invented the fly shuttle, which made for faster looms.

■ Botulism first appeared in Europe.

■ England's death rate began to fall dramatically; the birth rate rose. The population doubled over the century.

■ Houses in London were numbered.

■ Botany Bay became an English penal colony, which then moved to Sydney.

- In Germany, the first savings bank opened.
- Lord Charles Townshend, or "Turnip Townshend," rotated crops, increasing agricultural productivity.
- New York held its first St. Patrick's Day parade.
- Josiah Wedgwood transformed the pottery industry.
- John Wesley founded Methodism.
- German chemist J.H. Schulze proved that silver salts darken when exposed to light, later used in photography.
- Joseph Black discovered carbon dioxide.
- Humphry Davy made laughing gas.
- The Leyden Jar was invented to store static electricity.
- Benjamin Thompson, Count Rumford, theorized that heat is the motion of particles.
- P.L.M. de Maupertuis's writings on natural selection predated Darwin's.
- Astronomer Anders Celsius created his temperature scale and measured the magnitude of stars.
- Antoine Lavoisier wrote the first modern chemistry text.
- Aloys Senefelder invented lithography, a printing form that came to be favored by artists.
- Joseph Bramah invented a water closet, an early toilet.
- Joseph Priestley named *rubber* because he saw it rub out marks.
- Chlorine was used as a bleach.
- Captain Cook crossed the Antarctic Circle.
- Vitus Bering discovered Alaska.
- Daniel Defoe wrote *Robinson Crusoe*. Jonathan Swift wrote *Gulliver's Travels*. Alexander Pope wrote *The Dunciad*. The novel was fast-maturing as a literary form. Robern Burns revived Scottish folk stories. Playwrights like Oliver Goldsmith and R.B. Sheridan wrote comedies of manners.
- In France, philosophical writers dominated literature—Montesquieu, Voltaire, and Rousseau, who used the phrase "Let them eat cake," later erroneously attributed to Marie Antoinette.
- The *Encyclopaedia Britannica* was published in Edinburgh.
- *Tommy Thumb's Pretty Song Book* included some of the earliest versions of nursery rhymes. Thomas Fleet published *Mother Goose's Melodies* in Boston.
- Doctor Hans Sloane left 50,000 books, thousands of manuscripts, and artifacts to Britain. The collection was to become the British Museum.
- Painting was dominated by classical styles and themes until the Romantic age began late in the century. "Picturesque" became a category of art, particularly in reference to landscapes.
- The architectural Greek Revival movement arose.
- Great musicians of the century included Mozart, Hayden, Beethoven, Cimarosa, Paginini.
- Edmond Hoyle formalized the rules of whist, a precedessor of bridge.
- Joseph Merlin invented roller skates. He rolled into a party playing a violin.
- Richelieu invented mayonnaise.
- In Louisiana, Cajun cooking merged Canadian and Native recipes.
- The kipfel roll, brought by Marie Antoinette from her homeland, Austria, became the French croissant.
- European teacups added handles, unlike Asian cups.
- A diamond rush occurred in Tejuco, Brazil.

- Mount Fuji erupted for the last time.
- King Alaungapaya founded Rangoon.
- The worst famine in history killed 10 million in Bengal.
- Ts'ao Chan and Kao Eh wrote *The Dream of the Red Chamber,* a Chinese novel of manners.
- The Chakri Dynasty of Siam began and ruled for two centuries.
- Indian music adopted the violin after the English introduced it.

Romantics, Imperialists, Industrialists
Nineteenth Century

- After defeating Napoleon, who placed his brother Joseph on the throne, Spanish liberal groups led by Rafael Riego rebelled against the monarchy. The Spanish Inquisition formally ended.
- Simón Bolívar fought for independence in Bolivia, Colombia, Ecuador, Panama, Peru, and Venezuela alongside de Miranda, Nariño, Paéz, and de San Martín.
- Brazil declared independence from Portugal.
- Greece declared independence from the Ottoman Empire. France and England supported Greece in the war against the Turks.
- The Greek struggle influenced English poets such as Byron, and Keats, whose "Ode on a Grecian Urn" includes the lines "Beauty is truth, truth beauty— that is all/Ye know on earth and all ye need to know."
- France placed a naval blockade on Algeria, invaded, and occupied the land.
- Leon Gambetta escaped from Paris during a siege in a hot air balloon.
- Belgium won independence from the Dutch.
- Across the century, the Irish struggled with Britain for Home Rules. Repeated famines and English policy led to massive deaths and immigration.
- Giuseppe Garibaldi was an inspirational leader in the revolution, the Risorgimento, to unite Italy.
- In the Treaty of Waitangi, the British agreed to allow the Maoris full possession of their land, in return for sovereignty over New Zealand.
- Britain made slavery illegal.
- British laws restricted the hours children could work to 12.
- Women were granted the vote in New Zealand, the first time ever.
- William Garrison boycotted a London abolitionist convention because women were not allowed to attend.
- Britain founded Singapore.
- The Congress of Vienna, presided over by Metternich, remade Europe's borders. Attendees included Czar Alexander, the Duke of Wellington, and Talleyrand.
- The border between Canada and the U.S. was set at the 49th parallel.
- The U.S. government resettled Eastern Native Americans in the West, to gain control of territory east of the Mississippi.
- A Native American Paiute, Wovoka created the Great Ghost Dance, in a spirituality that looked to a messiah to end white domination. The Sioux wore ghost shirts at the Battle of Wounded Knee.
- John Fremont traveled to the West with Kit Carson as a guide. Fremont's writing made Carson a folk hero.
- Navajos fought against settler incursions in New Mexico. The U.S. built Fort Defiance in reaction. Raids continued until Kit Carson destroyed Native American crops and livestock.

■ Shoemakers went on strike in Lynn, Massachusetts. The first national strike was by railroad workers.

■ Switzerland's cantons united.

■ Massachusetts Governor Elbridge Gerry was falsely accused of shaping electoral districts to his advantage. The action was named *gerrymandering*.

■ The writers behind the French Revolution, and the struggle itself, led to the Romantic movement, which received added momentum from Wordsworth and Coleridge. Romanticism embraced literature, music, the visual arts, and philosophy. In the U.S., it was inherent in Transcendentalism. Reaction against Romanticism threaded through the arts and thinking late in the century, into the 1890s' Age of Decadence.

■ Walter Scott wrote the first historical novel, *Waverley*. Novel serializations were widely read, the most notable of them by Charles Dickens.

■ The Hudson River School was a group of American artists inspired by the Hudson River and Catskills. It included Thomas Cole and Frederick Church.

■ The pre-Raphaelites were mid-century English artists who reacted against increasing industrialism. They included Dante Gabriel Rossetti and John Millais.

■ William Morris was the founder of Art Nouveau. He designed fabric and furniture, wrote poetry, was an innovative printer, and a social reformer.

■ Paris's established art Salon refused to display the work of many new artists. Napoleon III commanded the Salon des Refusés, which included Manet, Cézanne, Pissarro, Whistler. A decade later, the Impressionists held the Salon des Indépendants.

■ Soren Kierkegaard, an early Existentialist, wrote on aesthetics and religion, and argued for self-examination and individual commitment.

■ Sir Arthur Conan Doyle created Sherlock Holmes.

■ Washington Irving published *Salamagundi,* humorous and satirical essays, and the satirical *A History of New York*. In the second half of the century, American humor soared with the writings of Samuel Clemens.

■ Negro spirituals, jazz, blues, ragtime, and Gospel music emerged.

■ Offenbach created the operetta. Gilbert and Sullivan took it to its heights.

■ Sarah Josepha Hale edited the *Ladies' Magazine* and *Godey's Lady's Book;* published *Poems for Our Children,* which included "Mary Had a Little Lamb"; promoted Thanksgiving; and supporterd women's education and writing.

■ Alessandro Volta devised the battery. Andre Marie Ampere learned how electric currents work. Hans Oersted discovered electromagnetism.

■ James Joule formulated the first law of thermodynamics: Energy can be converted but not destroyed. Rudolf Clausius formulated the second: Heat passes from a warmer to a cooler body.

■ Amadeo Avogadro hypothesized that equal volumes of gases at the same temperature and pressure contain the same numbers of molecules.

■ Viruses were discovered.

■ Sanitary reform was introduced in England. Ignaz Semmelweiss, a Hungarian, showed that washing hands could prevent childbed fever.

■ Bernard Courtois discovered iodine, used as an antiseptic and water purifier.

■ Crawford Williamson Long first used ether as an anesthetic.

- R.T. Laennec invented the stethoscope.
- John Lanark used the term *biology*.
- An anonymous woman wrote the first American book on the nurturing of children, *The Maternal Physician*.
- Jean-Louis Agassiz studied glaciers.
- Charles Stanhope, a British politician, invented a printing press that led to large sheet printing and thick advertising fonts. He also invented lenses, calculators, and fireproof stucco.
- The invention of a metal framework to support floors and walls led to the building of skyscrapers. The first was Chicago's Home Insurance Building.
- In New York, the Brooklyn Bridge and Metropolitan Opera House were built.
- The Metropolitan Museum of Art in New York and the Museum of Fine Arts in Boston were established.
- The Staten Island ferry, owned by Cornelius Vanderbilt, started up.
- Eugene Schieffelin brought starlings to New York City. They became quintessentially urban birds.
- Canned food was made in England.
- F.W. Bessel catalogued 50,000 stars.
- Earthquakes made the Mississippi flow upstream and pushed a town into the river.
- Oceanography began with the Challenger Expedition.
- Celluloid, the first plastic, was invented.
- The first artifical dye was produced, and named *mauve*.
- The Cumberland Road was begun. The first U.S. national road ran from Maryland to Missouri.
- John Burckhardt uncovered the ancient rock city of Petra, which had been a trade and religious center.

- Auguste Conte coined *sociology*.
- Sylvester Graham invented the graham cracker.
- The waltz, considered risque, became popular.
- The mouth organ, a Chinese instrument, was introduced in Vienna.
- The first county fair took place in Pittsfield, Massachusetts.
- The first Oktoberfest was held, as a wedding festival for a Bavarian prince.
- The Kentucky Derby was first run.
- The Boers took the Great Trek to find new territory in South Africa.
- Hung Hsiu-ch'üan led the Taiping Rebellion against the Manchu, or Chi'ing, dynasty. Hung aimed to start a dynasty called the Taiping, which means great peace. His movement was defeated, with the help of Western nations that didn't want to lose trade with China.
- The French colonized in Indochina, including Cambodia, Tonkin, and Laos.
- The British controlled most of India. The Sepoy Rebellion was a sign of political and cultural unrest. Indian soldiers mistakenly believed the British had given them cartridges coated with fat from cows and pigs, abominations to Hindu and Muslim belief.

The Modern Age
Twentieth Century

- Russia experienced revolutions in 1905 and, with the integral participation of Lenin, in 1917.
- André Maginot was responsible for the construction of a French defense wall, but it was unsuccessful against the Germans in World War I.
- A seminal and ultimate event in Irish history, the Easter Rebellion brought tragedy and independence

for the southern Irish counties.

■ The U.S. urbanized. By 1990, 70 percent of Americans lived in cities, with a detour by the post-World War II population to suburban enclaves such as Levittown. Early in the century, a social reform movement had grown out of urban problems; in 1920, Upton Sinclair, Clarence Darrow, Jane Addams, and Helen Keller, founded the ACLU.

■ The first housing projects were built in 1935 on New York's Lower East Side.

■ Fiorello La Guardia ended Tammany Hall's power in New York.

■ Congress passed the Pure Food and Drug Act.

■ Montana elected Jeannette Rankin to Congress, the first woman.

■ Black labor leader Asa Phillip Randolph fought for civil rights for the Brotherhood of Sleeping Car Porters, which threatened to march on Washington to protest employment discrimination during World War II.

■ Henry Ford paid workers $5 a day, twice the average, to avoid labor problems.

■ In response to the Great Depression, Franklin Roosevelt initiated the New Deal as a means of recovery. It encompassed social security, Works Progress Administration, and other reforms.

■ Rabbi Stephen Wise, a Zionist, attempted to inform Americans of the Nazi's Jewish extermination policies, most Americans remained unaware.

■ The oratorical gifts of Winston Churchill, Prime Minister of Britain, inspired the Allies during World War II.

■ The Daughters of the American Revolution refused to let opera singer Marian Anderson, who was black, sing at an event. Eleanor Roosevelt resigned from the DAR in protest.

■ Women were guaranteed equal pay for equal work under U.S. law in 1963.

■ Behind what Churchill called the Iron Curtain, the U.S.S.R. put down freedoms in Hungary, Czechoslovakia, Poland, but as the century closed, the curtain rose on new governments and the rise of names like Walesa and Havel.

■ Among the century's prominent Supreme Court justices were Oliver Wendell Holmes, who advocated judicial restraint; Benjamin Cardozo, an expert on social change and the law; Louis Brandeis, whose "Brandeis Brief" argued that it wasn't unconstitutional for women to be paid a minimum wage; Earl Warren, the Chief Justice during Brown v. Board of Education; Thurgood Marshall, the first black named to the Court, and a challenger of the separate but equal doctrine; and Sandra Day O'Connor the first woman, and a current Justice.

■ The U.S. lowered the voting age from 21 to 18 in 1969.

■ The 1913 Armory Show in New York heralded Modern Art in the U.S., to be followed decades later by Post-Modernism and Contemporary Art. Some of the important trends and artists of the century, internationally, were Fauvism, Expressionism, Cubism, the Ashcan School, Art Deco, Constructivism, Picasso, Braque, Mondrian, Klee, Ernst, Duchamp, Chagall, Dali, Kandinsky, Magritte, Pollock, Calder, Brancusi, Moore. Postmodernists or Contemporary artists included Johns, Warhol, Lichtenstein, Stella, Schnabel.

■ Major twentieth-century names in literature included Yeats, Shaw, Synge, Proust, Kafka, Lawrence, Galsworthy,

Woolf, Conrad, James, O'Casey, Eliot, Stein, Mann, Joyce, Fitzgerald, Ford, Hughes, Cather, Dreiser, Dos Passos, Hemingway, Frost, Faulkner, Orwell, Auden, Pasternak, Camus, Beckett, Stevens, Salinger, Pinter, Stoppard.

■ Major twentieth-century trends and names in music, popular and classical, were Ragtime, Jazz, Big Band; Stravinsky, Ives, Bartok, Gershwin, Delius, Elgar, Vaughan Williams, Copland, Cage.

■ The Original Dixieland Jazz Band toured Europe, making jazz a worldwide phenomenon.

■ Berry Gordy founded Motown.

■ The American musical dominated theater for a time, especially the works of Rodgers and Hammerstein and Lerner and Loewe.

■ The synthesizer developed as a musical instrument.

■ Among the major architects of the century were le Corbusier, White, Wright, Johnson, Pei.

■ New York held the first car show.

■ The Autobahn opened in Germany, the first road meant for motor vehicles.

■ Los Angeles's Arroyo Seco Parkway opened, its first highway 1940.

■ The hamburger was invented in New Haven, Connecticut.

■ America had a ping pong craze.

■ U.S. newspapers and magazines gained in breadth and importance: Hearst's empire; *The Christian Science Monitor; The New Yorker, Cosmopolitan;* Scripps-Howard newspapers; *Ebony; Rolling Stone;* and many more.

■ Honus Wagner forced a tobacco company to take his picture off baseball cards because of the possible influence on children.

■ Universal Pictures and Warner Brothers were founded early in the century, with movies to become a major U.S. industry over the century.

■ *Rinso* was the name of the first soap flakes.

■ Coco Chanel transformed fashion. Her perfume Chanel No. 5 was an enormous seller in 1921.

■ Barney's and Saks opened in 1924, the same year Macy's held the first Thanksgiving Day parade.

■ The *Delta Queen* launched on the Mississippi.

■ The *Graf Zeppelin* flew around the world.

■ Paris's Metro opened. Its entrances are examples of Art Nouveau.

■ The first Davis Cup tennis tournament took place at Harvard. Field hockey was introduced in the U.S. The first Tournament of Roses was played in California. The Tour de France originated. The first Soccer World Cup was played in 1930.

■ The comic book was invented.

■ The answering machine was invented—in 1904.

■ General Foods made instant coffee for the U.S. Army in World War II.

■ Smokey the Bear was created as a symbol after a bear cub was burned and orphaned in a forest fire.

■ New York's Museum of Modern Art and the Frank Lloyd Wright-designed Guggenheim Museum opened.

■ Jack Kilby and Robert Noyce invented the microchip. Noyce started Intel.

■ Jack Nicklaus won the U.S. Open at 22.

■ The first state lottery in the U.S. started in New Hampshire.

■ Mary Quant designed the miniskirt.

■ Ralph Nader published *Unsafe at Any Speed.*

- The First Philadelpia Bank installed the first version of the ATM.
- EMI Records was behind the development of the CAT scan.
- Word processors and faxes were first used in the 1970s.
- Cell phones first appeared in the U.S. in Chicago in 1983.
- Quantum theory was based on the work of Schordinger, Planck, Einstein, Bohr, Heisenberg.
- Ruth Benedict and Margaret Mead were anthropologists who studied child rearing and culture.
- The Leakey family became synonymous with human fossil discoveries.
- The photocopier was invented; the first Xerox copy was made in 1938.
- Insulin was isolated.
- Willis Carrier developed air conditioning.
- Bakelite, a fully synthetic plastic, was invented.
- Hiram Bingham discovered Macchu-Pichu.
- Passenger pigeons became extinct. The Department of the Interior issued the first endangered species list.
- Serengeti Park opened.
- Edward Hubble saw galaxies move away from each other.
- Barnum Brown discovered the first Tyrannosaurus rex skeleton.
- Frequency Modulation (FM) radio developed, reducing static.
- Arthur Compton and General Electric invented fluorescent lighting.
- A French child, Jacques Marsal, discovered cave paintings in Lascaux.
- Charles Drew, a black doctor, opened the first U.S. blood bank.
- IBM and Harvard built the first automatic computer.

- Hammurabi's Code was decoded.
- The transistor was invented.
- DNA's double helix was discovered.
- NASA was created in 1958.
- Michael De Bakey used the first artificial heart. Christian Barnard transplanted the first heart, but a heart transplant wasn't successful until 1982.
- In Canada, the first nuclear power accident in the world took place in 1952. The Three Mile Island accident occurred in 1979 and Chernobyl in 1986.
- Mid-century, decolonization took place across Africa: Senegal, Ghana, Nigeria, Madagascar, the Congo, Algeria.
- Chinese nationalists attempted to remove foreign influence in the Boxer Rebellion.
- The Dalai Lama escaped from Tibet after a failed revolution to free the country from China.
- Gandhi and Nehru struggled for India's independence. Rice crops were widely destroyed by a fungus, leading to the deaths of 1.6 million in 1942.
- Sun Yat-Sen was a leader of the Kuomintang and led the Chinese Revolution that continued after his death in 1927.
- The nation of Egypt formed.
- Reza Pahlevi renamed Persia Iran.
- Ho Chi Minh lived in England, the U.S. He helped found the Communist party in France. In his native Vietnam, he fought against the French and eventually the U.S. for an independent, united country.

Reference & Research

Researching Your Readers

By Jan Fields

Research is a necessary part of writing, fiction or nonfiction. It begins inside the subjects we write about and can inspire us to bring something fresh and interesting to readers. Research is exciting, challenging, and rewarding no matter the subject, but one area of investigation offers benefits, not only for our work in progress, but for all our future work: researching our readers.

As children's writers, we create a body of literature for an audience that is fundamentally different from ourselves. In some ways, it is like writing for a readership that is from another culture, with distinct challenges, various pastimes, and practically a unique language. How can we best reach our readers? How can we get to know them? How can we portray them authentically?

As we come to know our target audience better, we can understand why touch-and-feel books are so popular with toddlers or why *The Way Things Work* was such a wildly successful book.

British author Diana Kimpton says she makes it a point to remain aware of her reader's age as she plans her research approach. "When interviewing people, I always explain my target age group as I try to think myself into my readers' heads and ask the sort of questions they would ask if they were there." But she researches as she would for any age: "I don't consciously use different sources for different ages. The important thing is to get the facts right and that may mean going to a source my readers may never approach on their own."

To keep your audience in mind as you plan and create your work, you need to get to know the reader. How does a toddler differ developmentally from a preschooler? How do reading tastes change from middle-grade readers to teens? What are the cultural trends among the young, and what do they reveal about your readership? Answering these questions will help you create stories and articles that capture your reader's attention and leave a lasting impression.

What Are Kids Reading?

Ever wish someone could tell you what kids want to read? Asking your local children's librarian helps, and so can mail groups, and even university course materials available online.

Children's librarians can tell you which books are checked out most often, who the popular authors are, and the most requested types of book. A good working relationship with your local children's librarian is well worth cultivating. It is fascinating to hear what topics are hot reads for different age groups.

Laurie A. Cavanaugh, who works in a school library, says, "Nonfiction and fiction about dirt bikes, skateboarding, and snowboarding come to mind right away. Pet care books for younger readers, especially about kittens and puppies are very popular, but I don't know how many are out there already but just not in our library! And scary stories and funny stories are always in demand, definitely!"

"There are never enough books about cars, trucks, and other vehicles," says former children's librarian Diane Myr. "Little boys just can't get enough. Preschool boys seem to be more obsessive and will not take out anything other than cars and trucks, much to the dismay of the adult who has to read the books!"

Apart from sitting down for long chats with children's librarians, what can authors do to target particular ages and audiences? The Internet can help.

One possibility is a good library mail group. Yahoogroups, for example, has a list for children's librarians. Although the librarian-to-librarian posting is light, this group is quick to respond when you have a question about what children like and what books are getting the most traffic. To become part of this list, send a blank email to childlibrarian-subscribe@yahoogroups.com.

A wealth of information about children's literature and children's reading preferences can be found at the University of South Florida's School of Library Science class in Children's Literature. (www.cas.usf.edu/lis/lis 6585/ class/ intro2.html). Dr. Marilyn H. Stauffer has compiled information from a variety of studies on reading preferences by age and presents them as part of her Introduction to Children's Literature class. Her age-specific preferences are tied to children's psychological stages of development. The list, on the bottom third of the website page, is fascinating.

Another great method for finding out what kids want to read is to ask them. The International Reading Association (IRA) does just that on a large scale and compiles the resulting information into favorite book lists: The Children's Choices list and the Young Adult Choices list are invaluable for writers. These lists can be downloaded from the IRA website at www.reading.org/choices/index.html.

The lists' annotations alone are a wealth of information. We can see that humor is still the most common ingredient in the books on the Children's Choices list. Strong protagonists with just a bit of mischief seem to pop up over and over as you read through the annotations. Although fantasy does not dominate the list as you might expect, given the Harry Potter juggernaut, imagination and pretending (especially with adults going along with the game) are common elements in many of the stories for beginning readers.

Intermediate readers seem to have a fascination with the unknown and mysteries dominate the list—both fiction and nonfiction. There is far more nonfiction than you might expect in this age range, and fewer classroom stories.

The Young Adult Choices list shows that problem novels still rule with teens, although both humor and fantasy appear here and there. Nonfiction is scarce but reality is clearly in. Studying these lists can give writers a clearer idea of what readers choose for themselves. Of course, readers don't always get to choose what they will read. So writers may want to consider subjects that attract students by tying into school subjects.

What Are Kids Studying?

Stories, articles, and books linked to school curriculums are useful to teachers and students. Librarians report that children constantly search for books related to specific school subjects and that can be used in writing reports. Knowing what subjects are taught, and how extensively, can be important.

Public libraries often carry copies of the curriculum standards for your particular state but, the information may be much closer at hand if you have access to an Internet connection. Many state curriculums are available online, sometimes with ac-companying lesson plans and other add-ons that you may find useful.

One site to check out is Mid-continent Research for Education and Learning (www.mcrel.org). The McRel Standards are a compilation of educational standards in all subjects into a national guideline. This is probably the best place to find *what* is taught *when*, but it is not state-specific. The site also includes extensive links to lesson plans, educational publishers, and sites on educational theory.

Another online resource is Global Resources for Teachers (http:// resources. globalchalkboard.com). The source includes links to the state departments of education, many of which have state-wide curriculum standards online.

What Are Kids Perceiving?

Part of knowing about our readers is understanding where they are in developmental terms. Physical, social, and psychological development shape how children perceive and respond to the world around them. Understanding these developmental changes can help you create characters that ring true, keeping you from the trap of putting adult words and thoughts into young characters.

Most children's writers have a sense of their target audience based on direct observation. It is also useful to know what the experts on children and their emotional and physical development have to say. Jean Piaget, perhaps the most famous of child psychologists, analyzed the way children think and perceive the world as they age. He said people must be able to fit new information into their present worldview to understand it; children's ability to do this differs from age to age.

Understanding Piaget's explanation of children's cognitive stages can help writers understand what young readers are ready to enjoy and comprehend.

Piaget said that children from infancy to age two are in a *sensorimotor stage*, when everything must be experienced with their five senses if it is to be "real." Young children cannot perceive the world except where it intersects with them. Thus, books for the very young have few words but plenty of sensory experiences: simple shapes, bright colors, textures, even smells. From age two until about seven, children are in a *preoperational stage* where pretending is very important. Children at this age understand about the concepts of *past* and *future* and that experiences exist that they have not yet tried. Children are learning about cause and effect, but are not usually ready for complex abstract thought. Consider how much imagination, make-believe, and the sequences of cause and effect can apply to fiction and nonfiction for readers in this stage.

From 7 to 12, children begin to understand, through reading, things that are totally outside their experience. This is the *concrete operational stage* when children can understand symbolic representations for abstract thought and when most children develop cognitive conceit: a belief that they are as capable and intelligent as adults. Perhaps the attraction for mysteries and the burgeoning interest in problem novels at the higher end of this age range becomes clearer.

During the *formal operational stage*, from 12 to adulthood, young people learn to process complex information in formal, logical ways, including advanced mathematical and scientific formulas. Piaget believed that the introduction of the formal operational stage brought with it a brief return of the egocentric tendencies of early childhood: Teens tend to spend a lot of time thinking about themselves.

A closer look at these stages can be found at www.pbs.org/wgbh/aso/databank/entries/dh23pi.html and chiron.valdosta.edu/whuitt/col/cogsys/piaget.html Another source for research on child development is the National Network for Child Care (NNCC) (www.nncc.org), part of the U.S. Department of Agriculture. This site contains many articles about child development and about presenting educational material for young children. Hot topics such as diversity, conflict resolution, and building compassion are all covered. This is truly a one-stop resource for all aspects of child development, from intellectual to language to physical, to social.

Another excellent source for information about physical and emotional development is Bright Futures (www.brightfutures.org). The site is designed to prepare parents and health professionals to evaluate the healthy development of children at different ages. It offers a children's writer a peek into age-specific developmental milestones. You can download Bright Futures' booklets for whatever age range you address. The booklets include possible risk factors (both health and behavioral risks such as increased risk taking or gun safety) for different age groups. The Bright Futures' online guidelines cover issues for infancy, early childhood, middle childhood, and adolescence.

Kids Health (www.kidshealth.org) includes information on all aspects of healthcare and development for children and teens. The material on sports, identifying different sports for younger age groups, sports injuries, nutrition, and healthy competition are excellent. This site could keep a writer busy for quite a while.

Not all resources are online, of course. Worthwhile books on child development include: *Introduction to Psychology, Exploration and Application,* by Dennis Coon (West Publishing Company, 1989), and *Children, Development and Social Issues,* by Edward F. Zigler and Matia Finn-Stevensen (Yale University. D.C. Heath and Company, 1987).

What Do Kids Want to Know?

Because children's writers use adult resources for gathering the information they intend to present to kids, there can be some difficulty in rethinking the material, and in moving from the academic to the entertaining. Some children's authors find it helpful to turn to children's books, children's magazines, and even children's televi-

Research

sion to reorient them to address their target audience.

"Personally, I use Ask Jeeves, (www.askjeeves.com) more when I'm researching for kids," says Canadian children's writer Joanne Keating. "I figure that the research should also be directed at their age level. What is it that they want to know? By using that route, I get to all kinds of kids' sites that give me more insight. Or, I'll use the junior version of an encyclopedia, etc. Same thing: geared more to what kids are ready to learn, on average."

Knowing what interests kids can be tricky. One of the quickest ways to learn is to examine media who depend upon interesting young consumers right now. Children's magazines are often more trendy than children's books because books must be more conservative to remain viable for future readers. Magazines are disposable, so they narrow their content to what interests kids right now. Many children's authors, especially those who target teens, subscribe to several of the most popular magazines to stay on top of trends in fashion, music, and fun. Some of these popular magazines are also available in public libraries and in an online form, making such research a bit less expensive. The sidebar on page 297 includes some of the most valuable magazines and websites for learning what's hot.

Children's nonfiction writer Kimberly Baldwin Radford says, "When I start the actual writing process, I usually look for several different magazines that are geared toward the age group I am targeting and that deal with similar themes, but not necessarily the exact same topic. This helps keep me on track with gearing my words and ideas for the right age group. I don't actually like reading too many kids' magazine articles on the same exact topic, lest I compromise my own vision for the piece."

"Once basic facts are in place, I begin hunting for the extras—the tidbits that will make the article shine," says nonfiction writer Laura P. Salas. "For the youngest readers/audience, I would probably look for things I could tie into their world. Can I relate anything about the nonfiction piece to meals, parents, playing, and bedtime? Can I relate something in the piece to a place they might have been or something they have likely seen? I try to come up with ways the topic might intersect with a very young child's world, and then I look for more specific resources to find details about that intersection.

"For kids from 6 to 11, I would be looking instead for the gross-out factor or the really neat wow stuff. Usually, this involves skimming through longer academic, scholarly works to try to pick out the two sentences about a neat fact that are in a 338-page book! Very time-consuming," Salas adds. "It doesn't necessarily have to relate so much to their world. But it is fun to find facts that contain something they can relate to, like for an article on water or plumbing, maybe I would include the fact that when you flush a toilet, between 5 and 10 billion water droplets go into the air.

"For teens, I would also look for nifty facts, but I'd be more likely to

Trendy Sources

Young Children
■ **Nick Jr.:** www.nickjr.com/grownups/home/magazine/current/index.jhtml
   A magazine from the cable television station that reveals not just little kids' favorite television characters, but is a crash course in what they love.

Tweens
■ **CosmoGirl!:** www.cosmogirl.com
   Cosmo for the tween and young teen set, a good trend guide, but be prepared for what you'll find!
■ **Discovery Girls:** www.discoverygirls.com
   Softer focus but plenty of fashion.
■ **Girls' Life:** www.girlslife.com
   Lets writers, and parents, look at fashion trends, music trends, and slang for middle-grade girls.
■ **New Moon:** www.newmoon.org
   Focuses on empowering girls, a hot topic these days.
■ **Nickelodeon:** www.nick.com
   A peek into TV trend land: music, games, sports, and slang.
■ **Sports Illustrated For Kids:** www.sikids.com/index.html
   The place to learn what sports are in, both for watching and for playing.

Teens
■ **Fox Family** and the **WB** networks: www.fox.com/home.htm and www2.warnerbros.com/ web/main/index.jsp
   Two network television stations : You'll find it informative to look at what kids are watching.
■ **Seventeen:** www.seventeen.com
   For girls, but since the magazine spends considerable time telling girls what guys like, it can tell writers, too!
■ **YM:** www.ym.com/index2.jsp
   One of the most successful, and becoming one of the most enduring, preteen and young teen girl's magazines. Since it's enduring when many others are failing, it must be saying something to adolescent girls.

Research

look for personal stories of teens accomplishing something to add to the mix. If it were something involving history, I'd try to come up with a modern-day analogy to make it more real for them, which would involve different resources."

As we research the readers who will be reading our work, we become more able to create books that endure. When we know the heart of a child, we can touch that place, not just today, but for future generations.

Chatting Them Up

By Donna Freedman

One of the most delightful aspects of writing is the chance to be, well, a snoop. Think of it: a job description that *requires* you to march into people's lives and ask questions.

- "Did you always want to be a marine biologist?"

- "How do you get that clown makeup off?"

- "What's the subject of your next book?"

You can tour a candy factory, hang out with a champion figure skater, or observe the training of guide dogs for the blind—and you get *paid* for it.

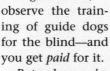

But unless you're good at interviewing, you won't get hired again. Interviewing can be a dry, who-what-where-why-when ordeal, or it can be a lively and revealing conversation. You have the chance to explain things, introduce new ideas, or provide a glimpse of a fascinating person or topic to young readers, but only if you know how to interview.

Getting Started

You may be lucky enough to be assigned a specific person to interview: a teen celebrity, a best-selling novelist, a famous astronomer. In that case, all you have to do is contact that person's agent, publisher, or employer. But suppose your assignment is "all about warthogs," or "girls' ice hockey"? Then it's time to (a) identify experts, and (b) convince them to speak with you.

Some possibilities for finding interviewees are through trade publications, professional groups (the American Medical Association, for example), speakers' bureaus, and the public relations offices of universities, hospitals, or businesses. And, of course, through the Internet. If you do a search for *warthogs*, you'll probably find lists of breeders, biologists, and businesses.

How do you get the interview? Often, all you have to do is ask. "When you say you're writing a children's

Research

book, how could anyone refuse?" says Gloria Skurzynski, author of more than 40 books for kids and young adults. How to contact potential interviewees depends on your own personal style. In this high tech age, some people still go the snail mail route. Fred Bortz thinks letters have more impact. In his interview requests, he writes very specifically of the project he's doing and what he hopes to accomplish. "I think that gives them a chance to reflect on it," says Bortz, author of numerous interview-based articles for children and adults, as well as books such as *Techno-Matter: The Materials Behind the Marvels*, and a book of profiles, *To The Young Scientist: Reflections on Doing and Living Science*.

Some writers have no qualms about picking up the telephone to ask for an interview. That's how Skurzynski does it. Candace Purdom, who writes for a number of children's publications, uses the phone, or a combination of phone and e-mail, because "deadlines are always looming. I try the quicker routes."

E-mail is a good compromise for those who don't feel comfortable cold-calling, but who don't have time to write letters. Nonfiction writer Debbie Miller, who talks with many scientists, uses e-mail to frame her questions and suggest some times for interviews. This "gives them more control over how they respond," says Miller, author of books that include *A Caribou Journey* and *Disappearing Lake*.

Sonya Senkowsky does phone potential interviewees—but she prefers to e-mail first. The freelance science writer announces her intentions in an electronic note explaining who she is and the details of her assignment. "I list my website as part of my signature, so subjects can check me out ahead of time if they want," says Senkowsky, whose work has appeared in daily and weekly newspapers, trade publications and, most recently, *Bioscience Magazine*.

Talking With . . .

How many experts should you interview? That depends on the publication for which you're writing. The newsletter *Children's Writer,* for instance, requires at least six to eight interviews for its lead articles. Other editors may ask for fewer, or more.

Keep in mind that if you contact five people, you might get three—or none. So make your requests early on and prepare to accommodate yourself to someone else's schedule. Of course, you may luck out and get all five, and right away. So you'd better be ready if they are. "You never know when a subject will take you off-guard by saying, 'Oh, I'm about to go to Europe on a phone- and computer-free vacation for six months, but I can talk to you for the next 10 minutes,'" Senkowsky notes.

Should this happen, you'd better have a decent understanding of the subject at hand and, ideally, some questions. That means research. The writers interviewed use a mix of sources, including newspapers, magazines, professional journals, popular magazines, college and university resources, and the Internet.

Writers cheer the Internet because it can connect them with sources they

Clicking at Interviews

After 17 years as a features writer at a daily newspaper, with a concurrent freelance career, I've learned a few things about interviewing. Here are some that have worked for me.

■ **Offer to do the interview at the subject's convenience.** That might mean you have to get up at 5 A.M. to accommodate a faraway time zone, or work on a Sunday afternoon. Do it. You're already asking a favor by requesting the interview; asking the person to rearrange a schedule might wreck your chances.

■ **Keep an eye on your tape recorder.** That way, you can say, "One moment, please," and flip the tape, rather than finding out later that you missed the last 10 minutes of the interview because the tape ran out.

■ **Get your biographical information somewhere else.** Don't waste the first 15 minutes finding out the person's age, educational or professional background, current job, etc.

■ **Try to find a *click* point.** Find something that will make this person warm to you. If your subject raises Rottweilers and you happen to own a Rottweiler, mention it. If the person was born in New Jersey and you were, too, say so. This is not ingratiating or falsely familiar. It simply lets the person know that there really *are* only six degrees of separation.

■ **Be open to suggestion.** If the person you're interviewing thinks something will be intriguing to your readers, listen to him. He'll become more expansive as he talks about what really interests him. At worst, you'll have to steer away from the subject. At best, you'll wind up with a new layer to your article, or an interesting fact no one else knows.

■ **Ask the toughest questions last.** These might include "How old are you? What's your salary? What'd you pay for that?" That way, if the person hangs up on you, you've still got the bulk of the interview.

■ **If they haven't hung up?** Your last question should always be, "Is there anything you'd like to bring up that I haven't asked?"

Research

might not otherwise have encountered. When young adult author Linda Joy Singleton decided to write a book about cheerleading, she knew next to nothing about the subject. So among other things, she joined an Internet listserv. "This online connection eventually led to an invitation to attend a four-day cheerleading camp," Singleton says.

Be selective about the sites you choose, however. Miller points out that "you may find information on the Internet that doesn't list the sources clearly."

If you're interviewing an author, read some of their recent works. For an entertainer, rent films or listen to CDs; read reviews, too. If time permits, seek out influences your interviewee has mentioned in the past. When *Booklist* devoted an issue to religion, Children's Book Editor Ilene Cooper sought out books one writer had mentioned as being influential to his writing.

Not everyone can do things like that. Freelancers, especially, know that time is money. But it's vital to do enough research so that you don't "look like an amateur," cautions Skurzynski, or waste the interviewee's time.

Ask a Stupid Question?

Suppose you've researched enough not to sound completely ignorant, but you're not sure you fully understand polar bear migration. Should you admit up front you're not entirely clear on the matter yourself?

Absolutely, says Wendie Old, author of 12 books for children and young adults. "Indicate that you have some general/popular knowledge about the subject, but that you've always wondered that/if/why," she suggests. "This makes the interviewee comfortable with you, because he is in familiar territory explaining things."

Purdom claims there really *is* no such thing as a stupid question. "How can I explain it to readers if I don't get it? So I don't have a problem saying I don't understand something," she says. "Or I repeat something back: 'So what you're saying is . . .' and make sure I have it right."

How much research is enough? "When I've exhausted my sources, or I'm finding the same information repeated," says Purdom. Bortz uses his own curiosity as a gauge. "When it is fairly well satisfied, that's when I can quit," he says. Old has a simple rule to determine when to quit researching: "When you run out of time."

Interview questions will develop as you research. Keep your audience in mind, but remember that whatever's really interesting about a subject should be interesting to anyone. "The fact that the mold that grows in the bathroom is alive is interesting to anyone. The fact that it digests its food outside of its body, then consumes it, is interesting, too," Purdom says.

If you're writing for a specific age group, ask questions that make famous people accessible, and therefore human. For a series of author biographies, Cooper posed queries like, "What were you like when you were a kid?" and "Who were your favorite authors when you were young?" When she's writing for *Booklist*, though, she takes care to ask questions designed to help librarians and teachers.

Should you send the questions in advance? Writers are sharply divided on this idea. Cooper doesn't want to limit the conversation by establishing parameters with a list of questions. Besides, she says, a prepared list may result in answers that "sound canned." Not that the interview is a total blind-side; when Cooper writes a letter to confirm her appointment to talk, she will mention a few of the points she'd like to cover.

Judy O'Malley, Editor of Cobble-stone Publishing's new *Ask* magazine and former Editor of *Book Links,* frequently interviews children's authors. She's found that many prefer to have the questions in advance, "to mull them over and compose a coherent, directed response." The result, she says, is "an interview that has an integral shape beyond a string of informative answers."

Chatting Them Up

Approach the interview with common sense and courtesy. If you have an appointment, by phone or in person, keep it. If the interviewee has only 15 minutes to talk, get right to your questions—but first, thank him for being willing to talk.

"The people I'm interviewing are giving me some of their time," notes Bortz. So he keeps an eye on the clock to make sure he doesn't go over the time he'd requested—"unless they seem really eager to tell me more."

Hang in there if things are a little awkward at first. Not everyone is at his best when he's on the spot, be it by phone or in person. And it's a little off-putting to have someone write down or tape your comments. (Empathy exercise: ask a friend to "interview" you. You'll be surprised how odd it feels.)

When Purdom senses resistance, she'll ask what the issue is. "There's usually a way to smooth things out," she says. Sometimes, that's with humor: "I convince them I don't have the mange and I won't bite and I'm not with *60 Minutes!*"

In her newspapering days, Sen-kowsky dealt with her share of difficult interviews. When one subject was "a little combative," she let him vent for 10 minutes straight. "Then I repeated back to him what he had said, in a way that indicated neutral interest," she says. "After he realized I had been listening to him quite intently, he was satisfied to let me go on with my part of the interview."

Not every interview involves listening—some writers find it easier to do some or all interviewing via e-mail. Singleton loves electronic Q&As, which are "quick and convenient." Old prefers e-mails, because they can be sent and received in her spare time. Whenever possible, though, she conducts interviews in person.

So does Bortz. "The purpose is to understand the person. I don't think it's possible to do that through electronic means," he says. "You need at least to talk to them on the phone, when you can hear the nuances of their speech."

Another wonderful by-product of person-to-person conversation: tangents. If your subject goes off-topic, you should go there, too, according to Skurzynski. "Tangents are wonderful, because they're about matters I didn't even think of," she says, "and that may be much more interesting."

Of course, you may have to rein in your interviewee. Keep an eye on the clock, so you don't spend too much of your allotted time with this conversational bushwhacking. "Let him go there for a short time, then ask your next question to bring him back to the subject you are interviewing him for," advises Old, who notes that sidetracks "help with characterization, and might make a good sidebar."

In a perfect world, your assignment would include travel money to visit the expert's turf. This certainly helps with the scene-setting, since it lets you describe the sound of whale songs, or the smell of a tiger's cage.

Cooper is working on a children's book about John F. Kennedy, Jr., so she went to Massachusetts for research at the Kennedy Library. When Bortz was researching *To the Young Scientist*, he visited seven states in six weeks. "Really crazy travel," he says, "but it was just so important for me to get to where they were working, to get a sense of the person."

Are You Getting This?

The best way to capture an interview is the way that works for you. Some people use only pen and paper, others only tape recorders. If you tape, be careful where you stage your interview. If it takes place in a public place, such as a restaurant or hotel lobby, "background noises and interruptions can be distracting and make tran-

scription a nightmare," according to O'Malley.

Even if you're a total tapehead, bring a notebook. You'll want to write down the matter-of-fact way the biologist handled the snake, or how the author's face lit up when he discussed Madeleine L'Engle. The writers interviewed do their own transcribing, since tapes may contain technical or esoteric information or pronunciations. Besides, listening to the words helps get them into the spirit of the interview once more.

If your topic is extremely technical, or relatively new to you, don't be too proud to ask for a reality check. This could be from someone else in the field, rather than your original interviewee. Miller asks three to five scientists to review her first draft. "For *A Woolly Mammoth Journey*, the man who knew more about mammoths than just about anybody lives in London. I sent it to him electronically," Miller says.

Should you show the entire article? That depends on your personal ethics and/or those of the publication for which you're writing. Some magazines routinely send articles out for an advance read; others do their fact-checking in-house, and may in fact prohibit writers from showing the work before it's published.

Skurzynski always offers prepublication review. "I may have gotten something wrong that needs clarification," she says. But Cooper wants her interviews to stand as they were recorded. "It's just human nature that anybody might want to take something back," she notes, "or make themselves sound better." Sending the article around also "slows down the process," says Singleton. "But if someone asks, I will probably agree."

Finally: Once is not enough when it comes to thank-yous. The writers interviewed always follow up with a note and/or a copy of the book or publication. This ensures future friendly relations and, according to Miller, makes the interviewee feel like a part of the finished project. "This lets them know that their work is valuable," she says, "and that because they shared it, I'm able to create engaging and factually accurate books for children."

Research

Content, Not Catalogues

By Mary Northrup

Remember when the World Wide Web was new and we were promised we would have the libraries of the world at our fingertips? Well, we can now connect to almost any library, but for the most part what we get is that library's catalogue. While this is very handy for the researcher who wants to know what's available, sometimes we want content, not a catalogue.

Yet some library websites deliver great content: literary texts, historical images, primary documents, maps, music, ads, and much more. Writers who research will be delighted with the treasures that await—with no need to travel.

The scope of these sites is wide, encompassing many subjects, although history is especially strong. Sample the sites listed below, then do your own searching. For local history, check out the websites of libraries in the geographical area you are researching. Many have digital collections of texts and photos highlighting their region. Because the information is provided through a university or public library, it's accuracy should be extremely high.

While researchers will always need to search out books, articles, memorabilia, and actual physical locations, more and more texts and images will show up on websites. What better place to find these than in online libraries?

■ The Library of Congress
www.lcweb.loc.gov

Just as our national library in Washington, DC, takes up an enormous amount of physical space, its presence on the Web is huge. In user-friendly format, the home page offers a tempting variety of information.

Click on American Memory, and you have access to more than five million items available for viewing, including such highlights as baseball cards of 1887 to 1914, folk music from Depression-era migrant worker camps, the papers of Alexander Graham Bell in his own writing, quilts and interviews with quilt-makers in America in the last 20 years, women's rights tracts from the National American Woman Suffrage Association of 1848 to 1921, and maps of the national parks. Browse through pamphlets, manuscripts, audio and video clips, letters, photographs, sheet music, portraits, and documents from all eras of American history. The collections are well-organized and searchable by keyword, topic, original format, or time period. This is a treasure trove for the researcher in Americana.

Go to *Exhibitions: An On-line Gallery* to find out about feature attractions at the Library of Congress. Even if you can't travel, you can gather much information at this site as you revel in the variety of cultural artifacts contained here.

The Library Today is an up-to-date collection of news and special events going on at the Library of Congress. Again, much information is available for the person who can access only through the Web. One sample day featured news of an online author chat; an announcement of a new exhibition about Chautauqua, New York, a historical center where artistic festivals, seminars, and events take place; a long, illustrated article about James Madison; a report, including a Web cast, on the New Digital Reference Service organized by the Library of Congress and other libraries; and information on a new collection of Communist Party USA records.

Clicking on *Thomas* takes you to almost everything you want to know about legislation: bills, their status and complete text, public laws, roll call votes, and committee reports. *Thomas*, of course, is named for Thomas Jefferson, whose donated library formed the first Library of Congress.

At the kids' site, *America's Library,* children and parents can read biographies of famous Americans; explore a time in history; find out about a particular state; investigate hobbies, recreation, and sports; view movies; hear songs; and much more.

The United States Copyright Office pages are also part of the Library of Congress site, and contain information, forms, and legislation.

The Library of Congress has created an outstanding site, a great example of the capabilities of the Web. On one hand, it is a typical library site that gives users a chance to search the catalogue, exhibits, special collections, and even view available jobs. On the other, it goes so much further in promoting the Library's services and making its collections available to all. If you are doing research on any aspect of the history or culture of America, don't hesitate to check out this site.

■ **Duke University Rare Book, Manuscript, and Special Collections Library**
http://odyssey.lib.duke.edu
Researchers in history should definitely stop at this site. The digitized collections include a wide variety of sources. Of special interest:

Emergence of Advertising in America: 1850-1920 includes more than 9,000 items (all types of print advertisements: leaflets, broadsides, cookbooks, books, pamphlets, posters, cards) are in this database, searchable by keyword or by type of illustration or special feature, such as children in illustration, sports in illustration, coupons, premiums, etc.

A related site is *Ad*Access*, which contains more than 7,000 advertisements appearing in print between

1911 and 1955. Search by keyword or browse through categories such as Beauty and Hygiene, Radio, Television, Transportation, and World War II. Illustrations and special features can also be searched. Both ad databases also include timelines.

Historic American Sheet Music presents over 16,000 pages published between 1850 and 1920. Browse by title page within dates or by subject, illustration type, advertising, or date. Historical information about the songs and a time line place them in their era in American culture.

Documents from the Women's Liberation Movement presents images of the real pages of pamphlets, fliers, and articles from 1969 to 1974. Keyword searching is available, as well as searches by subjects, such as Women of Color, Organizations and Activism, and Women's Work and Roles.

Duke Papyrus Archive features images of more than 1,300 papyri and much information about the papyri, its history, and Egypt. Search by topics, including Women and Children, Cultural Aspects, Archives, or by language.

Check out the Duke University site for much more: presidential campaign memorabilia, an Italian pamphlet collection, women's diaries from the civil war, slave experiences, and more.

■ **The New York Public Library Digital Library Collection**
http://digital.nypl.org

The Schomburg Center for Research in Black Culture, part of the New York Public Library, collects primary source material covering the history and culture of African Americans and Africans all over the world.

African American Women Writers of the 19th Century (http://digital. nypl. org/schomburg/writers_aa19/) attests to the fact that although it was a crime to teach American slaves to read and write, many slaves did learn, and some became published authors. Interest spurred by the civil rights movement brought these authors to light. Browse by title, author, or type of writing: fiction, poetry, biography and autobiography, and essays. The full text of the work is here, as well as biographies of the authors.

Images of African Americans from the 19th Century (http://digital.nypl. org/schomburg/images_aa19/) has a wide variety of photographs, engravings, and other images documenting the lives of African Americans in slavery and freedom. Search by keyword or choose from categories, such as Civil War, education, social life, politics, or individual portraits of men, women, or children. Each image is identified with a title, original caption, material type (stereograph, postcard, print, wood engraving, illustration, etc.), creator, date, source, location, and subjects (standard library subject headings).

■ **University of Pennsylvania Digital Library Programs & Projects**
http://digital.library.upenn.edu/

This site provides access to text, manuscripts, photos, maps, and audio. Read, in manuscript form, the diaries of women in the nineteenth and early twentieth centuries. Browse through a 1705 cookbook manuscript, with recipes and medicines. View corporate annual reports from a variety of companies from the 1910s to the 1960s. View the *Marian Anderson Collection of Photographs, 1898-1992*, then read about her life and listen to her sing. Search, and listen to, a sampling of more than 25,000 Yiddish and other Jewish songs in the *Freedman Jewish Music Archive*. There is much to explore here.

■ **Cornell University Prototype Digital Library**
http://moa.cit.cornell.edu
This site brings the pages of books and magazines to you in digital form. Represented in the *Making of America* Collection here are primary sources in American history. Over 260 volumes and more than 100,000 articles are featured in this collection. Browse through reproductions of the actual pages of *The New England* magazine from 1886 to 1900 or *Scientific American* from 1846 to 1869, or one of many others. Investigate official records of Union and Confederate armies and navies. Browse through historical math books, or agriculture books from the early part of the twentieth century. There is much to access at this site. Check it out for even more collections.

■ **The Indiana University Digital Library Program**
http://www.dlib.indiana.edu
Peruse the *Hoagy Carmichael Collection*, which includes music, song lyrics, photos, letters, scrapbook clippings, and personal effects. Search by word or phrase. Or find the text of a novel, poem, drama, or pamphlet in *The Victorian Women Writers Project*. Search full text by keyword. Keep up with this one as other collections are in progress, including American novels, twentieth-century slides, music, and steel mill photographs.

■ **Brown University Library Digital Projects**
http://www.brown.edu/Facilities/University_Library/digproj/index.html
Investigate the development of musical theater in the African American community through *AfricanAmerican Sheet Music, 1850-1920*. Read about each decade in *The Development of an AfricanAmerican Musical Theatre 1865-1910* and see actual sheet music displayed.

Or view the detailed, colorful "*Minassian Collection of Persian, Mughal, and Indian Miniature Paintings.*" Much textual material is provided, besides the images.

There are a number of special exhibitions, from military characters and World War II artists to early twentieth-century Christmas illustrations and illustrations from travel books. In some cases, only part of the collection is shown, but there is usually explanatory text and a sample of the collection.

■ **University of Kansas AMDOCS: Documents for the Study of American History**
http://www.ukans.edu/carrie/docs/amdocs_index.html
Arranged by century from the fifteenth to the nineteenth, then by

major events (Civil War, Reconstruction, First World War, etc.) up to the twenty-first century, each section contains charters, constitutions, reports, acts, letters, speeches, political platforms, and diaries. A great place to go for primary sources.

■ **Princeton University Library Digital Collections**
http://infoshare1.princeton.edu:2003/digital_collections/texts_images.html

A variety of texts, images, and projects await you at the Princeton Library. If you are interested in the West, check out the *Western Americana Collection, Prints and Photographs*, which includes manuscripts, Indian records, and personal papers.

Or try *Princeton University Library Papyrus Home Page*. Here you can view pieces of papyrus from many time periods, identified by author or contents, including Egyptian, Greek, Roman, and Arabic papyri, and literary, religious, and historical documents.

There are also some map sites, in particular New Jersey geological survey sheets and a sixteenth-century map of Rome to assist the study of art and architecture. This site also has links to sites at other universities that offer texts and images on line.

■ **The British Library**
http://www.bl.uk/

Click on *Digital Library* and you will find listed several projects that comprise the British Library Digital Library Programme. Here you can view facsimiles of the original *Beowulf*, Gutenberg Bible, Magna Carta, and other historical manuscripts. In addition, because Great Britain was involved in exploration and colonization all over the world, several projects from the Far East are included. One is a reproduction of the full text of *The Lion and Dragon: Britain's First Embassy to China,* a report from the 1790s.

According to information on this site, the Digital Library is a program that will continue to grow.

■ **University of North Carolina at Chapel Hill, Documenting the American South**
http://docsouth.unc.edu/dasmain.html

Southern history and literature are featured here: first-person narratives, Southern literature, slave narratives, Confederate documents, and African-American church documents and writings. More than 900 books and manuscripts are included, and some photos, covering colonial times to the beginning of the twentieth century.

■ **University of Miami Archives and Special Collections, Otto G. Richter Library**
http://www.library.miami.edu/archives/intro.html

Twenty collections make up this website, with a variety of specialties: sea journals and war diaries, Civil War letters, postcards, promotional literature, and maps. Some collections of note:

Reclaiming the Everglades: South Florida's National History, 1884-1934, is a collection of original papers, postcards, and photographs that document this era in the development of the Everglades.

Slave Resistance: A Caribbean Study includes texts as well as rare maps and engravings to offer a scholarly study of Caribbean slave life.

The Florida Postcard Collection contains 5,000 postcards of landmarks and buildings all around the state.

■ **University of California, BerkeleyDigital Library Project**
http//elib.cs.berkeley.edu/matrix.html

This site provides California plant and animal information, maps, California environmental reports, and photos of the region.

■ **The Denver Public Library Western History Photos**
http://gowest.coalliance.org

Search or browse 80,000 historic images and records from the library's Western History/Genealogy Department and the Colorado Historical Society. They cover Native Americans and pioneers, towns and railroads, mining, art, and more. Search by author, title, subject, or keyword.

■ **University of Georgia Libraries Rare Map Collection**
http://www.libs.uga.edu/darchive/hargrett/maps/maps.html

Eight hundred maps, from the 1500s through the early 1900s, are available, most depicting Georgia and that geographic region. Search by broad subject (New World, Colonial America, American Civil War, Transportation, etc.).

Electronic Texts Online: Library in a Box

Many books that are no longer covered by copyright appear on websites. Although not all these sites are offered by libraries, they all provide selections from a library's most famous commodity: a book. What can you find? Classics from the ancient Greeks and Romans, nineteenth-century poetry, Tarzan novels, Sherlock Holmes stories, historical documents, folktales, sacred books from many religions, and so much more.

■ **Project Gutenberg** http://www.gutenberg.net
  This is the granddaddy of all electronic text sites. It has been around for 30 years, even before the Internet's modern incarnation. Thousands of titles can be searched by author, title, subject, and language.

■ **Alex Catalogue of Electronic Texts** http://infomotions.com/alex
  Featuring American and English literature and Western philosophy, this site offers searching text by keyword or browsing by author, title, or date.

■ **Bartleby.com** http://www.bartleby.com
  Although this is a commercial site, access to titles is free. Search a number of reference books, anthologies, and volumes of verse, fiction, and nonfiction by author, title, or subject.

■ **Bibliomania** http://www.bibliomania.com
  Search by literary type (fiction, nonfiction, poetry, reference, short story, drama), author, title, or words within the work. Designed for students, the site also includes study guides.

■ **Folklore and Mythology Electronic Texts** http://www.pitt.edu/~dash/folk-texts.html
  Hundreds of tales from throughout the world appear here. The tales are translated and retold. Browse an alphabetical list of titles and authors.

■ **The Free Library of Classics** http://www.information-resources.com/Library/library.html
  More than 200 literary works and historical documents are featured, under the categories Novels, Children, Plays, Historical Documents, Poetry, and Short Stories. Browse an alphabetical list of titles or authors.

■ **Humanities Text Initiative** http://www.hti.umich.edu
  Look through 22 collections, from American verse to the King James Bible to Bosnian travel books. Search within the collection by a variety of search strategies.

■ **The Online Medieval & Classical Library**
  http://sunsite.berkeley.edu/OMACL
  Interested in fare such as Chaucer, Icelandic sagas, or the Song of Roland? Search by keyword in text, or browse by title, author, genre, or language.

Research

Writer Websites: Practical & Fun

By Mark Haverstock

Along with all the serious resources available to writers through the Internet, many websites are also just plain fun. Here is a selection of sites that deliver references, writers' tips, market listings, places to chat with fellow writers, that give you those practical answers you need quickly and painlessly, and sites that are entertaining, too. We chose sites based on their interest and usefulness to writers, with an eye toward free or inexpensive access. The best way to get to know them is simply to browse and see what's available. Many have help and FAQ (frequently asked questions) sections to help you on your self-guided tours.

Be aware that websites come and go. We checked all before *Children's Writer Guide to 2002* went to press, but any could fade away virtually overnight. If you can't link with the website for some reason, try typing the name into any of the search engines listed in the article before you give up. You might find the site at a new location or a site with similar content.

Don't just sit there—get clicking!

General References
- **Bartleby**
  www.bartleby.com
  In addition to the *World Factbook* and the classic version of *Bartlett's Familiar Quotations,* you'll find public-domain versions of more than a dozen widely used reference materials. You'll also find a quotation and a word for the day.

- **Encyclopedia Britannica**
  www.britannica.com
  Don't reach for the encyclopedia, go here instead. Britannica gives you access to their encyclopedia entries as well as outside links for additional information.

- **The Internet Public Library**
  www.ipl.org
  The collections of the Internet Public Library are divided into reference; exhibits; "especially for librarians"; magazines and serials; newspapers; and online texts. It has special collections for children and teens and many links to good sites on many subjects, including children's authors. The University of Michigan School of Information and

Bell & Howell Information and Learning sponsor the site.

■ **Grammar Lady**

www.grammarlady.com

This one-woman operation raises consciousness about correct language use and reminds everyone of the ways to have fun with language. If you've got a pressing question, the Grammar Lady even has a hotline from 9:00A.M. to 5:00P.M., Monday through Friday, with a toll-free number, 1-800-279-9708.

■ **Infomine**

infomine.ucr.edu

Infomine is especially valuable in academic searches. It includes databases, electronic journals, electronic books, bulletin boards, listservs, online library card catalogues, articles, and directories of researchers, among many other types of information.

■ **Merriam-Webster's Collegiate Dictionary**

www.m-w.com

Look up words, get help with a thesaurus, play daily word games, check out the word of the day, find language resources, and do much more on this useful and fun site.

■ **Microsoft Encarta Encyclopedia**

www.encarta.msn.com

Need some quick reference help on general topics, and without heavy reading? This is the place to go. The site also features a dictionary and atlas.

■ **Your Dictionary**

www.yourdictionary.com

Stumped by words like bloviate or diffident? Get definitions and synonyms here. If the quick lookup doesn't find them, there are links to other dictionaries and references as well, including specialty and foreign language dictionaries.

■ **United States Postal Service**

www.usps.com

Need to calculate the postage for a manuscript sent Priority Mail? Want to make sure you have the right zip code? Check this site for all you need to mail.

In Search Of . . .

■ **Amazon.com and Barnes & Noble**

www.amazon.com

www.bn.com

These online booksellers can help you locate books by author, title, and subject; get reviews; and help you purchase hard to locate books that may be out of print. Writers can do research from many directions on these sites—find research sources, do competition research, and much more.

■ **Dogpile**

www.dogpile.com/

Dogpile will fetch the information you seek from 17 popular search engines at once in all formats, including text, images, audio, and video.

■ **Google**

www.google.com

Keep it simple with just a search box, or use their expanded web directory. Google is still one of the best search engines around when it comes to accurate hits.

- **Library of Congress Online Catalogue**

  catalog.loc.gov

  Locate books by author, title, publisher, or ISBN. The possibilities for research on this massive site are endless.

- **Northern Light**

  www.northernlight.com

  This search engine provides general search capabilities as well as access to a collection of downloadable articles from periodicals. Articles generally cost less than $3, and there is a liberal refund policy if the material doesn't meet your needs.

- **Pilot Search**

  www.pilot-search.com

  This arts and technology search engine will help you find everything from author information to e-zines from a growing list of more than 11,000 links.

- **WhoWhere**
  InfoUsa

  www.whowhere.lycos.com

  www.infousa.com

  Find phone numbers, addresses, and e-mail addresses, including reverse phone number searches.

Expert Sources
- **AskMe**

  www.askme.com

  Post your question for free in any of the listed categories, from arts to travel, and wait for an answer from a professional in the field. Check the ratings to reveal the apparent reliability of your source.

- **Experts.com**

  www.experts.com

  Do you want to find an expert in a specific field? This site matches a diverse collection of professionals with your needs.

- **Expert Source**

  www.businesswire.com/
  expert source

  ExpertSource connects writers to authoritative academic and industry sources. ExpertSource is a partnership between Business Wire and Round Table Group, Inc.

- **Journalist Express**

  www.journalistexpress.com

  Free membership provides contacts for expert sources and a home page you can customize according to your interests. Their standard portal contains hundreds of links to specific research topics and directories.

- **Profnet**

  www.profnet.com

  Need a physicist for a science article or a psychologist to help explain the major fears of children? This free service connects writers to expert sources from colleges, universities, corporations, think tanks, laboratories, medical centers, nonprofit organizations, government agencies, and public relations agencies.

Internet Mailing Lists
- **Catalist**

  www.lsoft.com/lists/listref.html

  This official site for Listserv mailing lists is a quick and free source of information and resources on a variety of topics. If you're a nonfiction writer, try searching and subscribing to lists on topics you routinely cover.

■ Publicly Accessible Mailing Lists
www.paml.net

PAML bills itself as the Internet's premier mailing list directory, frequently updating its contents. The site contains additional links to other mailing lists, as well as a question-and-answer section on mailing lists.

■ Quick Topic
quicktopic.com

The Internet is full of discussion boards, mailing lists, and news-groups dedicated to specific topics. Here's a way to start your own. At Quick Topic, you simply enter a topic name and your address. You'll get an e-mail you can then forward to all the members of your group; it will contain the unique URL of an easy-to-use discussion page where folks can post messages.

Markets/Jobs
■ Guru.com
www.guru.com

This independent professional talent resource helps match freelancers with projects. Though not specifically for writers, it has easy-to-do custom searches for specific markets or you can create your own profile so contractors can find you.

■ Writer's Exchange
www.writers-exchange.com/job.htm

Check here for numerous links to jobs, news, and information about the writing profession.

■ Writer's Weekly
www.writersweekly.com

Freelance job listings and new paying markets are delivered to your e-mailbox every Wednesday when you sign up at this site.

Miscellaneous/Fun Stuff
■ Backwash
backwash.com

Wouldn't it be cool to have a Web-savvy pal who could clue you in to the coolest new sites? Start by picking out a personality type you're interested in: Marxist, skeptic, artsy type, etc. You'll get listings of recommended sites to check out, updated regularly.

■ Find Tutorials
www.findtutorials.com

Want to know how to tie basic knots, how to host a party, or how to drive a stick shift? Do a search at this site to find out these and other skills in dozens of categories.

■ How Things Work
rabi.phys.virginia.edu/HTW

Physics professor Louis A. Bloomfield has a mission: to answer questions about why things are the way they are in the physical universe.

■ LiveManuals
www.livemanuals.com

Forget how to set your inkjet printer? Program your cell phone? Find online manuals with support information for thousands of products.

■ Marshall Brain's How Stuff Works
www.howstuffworks.com

The hundreds of articles at this site

Mailing Lists

You've got mail. But if you're not taking advantage of Internet mailing lists, you're missing the boat. Mailing lists can be a nonfiction writer's best friend, supplying numerous quick and free sources of information. They're especially helpful if you specialize in writing on certain topics.

Mailing lists come in two flavors, *discussion* and *announcement*. If you subscribe to a discussion list, you'll receive a message each time a member posts information. You can then read the message, reply, or generate a message of your own. One caution: When members get verbose, you can find a full mailbox. Choose wisely.

Announcement lists are most often sent from companies or news agencies—think PR release. They contain breaking news about technology, industry gossip, and other topics.

So how can these lists help you? If you need an expert, it's likely you'll find a name and phone number on an announcement list. If you need to include a real-person story in your article, you can use a discussion list to solicit contacts discreetly. You can even keep in contact with writing colleagues that share similar interests.

To join, send an e-mail to the list administrator with your e-mail address and you'll soon be added to the list. Most are automated. In some cases, like ProfNet and PR News Wire, you'll be asked to fill out a more detailed form.

When in discussions, remember to keep to the topic, focus on your point, and show consideration for others on the list. Don't forget to help others when you join mailing lists: Active participation can pay off later in valuable sources.

cover categories from health to machines to the home to science. It seriously takes on questions like "which came first, the chicken or the egg?" and "how does your stomach keep from digesting itself?"

■ **SafeWeb**
www.safeweb.com
Surf the Web while maintaining online privacy through this site. Your web address is hidden and no one will know where you've been.

■ **Spyonit**
www.spyonit.com
Create a personal Internet spy to notify you when a web page changes, when your stock splits, or when an airfare drops into your price range.

■ **Useless Information Home Page**
home.nycap.rr.com/useless/
index.html
UIHP contains all the factoids you never needed to know, but your life would be incomplete without.

Getting Connected

Maybe this is your first experience getting online, or you're an old pro looking for better service. There are now more options available, with others on the horizon. Here's the scoop on the how and where to connect from your home office today, along with some tips.

DSL/Cable. Check with your local phone or cable company. You'll love the speed, which can beat typical dial-up lines by a factor of 10 or more. But that's provided that cable and DSL are even available in your location and that they've worked out the bugs. DSL, a phone line-based service, has gotten some bad press in the last year for numerous technical glitches and poor service. In some areas, a wait of several months for a DSL installation is not uncommon and DSL has some restrictions. You need to be within three miles of a telephone switching station for it to work, which rules out many suburban and rural customers. Check with current customers in your area before taking the plunge.

Cable Internet. This is my preference. Generally, it's been more reliable and installation times can be measured in days instead of weeks or months. There's only one downside—if lots of people in your neighborhood also choose cable Internet, your connection slows somewhat, especially during peak usage times.

Satellite. You'll find it through electronics dealers such as Best Buy, Radio Shack, or Circuit City. DirecTV currently is the leading provider of satellite

On Writing

■ **Absolute Write**
www.absolutewrite.com
A one-stop destination for freelancers with articles, market news, interviews, reviews, and a free newsletter.

■ **Famous Children's Author's Websites**
galileo.vigoco.k12.in.us/~fuqael/coolproj/summer2000/author.htm
Want to find out more about Will Hobbs? Katherine Paterson? Use the links here to find their home pages.

■ **The Institute of Children's Literature**
www.institutechildrenslit.com
This site, sponsored by the Institute of Children's Literature, provides tips for writers in the children's market, online interviews with experts, message boards, and open chat.

■ **KaZoodles**
klockepresents.com/kazoodles.html
KaZoodles is a biweekly featuring all the e-zines, lists, books, sites and more on writing that you would like to know about but don't have time to search out. Writers are welcome to send their own writing information for inclusion.

Getting Connected

Internet and can provide an alternative for those who cannot get cable or DSL. These systems work one-way: You call up the Internet through your phone line and the return information is sent back via satellite. The assumption is that loading a web page takes the most time, so the satellite speeds the process. Satellite service can be pricey, but may turn out to be in the same ballpark as cable or DSL, depending on usage. The downside is you must have an unobstructed path to the south (no trees or buildings in the way), and heavy precipitation can adversely affect reception. If you already have satellite TV and you're satisfied with its performance, it's a good bet it will work fine in your location.

Dial-Up Services. Check your nearest computer stores or your phone book for local services. Dial-up services like AOL, EarthLink, MSN, and others have been the mainstay of online services for years. Though 56K connections may seem slow compared to the services listed above, they still give most Internet users reliable service and tolerable download times. Shop for the best bargains available. Often, phone companies like Sprint and AT&T will bundle your Internet and long distance services and give you discounts on both. Stay away from long-term contracts, especially ones that last more than a year. Though several retailers may offer some sweet rebates for making a three-year commitment with certain ISPs, they may not be worth it in the long run.

■ **LiteraryAgent.com**
www.literaryagent.com
This database contains hundreds of agencies searchable by agency name, city, state, country, or area of interest. You'll also find columns on writing and forums, including one on children's literature.

■ **The Slot**
www.theslot.com
Maintained by Bill Walsh of the *Washington Post*, this site keeps a lengthy list of style points and issues, things you won't find in the *AP Stylebook*. It's a great site for the copyeditor in all of us.

■ **Suite 101**
www.suite101.com/welcome.cfm/childrens_writing
Suite 101 contains articles on children's writing, discussion boards, and links to other sites of interest. Go back to the main site, www.suite101.com, and you'll find 1,400 general reference topics accompanied by more than 43,000 articles.

■ **Writer's BBS**
www.writersbbs.com
You'll meet fellow writers and find many resources of interest to authors, poets, and journalists here. Join other writers for writing workshops, confer-

ences, or just to talk in our more than 50 Writers' Discussion and Critique Forums covering fiction and nonfiction. Open chat is also available.

■ Writer to Writer
www.writertowriter.com

Writer to Writer is a site for all writers from beginner to pro, and offers a mix of tips, articles, and advice.

■ Writing World
www.writing-world.com

This site picks up where the former Inkspot/Inklings website left off when it shut down last year. You can subscribe to their biweekly newsletter, peruse posted writing articles, or take advantage of fee-based writers' services.

Writers' Organizations
■ Canadian Society of Children's Authors, Illustrators and Performers
www.canscaip.org

Keep up-to-date with meetings, events, and member publications.

■ Society of Children's Book Writers and Illustrators
www.scbwi.org

Check out regional news and events of interest to authors writing in the children's market. There's also a good collection of articles and tips excerpted from the monthly newsletter.

■ Writer's Union
www.nwu.org

NWU is the only labor union that represents freelance writers who work in all genres, formats, and media. You'll find current information on political issues, contracts, and other issues of interest to all writers.

On Books
■ Book Browser, the Guide for Avid Readers
www.www.bookbrowser.com

Here's a site with reading recommendations arranged by genre, features on libraries, information about authors, and more. It adds about 40 book reviews a week and gives readers many ways to find more of the kinds of books they like to read, like its If You Like . . . Try list.

■ Carol Hurst's Children's Literature Site
www.carolhurst.com

While this is an educational site, with professional resources, it also posts reviews of children's sites and makes reading recommendations. On the curriculum areas page are lists of books to use in social studies, science, math, art, and language arts. It also has links to related sites.

Expert Encounters

By Carolyn P. Yoder

If your image of research involves blowing dust off musty primary sources or squinting hours on end at Web pages, your picture lacks an important component: people. Research for any kind of writing will lead you to a profusion of people as you scour libraries, special collections, or museums. The big picture includes encounters with these experts and more.

Writers and editors for children rely increasingly on professional opinions. Publishers demand accurate and complete information. They stress fairness in tone. Experts can help writers, editors, and illustrators locate the most reliable resources for a project, and as a result, help maintain a balanced tone, suggest places to visit, recommend other experts, and perhaps most important, explain the differences of opinion or discrepancies that always tend to come up in research. Experts can be involved in all stages of research from the early gathering of information, to the *digestion* process to the final draft. Writers and editors often use experts to review completed manuscripts or particular sections for information and tone.

Respect & Review

Laurence Pringle, the author of nearly 100 nonfiction titles, works with experts because it is "the best way to help ensure my writing is accurate. As a reader, I wouldn't trust any nonfiction book that was not checked by one or more experts in the field. As an author, I know that inaccuracies can damage my reputation."

Robert San Souci, who has written more than 60 books for young readers and is a regular contributor to *Faces* and *Cobblestone* magazines, often seeks out experts to help fill in the blanks when a book requires specific information that's beyond the scope of his reference library or his own knowledge. "Many of my books are cross-cultural studies often set in distant parts of the globe. I'll consult experts in linguistics, social and cultural values, geographical materials, etc. An error in these books never goes completely unnoticed. A significant error can bring the accuracy and value of the whole book into question. So *getting it right* is essential—especially since many of my books have found their way into classrooms and libraries as teaching tools."

Research

Compensation for an Expert Review

Most of the authors interviewed for this article do not pay for expert reviews, or if they do, not out of their own pockets. Author Pam Munoz Ryan says that most of the experts she has queried have worked at agencies, such as NASA, the White House, or a zoo, where part of their job is to assist those in need of direction. At Cobblestone magazines, the editors say the experts they consult are thrilled to be involved in putting together materials for children—future historians or scientists—on topics near and dear to their hearts.

If a fee is offered, author and editor James Cross Giblin offers this advice: "The fee or honorarium you offer to pay an expert should obviously be commensurate with the job you want done. A hundred dollars would probably be enough if you were seeking an evaluation by a herpetologist of a five-page picture book manuscript about killer snakes. But an expert might expect $500 or more for a detailed critique of a 200-page history of the Civil War." Giblin adds, "Before offering to pay the fee out of your own pocket, you should check first with your editor, assuming you've already sold the project. The publisher may have an expense category that covers experts' fees."

In author Laurence Pringle's experience, the publisher sets the amount of payment to the expert. "I assume it varies quite a bit. When I mention payment to an expert, I simply assure them they will be paid. I assume that the amount paid varies with the length of the manuscript."

Giving Credit

Almost all of the authors and editors acknowledge experts in their books or magazines. This is a great way to say thank you and to lend creditability to your work. Giblin, who usually recognizes experts on the acknowledgments pages of his books, says that this "carries weight with teachers and librarians, and can be an effective aid in promoting your book."

The Cobblestone magazines acknowledge experts on the mastheads along with brief biographical descriptions. Experts also receive complimentary copies and subscriptions to some of their magazines. Author Margery Facklam lists experts on the title page for a picture book or in the back matter or author's note for books for older readers.

Pringle adds that he always acknowledges the help of experts, "sometimes in a single short statement on the copyright page, sometimes in a more lengthy acknowledgment to all who helped."

Margery Facklam, who has written 36 nonfiction books on science and natural history, uses experts "to check facts, explain things, expand or narrow my focus, and for anecdotal information." She offers examples: "When I was writing *Spiders and Their Web Sites*, I took a class about spiders from the Curator of Entomology at the Buffalo Museum of Science. When the book was published, I included him in the dedication, along with a second-grade class that had let me visit their tarantula. It was fascinating to learn what they knew about their spider because it gave me a better sense of what they understood about spiders. I also learned what more I could include or expand on. When I was writing *What Does the Crow Know?*, which is about animal intelligence, I visited the Primate Cognition Center at Ohio State University and got firsthand knowledge of chimpanzees that were learning to add (one was learning fractions!). I also visited Dr. Pepperberg of the University of Arizona, who works with Alex, a gray parrot."

At *Highlights for Children*, authors are encouraged to seek expert reviews as part of their research. Another expert is often brought in once the article is purchased, to review the text or work with the editor to solve problems or any questions.

Highlights Science Editor Andy Boyles seeks expert help for virtually everything he edits and writes. "I research everything as thoroughly as possible, then I try to have it reviewed by someone who lives and breathes the subject." Boyles's reliance on experts is tied to the mission of the magazine. "*Highlights* has a tradition of working to earn the respect of people outside our target audience. If a scientist, teacher, or other professional who's knowledgeable in the subject were to read an article in *Highlights*, our aim is for that person to come away thinking, 'That's a factual and reasonable way to present that subject to young readers.'"

The Cobblestone Publishing magazines are known for their work with consulting editors, or experts in the field. Meg Chorlian, Editor of *Cobblestone*, looks for someone—historian, museum personnel, educational expert—who has a concentration in the theme of the issue. "We ask the consulting editors to review the uncopyedited manuscripts to make sure that we are including the right information, not using out-of-date sources, and to guide us correctly on spellings of specific terms or phrases. We also rely on them for feedback on the general tone of the issue."

Beth Lindstrom, Senior Editor of *Odyssey*, another Cobblestone publication, explains that consulting editors help set the tone of the issue, tell her where there might be pitfalls or controversy, suggest sources for interviews and writers, help with fact-checking, and, at times, write for an issue.

Illustrators often find that they too must seek out experts to help with specific details. Children's book illustrator Daniel San Souci says that the subject matter determines when and how to seek out professional advice. "Some subjects I have little or no knowledge of, so I must find someone who does. When I illustrated *Red Wolf Country*, through phoning and asking questions, I came up with Roland Smith's name. He was the Red Wolf Coordinator for the U.S. Fish and Wildlife Service. By the time I was through, I had seen what a red wolf looks like and had enough information and slides to illustrate volumes on the subject."

Expert Criteria

Experts can be found almost anywhere: at universities, historic sites or parks, museums, foundations, organizations, government agencies, locally and internationally. Experts may have a personal connection to the subject or work in the field; they may live in a particular area, or have been a relevant witness to an event. Facklam has even relied on her two sons, who do pharmaceutical research, for her book *Healing Drugs*.

James Cross Giblin, the author of more than 20 books for young readers and Contributing Editor at Clarion Books, sought out an old friend from graduate school, a professor of biochemistry, as an expert for *When Plague Strikes*.

Many times authors, editors, and illustrators work with combinations of experts. Individuals might have certain biases or are familiar with only one aspect of a subject, so writers and editors go to two or three people to achieve a balance of opinion. Of course, writers and editors run the risk of encountering experts who contradict or disagree with one another. In those cases, the writer and editor has to delve deeper into research and, as

---

Make Use of Differences of Opinion

If there are unresolved issues in your research Robert San Souci advises to let your readers in on them. "I will often try to indicate in an Author's Note that I have gone with the majority opinion in certain matters—but that other views also have credence. This often reassures the person who may subscribe to the 'minority report' that you are not arbitrarily or erroneously putting out information they believe wrong—but that you have come to a conclusion, and used it, based on balanced assessment of the best information available to you, the author."

Robert San Souci points out, come up with "which side the consensus weighs in on."

Author Diane Hoyt-Goldsmith, who specializes in multicultural photodocumentaries about Native American children and culture and ethnic holidays in America, explains that facts can always have different interpretations. "I try to go with the one that seems mainstream in the culture I am writing about."

Pam Munoz Ryan, who has written more than 20 books for young people and also works for a publisher in Japan, has no set number of experts to work with on a project. She says, "The more corroboration, the better. I look for experts with the highest credentials, but I also look to people who work for organizations that are known to archive information about the topic. I usually ask for curators or historians."

For Boyles and Lindstrom, the nature of the discipline—science—dictates what they look for in an expert. Being aware of the latest research is key. Lindstrom, who usually works with two consulting editors per issue of *Odyssey*, prefers that they be at the cutting edge of research in their field and also be familiar with the demands

of educational and trade publishing. "It's great when the person also has *Odyssey*-age children. Of course, that's a big order. Sometimes it's better to go with a lesser figure in a particular field who has more time to commit to an *Odyssey* project. But many big-name scientists are generous with their time because they are so enthusiastic about reaching young people and getting them turned on to science."

Boyles also looks for someone active in the area in question, a person who is typically affiliated with some institution or organization that has a tradition of research, such as a university, museum, aquarium, or federal agency. Boyles points out that "often the individual also does research of his or her own on the subject and publishes the results in peer-reviewed journals. In other cases, depending on the subject, the expert may be someone who works as a keeper of a museum or aquarium. I take those traits as signs that the individual is knowledgeable and stays informed about the latest findings in the field." Boyles feels that one expert is enough if the subject is straightforward. More experts are needed if the subject involves controversy or the latest research.

Pringle also seeks out experts who are actively involved in research, although he has sometimes worked with retired professionals who still have a good overview of the field. Pringle also likes to work with people nearby. "It helps to have an expert who is fairly close, geographically, for frequent contact or actual in-person communication. Each book project can present a different situation. For example, for *A Dragon in the Sky: The Story of a Green Darner Dragonfly*, I called two dragonfly experts, both of whom lived within 75 miles. I visited each once, later had several phone or e-mail communications, and each expert checked the manuscript and art sketches. Their comments were complementary; one could catch a mistake the other missed. I also was in contact with a dozen other experts on details." Depending on the project and its complexity, Pringle has worked with anywhere from 1 to 20 experts.

For her multicultural work, Hoyt-Goldsmith relies on many experts, the foremost the family featured in the book. "I find a family and a child in the community that I am writing about, and they become my most respected informants. I am trying for documentary-type realism, so their particular *truth* is what I am after. Of course, people are subjective and each person has his or her own set of values. But that works fine for me. In my books, I am going for the specific experience that will then shed some light on the universal, or so I hope."

Hoyt-Goldsmith agrees with Pringle that it is a good idea to meet your experts. "I believe you earn a measure of credibility when you appear in person. You can look at each other eye-to-eye and gauge a certain amount of character from that interaction. I make a point to travel to a place I am interested in writing about. I meet people and network. I ask questions and listen. I form impressions on my own."

Will They Talk to Me?

Most authors and editors have their own personal styles for locating experts. Some use the Internet and then e-mail or phone. Some find their experts through books or articles and then write (mostly e-mail) or phone. Some contact friends or experts they have worked with in the past. But no matter what path they choose to follow, most authors and editors agree that experts are approachable and more than willing to help out. Experts want to make sure the right information is published and that young readers are well-informed. All writers and editors also agree on another important point: It doesn't pay to contact an expert until you know the subject to be covered well. Experts don't have much time to spare and it isn't a good idea to waste it with unnecessary questions.

According to many of the authors and editors interviewed, relationships with experts are more casual than formal. Robert San Souci reveals, "I find that a more casual relationship is—for me, at any rate—a more comfortable way to approach people. By and large, it seems to work with others. Often, a phone call or visit to an expert spins off into a discussion of related ideas, and sometimes suggests a story line for a future project."

Peggy Thomas locates experts through her preliminary research and local universities. "I'm lucky to live in an area with many research facilities nearby. I usually call and do follow-up questions through e-mail." Thomas's books include The Science of Saving Animals series; *Talking Bones: The Science of Forensic Anthropology; Medicines from Nature; The Kids' World Almanac of Amazing Facts About Numbers; Math and Money Volcano!*

As an editor, Boyles locates experts in a variety of ways. "It sometimes takes a lot of patience and legwork. Often, the author's research gives me some tips, such as the name of the author of a book or paper, listed in the bibliography. Also, I already have a number of contacts. Many times, I have simply called trusted experts in related fields and asked them whom they would go to for help if they had a question about the subject. Professional societies often have contact information on their websites. A few services are offered over the World Wide Web for finding experts. I have not tried them, mainly because I haven't had to yet. In addition, I read a number of articles in science journals. From those papers, I can get the names of people who are working in a given field. Then I just call them or send them an e-mail. Usually, if they are not the best person to comment, they are quick to admit that fact and then direct me to someone who is."

The Internet has proved helpful to Chorlian and Lindstrom. Chorlian depends on the websites of colleges and universities, which post their faculties and departments. Lindstrom says, "I usually do Web research, narrow the possibilities, and then make some calls. Occasionally I'm lucky enough to make the call at the right moment and actually get the person. If not, I leave a voice mail and then send an e-mail. I almost always get a reasonably quick response."

As in the case of magazine publishers, book publishers often locate their own experts to read manuscripts. Ryan explains, "If one expert is considered quintessential on a subject, then my publisher may contract with that person after the book is complete to factcheck. More likely, my publisher will contact someone independent of my research." Pringle adds, "More commonly, one expert is contacted by the publisher to read the complete manuscript, and perhaps check illustrations. I often name one

or more experts for the publisher to use. Sometimes a publisher already has a stable of experts that it has used on other projects and doesn't need any nominees."

The Problem with Experts

Giblin rarely relies on experts in connection with his nonfiction writing. "Early on in my editorial career, I had the misfortune to get saddled with experts who either had an agenda that ran counter to the manuscript in question, or who did a much too superficial job. As a result, I came to rely far more on expert copyeditors to serve as factcheckers, and I've followed the same practice with my own books. For example, I've requested the same freelance copyeditor for all of my recent titles, and she's spared me a lot of potential embarrassments. In the case of my biography of Charles Lindbergh, she even caught *him* in an error."

Experts do sometimes have agendas. Robert San Souci recommends listening to an expert and taking what is needed for a particular project. Daniel San Souci agrees. "I have found that the experts I have worked with only care about getting things right. If they want to push their own agenda, that's fine. I guess it all adds up to getting more information. An author or illustrator can always edit out what they feel is appropriate."

Lindstrom admits that an agenda causes problems, "especially when late in the process you realize there is one. The most common agenda is to promote the research being done at the expert's university—that certainly isn't all bad, but it can be."

Pringle says, "If the subject is controversial—nuclear power or global warming, for example—experts can emphasize, omit, or downplay different facts, statistics, and so on. It is up to the editor and writer to agree on which is more fair and trustworthy in light of their own leanings."

Boyles points out that an expert may insist that you add or delete some particular information without giving much, or any, reasoning for the change. "I want to know *why* a change is being suggested. If I resist making a particular change, an unbiased reviewer will normally support the change with a calm, well-reasoned argument. A reviewer with an agenda may become angry or sarcastic or simply vague. When I sense some emotion or evasiveness on the part of the reviewer, a red flag goes up for me. I will not be satisfied until I know a lot more about that point. So I end up talking to more experts until I gain some insight into the situation, which sometimes has as much to do with personalities as it does science."

Even with agendas, Chorlian reveals that most experts are accommodating. "I have found that most consulting editors are happy to provide their expertise on the subject and then allow us the freedom to take their suggestions and work them in as we judge best."

It is primarily that accommodating nature that authors and editors like best about experts. Besides factual know-how and keen insight, experts are almost always reasonable, extremely helpful, and, most important, comforting. Giblin points out "that, in the end, reassurance is probably one of the main things an expert can give to a writer and editor."

Conference &
Contest Listings

Writers' Conferences

Conferences Devoted to Writing for Children —
General Conferences

**Butler University Children's
   Literature Conference**
Butler University
4600 Sunset Lane
Indianapolis, IN 46208

Participants in this one-day conference typically include an equal mix of librarians, teachers, writers, and illustrators from across the country. Sessions are conducted by internationally known, award-winning children's book authors and illustrators, as well as leaders in schools and libraries, renowned university professors, critics, and children's book editors and agents. Send an SASE for complete conference information.
Date: January 26, 2002.
Subjects: TBA
Speakers: Past speakers have included Avi, Lois Lowry, Patricia MacLachlan, Karen Hesse, Phyllis Reynolds Naylor, and James Cross Giblin.
Location: Butler University, Indianapolis, Indiana.
Costs: $85. Optional manuscript critique and optional portfolio critique, $25 each (available only to registered participants).
Contact: Valiska Gregory, Director.

Celebration of Children's Literature
Montgomery College
51 Mannakee Street
Rockville, MD 20850-1195
www.montgomerycollege.org

Writers, illustrators, teachers, librarians, and parents gather at this annual one-day conference to learn about new trends in children's and young adult literature.
Date: April 20, 2002.
Subjects: Last year's topics included "The Picture Book from Start to Finish," and "Teenage Readers."
Speakers: TBA
Location: Montgomery College, Germantown, Maryland, campus.
Costs: Approximately $70.
Contact: Sandra Sonner, Senior Program Director.

**Children's Book Festival/
   Haystack Program**
Portland State University
P.O. Box 1491
Portland, OR 97207-1491
www.haystack.pdx.edu

Held since 1998, this weekend

workshop has now developed into a week-long, hands-on event. It gives writers an opportunity to work with an outstanding faculty of experienced writers and illustrators, and to learn how to turn real life into great fiction for children.
Date: July.
Subjects: Last year's topics included "Writing for Children," "E-Publishing," and "Editing."
Speakers: The 2001 conference included Eve Bunting, Elsa Warnick, Nancy Coffelt, and Linda Zuckerman.
Location: Cannon Beach, Oregon.
Costs: For those seeking credits , $435; non-credit fee, $415.
Contact: Margaret Herrington, Conference Director.

Highlights Foundation Writers' Workshop
814 Court Street
Honesdale, PA 18431

———————————————

The Highlights Foundation sponsors a week-long conference on writing for children every summer in Chautauqua, New York. Participants are immersed in daily workshops and also take part in mentoring sessions. Each attendee must submit a manuscript in advance, which is critiqued in a one-on-one session with a faculty member. This conference covers writing for children of all ages, as well as marketing.
Date: July.
Subjects: Last year's conference workshops included writing for beginning readers; historical fiction; and biographies. They covered general writing topics as well, such as how to develop a plot, characterization, and point of view.
Speakers: Past faculty members include Patricia Lee Gauch, Pamela Greenwood, Joy Cowley, and *Highlights for Children* editorial staff.
Location: Chautauqua, New York.
Costs: $1,485 for first-time attendees; $1,900 for those who have attended in previous years.
Contact: Kent L. Brown, Jr., Director.

Writers Conference in Children's Literature
Department of English
University of North Dakota
Grand Forks, ND 58202-7209

———————————————

The Society of Children's Book Writers & Illustrators is one of the sponsors of this conference, which is held annually. Participants attend lectures and presentations scheduled throughout the day and have ample opportunity to meet and talk with other attendees.

For an extra fee, each participant may submit one manuscript of up to 1,500 words, or a synopsis and one chapter of a book, for evaluation. Each manuscript receives a written critique, and the writer meets with the author who evaluates the work.
Date: September.
Subjects: Topics at the 2001 conference were "Writing from the Prairie," and "Unfolding the Metaphor: Childhood Memories and the Kernel of the Story."
Speakers: Last year's speakers included Peggy Brooke, Jane Kurtz, Emily Johnson, and Jo Bannatyne-Cugnet.
Location: University of North Dakota.
Costs: $60 for SCBWI members; $65 for nonmembers. Evaluation fee, $30.
Contact: Ursula Hovet, Department of English, University of North Dakota.

Conferences Devoted to Writing for Children — Society of Children's Book Writers & Illustrators

Alabama
SpringMingle '02!
SCBWI–Southern Breeze Region
P.O. Box 26282
Birmingham, AL 35260
members.home.net/southernbreeze

The emphasis at this conference is on professionalism. Ninety-five percent of the attendees are published authors, though not necessarily in the children's field. Manuscript evaluations and portfolio reviews are offered for additional fees. Pre-registration is required; cut-off date for registration for the upcoming conference is February 20, 2002, at noon.
Date: February 22–24, 2002.
Subjects: SpringMingle '02! will cover writing and illustrating for children, success stories that celebrate the 10-year history of Southern Breeze, and encouragement for the future.
Speakers: Last year's speakers included Larry Dane Brimner, Wendy Lamb, Karen Stormer, and Paula Morrow.
Location: Gulf Shores, Alabama.
Costs: Costs range from $80–$100 for members; $95–$115 for nonmembers.
Contact: Joan Broerman, Regional Advisor.

"Writing and Illustrating for Kids"
Southern Breeze SCBWI
P.O. 26282
Birmingham, AL 35226
members.home.net/southernbreeze

This fall conference offers more than 30 workshops addressing every-thing from the basics to career strategies. The conference is beneficial to both new and experienced writers.

Children's writing of all genres for all ages will be covered. Manuscript critiquing will also be available. Send an SASE or visit the website for more information.
Date: October.
Subjects: Last year's topics include fantasy and mystery writing, and writing for religious magazine markets.
Speakers: The 2001 keynote speaker was Lin Oliver.
Location: Birmingham, Alabama.
Costs: Members, $70–$100; nonmembers, $80–$120.
Contact: Mary Ann Taylor, Fall Conference Coordinator.

California
SCBWI International Conference on Writing and Illustrating
Society of Children's Book Writers and Illustrators
8271 Beverly Boulevard
Los Angeles, CA 90048
www.scbwi.org

Writers and artists of children's books receive concrete information as well as creative stimulus from well-known writers and illustrators who speak at this conference. Send an SASE or visit the website for further details on this conference.
Date: February and August.
Subjects: Writing, illustrating, craft techniques, marketing, sales, promotion, speaking, and publishing.

Speakers: TBA

Locations: In February 2002, the conference will be held at the Roosevelt Hotel in New York City. The August 2002 conference will be held in Los Angeles.

Costs: Approximate cost for the two-day New York conference is $220. Approximate cost for the four-day Los Angeles conference is $375.

Contact: Lin Oliver, Executive Director.

SCBWI National Summer Conference

8271 Beverly Boulevard
Los Angeles, CA 90048
www.scbwi.org

This annual three-day conference blends general sessions with interactive workshops. It offers workshops for both new and experienced writers.

It also provides an opportunity to meet leading children's book authors, illustrators, editors, art directors, and agents.

Date: August.

Subjects: Last year's topics included "From Brainstorming to Bound Book: Turning Your Ideas into Books," "Negotiating Your First Contract Without an Agent," and "The Plot Puzzle and Making the Pieces."

Speakers: At the 2001 conference, Toni Buzzeo, Paula Danziger, and Bruce Hale were speakers.

Location: Los Angeles, California.

Costs: Fees for the complete conference range from $335 to $415. Manuscript consultation, $45.

Contact: Conference Director.

Canada

Canada Conference

130 Wren Street RR#1
Dunrobin, ON K0A 1T0
Canada

Sponsored by the Canadian Chapter of SCBWI, this annual conference provides authors with a one-day workshop to help writers hone their craft and achieve their goals of publication. The workshop features panel discussions, portfolio critiques, and book signings.

Date: May.

Subjects: Last year's subjects included marketing your writing, writing techniques, and illustrating.

Speakers: Past keynote speakers include Kaea Vincinelli from HarperCollins, and authors Stephen Mooser and Janet Wilson.

Location: Carleton University, Ontario, Canada.

Costs: TBA.

Contact: Noreen Kruzich Violetta, Regional Advisor.

Michigan

Writers & Illustrators Conference

SCBWI-Michigan
5060 Sequoia SE
Grand Rapids, MI 49512
www.kisbooklink.org

This three-day conference focuses on story creation and provides an opportunity for new and established writers to meet with editors, illustrators and authors. It offers discussion groups, and a silent auction, and an illustration spotlight. Send an SASE or visit the website for complete information.

Date: October.

Subjects: Topics from the 2001 conference include "Creating Characters Kids Will Love" and "Splashing Paint Together."

Speakers: At the 2001 conference, Audrey Couloumbis, Elaine Marie Alphin, Wendy Lamb, and Alison Keehn were speakers.

Location: Clarkston, Michigan.

Costs: TBA.

Contact: Shirley Neitzel, Regional Advisor.

New England
SCBWI New England Annual Conference
http://members.aol.com/nescbwi

Held annually, this conference is sponsored by the New England chapter of SCBWI. Each year the conference is held in a different location, and offers workshops on writing fiction, nonfiction, young adult literature; marketing; and publishing. Manuscript portfolios will also be offered. Visit the website for complete information.

Date: April.

Subjects: Past topics have included connecting with readers and publishers, marketing your work, and creating books for children.

Speakers: Patricia Reilly Giff, Mary Azarian, Diane Hess, and Yolanda Le Roy will speak at the 2002 conference.

Location: Sturbridge Hotel, Sturbridge, MA.

Costs: $150, lodging is not included.

Contact: Marilyn Salerno, Regional Advisor.

New York
SCBWI Illustrator's Conference
Society of Children's Book Writers and Illustrators
c/o Frieda Gates
32 Hillside Avenue
Monsey, NY 10952

This annual conference provides illustrators and author/illustrators the opportunity to have their portfolios reviewed by art buyers and agents from the publishing and allied industries.

Date: May.

Subjects: This conference focuses on the markets for children's picture books and illustrated books for young adults.

Speakers: TBA.

Location: Society of Illustrators, 128 East 63rd Street, New York, NY 10021.

Costs: With portfolio, $90 for members; $100 for nonmembers. Without portfolio, $60 for members; $65 for nonmembers. Portfolio evaluation, 30-minute session; $50. Book dummy evaluation, 15-minute session; $25.

Contact: Frieda Gates, Director.

North Carolina
The Magic of Writing & Illustrating for Children
SCBWI-Carolinas
104 Barnhill Place
Chapel Hill, NC 27514-9224
www.geocities.com/scbwi_c

Held annually in late September or in October, this conference provides information on writing and illustrating for children. Attendance is open to members of SCBWI as well as to nonmembers.

Date: TBA.

Subjects: Among the subjects covered at the last conference were illustration, writing chapter books, and conducting research for biographies.

Speakers: Jane O'Connor and Richard Peck were among the speakers scheduled to appear at last year's conference.

Locations: North or South Carolina.

Costs: $65 for members; $75 for nonmembers. Critiques, $35.

Contact: Earl L. Davis, Program Coordinator.

Oregon
SCBWI-Oregon Spring Conference
http://users.rio.com/robink

The Oregon Chapter of SCBWI sponsors this annual spring conference each year. It provides manuscript critiques, lectures, workshops, and social events for both new and established writers.

Visit the website for complete information. E-mail any questions to Robink@rio.com

Date: May.

Subjects: Among the 2001 conference subjects were "Being Your Own Editor," "Illustrating Children's Books: The Process," and "Donuts to Death Threats: An Insider's Guide to Dealing with the Media."

Speakers: Last year's speakers included Judy Cox, Kathryn Dawson, Tracey Adams, and Mary Whittington.

Locations: Tualatin, Oregon.

Costs: $65 for non-members.

Contact: Robin Koontz, Regional Advisor.

Tennessee
SCBWI-Midsouth Chapter Annual Spring Conference
P.O. Box 120061
Nashville, TN 37212

This day-long conference brings writers, illustrators, editors, and other publishing professionals together to focus on children's literature. Manuscript critiques and portfolio reviews are also available to participants for an additional cost.

Date: April 20, 2002.

Subjects: Children's literature, illustration, and marketing.

Speakers: Sid Fleischman.

Location: Nashville, Tennessee.

Costs: $65 for SCBWI members; $70 for nonmembers. Manuscript critique or portfolio review, $35.

Contact: Tracy Barrett, Regional Advisor.

Conferences with Sessions on Writing for Children — University or Regional Conferences

American Society of Journalists and Authors Annual Writers Conference
1501 Broadway, Suite 302
New York, NY 10036
www.asja.org

This conference is open to all interested writers, whether or not they are members of ASJA. Attendees sign up for workshops that are scheduled throughout the day on Saturday. On Sunday, they may sign up for one or two special three-hour workshops that delve more deeply into a particular subject. The conference workshops cover a variety of topics of interest to aspiring as well as professional writers, but nothing that specifically addresses the children's market. Send an SASE or visit the website for more complete conference information.
Date: May.
Subjects: Some of the workshops offered at the 2001 conference were "Nuts & Bolts of Narrative Nonfiction," "New Ways to Market Fiction," and "What Do Women's Magazines Really Want?"
Speakers: James Brady and Leonard Riggio were the keynote speakers at last year's conference.
Location: New York City.
Costs: Costs for the Saturday conference range from $195–$230; costs for the Sunday workshops range from $75–$85 each. A Saturday mentoring session is $30.
Contact: Ann Arnott, Director.

Annual Spring Writers' Conference
P.O. Box 1307
Mt. Pleasant, TX 75456
www.ntcc.cc.tx.us

Local residents have the opportunity to learn about writing from successful Texas authors at this annual one-day conference. Various genres are covered, including writing for the children's market.
Date: April 27, 2002.
Subjects: Topics presented at the 2001 conference included "Demystifying the Mystery," "From an Agent's Perspective," and "On Becoming a Columnist."
Speakers: TBA
Location: Northeast Texas Community College, Mt. Pleasant, Texas.
Costs: $50; $30 for students.
Contact: Toni LaBeff, Program Developer, Continuing Education.

Antioch Writers' Workshop
P.O. Box 494
Yellow Springs, OH 45387
www.antiochwritersworkshop.com

First held in 1985, this workshop has developed a reputation for informality and close interaction among the participants and faculty members. The authors who serve on the faculty are chosen based on their willingness to be accessible to workshop participants. Attendees are given ample opportunity to interact with the staff, editors, and agents. The workshops are known to be professional and intense, targeting beginning writers as well as those who are more experienced.

Date: July 6–13, 2002.

Subjects: Fiction, nonfiction, and poetry are covered in the workshops.

Speakers: Past faculty members have included Joyce Carol Oates, John Jakes, Sue Grafton, Natalie Goldberg, and Lawrence Block.

Location: Yellow Springs, Ohio.

Costs: $460; $410 for local or returning participants.

Contact: Mindy Carpenter, Director.

Aspen Summer Words Writing Retreat and Literary Festival

Aspen Writers' Foundation
P.O. Box 7726
Aspen, CO 81612
www.aspenwriters.org

The Writing Retreat consists of four mornings of intensive study in small group workshops. With a limit of 12 participants per workshop, students are encouraged to develop and perfect their writing skills in a demanding yet invigorating setting. Opportunities are also available for students to schedule private meetings with editors and agents. The Literary Festival, held in the afternoons and evenings, offers lectures, industry talks, and roundtable discussions, as well as the opportunity to meet authors, industry insiders, and fellow writers.

Enrollment is limited. Those who wish to attend the Writing Retreat must submit up to 10 pages of their best work, along with a cover letter explaining why they want to attend the retreat. Send an SASE or visit the website for further information.

Date: June.

Subjects: TBA.

Speakers: Speakers in 2001 included Pam Houston, Madeleine Blais, and Pete Fromm.

Location: Aspen, Colorado.

Costs: $460 for Retreat and Festival; $325 for the Writing Retreat only. Lodging is extra.

Contact: Write to the Aspen Writers' Foundation, or visit their website.

Big Apple Writing Conference

International Women's Writing Guild
P.O. Box 810, Gracie Station
New York, NY 10028
www.iwwg.com

Sponsored by the International Women's Writing Guild, this weekend conference is held twice each year. The Big Apple Writing Conference offers writing workshops as well as face-to-face meetings with authors and agents and provides insights into several genres of writing.

Date: April and October.

Subjects: TBA

Speakers: TBA

Location: New York City.

Costs: $130.

Contact: Hannelore Hahn, Executive Director.

The College of New Jersey Writers Conference

College of New Jersey
Department of English
P.O. Box 7718
Ewing, NJ 08628-0718

Helping writers improve their skills and achieve publication is the goal of this annual, one-day conference. It offers aspiring writers the opportunity to meet with other writers, editors, and agents.

Date: April.
Subjects: Workshops cover all genres, including poetry, fiction, nonfiction, journalism, and children's literature.
Speakers: TBA
Location: The College of New Jersey, Ewing, New Jersey.
Costs: $40, plus $10 per workshop.
Contact: Jean Hollander, Director.

Creative Writing Conference

English Department, 467 Case Annex
Eastern Kentucky University
Richmond, KY 40475
www.english.eku.edu/conferences

Now in its 40th year, this conference is held annually during the third week of June. Those seeking to improve their skills in writing fiction, poetry, or drama are welcome to attend. Lectures, workshops, private conferences, and readings are scheduled for each day of the five-day program. Participants are required to submit 3–5 poems or 10–15 pages of drama or fiction.

Date: June.
Subjects: Fiction, poetry, and drama.
Speakers: Visiting writers at last year's conference included Crystal Wilkinson, Jeffrey Skinner, and Gywn Hyman Rubio.
Location: Eastern Kentucky University, Richmond, Kentucky.
Costs: Tuition ranges from $106 for in-state undergraduates to $418 for out-of-state undergraduates.
Contact: Harry Brown, Director.

Critique Retreat for Writing Women

Writing Women
P.O. Box 14282
Pittsburgh, PA 15239
www.geocities.com/jmjwriter

These weekend retreats are held three times each year and are open to all women, regardless of experience or genre of interest. Each writer has her own focus time in each of the five sessions offered. Individual writing, including children's writing, is critiqued, and writers are offered professional feedback and suggestions.

Dates: June, July, and October.
Subjects: The retreat features critiquing and writing prompts, along with motivational talks.
Speakers: TBA
Location: Greensburg, Pennsylvania, and Alliance, Ohio.
Costs: $225/double; includes meals.
Contact: Mary Jo Rulnick, Director.

CWA/DWAA Writers Seminars

Cat Writers Association and Dog
    Writers Association of America
22841 Orchid Creek Lane
Lake Forest, CA 92630

This three-day event is held every year on the weekend before Thanksgiving. Here, the focus is on writing for the pet markets. It does not offer programs on writing for children.

Date: November.
Subjects: The 2001 seminar covered writing a query letter, fiction writing, interviewing, and media training.
Speakers: Speakers in 2001 included J. Anne Helgren, Steve Dale, Carole Nelson Douglas, Jan Grape, and Bill Crider.

Location: TBA
Costs: $65 for members; $88 for non-members.
Contact: Kim Thornton, President.

Gig Harbor Writers' Conference
P.O. Box 826
Gig Harbor, WA 98335-0826

Participants in this conference may sign up for seven different workshops scheduled over this three-day event. Topics covered include children's writing, poetry, screenwriting, and travel writing. Registered participants are invited to submit in advance up to 10 pages of a fiction, nonfiction, or children's manuscript for critique.
Date: May.
Subjects: Workshops at the 2001 conference included "The Nuts and Bolts of Writing for Children," "Getting the Dang Thing Sold," and "How To Bounce Proof Your Manuscript."
Speakers: Faculty at the 2001 conference included Heather McHugh and Bonny Becker.
Location: Gig Harbor, Washington.
Costs: $125–$135.
Contact: Kathleen O'Brien, Director.

Hofstra University Summer Writers' Conference
Hofstra University
Hempstead, NY 11549-1000
www.hofstra.edu

At this two-week conference, aspiring writers attend one or two workshops each day, take part in individual conferences with established authors, and hear readings and presentations by guest writers, publishers, editors, and agents. The workshops are designed to help developing writers sharpen their powers of expression by reading and discussing students' works, and by analyzing themes and techniques. The Summer High School Student Writers' Conference offers workshops in poetry and prose for mature high school students who demonstrate a serious interest in writing.
Date: July.
Subjects: Fiction, nonfiction, poetry, playwriting, and children's writing are the genres covered at this conference.
Speakers: Past instructors and speakers have included Maurice Sendak, Denise Levertov, and Robert Olsen Butler.
Location: Hofstra University.
Costs: $400 for one workshop; $625 for two. Graduate and undergraduate credits available at an additional cost.
Contact: For more information, visit the Hofstra website or write to the address above.

International Women's Writing Guild's Summer Conference
P.O. Box 810, Gracie Station
New York, NY 10028
www.iwwg.com

Seventy workshops are presented each day of this week-long conference, which has been held since 1976. Its goal is to empower women personally as well as professionally through the craft of writing.
Date: August.
Subjects: Last year's workshops included two on writing for children: "Writing the Fairy Tale," and "Writing and Illustrating Children's Books."
Speakers: TBA
Location: Skidmore College, Saratoga

Springs, New York.

Costs: $860; includes room and board on campus.

Contact: Hannelore Hahn, Executive Director.

Literacy Learning in the Classroom

Richard C. Owen Publishers, Inc.
P.O. Box 585
Katonah, NY 10536
www.RCOwen.com

Literacy Learning in the Classroom is a three-day institute held each summer at various locations across the US. Directed at primary, intermediate, and middle school teachers, it focuses on how to teach reading and writing and also covers classroom organization and management. The institute is presented as a mix of general sessions, in which guiding principles of teaching and learning are introduced, and dialogue groups, where participants explore these concepts in depth.

Date: Summer; visit the website for specific dates for your area.

Subjects: Subjects covered include how to assess and evaluate reading; using guided and shared reading approaches; how to assess and evaluate writing; how to develop effective writers; and preparing lesson plans.

Speakers: This institute is staffed by professional educators who are actively involved in teacher training and school development.

Location: Check website for a location in your area.

Costs: $350.

Contact: Contact Richard C. Owen Publishers at the address above, or visit their website.

Maritime Writers' Workshop

University of New Brunswick
Dept. of Extension & Summer Session
Box 4400
Fredericton, New Brunswick E3B 5A3
Canada
www.extension@unb.ca

A week-long program, the Maritime Writers' Workshop offers five classes, each one limited to 10 participants. Lectures, discussions, public readings, and special events are also part of each annual program. Participants are asked to submit a writing sample of 10–20 pages, along with a $25 processing fee. Limited financial assistance for tuition is awarded based on need and talent.

Date: July.

Subjects: Two fiction workshops and one each on nonfiction, poetry, and children's writing are offered.

Speakers: TBA

Location: The University of New Brunswick, Fredericton.

Costs: $350, plus meals and lodging.

Contact: Rhona Sawlor, Coordinator.

Midland Writer's Conference

1710 W. St. Andrews
Midland, MI 48640
www.midland-mi.org/gracedowlibrary

Sponsored by the Grace A. Dow Memorial Library, this yearly conference provides a forum for beginning and established writers to exchange ideas with publishing professionals. Each one-day conference features a keynote speaker and five workshops, one of which usually covers writing for children or young adults.

Date: Second Saturday in June.

Subjects: Last year's conference offered a workshop titled "Writing for Children: Hearing the Voice."

Speakers: Previous conference speakers included Judith Viorst, Mary Higgins Clark, Dave Barry, Pat Conroy, Peggy Noonan, Norman Cousins, Kurt Vonnegut, Jr., Cathy Guisewite, Tom Wolfe, and P. J. O'Rourke.

Location: Grace A. Dow Memorial Library, Midland, Michigan.

Costs: $50; $40 for seniors.

Contact: Ann Jarvis, Librarian.

Mississippi Valley Writers Conference

Midwest Writing Center
3403 45th Street
Moline, IL 61265
www.midwestwritingcenter.org

This conference offers beginning and advanced instruction in all areas of writing for children. It assists the novice as well as the professional writer on the road to publication. Participants may submit up to 10 pages of their work for critique.

Date: June 3–7, 2002.

Subjects: Last year's workshops included "Basics for Beginners," "Juvenile Manuscript Seminar," and "Marketing Your Work."

Speakers: Last year's conference staff included Mel Boring, Bess Pierce, and Ann Boaden.

Location: Augustana College, Rock Island, Illinois.

Costs: One workshop, $25; two workshops, $90; each additional workshop, $40; non-refundable registration fee, $25; room and board, $220.

Contact: David R. Collins, Director.

National Writers Association Summer Conference

3140 South Peoria Street, #295
Aurora, CO 80014
www.nationalwriters.com

This annual three-day conference covers general writing and marketing topics. It affords aspiring writers the opportunity to meet with accomplished authors, literary agents, editors, and film producers.

Date: June.

Subjects: TBA.

Speakers: Previous speakers included Marcia Preston and Scott Goldman.

Location: Colorado.

Costs: TBA.

Contact: Sandy Welchel, Director.

North Carolina Writers' Network Fall Conference

P.O. Box 954
Carrboro, NC 27510
www.ncwriters.org

Held annually on a November weekend, this conference provides high-quality workshops and roundtable discussions for North Carolina writers. It also facilitates networking among writers, agents, and publishers. While the conference focuses mainly on writing for adults, writing for young readers is also addressed.

Date: November.

Subjects: TBA.

Speakers: TBA

Location: North Carolina.

Costs: $200, plus room and board.

Contact: Linda Hobson, Director.

Odyssey Fantasy Writing Workshop
20 Levesque Lane
Mount Vernon, NH 03057
www.sff.net/odyssey

Considered one of the top science fiction, fantasy, and horror workshops in the US, Odyssey helps authors who specialize in these genres take their writing to the next level. It also covers genre fiction for children. Participants must submit a writing sample with their applications.
Date: June 10–July 19, 2002.
Subjects: Topics covered last year included "Creating Powerful Plots," "How To Get Published," and "Developing Characters."
Speakers: In past years, guest lecturers included Harlan Ellison, Dan Simmons, and Terry Brooks.
Location: New Hampshire College, Manchester, New Hampshire.
Costs: Tuition, $1,200; application fee, $25. Lodging is extra.
Contact: Jeanne Cavelos, Director.

Oklahoma Fall Arts Institutes
105 North Hudson, Suite 101
Oklahoma City, OK 73102
www.okartinst.org

Spread over four weekends in October, the Fall Arts Institutes consist of 27 arts workshops in six different disciplines, including visual arts, music, theater, photography, and writing. One weekend is set aside as a writers' retreat. Classes are open to adults with abilities ranging from beginner to advanced. Admittance is on a first-come, first-served basis. Scholarships are available for teachers.

Date: October.
Subjects: The 2001 writers' retreat covered writing for children, writing the memoir, poetry, and playwriting.
Speakers: TBA.
Location: Quartz Mountain, Oklahoma.
Costs: $500, includes room and board.
Contact: Mary Y. Frates, President.

Ozark Creative Writers, Inc.
#5 Colony Road
Little Rock, AR 72227
www.ozarkcreativewriters.org

This conference offers writers the chance to improve their skills by providing them with teachers who are high-quality, professional authors. Held annually since 1968, it welcomes high school students as well as adults at all levels, from beginner to advanced. The conference provides a forum for writers, illustrators, and agents, to meet and learn from one another. Send an SASE or visit the website for complete information.
Date: Second weekend in October.
Subjects: Last year's topics included "The Craft of Contemporary Fiction" and "Writing for the Christian-Based Market."
Speakers: Sarah Bird, Joe Vallely, and Lucia St. Clair Robson spoke at the 2001 conference.
Location: Eureka Springs, Arkansas.
Costs: $60–$75.
Contact: Chrissy Willis, Program Director.

Philadelphia Writers' Conference
107 Newington Drive
Hatboro, PA 19040-4508

http://pwcgold.com

A three-day program, this conference offers four concurrent workshops, agent/editor sessions, a roundtable buffet with an agent/editor panel, faculty consultations, manuscript readings and critiques, and an awards banquet. Beginners are welcome to attend, but participants must be at least 18.

Date: June.
Subjects: Writing for children and young adults, fiction, humor, journalism, mystery, nonfiction, autobiography/memoir, poetry, and marketing.
Speakers: Faculty at the 2001 conference included James Freeman, Eileen Spinelli, and Sylvia Goldfarb.
Location: Philadelphia.
Costs: $160–$180; scholarships are available.
Contact: I. Murden, Registrar.

South Carolina Writers Workshop Annual Conference
P.O. Box 7104
Columbia, SC 29202
www.4bnc.com/scww

Conducted annually on the third weekend in October, this conference has grown each year in scope and attendance since it was first held in 1990. Workshops cover all genres, including children's writing. For an additional $25, participants may submit 10 manuscript pages for critiquing by a faculty member.

Date: October.
Subjects: This conference offers workshops in all areas of writing.
Speakers: TBA
Location: Myrtle Beach, South Carolina.

Costs: $160.
Contact: Sandra Johnson, Conference Chair.

SouthWest Writers Annual Conference
8200 Mountain Road NE
Albuquerque, NM 87110
www.southwestwriters.org

This annual conference, sponsored by SouthWest Writers, provides participants with several workshops on all aspects of writing.

Date: September.
Subjects: Last year's topics included "Writing Realistic Dialogue," "Customize Your Writing Style," and "First Chapters."
Speakers: The 2001 conference featured Terry Brooks, Alice Walker, Catherine Ryan Hyde, and John Nance.
Location: Albuquerque, New Mexico.
Costs: Members: $195–$255. Non-members: $260–$320. Preconference sessions: $25–$100.
Contact: Conference Director.

Split Rock Arts Program
University of Minnesota
360 Coffey Hall
1420 Eckles Avenue
St. Paul, MN 55108
www.cce.umn.edu/splitrockarts

Split Rock features a variety of workshops that are held during the summer months. It offers a supportive, inclusive environment in which students may explore their creative sides. Workshops are open to writers at all levels.

Date: July–August.

Subjects: "Inventing the Truth," "New Approaches to Fiction," and "Writing Healing Narratives" were among the workshops held last year.
Speakers: Mary Jane Moffat, Paulette Bates Alden, and Percival Everett were among the leaders of last year's workshops.
Location: St. Paul, Minnesota.
Costs: TBA.
Contact: Andrea Gilats, Director.

Steamboat Springs Writers Conference

Steamboat Springs Arts Council
P.O. Box 774284
Steamboat Springs, CO 80477

Begun in 1982 and held each summer, this weekend conference offers top quality instruction to individuals with limited time or finances. To allow direct interaction among instructors and participants, registration is limited to 35 attendees. The focus of each conference varies from year to year, covering, in turn, all phases and forms of writing. Every four or five years, the focus is on writing for children.
Date: July.
Subjects: Among the topics covered at last year's conference were "The Professional Writer" and "Writing for Young People."
Speakers: Last year's workshops were conducted by James Tipton and Avi.
Location: Steamboat Springs, Colorado.
Costs: Early registration rates are $25 for members; $35 for nonmembers.
Contact: Harriet Freiberger, Director.

Summer Writers' Workshops

Manhattanville College
2900 Purchase Street
Purchase, NY 10577
www.manhattanville.edu

These workshops, offered annually during the last week in June, foster creative writing in various genres. Participants sign up for one of seven workshops that are conducted by professional writers or teachers of writing. Novice as well as advanced writers take part in this program. Submission of a writing sample is required with registration.
Date: June 24–28, 2002.
Subjects: Last year's workshops included "Tales of Children in the Contemporary World," "The Young Adult Novel," and "Reading & Discussion on Children's Literature."
Speakers: Janet Taylor Lisle, C. Drew Lamm, and Mary Gordon took part in the 2001 conference.
Location: Manhattanville College, Purchase, New York.
Costs: Non-credit, $560; 2 graduate credits, $840; registration fee, $30; activities fee, $30; lodging, $40 per night.
Contact: Ruth Dowd, RSCJ, Director.

Vancouver International Writers & Readers Festival

1398 Cartwright Street
Vancouver, BC V6H 3R8
Canada
www.writersfest.bc.ca

A five-day festival held on Granville Island, this event serves to bring book lovers and writers together. Scheduled events are aimed at early readers

through adults, and several programs are designed specifically for school children and their teachers.
Date: October.
Subjects: At last year's festival, programs conducted by accomplished authors addressed aspiring travel writers and those with an interest in science, inventions, and historical fiction.
Speakers: Past authors who have appeared at the festival include Ursula K. Le Guin, Aislinn Hunter, and David Rakoff.
Location: Granville Island, Vancouver.
Costs: Tickets range from $6 for students to $16.
Contact: Alma Lee, Artistic Director.

Whidbey Island Writers' Conference
Whidbey Island Writers' Association
P.O. Box 1289
Langley, WA 98260
www.whidbey.com/writers

The Whidbey Island Writers' Association sponsors this annual three-day conference. Lectures and workshops target writers of every genre. The workshops on children's writing cover picture books, chapter books, middle-grade and young adult titles, magazine writing, and marketing. Participants in this conference have the opportunity to meet agents, editors, and publishers.
Date: March 1–3, 2002.
Subjects: Topics covered at the 2001 conference included "Nailing Voice for the Middle Grade/Young Adult Novel," and "Picture Books and Poetry."
Speakers: Cherry Adair, Catherine Coulter, Eva Shaw, and Kirby Larson.
Location: Langley–Whidbey Island, Washington.
Costs: $308 (includes luncheons), plus lodging.
Contact: Celeste Mergens, Director.

Willamette Writers Conference
9045 SW Barbur
Portland, OR 97219
www.willamettewriters.com

Since 1976, Willamette Writers has sponsored this conference to help writers improve their craft while providing opportunities to meet agents, editors, and members of the film industry. The children's topics regularly covered include young adult books and picture books. Send an SASE or visit the website for details.
Date: August.
Subjects: The 2001 conference featured "Writing for Young Adults," "Writing Picture Book Text," and "ABC's of Children's Books."
Speakers: Robert Ray and Steven Barnes were among the speakers at last year's conference.
Location: Portland, Oregon.
Costs: $246–$276, plus lodging.
Contact: Cheri Walter, Conference Coordinator.

Writers' Conference
The Writing Center
Marymount Manhattan College
221 East 71st Street
New York, NY 10021
www.marymount.mmm.edu

The Writers' Conference, a one-day series of panel discussions, has been held annually since 1993. Here, emerging writers have the opportunity to meet and talk with editors and literary agents and learn how to succeed in the writing profession. Participants may also register for a Four Day Writers' Intensive—attendance at a workshop of their choice, which culminates in the writers' conference.

Date: June.

Subjects: Panel discussion topics at last year's conference included "Writing for the Children's Market," and "Writing Over the Age of 40: Trials and Triumphs."

Speakers: Speakers from the 2001 conference included Carol Higgins Clark, Trish Marx, and Russell Banks.

Location: Marymount Manhattan College, New York City.

Costs: Fees range from $135–$165 for the conference only; from $355–$415 for the Writers' Intensive only; and from $495–$530 for both.

Contact: Lewis Burke Frumkes, Director of The Writing Center.

Writers Institute

University of Wisconsin–Madison
Division of Continuing Studies
Room 616 Lowell Center
610 Langdon Street
Madison, WI 53703
www.dcs.wisc.edu/lsa

This annual conference offers a selection of workshops over a two-day period. It offers instruction on general topics, such as writing for the children's market, as well as on specific aspects of the craft of writing, including characterization and story structure. Send an SASE or visit the website for complete information on the conference.

Date: July 11–12, 2002.

Subjects: Last year's conference featured workshops on juvenile markets, writing the novel, and creating nonfiction proposals.

Speakers: TBA

Location: Madison, Wisconsin.

Costs: $195. Lodging is not included in the conference cost.

Contact: Christine DeSmet, Director.

Writers Workshop in Science Fiction

English Department
University of Kansas
Lawrence, KS 66045
http://falcon.cc.ukans.edu/~sfcenter

Sponsored by the Center for the Study of Science Fiction, this workshop began in the 1980s as a temporary replacement for the Intensive English Institute on the Teaching of Science Fiction. Each two-week session covers fantasy as well as science fiction. Application is by submission of a science fiction story presented in a professional format. For complete conference information, send an SASE or visit the website.

Date: Late June.

Subjects: These workshops cover the writing and marketing of science fiction and fantasy.

Speakers: TBA

Location: University of Kansas.

Costs: $400. Lodging and meals are not included.

Contact: James Gunn, Director.

The Writing Academy's Writers' Weekend
21445 Sunny Drive
Fergus Falls, MN 56537-9519
www.wams.org

The Writers' Weekend is aimed at established writers as well as those who are just beginning. It offers inspirational teaching, hands-on workshops, and fellowship with other writers. Informal critique groups are part of each conference, and attendees are invited to read from their works in progress.
Date: August.
Subjects: Short fiction, humor writing, and writing from personal experience were among the subjects featured at the 2001 seminar.
Speakers: TBA.
Location: Minneapolis, Minnesota.
Costs: TBA.
Contact: Chris Hefte, Coordinator.

Conferences with Sessions on Writing for Children — Religious Writing Conferences

American Christian Writers Conferences
P.O. Box 110390
Nashville, TN 37222
www.acwriters.com

American Christian Writers hosts three-dozen conferences each year in three-dozen US cities. Since 1988, the goal of these conferences has been to locate, train, and motivate writers. The two-day sessions cover topics related to writing for adults, young adults, and children.

Date: Contact American Christian Writers for dates and locations.
Subjects: Topics covered at last year's conferences included "Writing for Youth," "Be Your Own Best Editor," and "Selling What You Write."
Speakers: Speakers at last year's conferences included Lin Johnson, Sally Stuart, and James Scott Bell.
Location: These conferences are held in 36 cities across the US, including Houston, Anaheim, Phoenix, Atlanta, Detroit, and Washington, DC.
Costs: One-day attendance, $99–$109. Two-day attendance, $169–$189.
Contact: Reg A. Forder, Director.

Christian Seniors Fellowship National Winter Conference
Christian Seniors Fellowship
P.O. Box 46464
Cincinnati, OH 45246-0464

Workshops on topics of interest to seniors and church leaders are conducted at this annual three-day conference. CSF also sponsors other conferences throughout the year, which are held at various locations across the US. Contact the CSF at the address above for dates and locations.

Date: February.
Subjects: Workshops cover subjects of interest to Christian writers, seniors, and church leaders.
Speakers: The speakers at the 2001 winter conference were Robert Shannon, Jack Ballard, Charles McNeely, and Max Smith.
Location: The 2001 winter conference was held in Daytona Beach, Florida.
Costs: TBA.
Contact: For more information, contact the Christian Seniors Fellowship at the address above.

Christian Writer's Day
Orange County Christian Writers' Fellowship
P.O. Box 538
Lake Forest, CA 92609

Published authors and editors present workshops on a variety of topics related to writing at this day-long conference, which is held in the spring and in the fall. Children's writing is among the genres covered at each session.

Date: Spring conference, April 20, 2002. Fall conference, date to be announced.
Subjects: Last year's spring conference offered the following workshops: "Writing That Changes Children's Lives," "Creating Memorable Fiction Characters," and "Writing Your Life

Experiences."

Speakers: Ray and Anne Ortlund will be the keynote speakers at the conference on April 20, 2002.

Location: Mariners Church in Irvine, California.

Costs: $50; $45 for OCCWF members; $30 for students.

Contact: Beverly Bush Smith, Co-Director.

Mount Hermon Christian Writers Conference

Mount Hermon Christian Conference
Center
P.O. Box 413
Mount Hermon, CA 95041
www.mounthermon.org

Held annually since 1970, this conference seeks to encourage Christian writers in their ministry. Sponsored by the Mount Hermon Christian Conference Center, it covers all areas of the Christian market, including writing for children. Participants may submit two manuscripts in advance for free critique. For complete details on this conference, visit the website or send an SASE.

Date: March 22–26, 2002.

Subjects: Marketing, creativity, publishing, thinking like children, generating ideas, and knowing what publishers want are among the subjects generally covered.

Speakers: TBA

Location: Mount Hermon Christian Conference Center.

Costs: $325, plus room and board.

Contact: David R. Talbott, Director.

Montrose Christian Writers' Conference

Montrose Bible Conference
5 Locust Street
Montrose, PA 18801
www.montrosebible.org

The children's topics generally covered by this conference include writing for various age groups, writing fiction and nonfiction, book writing, marketing, trends in children's literature, and conducting classroom visits.

Date: Fourth week of July.

Subjects: Last year's workshops included "How to Jump Start Your Creativity," "Trends in Children's Publishing," and "How a Children's Story and a Picture Book Differ."

Speakers: Workshop leaders at last year's conference included Barbara Scott, Shirley Brinkerhoff, and Ellyn Sanna.

Location: Montrose Bible Conference, Montrose, Pennsylvania.

Costs: From $120, plus lodging and meals.

Contact: Patricia Souder, Director.

St. Davids Christian Writers' Conference

87 Pines Road East
Hadley, PA 16130
www.stdavidswriters.com

Private tutorials and professional critiques are available for an additional fee at this conference, which also offers lectures and workshops. Christian writers from all denominations, from beginners to advanced, are welcome to take part in this annual event.

Date: June.

Subjects: "Write for Kids' Eyes," "Crafting Stories with Power," and "Writing for Christian Magazines" were among the workshops offered in 2001.

Speakers: Speakers at the 2001 conference included Jane Kirkpatrick, Ethel Herr, and Amanda Lynch.

Location: TBA

Costs: Costs range from $80 for a one-day workshop to $240 for full-time; on-campus enrollment.

Contact: Audrey Stallsmith, Registrar.

Writing Academy Summer Conference
1128 Mule Lake Drive NE
Outing, MN 56662
www.wams.org

Open to both new and established writers, the Writing Academy Summer Conference is a weekend retreat to rekindle one's passion for writing through inspirational teaching, workshops, and meeting other writers and professionals in the field. Send an SASE or visit the website for complete information on the 2002 conference.

Date: August.

Subjects: Among the 2001 topics were "Writing for the Religious Market," and workshops on short fiction, publishing, and marketing your work.

Speakers: The speakers at the 2001 conference included Reverend Marlys Korman, Nancy James, Athena Dean, and Jerry Elsea.

Location: The 2001 conference was held in Minneapolis, Minnesota.

Costs: Full active members pay room and board only. Associate members and guests pay $125 plus room and board. Last year's room and board costs were $325 for a single room; $265 for a double room (with a roommate).

Contact: Marlys Korman, Treasurer.

Writers' Contests & Awards

Jane Addams Children's Book Award
Ginny Moore Kruse
1708 Regent Street
Madison, WI 53705

Established in 1953, this annual award is presented to a book that most effectively promotes the cause of peace, social justice, world community, and the equality of the sexes and all races.

Entries should have a target audience of children ages two through fourteen. Themes may include solving problems; overcoming prejudice; approaching life with self-confidence; broadening one's outlook to appreciate a variety of cultures; and understanding human needs with compassion.

All entries must be submitted by the book's publisher, or requested by the committee, and must have been published in the year preceding the contest.
Deadline: April 1.
Representative winners: *Esperanza Rising,* Pam Muñoz; *The Composition,* Antonio Skármeta.
Announcements: Winners are announced on June 6, the birthday of Jane Addams.
Award: Winners receive an illuminated scroll. Silver seals are also placed on the book jacket by the publisher. Honor scrolls may also be awarded.

Aesop Prize and Aesop Accolades
Box 428
2887 College Avenue #1
Berkeley, CA 94705

The Aesop Prize and Aesop Accolades are presented annually by the Children's Folklore Section of the American Folklore Society. They are presented to the best English language books in both fiction and nonfiction.

Folklore should be central to the book's content, and should enhance the readers' understanding of folklore. Sources must be fully acknowledged and referenced within the publication. Entries must have been published in the year preceding the contest. Send an SASE for complete competition guidelines.
Deadline: September.
Representative winners: *The Day the Rabbi Disappeared: Jewish Holiday Tales of Magic,* Howard Schwartz; *The Hunter: A Chinese Folktale,* Mary Casanova.
Announcements: Winning books will be announced in November.
Award: To be announced.

Listings

AIM Short Story Contest
AIM Magazine
Ruth Apilado, Associate Editor
P.O. Box 1174
Maywood, IL 60153

This contest for short stories looks to encourage new writers and seeks submissions with social significance. It accepts previously unpublished entries that encourage understanding, tolerance, and compassion without moralizing. Entries should show that all people, regardless of racial backgrounds, desire the same things.

It accepts entries up to 4,000 words. Limit one entry per competition; no entry fee. Include an SASE for return of manuscript. Send an SASE for complete contest guidelines
Deadline: August 15.
Announcements: Winners are announced in the autumn issue of *AIM*.
Award: First-place winners receive $100; second-place winners receive $75. Both receive publication in *AIM*.

Alcuin Citations
Alcuin Society
P.O. Box 3216
Vancouver, BC V6B 3X8
Canada

The Alcuin Citations look to recognize the work of Canadian book designers and publishers. The citations are awarded in five categories: fiction, nonfiction, children's books, pictorial, and poetry.

Eligible books must have been published in Canada during the year preceding the contest. Entry fee, $10 per submission. Send an SASE for further information and entry form.
Deadline: March 31.
Announcements: Winners will be announced in May.
Award: An award certificate is presented at an annual banquet.

Amelia Annual Contests
329 "E" Street
Bakersfield, CA 93304-4064

Amelia magazine sponsors numerous annual contests in several different categories including short story, fiction, poetry, chapter book, mystery, and fantasy.

Guidelines and word lengths vary for each category. Send an SASE for complete contest information. Entry fees range from $3 to $10 depending on category. Multiple entries are accepted. Send an SASE for return of manuscript.
Deadline: Deadlines vary for each category.
Announcements: Winners are announced about 8 to 10 weeks after the contest due date.
Award: Winners receive cash prizes and possible publication in the magazine.

American Association of University Women Award for Juvenile Literature
North Carolina Literary and
  Historical Association
4610 Mail Service Center
Raleigh, NC 27699-4610

Open to residents of North Carolina (minimum three-year residency), this award is presented for the year's best work of juvenile or young adult fiction.

All entries must have been published in the year preceding the contest. It accepts published submissions only. No entry fees required. Send an SASE for complete competition guidelines and further information.
Deadline: July 15.
Announcements: Winners will be announced in November.
Award: Winners are presented with an engraved cup.

Américas Award for Children's and Young Adult Literature
Consortium of Latin American
   Studies Programs
c/o Center for Latin America
P.O. Box 413
Milwaukee, WI 53201

This award is presented in recognition of US works of fiction, poetry, folklore, or selected nonfiction, published in English or Spanish during the year preceding the contest. All entries must authentically and positively portray Latin America, the Caribbean, or Latinos in the United States.

The Américas Award looks to reach beyond geographic boundaries, focusing instead on cultural heritages within the hemisphere. Winners are chosen based on distinctive literary quality; cultural contextualization; exceptional integration of text, illustration, and design; and potential for classroom use.
Deadline: January 15.
Representative winners: *My Sister Gracie*, Kong Njo; *Elton the Elf*, Marielle Maheu; *Yuck, A Love Story*, Kathryn Cole and Mary Louise Gay.

Announcements: Competition is announced each January. Winners are announced in June.
Award: A letter of citation is presented to the winning author and publisher.

Amy Writing Awards
The Amy Foundation
P.O. Box 16091
Lansing, MI 48901
www.amyfound.org

Open to all writers, this awards program was designed to recognize creative, skillful writing that presents the biblical position on issues affecting the world today.

The competition accepts entries that were previously published in a secular, non-religious publication. All entries must contain scripture to be eligible for consideration.

No entry fee. Send an SASE for complete competition guidelines and complete contest category information.
Deadline: December 31.
Announcements: Winners will be announced in May.
Award: First-place winners receive a cash prize of $10,000.

Hans Christian Andersen Awards
IBBY
Nonneweg 12
Postfach, CH-4003
Basel, Switzerland
www.ibby.org

IBBY presents these awards every other year to a living author and illustrator who has made an important contribution to children's literature through the outstanding value of their work. Nominations are made by the National Sections of IBBY and recipients are selected by a distinguished international jury of children's literature specialists.

Deadline: August 15.

Representative winners: Ana Maria Machado; Anthony Browne.

Announcements: Winners are announced during the Bologna Children's Book Fair in Italy.

Award: Winners receive a diploma and a gold medal at an awards dinner.

Isaac Asimov Award

University of South Florida
School of Mass Communications
4202 E. Fowler
Tampa, FL 33620

This contest honors the legacy of Isaac Asimov, one of the most distinguished authors in the genre of science fiction. The award is presented for an undergraduate work of science fiction or fantasy ranging from 1,000 to 10,000 words. It accepts previously unpublished entries only.

The contest is open to full-time college students. Entry fee, $3. Limit 3 entries per competition. Include a cover sheet with author's name, address, and university. Author's name and personal information should not be on the manuscript itself. Entries should be focused more on the characters than on science. Serious, thoughtful fiction will have the best chance for success.

Deadline: December 15.

Award: A cash award of $500 is presented to the winner. The winning entry will also be considered for publication in *Asimov's Science Fiction Magazine.*

ASPCA Henry Berg Children's Book Award

American Society for the Prevention
of Cruelty to Animals
424 East 92nd Street
New York, NY 10128-6804

Named for the founder of the ASPCA, this annual award was put in place to honor those books that promote humane ethics of compassion and respect for all living things. The competition accepts works of fiction, nonfiction, collections of stories, and poetry.

Entries must be in English, and published during the year preceding the contest. Send six copies of each entry along with a plot summary. Include the story's moral within the summary. For more information, send an SASE.

Deadline: October 31.

Announcements: Winners and honor recipients will be announced in June.

Award: Winners are honored with an award at an ASPCA reception in June.

Atlantic Writing Competition

Writers' Federation of Nova Scotia
113 Marginal Road
Halifax, Nova Scotia B3H 4P7
Canada
www.writers.ns.ca

Helping writers become ready for publication, this annual competition offers awards in several categories including writing for children, novel, magazine article, and short story.

Entries should be unpublished and

word lengths vary for each category. Limit one entry per competition. Accepts computer printouts and photocopies. Entry fee, $15 for non-members; $10 for members. For more information, visit the website or send an SASE.

Deadline: August.

Representative winners: Anne Kelly; Joanne Taylor.

Announcements: Winners will be notified in March.

Award: Cash awards ranging from $50 to $150 are presented to the winners at an annual gala for the Writers' Federation of Nova Scotia.

Baker's Plays High School Playwriting Competition

Baker's Plays
100 Chauncy Street
Boston, MA 02111
www.bakersplays.com

Open to high school students, this annual competition accepts plays dealing with "the high school experience." Entries may be any length, as long as the play can reasonably be produced on a high school stage.

All entries must be accompanied by the signature of a sponsoring high school drama or English teacher. Multiple submissions and co-authored scripts are accepted. Send an SASE for return of manuscript. Visit the website for complete details.

Deadline: January 30.

Representative winners: *Dreaming Tree,* Robert Markland.

Announcements: Winners will be notified in May.

Award: Winners receive cash prizes ranging from $100 to $500. First-place winners also have their play produced by Baker's Plays.

Margaret Bartle Annual Playwriting Award

Community Children's Theatre of
    Kansas City, Inc.
8021 East 129th Terrace
Grandview, MI 64030

The Margaret Bartle Award is presented to the best play written for elementary school children. It accepts previously unpublished plays with fewer than 8 characters. All plays are performed by adults and should have women in the primary roles.

The competition accepts original ideas, legends, folklore, historical incidents, biographies, and adaptations of children's classics. Entries should have a running time of less than 60 minutes. Manuscripts should be typed and securely bound. Send an SASE for complete competition details.

Deadline: January 30.

Announcements: Winners will be notified in May.

Award: A cash award of $500 is presented to the winner. The winning play is also produced by the Community Theater of Kansas City, Inc.

John and Patricia Beatty Award

California Library Association
Suite 200
717 20th Street
Sacramento, CA 95814
www.cla-net.org

The California Library Association sponsors this annual award that honors the author of a distinguished book for children or young adults that best promotes an awareness of California and its people.

Winners are selected by a committee of librarians from books published in the United States in the year preceding the contest. This award is continually gaining prestige due to the excellence of the books it has honored. Send an SASE or visit the website for complete contest information.

Deadline: To be announced.

Representative winners: *Hurry Freedom: African Americans in Gold Rush California,* Jerry Stanley.

Announcements: Winners are announced during National Library Week in April.

Award: Winners receive $500 and an engraved plaque.

**Geoffrey Bilson Award for
   Historical Fiction**
The Canadian Children's Book Center
35 Spadina Road
Toronto, ON M5R 2S9
Canada

Honoring excellence in the genre of historical fiction by a Canadian author, the Geoffrey Bilson Award for historical fiction is presented annually. Entries must be historically authentic and inform the reader significantly. All entries must be written by residents of Canada, and should be published in the year preceding the contest.

Winners will be chosen by a jury appointed by the Canadian Children's Book Centre. Send an SASE for complete guidelines.

Deadline: May 15.

Representative winners: Nominees for the 2001 award are: *A Bushel of Light,* Troon Harrison; *Charlie Wilcox,* Sharon E. McKay; *In My Enemy's House,* Carol Matas.

Announcements: Winners will be notified in November.

Award: Winners of this award receive a cash prize of $1,000 and a certificate.

**Irma S. and James H. Black Award
   for Excellence in Children's
   Literature**
Bank Street College of Education
610 West 112th Street
New York, NY 10025

Presented annually since 1973, this award commemorates the work of Irma S. Black's achievements in the field of children's literature. The award is given to an outstanding book for young children where the text and illustrations combine together and become inseparable as a whole.

The award is unusual in that children are the final judges of the winning book. A group of adult writers, librarians, and educators choose approximately 30 books that they consider the best candidates for the award. The books are then sent to students to read and judge.

Deadline: December 15.

Representative winners: *The Raft,* Jim LaMarche; *A Dog Like Jack,* DyAnne DiSalvo-Ryan.

Announcements: Winners will be announced in May at a ceremony at the Harvard Club in New York.

Award: The winner receives a scroll and a seal for their book at an awards ceremony.

Black-Eyed Susan Awards
P.O. Box 21127
Baltimore, MD 21228

The purpose of the Black-Eyed Susan Awards is to promote life-long reading habits by encouraging students to read and enjoy quality, contemporary literature that broadens understanding of the human experience. Nominated books will broaden the human experience and provide accurate, factual information. Although anyone may nominate titles to be included on the list, the final books are chosen by school library media specialists and educators. Once the list of nominations is complete the books will be read and voted upon by students in Maryland. Send an SASE for complete information.

Deadline: April 30.

Representative winners: *The 6th Grade Nickname Game*, Gordan Korman; *Holes*, Louis Sachar; *Someone Like You*, Sarah Dessan.

Award: Winners receive a pewter plate engraved with the year and the Black-Eyed Susan logo.

Waldo M. and Grace C. Bonderman Youth Theatre Playwriting Competition
Indiana University-Purdue University at Indianapolis
CA305
425 N. University Boulevard
Indianapolis, IN 46202-5140

Established in 1985, this competition is held every other year in support of youth theater. All entries must be previously unpublished.

Entries should be written for an audience of children in grades 3 through 12, although no play is expected to appeal to all ages simultaneously. Authors should include age range of submission on the entry form. Entries should have a running time of about 45 minutes.

Limit one entry per competition. Musicals are not accepted. Author's name should not appear on manuscript. Include a separate cover sheet with name, address, age range, running time, and scene-by-scene summary of action. No entry fee; all entries must be accompanied by an entry form. Send an SASE for complete guidelines.

Deadline: September 1, 2002.

Representative winners: The 2001 finalists include: *Two Donuts,* Jose Gonzalez; *Threadheads,* Dean Corrin; *Tortilla Moon,* Margaret Larlham.

Announcements: Winners will be announced in January 2003.

Award: The top four winners receive a cash award of $1,000 and a staged production of their play.

Boston Globe-Horn Book Awards
The Horn Book
Suite 200
56 Roland Street
Boston, MA 02129
www.hbook.com/bghb.html

Co-sponsored by *The Boston Globe* and *The Horn Book*, Inc., these annual awards are presented for excellence in literature for children and young adults. These awards are considered among the most prestigious in the nation. Entries are evaluated by a committee of three judges. Winners are selected based on their overall creative excellence.

Books to be considered for this award may be submitted in four categories: fiction, poetry, nonfiction, and picture book. Please specify the category when submitting an entry. Eligible books will have been published in the year preceding the contest.

A copy of each entry should be sent to each of the three judges. Send an SASE or visit the website to access judges names and competition guidelines.

Deadline: May 15.

Representative winners: *Carver: A Life in Poems*, Marilyn Nelson; *Cold Feet*, Cynthia De Felice; *The Longitude Prize*, Joan Dash.

Announcements: Contest is announced each February. Winners will be announced in October.

Award: Winners in each category receive $500 and an engraved silver bowl. Honor books may also be awarded. Award recipient's speeches will be published in *The Horn Book Magazine*.

Brant Point Prize

What's Inside Press
P.O. Box 18203
Beverly Hills, CA 90209
www.whatsinsidepress.com

What's Inside Press sponsors this annual award that recognizes excellence in children's and young adult writing. The contest is open to published and unpublished writers and has a theme that changes yearly.

All entries must be previously unpublished. Length requirements vary each year. Entry fee, $10. Multiple entries are accepted if each is accompanied by an entry form and entry fee. Manuscripts should be targeted to children ages 2 through 8 or young adults ages 12 through 17. Manuscripts will not be returned. For further information and entry forms, visit the website or send an SASE.

Deadline: Entries will be accepted between May 1 and August 31.

Representative winners: *The Tree in the Field of Mathingamy*, Walter Caldwell.

Announcements: Winners will be notified by mail.

Award: Grand-prize winners receive $2,500 and a publishing contract with What's Inside Press, LLC, with a minimum first-run printing of 10,000. Each book will also be embossed with the prize logo.

Ann Connor Brimer Children's Literature Award

Nova Scotia Library Association
P.O. Box 36036
Halifax, Nova Scotia B3J 3S9
Canada

This award is presented for a distinguished contribution to children's literature in Atlantic Canada. The award is presented annually for books written for children up to the age of 15. Writers must be residents of Atlantic Canada to enter.

The competition accepts submissions of both fiction and nonfiction that were published between May of the year preceding the contest and April 30 of the contest year. Send an SASE for complete competition guidelines.

Deadline: January 30.

Representative winners: *The Secret Under My Skin,* Janet McNaughton; *The True Meaning of Crumbfest,* David Weale.

Announcements: Winners will be announced at the Atlantic Writing Award ceremony during May of each year.

Award: Winners are honored with a cash award of $1,000 and a framed certificate.

Buckeye Children's Book Award

State Library of Ohio
65 South Front Street
Columbus, OH 43215
www.bcbookaward.org

Beginning in 1981, the Buckeye Children's Book Award was designed to encourage children in Ohio to read literature, to promote teacher and librarian involvement in children's literature programs, and to give recognition to the authors of children's literature.

The awards are presented in three categories: Kindergarten through second-grade; third- through fifth-grade; and sixth- through eighth-grade. Students are given the master voting list, and may vote for one book in each category. The master list consists of books by American authors that were published in the past three years.

Beginning this year, children may now vote directly on the website. Votes may also be cast by mail or through schools in Ohio.

Deadline: February.

Representative winners: *Bark, George,* Jules Feiffer; *The Adventures of Captain Underpants,* Dav Pilkey; *Holes,* Louis Sachar.

Announcements: Winners are announced in February or March.

Award: Winning books become part of the Buckeye Children's Book Hall of Fame, housed in the Columbus Metropolitan Library.

Byline Magazine Contests

P.O. Box 130596
Edmond, OK 73013-0001
www.bylinemag.com/contests.html

Each year, *Byline Magazine* presents several writing contests in categories including children's poem, pet or wildlife article, nostalgia, flash fiction, short-short story, and editorial essay. Entry fees vary for each category. Multiple entries are accepted. All entries must be unpublished at the time they are entered in the contest.

Word lengths vary for each category. Visit the website or send an SASE for complete category information.

Deadline: Deadlines vary.

Announcements: Winners are announced in *Byline Magazine.*

Award: Winners in each category receive cash awards ranging from $10 to $70.

Randolph Caldecott Medal

American Library Association
50 E. Huron
Chicago, IL 60611
www.ala.org/alsc

This prestigious medal, awarded by the American Library Association, is presented to the most distinguished American picture book for children published in the year preceding the contest.

It is open to all US citizens. Illustrations must be original artwork and

demonstrate excellence in execution of the artistic technique and of pictorial interpretation of the story, theme, or concept, and illustration style. Visit the website or send an SASE for complete guidelines and further information.
Deadline: December 31.
Representative winners: *So You Want to Be President?*, David Small (text by Judith St. George).
Announcements: Winners will be announced at the ALA mid-winter meeting.
Award: The Caldecott medal is presented at an awards banquet.

California Writers Contest

Friends of the Sacramento
　Public Library
Suite 309
Department TA
828 I Street
Sacramento, CA 95814
www.saclib.org

Open to all California writers, this annual contest looks to encourage and reward its entrants. Entries are accepted in the categories of script, short story, first novel chapter, poem, nonfiction article, book or article for children and first chapter of a young adult fiction or nonfiction book.

Entry fee, $5 per submission. Word length requirements and guidelines vary for each category. Accepts previously unpublished entries only. Limit 5 entries per competition. Manuscripts will not be returned. For complete category guidelines and further information, send an SASE or visit the website.
Deadline: August.

Announcements: Winners will be announced in October.
Award: Winners in each category will receive cash awards ranging from $50 to $200.

Calliope Fiction Contest

Sandy Raschke, Fiction Editor
P.O. Box 466
Moraga, CA 94556-0466

This annual contest accepts fiction in all genres, including young adult and juvenile fiction, mystery, fantasy, light horror, romance, science fiction, and magical realism. Entries containing violence or graphic themes will not be accepted. Sponsored by the Writers' Special Interest Group of American Mensa, it looks to create a fun writing experience for members, subscribers, and entrants. The competition is open to all writers.

Entries must be original work that is previously unpublished. Entries should not exceed 2,500 words. Entry fees, $2 per submission (*Calliope* subscribers receive one free entry). Limit 5 entries per competition. All entries must come via regular mail; electronic entries are not accepted at this time. Send an SASE for complete competition guidelines and further information.
Deadline: Entries are accepted between April 16 and September 30.
Representative winners: *Exodus*, Tammy Kaiser; *Away from the Seen*, Stefano Danati; *Cat and Mouse*, Donald H. Sullivan.
Announcements: Winners will be notified by mail, and in the January/February issue of *Calliope*.
Award: Winners receive cash prizes

ranging from $5 to $20 and honor certificates. Winning entries will be published in *Calliope* (one-time rights required).

Canadian Library Association's Book of the Year for Children Award

328 Frank Street
Ottawa, Ontario K2P 0X8
Canada
www.cla.ca

Established in 1947, the Book of the Year Award is presented annually by the Canadian Library Association. The award was put in place to honor the author of an outstanding children's book published during the previous calendar year. To be eligible for consideration, entries must be suitable for children up to the age of 14, and have been published in Canada, by a Canadian citizen or permanent resident of Canada.

Entries may be fiction, poetry, or re-telling of traditional literature. Send an SASE for complete competition guidelines, or visit the website for further information.
Deadline: Nominations should be sent by January 1.
Representative winners: *Wild Girl & Gran*, Nan Gregory; *Sunwing*, Kenneth Oppel.
Announcements: Winners will be announced at the Canadian Library Association's annual conference in June.
Award: Winners are presented with a medal at an award ceremony during the annual conference.

Canadian Library Association's Young Adult Canadian Book Award

328 Frank Street
Ottawa, Ontario K2P 0X8
Canada
www.cla.ca

Sponsored by the Canadian Library Association, this annual award recognizes an author of an outstanding English language Canadian book appealing to young adults between the ages of 13 and 18. All entries must have been published during the year preceding the contest.

Eligible entries must be works of fiction, and may be short stories or novels. Entries must be published in Canada, and must be written by a Canadian citizen or landed immigrant.
Deadline: December 31.
Representative winners: *Before Wings*, Beth Goobie; *Alone at Ninety Foot*, Katherine Holubitsky.
Announcements: Call for nominees begins in October. Winners are announced in June at the CLA annual conference.
Award: Winners receive a leather bound book with the title, author, and award seal embossed in gold on the cover.

Raymond Carver Short Story Contest

Humboldt State University
Department of English
Arcata, CA 95521
www.humboldt.edu/~carver

This short story contest honors Raymond Carver and his connection to

Humboldt University. This annual contest is open to citizens of the US only. It accepts previously unpublished entries.

Entry fee, $10. Multiple entries are accepted as long as each is accompanied by an entry fee. Send two copies of each entry. Author's name, address, phone number, and e-mail address should be included on cover sheet only. Entries should not exceed 6,000 words.

Deadline: December 1.

Representative winners: *How the Dead Live,* Gina Ochsner; *Hitting the Wall,* Martha Kinney.

Announcements: Winners will be announced in June.

Award: First-place winners receive $500 and publication in *TOYON*, the literary magazine of Humboldt University. Second-place winners receive $250 and publication.

Rebecca Caudill Young Readers' Book Award

Illinois Reading Council
P.O. Box 6536
Naperville, IL 60567-6536

The Rebecca Caudill Young Readers' Book Award is sponsored by the Illinois Reading Council. Held annually, it was developed to encourage children and young adults to read for personal satisfaction. Books are nominated by children in grades 4 through 8.

A master list of 20 titles is sent to participating elementary and middle schools. Students read the books and vote on their favorites each February. This program may be sponsored by public libraries if the schools in the area choose not to participate.

Deadline: Students vote in February.

Representative winners: *Harry Potter and the Sorcerer's Stone,* J. K. Rowling.

Announcements: Winning title is announced in March.

Award: Winners receive a plaque.

Children's Writer Contests

Children's Writer
95 Long Ridge Road
West Redding, CT 06896
www.childrenswriter.com

Children's Writer newsletter sponsors two contests each year with different themes for original, unpublished fiction and nonfiction. In 2002, the themes will be profiles in history and YA fiction.

Entry fee, $10 for non-subscribers (includes an eight-month subscription); no entry fee for subscribers. Multiple entries are accepted. Entries are judged on originality, writing quality, characterization, plot, and age-appropriateness. Submission lengths range from 200 to 1,200 words, but vary for each contest; send an SASE for complete details.

Deadline: February and October of each year.

Representative winners: *Butterfly Picnic,* Beverly Letchworth; *The Night of Radishes,* Denise Marchionda.

Announcements: Winners will be announced by mail and in *Children's Writer.*

Award: Winners receive cash prizes ranging from $250 to $500 depending on the contest. Winning entries will be published in *Children's Writer.*

Mr. Christie's Book Award

Nabisco Ltd.
95 Moatfield Drive
Toronto, Ontario M3B 3L6
Canada
www.nabisco.ca

The purpose of the Mr. Christie's Book Award is to honor excellence in the writing and illustration of Canadian children's literature and to encourage the development and publishing of high-quality children's books that will promote a love of reading. The competition is open to all Canadian writers, and accepts books published in the year preceding the contest.

Entries are judged on intellectual and emotional values, high integrity, and their effectiveness in reflecting and exploring the world of childhood. Send an SASE for complete competition guidelines and further information.

Deadline: January 31.

Representative winners: *The Polar Bear's Gift,* Jeanne Bushley; *Cat's Eye Corner,* Terry Griggs; *Before Wings,* Beth Goobie.

Announcements: Winners will be announced in June.

Award: The grand-prize winner receives a cash award of $7,500. Other winners receive a gold or silver seal on their books and are honored at an awards dinner.

Christopher Award

The Christophers
12 East 48th Street
New York, NY 10017
www.christophers.org

Established in 1949, the Christo-pher Awards are presented each year to the producers, writers, and directors of books, motion pictures, and television specials that affirm the highest values of the human spirit. The awards look to recognize creative work that goes beyond entertainment to educate and inspire their audience.

No entry fees. To be eligible for the book categories, entries must be published in the year preceding the contest. Send four copies of each title with a press kit, press release, or catalogue copy. Send an SASE for complete competition guidelines.

Deadline: November.

Representative winners: *How Do Dinosaurs Say Goodnight?,* Jane Yolen; *The Wanderer,* Sharon Creech; *The Mousery,* Charlotte Pomerantz.

Announcements: Winners are announced in February.

Award: Winners are presented with bronze medallions at a ceremony in February.

CNW/FFWA Florida State Writing Competition

CNW/FFWA
P.O. Box A
North Stratford, NH 03590
www.writers-editors.com

Open to all writers, this annual contest offers prizes in several divisions including nonfiction, fiction, children's literature, and poetry. Each division also has two subcategories.

Entry fees for members of CNW/FFWA, $5 for entries of less than 3,000 words; $10 for entries of more than 3,000 words; and $3 for poetry submissions. Entry fees for non-members, $10 for entries of less than 3,000 words; $20 for entries of more than 3,000 words; and $5 for poetry submissions. All entries must be previously unpublished. Multiple entries are accepted provided an official entry form accompanies each submission. Author's name must not appear on manuscript itself. Include a separate cover sheet with name, address, and phone number. Send an SASE for complete competition guidelines and entry forms.

Deadline: March 15.

Representative winners: "The Last Best Gift," Kathryn Umbarger; "Pickles, Pumpkins and Parents," Ellaraine Lockie; "Challenge the Wind," Debra Tash.

Announcements: Winners are announced on the website after May 31.

Award: Winners receive cash awards ranging from $25 to $75 for first-through third-place. First-place winners also receive a certificate.

The Dana Awards

Mary Elizabeth Parker, Chair
7207 Townsend Forest Court
Browns Summit, NC 27214-9634
www.pipeline.com/~danaawards

The Dana Awards offer cash prizes for work that has not yet been published. Awards are presented in three categories: short fiction, novel, and poetry. Entries should be clear and concise, with well-developed themes.

Entry fees, one short story or five poems, $10; novel entries, $20. Visit the website or send an SASE for specific word length requirements and guidelines. Include a cover sheet with author's name,

address, telephone number, e-mail address, title of work, and category. Author's name should be on the manuscript itself. Multiple submissions are accepted provided each submission is accompanied by a separate cover sheet and entry fee. Manuscripts will not be returned; all are recycled. Send an SASE for winners' list. For questions regarding the Dana Awards e-mail to danaawards@pipelines.com.

Deadline: October 31.

Representative winners: *The Final Effort of the Archer,* Michael Pritchett; *The Stephen Hawking Death Row Fan Club,* Robert C. Goodwin.

Announcements: Winners will be notified by the end of the year.

Award: Winners in each of the three categories receive a cash award of $1,000.

Marguerite de Angeli Contest

Delacorte Press Books for Young
  Readers
1540 Broadway
New York, NY 10036

Open to US and Canadian writers who have not yet published a novel for middle-grade readers, the Marguerite de Angeli Contest is held annually.

Entries should be targeted to children ages 7 to 10 and may be contemporary or historical fiction that is set in North America. Manuscripts should be between 80 and 144 typewritten pages. Include a cover letter containing a brief plot summary. Send an SASE for return of manuscript.

Manuscripts submitted to this competition may not be submitted to other publishers while under consideration for this contest. Limit two entries per competition.

Deadline: Manuscripts must be postmarked between April 1 and June 30.

Representative winners: *Some Kind of Pride,* Maria Testa; *A Letter to Mrs. Roosevelt,* C. Coco De Young.

Announcements: Announcement of winners is made on October 31.

Award: Winners receive publication of their book, a $1,500 cash prize, and a $3,500 advance against royalties.

Delacorte Press Prize for a First Young Adult Novel

Delacorte Press/Random House
    Children's Books
1540 Broadway
New York, NY 10036
www.randomhouse.com

Open to all US and Canadian writers who have not yet published a young adult novel, this award is presented annually to encourage the writing of contemporary young adult fiction. Manuscripts previously submitted to Delacorte Press are not eligible for submission to this contest.

Submissions should consist of a book-length manuscript with a contemporary setting that is suitable for readers ages 12 to 18. Manuscripts should be between 100 and 224 pages.

Each manuscript should include a cover letter with author's name, address, and telephone number. It should also include a note on whether the submission is to be returned. Manuscripts submitted to Delacorte Press may not be submitted to other publishers while under consideration for the prize.

Deadline: Entries should be postmarked between October 1 and December 31.

Representative winners: *Night Flying,* Rita Murphy; *Breaking Boxes,* A. M. Jenkins; *Life Belts,* Jane Hosie-Bounar.

Announcements: Contest results will be announced no later than April 30. Winners will be announced in *Publishers Weekly* and *School Library Journal.*

Award: A book contract covering world rights for hardcover and paperback is awarded. Winner receives $1,500 in cash, and $6,000 advance on royalties.

Distinguished Achievement Awards

The Association of Educational
    Publishers
201 Mullica Hill Road
Glassboro, NJ 08028
www.edpress.org

The Association of Educational Publishers, known as EdPress, sponsors these annual awards. Through these awards, EdPress looks to recognize the industry's very best in writing, editing, art, and design in print publications and audio/visual media. Entries are accepted in 64 categories including short story, nonfiction, instructional material, and software for children, young adults, and adults.

Entry fee, $125 per submission for non-members; $75 per piece for members. Multiple submissions will be accepted. Requirements vary for each category. Send an SASE or visit the website for complete list of categories and further information on the competition.

Deadline: Entries should be postmarked by January 14.

Representative winners: 2001 winning publications: *Student Discovery; Careers & Colleges; American School Board Journal.*

Announcements: Winners will be announced in the spring.

Award: Winners in each category will be presented with a plaque at the EdPress annual awards banquet.

Violet Downey Book Award

The National Chapter of
   Canada IODE
Suite 254
40 Orchard View Blvd.
Toronto, Ontario M4R 1B9
Canada
www.iodecanada.com

Presented annually by the National Chapter of Canada IODE, this award is given for the best English language book suitable for children up to age 13, which has less than 500 words.

All entries must have been written by Canadian citizens, and published in Canada. Submissions are made by publishers. Although entries may be on any subject, preference is shown to entries with Canadian content. Send an SASE or visit the website for complete guidelines.

Deadline: December 31.

Representative winners: *Alone at Ninety Foot,* Katherine Holubitsky; *Janey's Girl,* Gale Friesen.

Announcements: Winners will be announced at the annual meeting in May or June.

Award: Winners receive a cash prize of $3,000.

Arthur Ellis Awards

Crime Writers of Canada
3007 Kingston Road
Box 113
Scarborough, Ontario M1M 1P1
Canada
www.crimewriterscanada.com

Established in 1984 by the Crime Writers of Canada, this award honors the best work published by Canadian authors in the crime writing genre. All entries must have been published in the year preceding the contest.

Awards are presented in five categories: best true crime; best short story; best novel; best first crime; and best juvenile award.

Entries may deal with espionage, suspense, mystery, and thriller fiction. Entrants must be residents of Canada or Canadian citizens living in other countries. For complete category guidelines and further information, send an SASE or visit the website.

Deadline: January 31.

Representative winners: *Sins of the Father,* Norah McClintock; *Sudden Blow,* Liz Brady; *Last Inning,* Scott MacKay; *No Claim to Mercy,* Derek Finkle.

Announcements: Winners are announced in May.

Award: Award winners receive the "Arthur Statuette."

Empire State Award

New York Library Association
Youth Service Section
252 Hudson Street
Albany, NY 12210-1802

Sponsored by the Youth Service Section of the New York Library Association, this award is presented annually for a body of work by a New York author that represents excellence in children's or young adult literature. Nominated books should make a significant contribution to literature for young people. Books may be nominated by members of the Youth Service Section or committee members of the New York Library Association. Send an SASE for complete details.

Deadline: November 30.

Representative winners: Jean Fritz, Peter Spier, Vera B. Williams.

Announcements: Winner will be announced in May at the spring conference.

Award: Winner receives an engraved medallion.

Shubert Fendrich Memorial Playwriting Contest
Pioneer Drama Service
P.O. Box 4267
Englewood, CO 80155-4267
www.pioneerdrama.com

In tribute to Shubert Fendrich, the founder of Pioneer Drama Service, this contest is held annually to encourage the development of quality theatrical material for educational and community theaters.

Individuals currently published by Pioneer Drama Service are not eligible to enter into this competition. The competition accepts unpublished plays on any subject, but should be suitable for family-oriented audiences and theater groups. Plays should have a running time of 20 to 90 minutes, and must have been produced at least once. Send an SASE for complete contest information, or visit the website.

Deadline: March 1.

Representative winners: Peg Kehret, Bill Francoeur, Vern Hardin, Jack Kocher.

Announcements: Winners will be announced in June.

Award: Winners will receive a $1,000 royalty advance in addition to publication.

Dorothy Canfield Fisher Award
DCF Committee
Northeast Regional Library
State of Vermont Department of
   Libraries
23 Tilton Road
St. Johnsbury, VT 05819

The competition for this award encourages Vermont children to become discriminating and enthusiastic readers. During the school year, a master list of 30 of the most distinguished books for children, published in the previous year, is given to children in grades four through eight. The students then vote on their favorite books.

Nominations to be included in the master list will only be accepted from publishers. Send an SASE for complete competition guidelines.

Deadline: January.

Representative winners: *Bud, Not Buddy,* Christopher Paul Curtis; *Holes,* Louis Sachar.

Announcements: Announcement of winners is made in March.

Award: Winning authors receive a scroll and are keynote speakers at the Claremont Reading Conference.

Norma Fleck Award

The Canadian Children's Book Centre
Suite 101
400 Orchard View Boulevard
Toronto, Ontario M4R 1B9
Canada
www.bookcentre.ca

Honoring Norma Fleck's extraordinary contribution to the field of children's literature, this annual award is presented to an author or illustrator of Canadian nonfiction for children. Entries must show exceptional quality and present the subject matter in a way that excites interest.

Recipients are chosen by a jury, with each member possessing a deep understanding of Canadian children's books, as well as a deep involvement in the field. Send an SASE or visit the website for complete competition guidelines.

Deadline: April 30.
Representative winners: Nominees for the 2001 award include: *Born to Be a Cowgirl: A Spirited Ride through the Old West,* Candace Savage; *The Kids Book of the Far North,* Ann Love and Jane Drake.
Announcements: Winners were announced in October.
Award: A $10,000 cash award will be presented to the winner.

Foster City International Writers' Contest

Foster City Art & Cultural Committee
650 Shell Boulevard
Foster City, CA 94404

Open to all writers, this annual contest is sponsored by the Foster City Art & Culture Committee. It accepts previously unpublished entries in the categories of short fiction, humor, short children's story, rhymed verse, and blank verse.

Entry fee, $10 per submission. Accepts photocopies and computer printouts. Entries should be typed, double-spaced, and should have a 3x5 card attached with the author's name, address, phone number, manuscript title, and category. Manuscripts will not be returned. Send an SASE for complete competition guidelines and specific category information.
Deadline: October 31.
Announcements: Winners are announced in December.
Award: First-place winners in each category receive a cash award of $250. Honorable mentions receive $125.

H. E. Francis Short Story Competition

English Department
University of Alabama, Huntsville
Huntsville, AL 35899

Sponsored by the Ruth Hindman Foundation and the University of Alabama, this annual contest is open to all writers. It accepts previously unpublished entries up to 5,000 words.

Entry fee, $15 per submission. Send three copies of each manuscript. Include a cover sheet with author's name, address, and phone number; author's name should not appear on manuscript. Simultaneous submissions are accepted as long as the competition is notified immediately if that manuscript is accepted elsewhere. Entries will be judged by a panel of recognized, award-winning authors, directors of creative writing programs, and editors of literary journals.

Deadline: December 31.

Representative winners: 2001 winner: *This Is So Not Me,* Natalie Serber. 2001 runners-up: *Waiting for the Pink,* Laura Hunter; *Long Past Time,* James Hunter; *Blue Moon Mountain,* Michael G. Johnson.

Announcements: Winners will be notified in March.

Award: Winners of this contest receive a cash award of $1,000.

Don Freeman Memorial Grant-In-Aid

Society of Children's Book Writers
& Illustrators
8271 Beverly Boulevard
Los Angeles, CA 90048
www.scbwi.org

The Don Freeman Memorial Grant-In-Aid was established by SCBWI to enable picture book artists to further their understanding, training, and work in the picture book genre.

This grant is available to both full and associate members of SCBWI who, as artists, seriously intend to make picture books their chief contribution to the field of children's literature. If you are not currently a member, visit the website for further information.

Applicants are required to submit artwork, either a rough book-dummy accompanied by two illustrations or ten finished illustrations suitable for a picture book portfolio presentation. Send an SASE for complete guidelines and artwork specifications.

Deadline: Requests for applications may be made beginning June 1 of each year. Completed application and materials will be accepted between January 10 and February 10.

Representative winners: Yuri Morales.

Announcements: Winners will be announced in June.

Award: The winner receives a grant of $1,500. One runner-up receives a $500 grant.

Danuta Gleed Literary Award for First Book of Fiction

The Writers' Union of Canada
Third Floor
40 Wellington Street East
Toronto, Ontario M5E 1C7
Canada
www.writersunion.ca

This award presents a cash prize for the best collection of short fiction, written in the English language. The award was initiated by John Gleed in honor of his late wife, and celebrates the genre of short fiction, which she loved.

The competition is open to Canadian writers who have published their first collection of short fiction in the year preceding the contest. Entrants should submit four copies of each entry for the judges. Visit the website or send an SASE for complete information on this competition.

Deadline: January.

Representative winners: *Message for Mr. Lazarus,* Barbara Lambert.

Announcements: Winners will be announced on Canada Book Day, April 23.

Award: Winners of this award receive a cash prize of $5,000. Honorable mentions receive $500.

Golden Archer Awards
Wisconsin Educational Media
    Association
Mary Ann Blahnik
Sturgeon Bay Public Schools
1230 Michigan Street
Sturgeon Bay, WI 54235

The Golden Archer Awards are presented in three categories: primary, intermediate, and middle/junior high. Nominations for books are solicited from students. Librarians will then choose five nominations that meet the eligibility criteria. Books should be recognized as noteworthy in quality and of special interest to children. Books must have been published in the United States and should be currently in print and readily available

A nominations committee determines the titles for each age level to be a part of the competition. This list of titles is sent to each librarian that is a member of the Wisconsin Educational Media Association, and others upon request. They then vote on the winners.
Deadline: Final votes are due March 15.
Announcements: Winners are announced in April.
Award: Winners are presented with bronze medals and certificates.

Golden Kite Award
Society of Children's Book Writers
    & Illustrators
8271 Beverly Boulevard
Los Angeles, CA 90048
www.scbwi.org

This award is presented to children's book authors and illustrators by their fellow authors and artists, for work that the judges feel exhibit excellence in writing or illustrating.

Accepts entries from SCBWI members only, and encourages those who are not members to sign up. Awards are presented in several categories including fiction, nonfiction, picture illustration, and collections of stories.

Submit 3 copies of each entry. Limit one entry per competition. Send an SASE for complete information.
Deadline: Entries may be submitted between February 1 and December 15.
Representative winners: *The Boxer,* Kathleen Karr; *River Friendly, River Wild,* Jane Kurtz; *Darkness Over Denmark,* Ellen Levine.
Announcements: Winners will be announced in April.
Award: Winners are presented with a statuette at the Golden Kite Luncheon during the annual SCBWI summer conference.

Gold Medallion Book Awards
Evangelical Christian Publishers
    Association
Suite 2
1969 East Broadway Road
Tempe, AZ 85282
www.ecpa.org

Established in 1978, the Gold Medallion Book Awards recognize the absolute highest quality in Christian Books. The awards program looks for books that are the finest examples of evangelical publishing.

Awards are presented in several categories including preschool, elementary, youth, reference, marriage, Christian education, family and parenting, biography, devotional, and nonfiction. Winners are based on excellence in content, literary quality, design, and significance of contribution.

Books must be submitted by the publishers. Entry fee, $125 per title for EPCA members; $275 for non-members. Send an SASE or visit the website for complete category list and further guidelines.

Deadline: December.

Representative winners: *Paul: A Novel*, Walter Wangerin; *Extreme Faith*, Tim Baker; *A Faith to Grow On*, John MacArthur.

Announcements: Entry forms are sent in October. Winners are announced at the annual Gold Medallion Book Awards Banquet.

Award: Winners receive a plaque at the annual banquet.

Governor General's Literary Awards

Canada Council for the Arts
350 Albert Street
Ottawa, Ontario K1P 5UB
Canada
www.canadacouncil.ca

The Governor General's Literary Awards are given annually to honor the best English-language and best French-language work by a Canadian writer, translator, or illustrator. It offers seven categories including fiction, children's literature, nonfiction, drama, and poetry.

Eligible titles will have been published in the year preceding the contest. Books may be published in Canada or abroad, but all entries should be written or illustrated by Canadian citizens. Entries should be at least 48 pages long, except for chil-

dren's picture books, which should have a minimum of 24 pages. Works by more than one author are not eligible. Send an SASE or visit the website for complete competition guidelines.

Deadline: August.

Representative winners: *Looking for X*, Deborah Ellis; *Anil's Ghost*, Michael Ondaatje.

Announcements: Winners will be announced in November.

Award: A $15,000 cash award will be presented to the winners in each category.

Aurand Harris Memorial Playwriting Award

New England Theater Conference
Northeastern University
360 Huntington Avenue
Boston, MA 02115
www.netconline.org

The Aurand Harris Memorial Playwriting Award is looking for full-length play submissions targeted to young audiences. Created in 1997, it honors the late Aurand Harris for his lifetime dedication to all aspects of professional theater for young audiences.

The contest is open to all playwrights that are living in New England and NETC members (playwrights living outside New England can join NETC to enter this contest). Entries must be previously unpublished. Musicals will not be accepted. Limit one entry per year. Entry fee, $20. Manuscripts will not be returned. Send an SASE or visit the website for complete competition guidelines.

Deadline: May 1.

Representative winners: *Riding the*

Wind: Story Plays from Old China, Carol Korty.

Announcements: Competition is announced in December. Winners will be notified by mail and on the website in September.

Award: First-place winners receive $1,000 and a staged reading of their play. Second-place winners receive a cash prize of $500.

Lorian Hemingway Short Story Competition

P.O. Box 993
Key West, FL 33041
www.shortstorycompetition.com

This competition was established in honor of Lorian Hemingway to recognize and encourage the efforts of those who have not yet received major success in publishing. It accepts short stories in several genres of fiction. Submissions should not exceed the 3,000-word limit.

Entry fee, $10 for submissions postmarked by June 1; $15 for submissions postmarked between June 1 and June 15. Multiple entries are accepted as long as each entry is accompanied by the entry fee. Send an SASE or visit the website for complete competition guidelines and further information.

Deadline: June 15.

Representative winners: *Mira Instead,* Kate Small; *Only Children,* Greg Tebbano; *The Lighthouse Keeper,* Neale McDevitt.

Announcements: Winners will be announced in August.

Award: Winners receive a cash prize of $1,000; honorable mention receives $500.

Highlights for Children Fiction Contest

Marileta Robinson, Senior Editor
Highlights for Children
803 Church Street
Honesdale, PA 18431
www.highlights.com

Highlights for Children sponsors this annual fiction competition with a different theme each year. The theme for 2002 is "Stories About Today's Kids." The contest was put in place to recognize and encourage those who create high-quality writing for children.

No entry fee. Entries should not exceed 900 words. Multiple entries are accepted; each entry must be accompanied by an SASE. Accepts photocopies and computer printouts. Send an SASE or visit the website for complete details.

Deadline: February 28.

Announcements: Winners will be announced in the spring after the contest.

Award: Three prizes of $1,000 will be awarded. The winning entries will be published in *Highlights for Children.*

Insight Writing Contests

Insight Magazine
55 West Oak Ridge Drive
Hagerstown, MD 21740
www.insightmagazine.org

This annual contest values the power of stories and poems, written from a spiritual perspective, and their power to change lives for eternity. It accepts short nonfiction and poetry written for young adults ages 14–22.

Multiple entries are accepted. No entry fee. Accepts computer printouts and e-mail submissions to insight@rhpa.org. Entries should not exceed 1,500 words.

All entries will be considered for publication in *Insight*. Entries will be judged on grammar, storyline, description, and dialogue.

Deadline: June 1.

Representative winners: *"I Just Wanna Be A Sheep,"* Christina Dotson; *"My Night in a Compost Pile,"* Ash Howe.

Announcements: Winners will be announced in a special winners' issue.

Award: Cash awards ranging from $150 to $250 will be awarded. Winning entries will be published in *Insight* (first rights are required).

Inspirational Writers Open Competition

Inspirational Writers Alive
6038 Greenmont
Houston, TX 77092-2332

Sponsored by Inspirational Writers Alive!, this annual competition encourages both new and beginning writers to sharpen their skills. Each entry will be returned with a full critique.

Entry fee, $7 for members; $10 for non-members. Entries must be previously unpublished and may be short stories of up to 1,200 words, poetry, or a book synopsis with three sample chapters (limit 50 pages). Multiple entries will not be accepted. Send an SASE for complete competition guidelines and further information.

Deadline: May 15.

Announcements: Winners will be announced in August.

Award: Cash prizes ranging from $10 to $25 will be awarded.

IRA Children's Book Awards

International Reading Association
P.O. Box 8139
Newark, DE 19714-8139
www.reading.org

These awards are presented annually for an author's first or second published book in the genres of fiction and nonfiction. Two awards will be presented in each genre: one for young readers (ages 4–10); and one for older readers (ages 11–17).

Entries may be submitted by the author or publisher. Entries should not contain racism, violence, or sexism, but rather encourage young people to read by giving them something they will profit from reading. Entries must be sent to the designated IRA Children's Book Award Committee Members. Send an SASE for further information.

Deadline: November 1.

Representative winners: Carl R. Sams and Jean Stoick; Peggy Brooke; Sophie Webb.

Announcements: Winners will be announced at the beginning of the year.

Award: Winners are presented with a cash award of $500 and a medal.

Barbara Karlin Grant

Society of Children's Book Writers
    & Illustrators
8271 Beverly Boulevard
Los Angeles, CA 90048
www.scbwi.org

The Barbara Karlin Grant was established to recognize and encourage the work of aspiring picture book writers. It is available to full and associate members of SCBWI who have not yet published a picture book. If you are not currently a member of SCBWI, visit the website for complete details.

One picture book manuscript per applicant may be submitted. The text may be an original story, work of non-fiction, or a re-telling or adaptation of a fairy tale, folktale, or legend. Send an SASE or visit the website for complete information and application.

Deadline: Requests for applications may be made beginning October 1 of each year. Complete application and materials will be accepted between April 1 and May 15.

Representative winners: Toni Buzzeo.

Announcements: Winners will be announced in August.

Award: One grant of $1,500 will be presented to the winner. One runner-up grant of $500 will also be awarded.

Ezra Jack Keats New Writers Award
The New York Public Library
Early Childhood Resource and
   Information Center
66 Leroy Street
New York, NY 10014

Honoring books that portray the universal qualities of childhood, strong family and adult relationships, and the multicultural nature of our world, this award is given to a new writer of picture books for ages 9 and under. All entries should reflect the style of award-winning author and illustrator, Ezra Jack Keats.

To be eligible for this contest, writers should have published no more than five books. No entry fee. Winners must be present to accept this award.

Send an SASE for complete contest information.

Deadline: December 15.

Representative winners: *Dear Juno*, Soyung Pak.

Announcements: Award winners will be announced in January.

Award: Winners will receive a cash award of $1,000 and an Ezra Jack Keats silver medallion.

The Kerlan Essay Award
Kerlan Collection
113 Andersen Library
222 21st Avenue South
Minneapolis, MN 55455
http://special.lib.umn.edu

The Friends of the Kerlan Collection present this annual award for an outstanding paper written during the preceding school year by a college or university student using the resources of the Children's Literature Research Collections. The purpose of the award is to promote the Kerlan Collection, and it is given in recognition of outstanding research utilizing the original resources available in the Kerlan Collection. Judges will look for topics that have been fully researched. Writing style and organization are key components of this competition.

No entry fee. Accepts computer printouts and clear photocopies. Send an SASE or visit the website for complete competition guidelines.

Deadline: June 1.

Announcements: Winners will be announced in early or mid-summer.

Award: The award consists of a citation and a cash prize of $300.

Coretta Scott King Award

American Library Association
50 East Huron
Chicago, IL 60611
www.ala.org

The Coretta Scott King Task Force of the American Library Association's Social Responsibilities Round Table sponsors this annual award. Recipients are authors and illustrators of African American descent whose distinguished books promote an understanding and appreciation of the "American Dream."

The Coretta Scott King Award celebrates the life and work of Dr. Martin Luther King, Jr., and is named for his widow. Winners will be chosen by a seven-member jury. Visit the website or send an SASE for complete competition guidelines and further information.

Deadline: Ongoing.

Representative winners: *Miracle Boys,* Jacqueline Woodson.

Award: Winners receive a framed citation, an honorarium, and a set of Encyclopaedia Brittanica or World Book Encyclopaedia.

Ursula Le Guin Award for Imaginative Fiction

Rosebud Magazine
P.O. Box 459
Cambridge, WI 53523
www.rsbd.net

Sponsored by *Rosebud Magazine,* this award is presented annually for imaginative fiction in the genres of fantasy, horror, and science fiction. It accepts previously unpublished entries only.

Entry fee, $10 per piece. Accepts computer printouts and multiple submissions. Entries should be 3,000 words or less. Final judging will be done by Ursula Le Guin. Send an SASE or visit the website for complete competition guidelines.

Deadline: October 31.

Announcements: Winners will be announced at the beginning of the year.

Award: Competition winner receives a cash award of $1,000 and publication in *Rosebud* (requires first serial rights). Four honorable mentions will also be announced with the possibility of publication.

Magazine Merit Awards

Society of Children's Book Writers
and Illustrators
8271 Beverly Blvd.
Los Angeles, CA 90048
www.scbwi.org

This awards competition is open to members of SCBWI. The awards recognize and honor fiction and nonfiction magazine articles for young people published during the previous calendar year.

No entry fee. Send four copies of the published work showing proof of publication: name of magazine, and publication date. Multiple entries are accepted. Send an SASE or visit the website for complete details.

Deadline: Entries accepted between January 31 and December 15.

Representative winners: *Si-Linh and the Dragon,* Joan Harlow; *No Cross Words Allowed,* Natalie M. Rosinsky; *Mountain Spring,* Stefi Weisburd.

Announcements: Contest is announced in January. Winners are announced in April.

Listings

Award: Winners receive a plaque. Honor certificates are also awarded.

David McCord Children's Literature Citation

Framingham State College
100 State Street
P.O. Box 9101
Framingham, MA 01701-9101

The David McCord Children's Literature Citation was put in place to honor David McCord's long and enduring contribution to the genre. The award looks to honor an author or illustrator for a body of work that has made a significant contribution to excellence in the field of children's literature.

Winners are chosen by a committee of four librarians and teachers. Send an SASE for complete competition details.
Deadline: Ongoing.
Representative winners: Jack Prelutsky; Kevin Henkes.
Announcements: Winners will be chosen in November.
Award: The winner is honored at the David McCord Children's Literature Festival in November.

Merlyn's Pen Short Story Contest

Merlyn's Pen
P.O. Box 910
East Greenwich, RI 02818
www.merlynspen.com

Merlyn's Pen sponsors this annual contest and accepts stories on all topics and in all story genres including personal narratives and true stories. The contest is open to writers in grades six through twelve. Prizes will be awarded in two categories: grades 6–9 and grades 10–12.

Entries should be between 600 and 7,500 words. Entry fee, $1. Multiple entries are accepted; each entry must be stapled to its own cover sheet. The contest cover sheets are available with an SASE or through the website.
Deadline: March 1.
Announcements: Winners will be announced in June.
Award: Top-prize winners in both categories will receive a cash award of $500. Winning entries will be published in *Merlyn's Pen*.

The Vicky Metcalf Awards

Canadian Authors Association
P.O. Box 419
320 South Shores Road
Campelford, Ontario K0L 1L0
Canada
www.CanAuthors.org

Established in 1963 by the Toronto librarian whose name they bear, these awards are presented in three categories: body of work; short story published in English; and to the editor responsible for publishing the prize-winning short story, if it was published in a Canadian periodical or anthology.

These awards are presented to stimulate writing for children by Canadian writers.
Deadline: December 31.
Representative winners: Linga Granfield; Wendy Lewis.
Announcements: Winners will be announced in June.
Award: The body of work categories offers a cash award of $10,000. The short story award offers a cash award of

$3,000; and $1,000 is awarded to the short story editor.

Milkweed Editions Prize for Children's Literature

Milkweed Editions
Suite 400
430 First Avenue North
Minneapolis, MN 55401-1473
www.milkweed.org

This annual prize is awarded to the best novel for children ages 8 through 13. Milkweed stresses the importance for quality writing for this age group because they feel this group is not well served by many publishers.

All submissions should be previously unpublished. Picture books and collections of stories are not eligible. Send an SASE for complete guidelines and further information.

Deadline: Ongoing.
Representative winners: *The $66 Summer,* John Armistead; *The Ocean Within,* V. M. Caldwell.
Announcements: Winner will be announced no later than October 31.
Award: Winner receives a cash advance of $10,000 on royalties.

Milkweed National Fiction Prize

Milkweed Editions
Suite 400
430 First Avenue North
Minneapolis, MN 55401-1473
www.milkweed.org

Milkweed Editions, a nonprofit literary press, presents this annual prize for the most outstanding work submitted to Milkweed during the calendar year. The prize will only be awarded to those not previously published by Milkweed.

Manuscripts may be a collection of short stories, one or more novellas, or a combination of short stories. No length requirements. No entry fee. Send an SASE or visit the website for complete details.

Deadline: Ongoing.
Representative winners: *Falling Dark,* Tim Tharp; *Tivolem,* Victor Rangel-Ribeiro; *The Tree of Red Stars,* Tessa Bridal.
Announcements: Announcement of winner is made upon publication.
Award: Winner receives a cash advance of $7,500 on royalties.

Minnesota Book Awards

Minnesota Center for the Book
987 East Ivy Avenue
Saint Paul, MN 55106
www.mnbooks.org

The Minnesota Book Awards looks to honor authors from Minnesota. Entries may be submitted in 10 categories: young adult literature; children's literature; fine press; autobiography; anthology and collections; history and biography; nature and Minnesota; poetry; mystery; novel and short story; and popular fiction.

No entry fee. Entries must have been published in the year preceding the contest. All submissions must be accompanied by an entry form and three copies of the book. Send an SASE or visit the website for complete category guidelines.

Deadline: December 15.
Representative winners: *Packinghouse Daughter: A Memoir,* Cheri Register; *The*

Hunter, Mary Casanova; *Curse of the Winter Moon,* Mary Casanova.

Announcements: Winners will be notified in January.

Award: Winners will be honored at an awards celebration.

Mythopoeic Awards
P.O. Box 320486
San Francisco, CA 94132-0486
www.mythsoc.org

The Mythopoeic Society sponsors these awards annually to encourage writers to pursue the fantasy genre. Four awards will be presented: Fantasy Award for Adult Literature; Scholarship Award in Inklings Studies; Fantasy Award in Children's Literature; and Scholarship Award in General Myth and Fantasy Studies. The Fantasy in Children's Literature Award honors books for younger readers to young adults and includes picture books.

Books are nominated and judged by members of the Mythopoeic Society. All nominations must have been published in the year preceding the contest. Send an SASE for complete information and guidelines.

Deadline: February 28.

Representative winners: *Aria of the Sea,* Dia Calhoun; *The Innamorati,* Midori Snyder; *King Arthur in America,* Alan and Barbara Tepa Lupack.

Announcements: Competition is announced in December. Winners are announced at the annual Mythopoeic Conference during the summer.

Award: Winners are presented with a statuette of a lion, intended to evoke Aslan from C. S. Lewis's Chronicles of Narnia.

The National Book Awards
The National Book Foundation
95 Madison Avenue
New York, NY 10016
www.nationalbook.org

These annual awards honor great American literature in fiction, nonfiction, poetry, and young people's literature, and to increase the popularity of reading in general. The competition looks to enhance the public's awareness of exceptional books written by Americans, to encourage a love of reading.

Entries must be submitted by publishers. Entry fee, $100. All entries must have been published in the United States, during the year preceding the contest. E-books will also be accepted.

Deadline: July.

Representative winners: *Homeless Bird,* Gloria Whelan; *In America,* Susan Sontag; *In the Heart of the Sea: The Tragedy of the Whaleship Essex,* Nathaniel Philbrick.

Announcements: Announcement of winners is made in November.

Award: Winners in each category receive $10,000. Finalists receive $100.

National Children's Theatre Festival Playwriting Competition
Actors' Playhouse at Miracle Theatre
280 Miracle Mile
Coral Gables, FL 33134
www.actorsplayhouse.org

Sponsored by Actors' Playhouse at Miracle Theatre, this annual competition looks for original musical scripts for judging by a distinguished panel from both professional and academic theater. Scripts should be intended for a target audience of ages 5 through 12 and have a 45–60 minute running time. The competition accepts previously unpublished scripts, but works that have limited production exposure, or staged readings are encouraged.

Entry fee, $10 per submission. Accepts photocopies and computer printouts. Send an SASE for the return of manuscript. Competition guidelines are available on the website or with an SASE.

Deadline: August 1.

Announcements: Winners will be notified in October.

Award: Winners receive a cash prize of $500 and full production of their play (requires performance rights for a limited time).

National Written By and Illustrated By...Awards Contest for Students
Landmark Editions, Inc.
P.O. Box 270169
Kansas City, MO 64127

This annual contest is open to students and presents awards in three categories: ages 6 to 9; ages 10 to 13; and ages 14 to 19. Most genres are accepted including biography, humor, mystery, science fiction, and fantasy. Entries may be either prose or poetry and should be between 16 and 24 pages.

Books are judged on the merits of originality and the writing and illustrating skills displayed. Entry fee, $2. All entries must be accompanied by an entry form, and must be signed by a teacher or librarian to qualify. For complete competition guidelines and further information, send an SASE.

Deadline: May 1.

Announcements: Winners will be announced in October.

Award: Winners in each category will have their work published.

John Newbery Award
Association for Library Service to
    Children
American Library Association (ALA)
50 East Huron Street
Chicago, IL 60611
www.ala.org/alsc/newbery.html

The John Newbery Award is recognized as the most prestigious award in the field of children's literature in the US. It has been presented annually since 1922 and honors the authors of the most distinguished original contributions to children's literature during the preceding calendar year. This competition accepts entries by US citizens or residents of the US.

No entry fee. Multiple submissions are accepted. Entries should demonstrate respect for children's understandings, abilities, and appreciations. Co-authored books are also accepted. Visit the website or send an SASE for complete information.

Deadline: December 31.

Representative winners: *A Year Down Yonder*, Richard Peck; *Bud, Not Buddy*, Christopher Paul Curtis.

Announcements: Winners will be announced at the ALA mid-winter meeting in January or February.

Award: The Newbery Medal is presented at an awards banquet. Honor books may also be chosen.

New Voices New Worlds First Novel Award

Hyperion Books for Children
8271 Beverly Blvd.
Los Angeles, CA 90048
www.hyperionbooksforchildren.com

Sponsored by Hyperion Books for Children, the New Voices New World First Novel Award looks for the best work of contemporary or historical fiction for ages 8 to 12, set in the US, that reflects the diverse ethnic and cultural heritage of our country. The competition is open to all US writers who have not yet published a novel.

No entry fee. Entry should be between 100 and 240 pages. An entry form is required. Entry forms are available on the website or with an SASE. Entries will be judged by the editors of Hyperion Books for Children. No simultaneous submissions. Send an SASE for return of manuscript.
Deadline: April 30.
Announcements: Winners are announced in August.
Award: Prizes include a standard book contract with a $7,500 advance, and a $1,500 cash prize.

No Noun-Sense Contests

Box 147-2211
No. 4 Road
Richmond, BC V6X 3X1
Canada
www.nonounsense.com

These contests are sponsored by *No Noun-Sense* and are presented in several categories including writing for children, romance, mystery, and nonfiction. The competition is open to all writers, new and experienced. The competition only accepts entries that are previously unpublished.

No length requirements. Entry fees vary for each category. Include a separate cover sheet with all contact information, story title, category, and word count. Visit the website or send an SASE for complete category list and further guidelines.
Deadline: Varies for each category.
Representative winners: *No Sneezes Please*, Tania Clarebrook; *Baby & the Bagpipes*, Andrew Osborne.
Announcements: Announcements of winners are made two months after competition deadline.
Award: First- through third-place winners receive cash prizes ranging from $25 to $200.

NWA Short Story Contest

National Writers Association
3140 S. Peoria Street #295
Aurora, CO 80014
www.nationalwriters.com

The National Writers Association presents this annual contest to encourage the development of creative skills and reward outstanding ability in the field of short story writing. Any genre of short story may be entered in this contest.

Entries should not exceed 5,000 words, and will be judged on marketability, originality, research, and reader interest. Entry fee, $15. Entrants that include an SASE with their entry will receive a judges' evaluation sheet. Entrants may also have a critique of their manuscript for a fee of $5 per 1,000 words.

All submissions must be typed, double-spaced, and written in English. Simultaneous submissions will be accepted, provided that the entry is not published prior to the contest winners being announced. Entries will not be returned without an SASE. Visit the website or send an SASE for complete information.

Deadline: July 1.

Announcements: Contest opens each April.

Award: First- through third-place winners receive cash awards. Fourth- through tenth-place winners will receive a book. Honorable mentions receive certificates.

Scott O'Dell Award
1700 East 56th Street
Chicago, IL 60637

The Scott O'Dell Award honors quality writing in the genre of historical fiction. Presented annually, it accepts entries from American citizens whose work was published during the year preceding the contest. Entries must be set in North, South, or Central America to be eligible for this award.

Entries are usually submitted by publishers, but authors may also submit their own work. Send an SASE for complete contest guidelines and entry forms.

Deadline: December 31.

Representative winners: *Forty Acres and Maybe a Mule,* Harriette Gillem Robinet.

Announcements: Award winners will be announced in the spring.

Award: Winners will receive a cash prize of $5,000.

Once Upon a World Children's Book Award
Simon Wiesenthal Center
Museum of Tolerance
1399 S. Roxbury Drive
Los Angeles, CA 90035-4709

This award honors the best English language books written for children ages 6 to 10. All books must have a theme of tolerance, diversity, human understanding, and social justice. Accepts entries of fiction, nonfiction, and poetry. All entries must have been published in the year preceding the contest.

No entry fees. Multiple entries are accepted. Send an SASE for competition guidelines.

Deadline: August.

Representative winners: *The Year of Miss Agnes,* Kirkpatrick Hill; *Through My Eyes,* Ruby Bridges.

Announcements: Winners will be announced in May or June.

Award: Winners receive a cash award of $1,000 and a trip to Los Angeles for an awards presentation.

Orbis Pictus Award for Outstanding Nonfiction for Children
National Council of Teachers of English (NCTE)
11 W. Kenyon Road
Urbana, IL 61801
www.ncte.org

Given annually, this award was established to promote and recognize excellence in the field of nonfiction for children.

Entries are nominated by NCTE members and the educational community. Nominated entries must be factually correct, with a clear sequence. The nominated entries should peak the interests of young people, revealing the authors enthusiasm.

All entries must have been published in the United States during the previous calendar year. Send an SASE or visit the website for complete competition guidelines and further information.

Deadline: November 30.

Representative winners: *Hurry Freedom: African Americans in Gold Rush California,* Jerry Stanley; *Through My Eyes,* Ruby Bridges and Margo Lundell.

Announcements: Winners will be announced at the NCTE Spring Conference.

Award: Winners receive a plaque and honor certificates.

Pacific Northwest Library Associations' Young Readers Choice Award

Marshall Public Library
113 S. Garfield
Pocatello, ID 83204
www.pnla.org

This annual award, sponsored by the Pacific Northwest Library Association, was established in 1940 and is the oldest children's choice award in Canada and the United States. The goal of this award is that every child will find a book that interests and entertains them.

Nominations are taken from children, teachers, parents, and librarians of the Pacific Northwest, which includes Washington, Oregon, Alaska, Idaho, Montana, British Columbia, and Alberta.

Books nominated for this award must have been published three years prior to the award year. All nominations must have been printed in the US or Canada. Titles are then voted on by students in fourth- through tenth-grade.

Deadline: February 1.

Announcements: Winners will be announced in April.

Award: Contest winners receive a cash award of $150 and a silver medal that is presented at an annual meeting and banquet.

Paterson Prize for Books for Young People

Maria Mazziotti Gilan, Director
The Poetry Center at Passaic County Community College
1 College Boulevard
Paterson, NJ 07505-1179

The Paterson Prize for Books for Young People honors the most outstanding book for young people, published in the year preceding the contest. The prize is awarded in three categories: Pre-K–Grade 3; Grades 4–6; and Grades 7–12. It accepts short stories, collections, short nonfiction, books, and poetry.

Publishers should submit three copies of each entry along with an entry form. Multiple submissions are accepted. Entries will not be returned; they will be donated to the Poetry Center Library at Pasaic County College. Include an SASE for list of winners. For additional information, send an SASE.

Deadline: March 15.

Representative winners: *Dear Juno,* Soyung Pak; *The Cello of Mr. O,* Jane Rutler; *Frenchtown Summer,* Robert Cormier.

Announcements: Competition is announced in September. Winners are announced in June.

Award: Winners receive a cash award of $500 and publication in *Poets & Writers Newsletter.*

PEN Center USA West Literary Award in Children's Literature

PEN Center USA West
Suite 41
672 S. Lafayette Park Place
Los Angeles, CA 90057
www.pen-usa-west.org

Recognizing outstanding works published or produced by writers who live in the western United States, this contest is held annually. Winners are selected in 10 categories including fiction, drama, nonfiction, and journalism.

The competition is open to authors who live west of the Mississippi River. Entries may be submitted by authors, publishers, or agents. All entries must have been published in the year preceding the contest. Send four copies of each entry. Entry fee, $20. Send an SASE or visit the website for complete competition guidelines.

Deadline: December 31.

Representative winners: *Ins and Walter,* Elissa Haden Guest; *Weslandia,* Paul Fleischman.

Announcements: Winners are announced in June.

Award: A cash award of $1,000 is presented to the winner in each category.

PEN/Norma Klein Award for Children's Fiction

PEN American Center
568 Broadway
New York, NY 10012
www.pen.org

This award commemorates the late children's book author Norma Klein. The biennial prize recognizes an emerging voice of literary merit among American writers of children's fiction. Candidates for this award are new authors whose books demonstrate the adventuresome and innovative spirit that characterizes children's literature.

Entries should be between 64 and 200 typewritten pages. No entry fee. Accepts photocopies and computer printouts. Entries must be nominated by authors and editors of children's books. Candidates may not nominate themselves.

Deadline: December 15.

Representative winners: Cynthia Grant, Graham Salisbury, Angela Johnson.

Announcements: Winners will be announced in the spring.

Award: A cash award of $3,000 will be presented to the winner.

PEN/Phyllis Naylor Working Writer Fellowship

PEN American Center
568 Broadway
New York, NY 10012
www.pen.org

Beginning in 2001, the PEN/Phyllis Naylor Working Writer fellowship will be offered annually to an author of children's or young adult fiction. This fellowship was developed in recognition of writers whose work is of high literary quality, but has not yet attracted a broad readership.

The competition is open to any writer in financial need, who has published at least two books, and no more than three, during the last 10 years. Writers should be nominated by either an editor or fellow writer. It is strongly recommended that the nominator write a letter of support describing in detail how the nominee meets all the criteria of the competition. Send an SASE for complete information.

Deadline: January.

Announcements: The fellowship will be awarded in May.

Award: Winner receives a fellowship of $5,000.

Please Touch Museum Book Award
210 N. 21st Street
Philadelphia, PA 19103
www.pleasetouchmuseum.org

The purpose of this award is to recognize and encourage the publication of books for children that are of the highest quality and to contribute in an exceptional way to children's literature. One award is presented to a picture book, published in the year preceding the contest, that is particularly imaginative and effective in exploring concepts for children ages 3 and under, and another award is presented to a book of the same quality for children 4 through 7.

All entries must be published by an American publisher. Send two copies of each entry. For further information and complete competition guidelines, visit the website or send an SASE.

Deadline: September 30.

Representative winners: *Cat and Mouse in the Snow,* Tomek Bogacki; *Can You Do This, Old Badger?,* Eve Bunting.

Announcements: Winners are announced in February.

Award: Winners are honored at an awards presentation and dinner.

Pockets Magazine Fiction Writing Contest
Lynn Gilliam, Associate Editor
P.O. Box 340004
Nashville, TN 37203-0004
www.upperroom.org

Pockets, a devotional magazine for children in grades 1 through 6, sponsors this annual fiction contest in the hopes of discovering new writers. It accepts previously unpublished stories that promote a Christian lifestyle. Works of historical fiction are not eligible.

Entries should be between 1,000 and 6,000 words; accurate word count must be noted on cover sheet. The competition accepts previously published material only. No entry fee. Previous winners of this contest will not be eligible.

Include an SASE for return of manuscript. Include a cover sheet with author's name, Social Security number, address, title, word count, and "Fiction Contest." Author's name should not appear on the manuscript itself. Complete competition guidelines and further information are available on the website or with an SASE.

Deadline: Entries must be postmarked between March 1 and August 15.

Announcements: Announcements of winners are made in November.

Award: Winners receive a cash prize of $1,000.

Edgar Allan Poe Awards

Mystery Writers of America
6th Floor
17 East 47th Street
New York, NY 10017
www.mysterywriters.org

Mystery Writers of America sponsors this annual competition that offers awards in several categories including children's mystery and young adult mystery. The awards look to honor the best mystery writing published in the year preceding the contest. Through these awards, MWA looks to enhance the visibility of the mystery genre.

No entry fee. Word lengths vary for each category. Entries may only be submitted in one category at a time. Submit one copy of the entry to each member of the appropriate judging committee. An official entry form is also required. Visit the website or send an SASE for complete category list, entry forms, and further guidelines.

Deadline: Varies for each category.

Representative winners: *Counterfeit Son*, Elaine Marie Alphin; *Dovey Coe*, Frances O'Roark Dowell; *Missing in Action*, Peter Robinson.

Announcements: Winners are announced in late April.

Award: An Edgar is presented to each winner. Cash prizes may also be awarded.

Michael L. Printz Award for Excellence in Young Adult Literature

American Library Association
50 E. Huron
Chicago, Il 60611
www.ala.org

This award is presented annually by the American Library Association to a book that exemplifies literary excellence in young adult literature. Entries may be fiction, nonfiction, poetry, or an anthology. All entries must be published in the year preceding the contest.

Entries should be targeted to young adults ages 12 to 18. Nominations may come from members of ALA. All nominations are kept confidential. Winners are chosen by a selection committee, and as many as four honor books may also be awarded.

Judges are looking for books that readers will talk about. Judges note that winning titles won't necessarily have a profound message, and that controversy is not something they avoid. Visit the website or send an SASE for complete details.

Deadline: December 31.

Representative winners: 2001 Winners: *Kit's Wilderness*, David Almond. 2001 Honor Books: *Many Stones*, Carolyn Coman; *The Body of Christopher Creed*, Carol Plum-Ucci.

Announcements: Winners are notifed at the American Library Association's mid-winter conference.

Award: Winners are honored during the conference.

Quill & Scroll International Writing/Photography Contest

Quill & Scroll Society
School of Journalism and Mass Communication
University of Iowa
Iowa City, IA 52242
www.uiowa.edu/~quill-sc

This awards program for currently enrolled high school students, looks to recognize student journalists for their writing, reporting, and photojournalism. Awards are presented in 12 categories including editorial cartoon, new story, feature story, and review columns.

Entry fee, $2 per piece. To qualify, entries must be accompanied by the school registration form. Each entry must have been published in a high school or professional newspaper, during the year preceding the contest. Visit the website or send an SASE for complete information.

Deadline: Entries must be postmarked by February 28.
Representative winners: Larissa Silva, Carl Hulsey, Lenee Rainey.
Announcements: Winners will be announced in March.
Award: Winners receive a National Award Gold Key, and if they are high school seniors, are eligible to apply for a $500 scholarship.

SCBWI Work-in-Progress Grants

Society of Children's Book Writers & Illustrators
8271 Beverly Boulevard
Los Angeles, CA 90048
www.scbwi.org

These grants are offered to assist children's book writers in the completion of a specific project. Four grants are presented annually: General Work-in-Progress Grant; Grant for Contemporary Novel for Young People; Nonfiction Research Grant; and a grant for a work by an author who has never had a book published.

The grants are available to full and associate members of SCBWI; if you are not a current member, visit the website for information. The grants are not available for works that are already under contract.

Deadline: Requests for applications may be made beginning October 1 of each year. Complete application and materials will be accepted between February 1 and March 1.
Representative winners: Paula Yoo, Cara Haycak, Jonathan Solomon, Mary Amato.
Announcements: Winners will be announced in August.
Award: Each of the four grant winners receives a cash award of $1,500. Four runner-up grants of $500 will also be awarded.

Scribes Hill Children's Short Story Contest

Scribes Hill Publishing
312 Colorado Street
Salem, VA 24153
www.scribeshill.com

Sponsored by Scribes Hill Publishing, this contest is open to both new and experienced writers. It accepts original, previously unpublished stories, written for children up to age 10.

Entries should not exceed 3,000 words. Entry fee, $5 per story. Multiple entries are accepted. Manuscripts will not be returned. Simultaneous submissions will be permitted, but if the manuscript is published elsewhere before the close of the contest, authors must notify Scribes Hill. Include an SASE for winners' list.

Deadline: December 31.

Announcements: Winners will be notified by mail.

Award: Winners will receive cash prizes based on contest participation.

Skipping Stones Awards

P.O. Box 3939
Eugene, OR 97403
www.efn.org/~skipping

Sponsored by *Skipping Stones,* this annual contest focuses on cultural and ethnic diversity. Awards are presented in four categories: Ecology & Nature, Educational Videos, Multicultural & International, and Teaching Resources. Entries are judged on authenticity and presentation.

The competition accepts previously unpublished entries and may be short stories, short nonfiction, plays, collections, and videos. Each category has specific guidelines; visit the website or send an SASE for complete information. Interested entrants may e-mail questions to skipping@efn.org.

Deadline: January 15.

Announcements: Competition is announced in August. Winners are announced in April.

Award: Honor certificates and award seals are presented to the winners. Winning entries will also be reviewed in *Skipping Stones.*

Skipping Stones Youth Honor Awards

Skipping Stones
P.O. Box 3939
Eugene, OR 97403
www.efn.org/~skipping

Promoting multicultural and nature awareness, the *Skipping Stones* Youth Honor Award competition is held annually. It looks for creativity, and community and cooperative values. The competition is open to young writers, ages 7 to 17.

Entries should be approximately 750 words. Accepts photocopies, computer printouts, and neatly handwritten entries. Entry fee, $3 (waived for subscribers and lower-income families). Non-English submissions are equally welcome. Send an SASE or visit the website for complete competition guidelines and further information.

Deadline: June 20.

Representative winners: Sam Miller; Corrine Nicole Kline; Samantha Brady; and Amanda Maruisch.

Announcements: Announcement of winners is made in September.

Award: Winners of these awards receive publication in *Skipping Stones* (requires first serial and non-exclusive reprint rights). Honor certificates are also awarded.

Kay Snow Writing Contest

Willamette Writers
Suite 5A
9045 SW Barbour Boulevard
Portland, OR 97219-4027
www.willamettewriters.com

Promoting new writers, this annual contest is given in honor of the founder of the Willamette Writers, Kay Snow. It accepts unpublished submissions in many categories including juvenile fiction, fiction, scripts, poetry, and nonfiction. The contest also offers awards to children for their short stories.

Entries should be 2,500 words. Entry fee, $10 for members; $15 for non-members. Multiple submissions are accepted. Accepts photocopies and computer printouts.

Submit three copies of each entry. Manuscripts will not be returned. For more information, visit the website or send an SASE.

Deadline: May 15.

Representative winners: *Her Husband's Wife,* Carolyn Pizzuti; *Shu's Story,* Karen J. Coates; *Hawk and Redwing,* Kathryn O. Umbarger.

Announcements: Competition is announced in January. Winners are announced in August.

Award: Winners in each category receive monetary awards ranging from $50 to $300.

Society of Midland Authors Awards

P.O. Box 10419
Chicago, IL 60610
www.midlandauthors.com

Sponsored by the Society of Midland Authors, these awards look to encourage writers to practice their craft of writing in the heartland. Awards are presented in several categories including juvenile fiction, juvenile nonfiction, poetry, adult fiction, adult nonfiction, and biography.

This awards competition is open to writers living in the Midwest only. Entries should be at least 2,000 words. Multiple submissions are accepted. No entry fee. Send an SASE or visit the website for competition guidelines.

Deadline: January 30.

Representative winners: *Destiny,* Vicki Grove; *Bound for the North Star: True Stories of Fugitive Slaves,* Dennis Brindell Fradin; *Fool's Gold,* Jane S. Smith.

Announcements: Award winners will be announced at the Society of Midland Author's annual banquet in May.

Award: Winners receive cash prizes.

Southwest Writers Contests

Southwest Writers Workshop
1338-B Wyoming Boulevard NE
Albuquerque, NM 87112
www.southwestwriters.org

Southwest Writers Workshop sponsors these contests in conjunction with their annual workshop. Awards are presented in several categories including children's picture book, young adult novel, science fiction, fantasy, spiritual essay, and romance.

These contests give writers the opportunity to have their work read and judged by professional editors and agents.

Submit two copies of each entry. Each entry must be accompanied by an official entry form. Author's name and personal information should appear only on the entry form. Entries are subject to blind judging. Send an SASE or visit the website for category word length requirements and complete competition guidelines.

Deadline: May 1.

Representative winners: Aileen Baron, April Kopp, Kelly Cannon,

Gordon Mustain, Nancy Hatch.
Announcements: Finalists in each category will be notified by mail. Winners are announced in September.
Award: Cash prizes ranging from $100 to $250 are awarded to the winners.

The Spur Awards
Western Writers of America
60 Sandpiper
Conway, AR 72032
www.westernwriters.org

Presented for distinguished writing about the American West, The Spur Awards are among the oldest and most prestigious in American literature. The awards are sponsored by Western Writers of America and are presented in several categories including juvenile fiction, short story, Western novel, and juvenile nonfiction.

To be eligible, entries must be set in the American West, the early frontier, or relate to the Western frontier experience. All entries must have been published in the year preceding the contest. Authors may submit multiple works provided that they are by different publishers.

Entries are judged on accuracy, grammar, clarity, and overall content. Send an SASE or visit the website for further information.
Deadline: January 31.
Representative winners: *The Midnight Train*, Erika Tamar; *Stories of Young Pioneers in Their Own Words*, Violet T. Kimball; *Summer of Pearls*, Mike Blakely.
Announcements: Winners are announced in the spring.
Award: Winners in each category receive a cash award of $2,500.

Stanley Drama Award
Wagner College
Department of Theatre and Speech
631 Howard Avenue
Staten Island, NY 10301

Held annually, this competition accepts original, full-length plays, musicals, or one-act plays, that have not been produced professionally or published in trade book form. Musical entries should be accompanied by an audio cassette with all of the music included in the play.

Only one submission per playwright will be permitted. Previously entered plays are not eligible. Entry fee, $20. For complete competition guidelines, send an SASE.
Deadline: October 1.
Announcements: Winners are announced in April.
Award: Winning entry receives a cash award of $2,000.

Stepping Stones Writing Contest
P.O. Box 8863
Springfield, MO 65801

This contest looks to promote writing for children by giving writers an opportunity to submit their work in competition. It accepts entries up to 1,000 words that are suitable for children and have excellent clarity, punctuation, grammar, and imagery.

Entry fee, $5 for the first entry; $2.50 for each additional entry. The competition accepts unpublished entries only. All entries must be accompanied by an entry form (available with an SASE). Accepts photocopies and computer printouts.

Listings

Deadline: July 31.

Representative Winners: *Happy Half Day,* Sue Corbett; *A Friend in Need,* Joseph P. Latorraca.

Announcements: Winners will be notified 4 to 6 weeks after the deadline.

Award: Cash prizes will be presented to the winners.

Sugarman Family Children's Award for Jewish Children's Literature

D.C. Jewish Community Center
1529 16th Street NW
Washington, DC 20036
www.dcjcc.org

The Sugarman Family Award is presented every other year to recognize and encourage writers and illustrators of books for Jewish children. It is open to books published in the 18 months prior to the contest. Entries must be targeted to an audience of children ages 3 to 16, and may be fiction, non-fiction, or picture books.

All entries should represent a Judaic perspective or include Jewish characters worthy of emulation and accurately reflect Jewish heritage in an honest, meaningful way. All entries must be published in the United States.

Send three copies of each book along with the entry form and entry fee of $25. For complete contest guidelines and further information, visit the website or send an SASE.

Deadline: July 15.

Announcements: Winners will be announced by the DCJCC at an awards presentation.

Award: The winner of this award receives a cash prize of $750.

Peter Taylor Prize for the Novel

Knoxville Writers' Guild
P.O. Box 2565
Knoxville, TN 37901-2565
www.knoxvillewritersguild.org

The goal of this annual contest is to identify and publish novels of high literary quality. The competition is open to published and unpublished writers living in the United States. It looks for full-length, unpublished novels

Entry fee, $20. Manuscripts should be a minimum of 40,000 words and should be accompanied by two title pages: one with only the title; and one identifying the author's name and address. Send an SASE or visit the website for complete competition information.

Deadline: Manuscripts must be postmarked between February 1 and April 30.

Representative winners: *The Marriage of Anna May Potts,* DeWitt Henry.

Announcements: Winners will be notified during the summer after the contest deadline.

Award: The prize includes a $1,000 cash award, publication of the novel by the University of Tennessee Press, and a standard royalty contract.

Sydney Taylor Manuscript Competition

Association of Jewish Libraries
315 Maitland Avenue
Teaneck, NJ 07666
www.jewishlibraries.org

The Sydney Taylor Manuscript Competition looks to recognize aspiring writers of children's books. The competition is open to unpublished writers and accepts fiction manuscripts appropriate for readers ages 8 to 11. Manuscripts should have a universal appeal, and strive to deepen the understanding of Judaism and reveal positive aspects of Jewish life.

Limit one entry per competition. Entries should be a minimum of 64 pages and a maximum of 200 pages. Entries should be typed, double-spaced, in Times New Roman font. Author's name should appear on cover sheet only. Include title on each page of manuscript. Send an SASE or visit the website for complete details.
Deadline: April 30.
Representative winners: "Zayda Was a Cowboy," June E. Nislick; "Devorah," Linda Press Wulfe.
Announcements: Winners will be announced in November.
Award: A cash award of $1,000 is presented to the winner.

Teddy Children's Book Award
Austin Writers' League
Ste. E-2
1501 W. Fifth Street
Austin, TX 78703
www.writersleague.org

This award was created to honor an outstanding children's book published by a member of the Austin Writers' League. Although the competition only accepts submissions from AWL members, entrants can join the league when entering the contest. Entries must have been published in the previous calendar year to be eligible.

Entry fee, $10. Send two copies of the book along with an official entry form, available with an SASE or on the website. Books will not be returned.

Winners will be selected by a panel of judges who are not members of the Austin Writers' League.
Deadline: May 1.
Representative winners: *Stories from the Hen House,* Carol Ann Sayle.
Announcements: Winners will be announced during the summer.
Award: A $1,000 cash award is presented to the winner. Special citations will also be presented to honor books.

Tennessee Williams One-Act Play Competition
Tennessee Williams New Orleans
  Literary Festival
UNO Lakefront
New Orleans, LA 70118
www.tennesseewilliams.org

Each year the Tennessee Williams New Orleans Literary Festival sponsors this one-act playwriting competition. Submissions are accepted from previously unpublished playwrights only. Entries should be one-act plays that demonstrate the strength and quality of the work.

Entry fee, $15 per entry. Accepts photocopies and computer printouts. Multiple submissions are also accepted. Visit the website or send an SASE for complete competition guidelines and further information.
Deadline: December 5.
Announcements: Winners will be announced during the annual festival in March or April.
Award: Winners of this competition receive a cash award of $1,000 and a reading and staging of their winning entry.

Vegetarian Essay Contest

The Vegetarian Resource Group
P.O. Box 1463
Baltimore, MD 21203
www.vrg.org

Held annually, this contest looks to increase awareness of the vegetarian lifestyle. The contest is open to children ages 8 to 18. Entrants do not need to be vegetarians to participate.

Entries may be written about any aspect of vegetarianism including culture, health, ethics, or the environment. Entries should be two- to three-page essays that are based on research, interviews, and/or personal opinion. Prizes will be awarded in three categories: 8 and under, 9 to 13, and 14 to 18. Visit the website or send an SASE for complete details.

Deadline: May 1.
Representative winners: Kylie Magnuson, Adia Dawn, Gabriella Neusner.
Announcements: Winners will be announced in *The Vegetarian Journal* at the end of the year.
Award: A $50 savings bond will be presented to the winner in each category.

Stella Wade Children's Story Award

Amelia Magazine
329 E Street
Bakersfield, CA 93304

Sponsored by *Amelia Magazine,* this award is presented annually for unpublished children's stories that are innovative, fresh, and contain strong characterization. It is one of several contests sponsored by the magazine.

Entries should not exceed 1,500 words. Entry fee, $7.50 per submission. Entries by children under 17 must be signed by a parent or guardian to verify originality. Accepts photocopies and computer printouts. Multiple entries are accepted. Include a separate cover sheet with author's name, Social Security number, address, and telephone number. Author's name should not appear on the manuscript itself.

Deadline: August 15.
Announcements: Winners will be notified within 12 weeks.
Award: Winners have their stories published in *Amelia Magazine* (requires First North American serial rights), and receive a cash award of $125.

Western Heritage Awards

National Cowboy Hall of Fame
1700 NE 63rd Street
Oklahoma City, OK 73111
www.cowboyhalloffame.org

Honoring writers that contribute to the preservation of Western heritage, this contest is presented by the National Cowboy Hall of Fame. All entries must deal with subject matter concerning the American West or the Western experience. Entries may be adult novels, juvenile novels, magazine articles, short stories, or poetry.

Entries will be judged on originality, quality of writing, organization, and grammatical structure. Send an SASE for complete details.

Deadline: November 30.
Announcements: Competition is announced each January. Winners are announced by mail in the spring.
Award: Winners receive "Wrangler Trophies" during a ceremony at the National Cowboy Hall of Fame.

Jackie White Memorial National Children's Playwriting Contest

Columbia Entertainment Company
309 Parkade Boulevard
Columbia, MD 65202

The Jackie White Memorial National Children's Playwriting Contest is looking for large cast scripts that are suitable for production by the Columbia Entertainment Company. Scripts that reach all ages are most appealing.

The contest is open to all writers, and has an entry fee of $10 per piece. Plays must be previously unpublished, and should have a running time of approximately 90 minutes (90 pages). Accepts photocopies and computer printouts.

All entries are read by at least three experienced judges. All authors receive a written report on the strengths and weaknesses of their plays.
Deadline: June 1.
Representative winners: "Musical! The Bard is Back," Stephen Murray.
Announcements: Winners will be announced in August.
Award: Winners receive a cash prize of $250 and have their play produced. In most cases, travel money to view the production is also provided.

William Allen White Children's Book Award

Emporia State University
Box 4051, 1200 Commercial Street
Emporia, KS 66801-5092
website: www.emporia.edu/libsv/

This contest was established by Emporia State University and was put in place to honor the memory of one of the state's most distinguished citizens by encouraging the boys and girls of Kansas to read and enjoy good books.

Each year a master list is compiled by the Book Selection Committee, which represents educational institutions in Kansas. Books on the list must be nominated by a member of the Book Selection Committee. Suggestions for nomination may be submitted to the Executive Secretary of the William Allen White Children's Book Award program.

All nominations must have been published in English, during the year preceding the contest. Only books whose authors reside in the United States, Canada, or Mexico are eligible.

Children in fourth through eighth grade read the books from the master list and vote on the winner.
Deadline: April 1.
Representative winners: *The Ghost of Fossil Glen,* Cynthia DeFelice; *White Water,* P. J. Petersen.
Announcements: Winners are announced at the end of April.
Award: Winners receive the bronze White Award Medal, designed by Elden Tefft. Winners are celebrated at a luncheon or dinner.

Laura Ingalls Wilder Award

American Library Association
50 East Huron Street
Chicago, IL 60611

Sponsored by the American Library Association, this award looks to recognize an author or illustrator whose books have, over a period of years, made a substantial and lasting contribution to literature for children. The

Laura Ingalls Wilder Award is presented every three years. Nominees are US residents, and must have had their books published in the United States.

Nominees are presented to the award committee by members of ALA.
Deadline: Ongoing.
Representative winners: Russell Freedman, Virginia Hamilton, Marcia Brown, Jean Fritz.
Award: Winner receives a medal at an awards presentation.

Paul A. Witty Short Story Award
International Reading Association
P.O. Box 8139
Newark, DE 19714-8139
www.reading.org

Presented annually, this award is given to the author of an original short story published for the first time in the year preceding the contest, in a periodical for children. Entries should serve as a literary standard that encourages young people to read periodicals.

No entry fee. No length requirements. Accepts photocopies accompanied by a copy of the periodical. Limit three entries per periodical. Publisher or authors may nominate stories for consideration for this award. Send an SASE or visit the website for complete information on this contest.
Deadline: November 1.
Representative winners: G. Clifton Wisler, Bill Pronzini, William J. Buchanan.
Announcements: Winners will be notified in January.
Award: Winners receive a cash award of $1,000.

Women in the Arts Annual Contest
Women in the Arts
P.O. Box 2907
Decatur, IL 62524

Sponsored by Women in the Arts, this contest looks to encourage beginning writers by offering awards in several categories including essay, fiction, juvenile fiction, poetry, and plays.

Entry fee, $2 per submission. Length requirements vary for each category. Accepts computer printouts and photocopies. Include a cover sheet with author's name, address, phone number, title of work, and category. All entries will be subject to blind judging; authors name should not appear on manuscript itself. Send an SASE for complete list of categories and further guidelines.
Deadline: November 15.
Representative winners: *Women's Work,* Jane Sherwood; *Yesterday and Today—Muskogee*, Barbara Deming.
Announcements: Winners will be notified by November 15.
Award: A $50 savings bond will be awarded to the winners.

Carter G. Woodson Book Award
National Council for the Social
    Studies
Manager of Awards and Special
    Projects
3501 Newark Street NW
Washington, D.C. 20016
www.ncss.org

The National Council for the Social Studies presents this award for the most distinguished social science books appropriate for young readers that depict ethnicity and diversity in the United States. It looks to encourage the writing, publishing, and dissemination of outstanding social science books for young readers. The award is presented in two categories: elementary and secondary. Honor books in each category will also be named.

This competition accepts work published in the United States during the preceding year. Send an SASE for competition guidelines.

Deadline: February.

Representative titles: *Story Painter: The Life of Jacob Lawrence,* John Duggleby; *Celebrating Chinese New Year,* Diane Hoyt-Goldsmith.

Announcements: Competition is announced in January. Winners are chosen in the spring.

Award: Certificates are given to the winners in each category during the NCSS annual conference in the fall.

Writer's Digest Annual Writing Competition
1507 Dana Avenue
Cincinnati, OH 45207
www.writersdigest.com

Writer's Digest sponsors this annual competition that awards prizes in several categories including children's fiction, poetry, inspirational fiction, personal essay, stage play script, and short story. It accepts original, unpublished material that has not previously been submitted to *Writer's Digest.*Word lengths vary for each category (children's fiction, 2,000 words). Entry fee, $10 per submission. Multiple submissions, photocopies, and computer print-

outs are accepted. No simultaneous submissions. Send an SASE or visit the website for complete list of categories and further competition guidelines.

Deadline: May 31.

Representative winners: *Youth on the Frontlines in Botswana's War Against AIDS,* Sandra Barron.

Announcements: Competition is announced in January. Winners are announced in the November issue of *Writer's Digest.*

Award: Grand-prize winners receive $1,500 and a trip to New York City to meet with four editors or agents. Other prizes include cash awards ranging from $25 to $750 and books from *Writer's Digest.*

Writer's Digest Short Story Prize Competition
1507 Dana Avenue
Cincinnati, OH 45207
www.writersdigest.com

This competition, sponsored by *Writer's Digest,* looks for fiction that is bold, brilliant, and brief. It accepts entries that do not exceed 1,500 words. Entries outside the word limit will be disregarded.

Entry fee, $10. Multiple entries are accepted. All entries must be original and previously unpublished. Simultaneous submissions are not accepted. Manuscripts will not be returned.

All entries should be typed, double-spaced and must include an entry form. Entry forms and complete competition guidelines are available on the website or with an SASE.

Deadline: December.

Representative winners: *Commerce,*

Diane Farrington; *The Whole Truth,* Karin Beuerlein; *Evil Eye,* Beth Manca.

Announcements: Winners will be notified by February 1 and their names will be posted on the website. Winners' names will also appear in the June issue of *Writer's Digest.*

Award: The first-place winner receives $1,500. Second- through tenth-place winners receive cash awards ranging from $100 to $750. Eleventh- through twenty-fifth-place winners receive a $50 gift certificate for Writer's Digest Books. First- through tenth-place winners will also have their stories published in the June issue of *Writer's Digest.*

Writers' Journal Writing Contests
P.O. Box 394
Perham, MN 56573-0394
www.writersjournal.com

Presented by *Writers' Journal,* these annual contests are offered in several categories to promote the work of up-and-coming writers. Categories for these contests include short story, horror, travel, fiction, romance, and poetry. Word lengths and guidelines vary for each category; visit the website or send an SASE for more information.

All entries must be previously unpublished. Submit two copies of each entry. Accepts photocopies and computer printouts. Entry fees range from $5 to $10 depending on the category. Enclose a #10 SASE for a winners' list.

Deadline: Varies for each category.

Representative winners: *Blues in the Rafters,* Jan R. Carrington; *The Museum,* C. L. Santin; *Burning Embers,* Jennifer Morey.

Announcements: Winners will be announced after the contest deadline in *Writers' Journal* and on the website.

Award: Winners receive cash prizes ranging from $15 to $50 and publication of their winning entry.

Writers' Union of Canada Short Prose Competition
The Writers' Union of Canada
Third Floor
40 Wellington Street East
Toronto, Ontario M5E 1C7
Canada
www.writersunion.ca

Open to Canadian citizens or landed immigrants who have not been published in book format and do not have a contract from a book publisher, this annual competition looks for original fiction or nonfiction up to 2,500 words.

Entry fee, $25 per submission. Author's name should not appear on the entry. Include a separate cover letter with author's name, address, phone number, e-mail address, word count, and indicate whether the submission is fiction or nonfiction. Manuscripts will not be returned. Include an SASE for competition results. Visit the website or send an SASE for complete contest information.

Deadline: November.

Announcements: Winners will be announced in January.

Award: Winners receive a cash award of $2,500 and publication in *GIEST,* a Canadian literary journal.

Writers' Union of Canada Writing for Children Competition

The Writers' Union of Canada
Third Floor
40 Wellington Street East
Toronto, Ontario M5E 1C7
Canada
www.writersunion.ca

Sponsored by the Writers' Union of Canada, this annual contest looks for fiction or nonfiction prose written for children. It accepts entries up to 1,500 words, written in English. All entries must be previously unpublished.

The competition is open to Canadian writers or landed immigrants who have not been published in book format, and do not have a contract from a book publisher.

Entry fee, $15 per piece. Multiple entries are accepted, provided that each is accompanied by an entry fee. Electronic submissions are not accepted at this time. Entries should be typed, double-spaced. Include a separate cover letter with author's name, address, phone number, word count, and fiction or nonfiction. Author's name and personal information should not be on the manuscript itself. Manuscripts are not returned. Include an SASE for winners' list.

Deadline: April 23.

Representative winners: *Harold and Me*, Wendy M. Hogarth.

Announcements: Winners will be announced in July.

Award: The winning entry receives $1,500. The winning entry and the entries of 11 finalists will be submitted to a Canadian publisher of children's books.

Writing Conference Inc., Writing Contests

The Writing Conference
P.O. Box 27288
Overland Park, KS 66225
www.writingconference.com

These annual contests are for young writers in elementary, junior high, and high school. Entries may be a narrative, essay, or poem. Limit one entry per competition. All entries must be original, and previously unpublished. There are no word length limits for this competition.

Each year the contests have a new theme on which the entries must be based. The theme for the 2001-2002 school year is competition, whether it be in professional sports, school activities, or everyday life. No entry fee. Send an SASE or visit the website for complete guidelines and contest entry form.

Deadline: January.

Announcements: Announcements of winners are made in late February.

Award: Winners will have their work published in *The Writers' Slate*. They are also honored at an awards presentation.

Young Hoosier Book Awards

Carmel Clay Public Library
Carmel, IN 46032

This annual award was established in 1992 and encourages recreational reading in Indiana students. The award consists of three categories: kindergarten through third-grade; fourth-through sixth-grade; and sixth-through eighth-grade.

Each year students, teachers, librarians, parents, and media specialists submit sugestions for nominations for the Young Hoosier Award. Nominations must adhere to all of the competition guidelines (available with an SASE). Student will then read a certain number of the books on the nomination list during the school year.

In April, the students vote for their favorite books.

Deadline: Voting results are due by April.

Announcements: Winners will be announced in April.

Award: An engraved plaque is presented to each of the winning authors.

Charlotte Zolotow Award

Cooperative Children's Book Center
4290 Helen C. White Hall
600 North Park Street
Madison, WI 53706

The Charlotte Zolotow Award, honoring her distinguished contributions to children's literature, is presented to the author of the best picture book text published in the year preceding the contest. All entries must be written by a citizen of, and published in, the United States. Entries may be of any genre of writing including fiction, nonfiction, poetry, or folklore, as long as it is presented in a picture book format and aimed at a young audience.

Winners are chosen by a committee of children's literature experts. The committee may also select up to three honor books. Send an SASE for complete guidelines.

Deadline: December.

Representative winners: *The Night Worker,* Kate Banks.

Announcements: Winners are announced in January.

Award: A bronze medallion and cash prize of $1,000 are given to the winner.

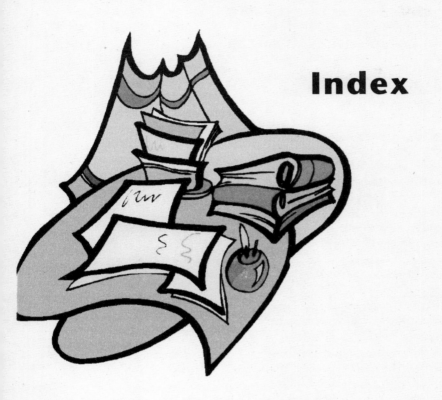

Index

Index

Index

Index